Nieuport Aircraft of World War One

Other titles in the Crowood Aviation Series

Aichi D3A1/2 Val	Peter C. Smith
Airco – The Aircraft Manufacturing Company	Mick Davis
Avro Lancaster	Ken Delve
BAC One-Eleven	Malcolm L. Hill
Bell P-39 Airacobra	Robert F. Dorr with Jerry C. Scutts
Boeing 737	Malcolm L. Hill
Boeing 747	Martin W. Bowman
Boeing 757 and 767	Thomas Becher
Boeing B-17 Flying Fortress	Martin W. Bowman
Consolidated B-24 Liberator	Martin W. Bowman
Douglas AD Skyraider	Peter C. Smith
English Electric Canberra	Barry Jones
English Electric Lightning	Martin W. Bowman
Fairchild Republic A-10 Thunderbolt II	Peter C. Smith
Fokker Aircraft of World War One	Paul Leaman
Hawker Hunter	Barry Jones
Hawker Hurricane	Peter Jacobs
Junkers Ju 87 Stuka	Peter C. Smith
Junkers Ju 88	Ron Mackay
Lockheed C-130 Hercules	Martin W. Bowman
Lockheed F-104 Starfighter	Martin W. Bowman
Luftwaffe – A Pictorial History	Eric Mombeek
McDonnell Douglas A-4 Skyhawk	Brad Elward
McDonnell Douglas F-15 Eagle	Peter E. Davies and Tony Thornborough
Messerschmitt Bf 110	Ron Mackay
Messerschmitt Me 262	David Baker
North American B-25 Mitchell	Jerry Scutts
North American F-86 Sabre	Duncan Curtis
North American T-6	Peter C. Smith
Panavia Tornado	Andy Evans
Short Sunderland	Ken Delve
V-Bombers	Barry Jones
Vickers VC10	Lance Cole

NIEUPORT AIRCRAFT
of World War One

Ray Sanger

The Crowood Press

First published in 2002 by
The Crowood Press Ltd
Ramsbury, Marlborough
Wiltshire SN8 2HR

© Ray Sanger 2002

All rights reserved. No part of this publication may be reproduced or transmitted in any form or by any means, electronic or mechanical, including photocopy, recording, or any information storage and retrieval system, without permission in writing from the publishers.

British Library Cataloguing-in-Publication Data
A catalogue record for this book is available from the British Library.

ISBN 1 86126 447 X

Typefaces used: Goudy (*text*),
Cheltenham (*headings*).

Typeset and designed by
D & N Publishing
Baydon, Marlborough, Wiltshire.

Printed and bound in Great Britain by Butler and Tanner, Frome.

Contents

Acknowledgements 6

1 THE COMPANY 7

2 NIEUPORT AIRCRAFT BEFORE WORLD WAR ONE 17

3 NIEUPORT AIRCRAFT OF WORLD WAR ONE 30

4 FRENCH OPERATIONS OF NIEUPORT AIRCRAFT DURING WORLD WAR ONE 77

5 BRITISH OPERATIONS OF NIEUPORT AIRCRAFT DURING WORLD WAR ONE 93

6 NIEUPORT AIRCRAFT IN RUSSIA AND ON THE EASTERN FRONT 109

7 NIEUPORT AIRCRAFT IN ITALIAN SERVICE 131

8 NIEUPORTS WITH THE AMERICAN EXPEDITIONARY FORCE AND OTHER AIR FORCES 147

9 POSTWAR DEVELOPMENTS OF WARTIME DESIGNS 159

Bibliography 188
Index 189

Acknowledgements

Nieuport aircraft were manufactured and used in many countries. Not being a linguist, it was not a practical proposition for me to refer to original documents in foreign languages, even if they were to be still in existence after many years and the ravages of two world wars. Of necessity I have therefore had to make extensive use of secondary references; some of these have proved to be unreliable, but others have proved of utmost value, and these are listed in the appendix. I must make particular mention of the many publications written by Jack Bruce, principally for Putnam and Albatros Publications; also of *L'Aviation Maritime Française Pendant la Grande Guerre* by Morareau, Feuilley and Courtinat; *I Reparti dell'aviazione italiana nella Grande Guerra* by Gentilli and Varriale; and the numerous articles that have appeared in the excellent French magazine *Avions*.

I also gratefully acknowledge the assistance given by Stuart Leslie and Jack Bruce in making their collection of photographs available; and wholeheartedly thank Harry Woodman for supplying photographs and giving me the benefits of his extensive knowledge of armament and Russian aviation history. I also thank Greg van Wyngarden, Lucien Morareau, Tomasz Kopanski, Giorgio Apostolo, Paul Leaman and Philip Jarrett for supplying photographs and giving encouragement.

Finally, I would like to thank Mick Davis, who took time off from his own research to draw the diagrams.

Designation System

The French system of designating military aircraft and squadrons became very complex during the war, and was further complicated by an overlap in type numbers between the prewar Nieuport monoplanes and wartime biplane designs.

To avoid confusion over the Nieuport type numbers, in this book Roman numerals have been retained for the prewar Nieuport monoplanes, but arabic numerals have been used for all Nieuport biplanes, although these were not officially adopted until later in the war. The Nieuport company sometimes added letters to its type numbers: for example, 'M' stood for 'Military' in the Type IVM designation; the biplane derivative of the Type X and Type XI monoplanes were designated the Type XB and Type XIB respectively – and for the Type XIB the company also used the designation B=XI.

In 1915 the Service des Fabrications Aéronautiques decided on an aircraft identification system in which aircraft from the various manufacturers were given Roman type numbers and the suffix M for *monoplan* and B for *biplan*. Thus the biplane derivative of the Type X became the Nie-XB (Nieuport 10 in this book). This was augmented a year later by adopting additional suffixes: A for observation aircraft, B for *avion de combat léger* or light combat aircraft, C for *avion de combat* or heavy multi-seat fighters, D for cannon-armed aeroplanes and E for bombers. In this way the Nie-XI was designated the Nie-XI BB (Nieuport 11 in this book). These designations were further modified shortly afterwards, A still referring to observation aircraft, but B becoming *bombardier* or bomber, and C *chasseur* or fighter or scout; the suffixes for the number of mainplanes was still retained. In 1917, Roman type numbers were totally replaced by arabic numerals, and the number of seats was shown by an arabic numeral after the suffix: for example, the Nie-XXIX became the Ni D-29C-1, the system also adopted in this book.

Other designations were applied to Nieuport aircraft, which can lead to confusion. For example, the Nieuport-Macchi-produced Nie-10 was sometimes referred to as the Ni.18 or Ni.18mq in Italian service, a nomenclature which referred to the wing area of 18sq m (194sq ft).

French escadrille numbers were given a prefix designating the main type of aircraft used in the escadrille: for example, Escadrille N.12 operated Nieuport monoplanes until it re-equipped with Morane-Saulnier Parasols, at which point it was re-designated MS.12. However, escadrilles did not exclusively operate the type indicated by the letter prefix: for example, one or two Nieuport scouts operated in most escadrilles early in the war, and during its latter part Nieuports and Spads operated side by side in Nieuport escadrilles for some time before the 'Spa' prefix was adopted.

Serial numbers allotted to aircraft by the Aviation Militaire indicated the sequence in which they were procured from each manufacturer, and not total aircraft procurement as in the case of the British and American systems. Thus they began with a letter prefix denoting the manufacturer, the letter naturally being 'N' in the case of Nieuport. Serial numbers were normally written in black letters on both sides of the fin and rudder, and the aircraft model designation was commonly written below the serial number; in the case of Nieuport aircraft this was often simplified to a type number, e.g. 'Type 28'. While the American forces had their own serial number system, it was not applied to aircraft obtained from their Allies, which retained those originally applied by the manufacturer even if the aircraft was subsequently exported to the USA. British serials were allocated to British manufacturers with each batch at the time the contract was assigned, and were substituted for the original French serial numbers on Nieuport aircraft manufactured by the parent company. Confusion may arise as the British serial number system also included 'N' letter prefixes.

Although, in general, foreign language names have been used, Russian unit nomenclature has been translated. The term 'detachment' has been used regularly in the literature to describe Russian aviation units, but they were in fact separate units and not generally detachments from larger establishments; so in this book the term 'section' has been used instead.

CHAPTER ONE

The Company

Edouard de Niéport was born on 24 May 1875 at Blida, a small town in Algeria, where his father, a colonel in the artillery, was commander of the garrison. After a sound technical education, he prepared for an entrance examination at the École Polytechnique in Paris; but in 1897 he abandoned his studies to devote his time to cycle racing. For young men at the end of the nineteenth century, cycling was a readily accessible sport for those with a mechanical bent. The races, a great novelty for the period, attracted a fashionable following, rather like golf or tennis today. It was not uncommon for future exponents of cars and aeroplanes – for instance Henry and Maurice Farman, and Roger Sommer, amongst others – to begin their careers in cycle racing.

He won a dozen races as an amateur at the Paris Vélodrome d'Hiver. During 1897 the young Edouard showed sufficient proficiency to turn professional, winning the Zimmerman Prize for the 1km tandem race; one year later he finished third in the championship of France, and the freedom of action this gave him allowed him to participate in a course at the École Supérieure d'Electricité. He lacked the physique to reach the top flight, but he compensated for his lack of strength by courage and the application of aerodynamics: he used a Rudge-Whitworth cycle with a long frame and low handlebars, which gave him a low stance and thus reduced wind resistance. By this time he was known as Nieuport.

Nieuport-Duplex

Forced to look for a living elsewhere, in 1902 Nieuport established a small business in Suresnes to manufacture electrical accessories for internal combustion engines under the brand name Nieuport-Duplex. His backers included de Joug, Gustin, Altschuller and Citroën, and the products included high-tension magnetos, accumulators and sparking plugs. He soon made a reputation in the automotive and aeronautical world, and his equipment was used in the Darracq, which in

Edouard de Niéport. *The Aero*

1902 became the first automobile to exceed 200km/h (124mph). At this time he did not appreciate the future of aviation; commenting in the magazine *La Locomotion* in November 1902 on Ferdinand Feber's glider experiments he wrote:

> This will become a game and a sport, nothing more ...We shall never see the sky traversed by air machines, or frontiers abolished by high-flying vehicles described by poets...or forecast by inventors. The laws of gravity, above all of geometry, will never be altered by the progress of science. ...it will be impossible to construct machines by which the wings can support its corresponding weight.

He had cause to change his opinion, however, largely as a consequence of the disastrous Paris to Madrid Rally of 1902, which caused the French administration to ban automotive competitions, a decision that had a serious adverse effect on the car industry. This led companies to turn to the fledgling aviation industry as an outlet for their energies and products.

La Société Générale d'Aero-locomotion

In 1907, Léon Levavasseur adopted the Nieuport-Duplex ignition system for the Antoinette engine, and Henry Farman completed the first closed circuit of 1km in a Voisin biplane powered by such an engine. Shortly afterwards Edouard founded the Société Générale d'Aero-locomotion, supported with finance by his brother Charles and other members of his family and the principal shareholder, the Lieutenant de Caumont La Force (one of the first military pilots in France). M. Zemette became the director of the new company, and Henri Depasse the financial director. The latter had also been a cyclist, and was the son of the member of parliament for Neuilly, who was destined to become a future minister. The production manager was Frank Schneider, a Swiss, and he was assisted by the two brothers and other collaborators including Cizeck, Desbordes, Rispal and Armand Gobé.

It is said that Edouard bought a Voisin in 1909, to practise flying and to test the electrical accessories that he was producing at the time; but this was destroyed on 18 April 1910 when it caught fire in the air, and Edouard was lucky to escape uninjured. The collaborators had no better luck with their first indigenous design, as it was destroyed by the flooding of the Seine soon after its completion in January 1910. Shortly afterwards Edouard established a factory for the production of aeroplanes, and also a flying school, at Mourmelon. He was joined there by François Dumoulin, André Levasseur and Georges Kirsch amongst others. Kirsch, who later became mechanic to Charles Weymann, had his first experience of flying as a passenger with Hubert Latham in an Antoinette. He later fought as a pilot in the war and was badly wounded. He returned to Nieuport after the war, and for a time was a successful test and competition pilot.

Edouard, flying his second design of aircraft, obtained his pilot's certificate (No.

Nieuport advert from 1910. *L'Aérophile*

Charles Weymann. *Flight*

Charles Weymann was the son of an American sugar planter in Haiti; he was born at Port-au-Prince on 2 August 1889, but was educated in France. He was an unassuming type, with the air of a country gentleman, and rather short in stature. He generally wore a pince-nez, and went around in a loose-fitting raincoat over a turtle-neck sweater, with cap and goggles instead of a crash helmet. He had passed his tests for the French brevet on 6 June 1910, and the Aero Club of America issued him with its own licence (No.14) on the same date, enabling him to compete as an American pilot.

105) from the Aéro-Club de France on 10 June 1910. Less than a month later he entered three monoplanes, powered by Darracq engines, in the second Grande Semaine d'Aviation de Reims; however, his only success was to come third in the cross-country race.

The year ended badly for Nieuport with the death of the principal shareholder, Lt de Caumont, who was killed while experimenting with a REP Type III at Buc. His rudder jammed and he omitted to cut off his engine, with the result that he hit the ground hard and smashed both his legs. He died the same day, though might have survived if he had been treated on the spot instead of being carted in a farm wagon from Buc to St Cyr and thence to Versailles. His death caused difficulties for the company, as it was not selling its machines in sufficient numbers to be financially viable.

Having gained self-confidence as a pilot, Edouard became more active in promoting the company's aeroplanes, and gained an international reputation for himself and his aircraft. In the period from March to June he obtained several speed and distance records, and achieved better success in competitions. For instance, at Mourmelon on 6 March he managed to exceed a speed of 101km/h (62mph) with an engine of only 28hp, and over the next few weeks flew a number of record flights.

On 1 July, Charles Weymann in a Nieuport carried off the Gordon Bennett Trophy at the meeting held at Eastchurch, and Edouard finished third in a similar time. However, no success was achieved in the Circuit de l'Est, nor in the Paris to Madrid, and Paris to Rome events. However, these failures were due to a number of reasons that were generally no fault of the aircraft.

Nieuport et Deplante

In May 1911, a new company was formed to build monoplanes. This was registered under the name of Société Nieuport (E) et Deplante, with offices at 9 rue de Seine at Suresnes, and it was expected that the company would be sufficiently well founded not to run into financial difficulties. But on 15 September, Edouard Nieuport was killed in an accident.

At the end of every summer it was customary to hold military manœuvres, and in 1911 these took place in the Ardennes, when twenty-two aircraft took part. Edouard was summoned as a reservist, with one of the Nieuport monoplanes powered by a 50hp or 70hp Gnome rotary, to a squadron commanded by LV Gustav Delage (much more of whom later).

Edouard was sent to Verdun. He arrived there in a gale, with squalls reaching more than 80km/h (50mph). He landed in front of a group of astounded officers, amongst whom was Colonel Estienne, Commandant of the Military Aviation Laboratory at Vincennes. Asked to give a demonstration flight, Edouard took off again, climbed to around 800m (2,600ft) before cutting his motor to glide down to land. Unfortunately he could not restart his engine, and as he approached the ground he was hit by a gust and crashed. Edouard was not strapped in and was thrown out, hitting a plank that had been set up to lay out maps. Gravely injured, he died that night from an internal haemorrhage, despite the attentions of the eminent surgeon Professor Doyen, who had been rushed to the scene by car from Paris. It had been intended to award Nieuport the Legion d'Honneur after the manoeuvres in recognition of his services, but in the event the Minister of War pinned the cross to the aviator's chest a few hours after he passed away.

Without its head the company would most probably have floundered but for the support of Henri Deutsch de la Meurthe.

In the meantime, in order to select suitable aircraft for the army, a competition was held during October and November 1911 by General Rocques, engineering director of the Ministry of War and responsible for military aeronautics. As a result of these trials the army ordered ten three-seat Nieuport monoplanes: these had been found to be fast and robust, having achieved an average speed of 116.9km/h (72.67mph) over 250km (155 miles).

Henri Deutsch de la Meurthe

In the early 1860s Henri had diligently studied engineering at the École Centrale; after this, together with his brother Émile, he guided the family petroleum business, known as Les Fils de Alexandre Deutsch, to increasing profitability. In his own laboratory he developed a means of refining petrol as a fuel for the internal combustion engine, and from the family fortune encouraged the development of cars and aircraft by putting up prizes for car, balloon and aeroplane competitions. In 1904 he established a joint prize of 50,000 francs for the first airman to fly a closed circuit of 1 km; this was won by Henri Farman. He then set up the Prix Deutsch de la Meurthe, valued at 70,000 francs, for an air race round Paris. He created the Institute Aéronautique de Saint-Cyr; he also re-established the Etablissements Surcouf company as the Astra company, to build aeroplanes, balloons and airships; and he became the patron of many of the fledgling aeroplane manufacturers, including Voisin and Nieuport.

Henri Deutsch de la Meurthe with Roland Garros in 1913. *The Aero*

Société Anonyme des Establissements Nieuport

In December 1911, the Nieuport engine of 28hp was placed first in the Ligue Aérienne competition. The day before Christmas, Armand Gobé beat the world distance record, covering 740km (460 miles) non-stop in 8hr 16min. Charles Nieuport succeeded his brother following his death: in 1912, after training as a pilot, he obtained his civil certificate (No. 742) on 22 January, and his military one (No. 156) on 9 February. Henri Deutsch de la Meurthe bought all the Nieuport patents and created the Société Anonyme des Establissements Nieuport with a capital of 1.2 million francs, with Léon Bazaine as commercial director and Henri de la Fresnaye as technical director. Another company, Anonyme des Equipements Electriques, continued to manufacture Nieuport magnetos and sparking plugs. In November a new factory was built at Issy-les-Moulineaux, and a flying school was set up at Villacoublay.

More aircraft constructors were coming on the scene at a time when aircraft sales were stagnating. However, Nieuport received an order from the French navy for monoplanes fitted with floats.

On 24 January 1913, prior to delivering three Nieuport three-seaters and in the company of Espanet and Gobé, Charles Nieuport flew to the military field at Etampes with his mechanic Guillot to carry out some flights before an army reception committee. He landed rather heavily following one flight, having achieved a height of 500m (1,640ft) in fifteen minutes with a load of 500kg (1,100lb), but set out again – but on reaching an altitude of about 300m (980ft), he side-slipped while making a steep turn, and crashed. Both occupants were killed.

In April, the Nieuport floatplanes of Weymann and Espanet took part in the Schneider Cup; but in spite of qualifying easily, they were both eliminated from the finals due to mechanical faults.

The Nieuport designs had hardly evolved since 1910, and were less advanced than those of Deperdussin, and especially Morane et Saulnier. At the end of 1913, Deperdussin brought out a monoplane of a new generation, the Type XI, with which Maurice Legagneux beat the world altitude record. However, it was not as fast as earlier designs, and the army, the only likely customer, required something even better, with improved visibility and shorter take-off and landing distances. As early as the beginning of 1913 Morane et Saulnier had produced a monoplane with a parasol wing, giving the crew an unparalleled view. But when Gustave Delage was made technical director of Nieuport in January 1914, he did not follow this line of development, and it was left to Nieuport-Macchi to develop a parasol wing design.

Production of Nieuport aircraft prior to the war is not known in any detail. Although its designs were used in the USA, UK, Sweden, Italy, Russia and Japan, it is unlikely that total production exceeded 250 (as indicated from constructors' numbers applied to tails). The Astra-Nieuport group were making heavy financial losses in 1914, having sold just fifty aircraft to the army and seven to the navy between 1912 and 1914, at a time when civil sales were negligible.

At the time of the general mobilization on 2 August 1914, aviation was judged to be of insignificant value for a conflict that was not expected to last very long. All the engineers and nearly half of the workforce and employees of Nieuport were called up. Gustave Delage found himself in Port Said with a detachment of Nieuport floatplanes from December 1914 until February 1915, when he returned to France. Nevertheless, it was vital to preserve the means of production, and the rest of the personnel were transferred to Tours, during which time production suffered severely.

Manufacturing facilities at the Issy-les-Moulineaux factory. SHAA

Gustave Delage

Delage was born at Limoges on 8 March 1883; following his formal education in Brest, he attended the École Navale and became a naval officer. He pursued an interest in aviation, and obtained his French Aero Club brevet (no. 219) on 19 September 1910. As recounted elsewhere, he commanded the first squadron of Nieuport monoplanes during the 1911 manœuvres. He nevertheless continued his technical studies at Vincennes, where he found time to be involved in the design of hydroplanes, an experience that was to be a considerable advantage later in his career.

At the beginning of the war, of the twenty-four squadrons of the French Military Air Force, only one squadron (N.12) was equipped with Nieuport monoplanes, some six or seven ordered in 1914. The navy possessed one squadron of Nieuport floatplanes, which, although considered by the French to have inadequate performance for military operations, gave a good account of themselves alongside the British in the Red Sea area.

When appointed as head of Military Aviation in October 1914, General Hirschauer decided to limit the number of aircraft types in service to four: the Morane et Saulnier Parasol, the Farman reconnaissance biplane, the Caudron G.III for artillery spotting, and the heavy Voisin biplane bomber. Nieuport successfully objected to its exclusion, and had the production of its monoplane reinstated, though this was only for export. These machines were therefore produced in only small numbers, and Nieuport found itself acting as a subcontractor producing Voisin 3 biplanes. In November 1914, the factory returned to Issy-les-Moulineaux, which was not threatened by the German advance. Delage returned in February to his post as technical director, and by April the business had recovered most of its specialized personnel from military service. Appreciating the drawbacks inherent in their earlier designs, the company had developed a new series of sesquiplanes of 80hp, the first of which reached the front in May.

The factory was enlarged by the construction of six new buildings. Sixty-six Nieuport 10s had left the factory by August 1915, a further fifty-one by October and forty by January 1916. During this time the technical office designed a new scout, the Nie XIB, nicknamed Bébé, which re-established Nieuport's reputation for building excellent aircraft. Some 7,200 of these were built, serving in twenty squadrons and also the famous Escadrille Lafayette, manned by American volunteers, and helped to re-establish Allied supremacy on all fronts.

The output of the Nieuport company during the war was prodigious; in these four years the firm produced some twenty different types, all remarkable in their own way. In 1915, the first two-seat sesquiplane scout, the Nieuport 10, and the Nieuport 12 reconnaissance machine were produced. By 1916, the famous Nieuport 11 was introduced: this aircraft not only rapidly equipped the Aviation Militaire, but also found service in the RFC and RNAS. Many of the French aces scored with this aircraft, including Guynemer with fourteen victories, Deullin, Dorme, Heurtaux, Pelletier d'Oisy, Pinsard, Navarre and Nungesser. These two-seater and scout designs were further developed, notably the Nieuport 17, 24 and 27, which saw extensive service with the Aviation Militaire, the Royal Flying Corps and the Imperial Russian Air Service. The manufacture of some Nieuport 11s and 17s was subcontracted to Borel, Duperon, Niepce et Fetterer (DNP), R. Savary et Henri de la Fresnaye and Société Anon. Française de Construction Aéronautiques (SCAF), and from licensees Nieuport-Macchi and Elettro-Ferroviera in Italy, and Duks, Mosca and Anatra in Russia. The Nieuport 28 appeared in 1917 and was allocated to the United States Air Service, which received about 300. The Nieuport 29 came too late to see service in the war, but carried on for eleven years afterwards and also served with overseas air forces. There were other aircraft, too, in particular a two-seater reconnaissance machine that was also capable of bombing.

In August 1918, Société Nieuport bought the company Société A. Tellier et Cie, which before the war had manufactured marine engines and until 1916 had produced a succession of multi-engined flying boats for the French navy. Its founder Alphonse Tellier became technical director of the marine department of the Nieuport company, and engineer Robert Duhamel became its chief designer. Two yards belonging to Société Tellier, at Isle de la Jatte and at Argenteuil, were linked up with the facilities at Issy-les-Moulineaux and continued to manufacture hulls and assemble flying boats. At this time Nieuport acquired an extensive area of land at Bordeaux with the intention of building yards and giant hangars, presumably with the objective of building large flying boats, starting with the four-engined Tellier 4R 450. This policy was confirmed by the whole range of Tellier flying boats appearing in the Nieuport catalogue. But the Nieuport management evidently had a change of heart, as flying boat development and construction ended with the Nieuport-Tellier TM, and construction of the two Tellier 4R 450 machines was abandoned. Alphonse Tellier was terribly affected by this decision and fell gravely ill, and in 1919 he gave up all his professional activities and retired to Grasse.

When the war ended, virtually all contracts were cancelled. This came as a severe blow to the French aircraft industry, which had expanded in the expectation of manufacturing large quantities of aircraft to support the final offensives in 1919. Instead it had to adapt its expertise in the design and manufacture of aircraft acquired during the war to the rigours of the new world peacetime economy.

Nieuport-Astra

The demobilization of the armed forces at the end of the war led to huge stocks of unwanted aircraft, engines and components. These were not only vastly in excess of the requirements of the civil market, but were not entirely suitable for peacetime use. Thus although the Nieuport company ended the war with the Ni 29C1, a scout with an excellent performance, demand was slow to materialize, and the company was forced to lay off the majority of its workforce.

Gustave Delage continued to manage the company, with the financial support of the heirs of Henri Deutsch de la Meurthe, who had died on 24 November 1919 aged seventy-three. But in August 1921 the company amalgamated with the Société Astra and the Compagnie Générale Transaérienne, to form a new company called Nieuport-Astra. Nieuport were no strangers to Astra, as it had taken over the construction of Astra aircraft designs in 1913, to allow the latter company to concentrate on airships. M. Gradis, son-in-law of Henri Deutsch de la Meurthe, became chairman and managing director; M. Thomas and M. Bazaine became respectively the director of administration and the commercial director. Gustave Delage remained as the technical director and became chief designer, and he also ran the factory that produced naval vessels. The airship department, at the time an essential part of Astra, stayed with its technical director Henry Kapférer; but this department ceased production in 1925, and the name Astra disappeared with it.

The new company made its first public appearance at the Seventh Salon d l'Aviation in Paris in November 1921. Shown on the stand were the NiD 30T2, and the sesquiplane that had won the 1921 Coupe Deutsch carrying the racing number '7'.

Nieuport was very successful in competitive events, as will be recounted later, and was fortunate in having a number of experienced pilots to fly their machines, including Kirsch, who has been mentioned before, Lasne, and particularly Sadi Lecointe.

Lasne was born in November 1894 at La Ferté-St-Aubin, several miles south of Paris. Intensely interested in aviation, when the war broke out he was posted to Escadrille MS.38 – but as a lorry driver. He got himself transferred to flying training at Avord in 1916, where his instructor was Sadi Lecointe, and he qualified in March 1917 (brevet no. 5870) He then flew with Escadrille N.93 in the Vosges from May 1917 to August 1918, when he was posted to the flight test escadrille at Villacoublay. He joined Nieuport on 1 April 1920.

Unlike other companies, Nieuport-Astra suffered little from the massive surplus of war material, since between 1922 and 1924 the demand for small fighter aircraft was still strong in France and elsewhere: thus eighteen government contracts and export orders totalled some 700 NiD 29C1 aircraft. In fact this total exceeded the production capacity of the factory at Issy-les-Moulineaux, and it became necessary to subcontract a large part of this production to other manufacturers, including Blériot, Buscaylet, Farman, Letord, Levasseur, Potez and Schreck.

In 1925, twenty-five squadrons of the Aéronautique Militaire were equipped with these aircraft, which remained in front-line service until passed on to the flying schools in 1928. They were also exported to six other countries, and were built under licence by four of these.

Nieuport experienced a very prolific period after 1928: it produced some 700 NiD 62 scouts and derivatives, and it also bought the Société Dyle et Bacalan, the flying school near Bacalan in Bordeaux.

Sadi Lecointe and the 1922 Eugène Gilbert aircraft. *Flight*

Sadi Lecointe was born to a family of farmers at St Germain-sur-Bresles in the valley of the Somme on 11 July 1891. When only nineteen, after flying lessons at the Anzani school at Issy, he gained his brevet (no. 431) in a Blériot on 3 March 1911. After eighteen months as a pilot from the beginning of the war he was awarded the Croix de Guerre, and spent the remainder of the war testing aeroplanes and instructing student pilots. He worked for a time for Blériot-Spad before joining Nieuport. He had a fascination for racing, whether it was with cars or aeroplanes. With Nieuport-Delage he won a national reputation as a record-breaking and racing pilot, but after winning the Coupe Beaumont of 1925, he retired from racing and concentrated on test-flying for the company. As a capitaine de réserve during 1925–26, he was seconded from the company and put in charge of the Sherifian Escadrille in French Morocco, where he successfully subdued the Riff incursion into French Morocco led by Abd-el-Krim. Always well groomed, he was raised to the status of an Officer of the Légion d'Honneur, and had a brief flirtation with politics in 1929, becoming inspector general for aviation in the prewar Popular Front government. But after the fall of France in 1940, as a de Gaulle sympathizer he fell foul of the Vichy regime. He died in Paris on 17 July 1944.

With the aid of local finance, on 25 July 1925 it set up a company, the Société Aéronautique Bordelais, with its head office at 91 rue Blanqui, Bordeaux.

At the request of the Service Technique de l'Aéronautique (STAé), in June 1922 the company organized a competition for parachute design, in which it donated several prizes. But the STAé were not satisfied with the overall standard, and ordered a new series of trials; these took place in November 1923, but were equally unsuccessful. A third trial was considered, but not carried out.

The Tellier naval factory at Argenteuil produced tugs, barges and tankers. The yards at the Isle de la Jatte, surviving from the times of Alphonse Tellier, were making pleasure boats, yawls, yachts and speedboats, the latter winning many prizes in France and abroad.

The Société Générale Aéronautique (SGA)

Following his appointment as Minister of Aviation on 11 November 1928, Victor Laurent-Eynac advocated two fundamental principles: decentralization and concentration; in his opinion these policies would revitalize the French aviation industry. With few exceptions, of which Nieuport was one, the industry in general had not recovered from the period of stagnation following the war. A multitude of constructors, not always with adequate manufacturing facilities and with a proliferation of prototypes, many of no practical use, was causing the dispersion of available funds to little useful purpose, and the minister urged the industry to amalgamate. So between November 1929 and February 1930, a large enterprise under the name of the Société Générale Aéronautique (SGA) was formed in Paris. The initiator of this grouping was the automotive manufacturer Lorraine-Dietrich, supported financially by the Banque Nationale de Credit.

The SGA, with a capital of 400 million francs, regrouped the various factories – four in the Paris region, three in the provinces and two affiliates in Aquitaine – into six aeronautical enterprises; these were:

- Lorraine-Dietrich, manufacturer of aero-engines with a factory in Argenteuil
- Hanriot, which manufactured trainers at its works at Bourges
- Chantiers Aéro-Maritimes de la Seine (CAMS), which made seaplanes at Sartrouville
- Amiots-SECM, which produced reconnaissance aircraft and bombers at Colombes
- Nieuport with its factory at Issy-les-Moulineaux
- The Société Aéronautique Boedelais (SAB), an affiliate of Nieuport with a factory at Bacalan.

In practice each company retained its own administrative autonomy, design offices and means of production. At the time Lorraine-Dietrich hoped that the amalgamation would foster its own customer base, but as it turned out this objective was never attained, in the face of severe competition from Gnome-Rhône and Hispano-Suiza.

Société Nieuport joined the consortium on 11 February 1930, contributing 75 per cent of its capital; but the integration did nothing for Nieuport's prospects, and did not revitalize the previously busy production lines. Seeing the writing on the wall, at the end of 1932 Gustave Delage left the company, where he had directed the technical advances for the previous twenty years. Instead he dedicated himself entirely to his other creation, Jaeger-France, which he had formed in 1917 to produce precision instruments for the automotive and aviation industries.

After two years of existence, it was evident that SGA was in serious financial trouble. The profit levels of 1930 could not be sustained in 1931 and 1932, although generous dividends continued to be paid to shareholders. Bad management and a failure to integrate or coordinate the production of its component companies led to the disintegration of the consortium towards the end of 1932. Nieuport and SAB regained their independence at the beginning of 1933, though were incapable of existing alone. Nieuport therefore found a new partner in Chantiers de la Loire, but it was required to cede its Bordeaux affiliate SAB to Marcel Bloch, which soon became part of the Société Nationale de Construction Aéronautiques du Sud-Ouest (SNCASO).

In August 1936, the aviation industry was nationalized by the Front Populaire left-wing government that had been elected on 3 May 1936. Thereby Loire-Nieuport became part of the Société Nationale de Construction Aéronautiques de l'Ouest (SNCAO).

With the loss of Gustave Delage, its guiding influence, and its independent identity, the products of the Nieuport company were no longer recognizable as descendants of the line that began before World War One.

Società Anonima Nieuport-Macchi

In 1912 the Italian War Ministry announced a competition to select an aeroplane for the armed forces. One tender came from Carlo Felice, a sportsman and inventor: together with Roberto Corsi, a businessman with an engineering background, and an artillery officer, Captain Costantino Biego di Costa Bissara, he proposed to form a company to manufacture Nieuport aircraft under licence. These gentlemen approached Giulio Macchi, an engineer who owned a small foundry and sawmill in Varese, to finance the company. An agreement was signed to form the Nieuport-Macchi company with a capital of 200,000 lira on 1 May 1913: this took place at a meeting between Léon Paul Maurice Bazaine, representing the Nieuport company; Paolo Molina, the legal representative of the Macchi brothers; and Giovanni De Martini of the Wolsit company of Legnano. The aims of the company were 'the manufacture and sale of apparatuses for aerial locomotion and components, accessories, tools and other articles relevant to such devices, their operation and repair etc'. The technical manager was Enrico Amman, and Felice Buzio became his deputy. Nieuport sent pilots and technicians to train the Italian personnel, and also arranged a supply of Gnome engines.

Nieuport-Macchi 11s under construction at Varese. Giorgio Apostolo

The new company did not win the War Ministry contract. However, the government did buy three 100hp Nieuports assembled from French components by seven workmen at Varese in a shed rented from the Macchi car body factory, and later in the year it ordered another fifty-six. These machines, designated Nieuport 10.000, were two-seat biplanes powered by 80hp Gnome engines, and intended for tactical reconnaissance.

During 1913 the company designed its first indigenous machine, a parasol derivative of the two-seat Nieuport monoplane, and it underwent further development in the hands of Clemente Maggiora, a pilot who arrived at Varese early in 1914. Altogether some forty-two were built for artillery spotting. On 4 December 1914 Maggiora established a new world altitude record in one of these, climbing to a height of 2,700m (8,860ft) with two passengers, Count Patriarca and Zanibelli, a pioneer aviator. More records followed: on 19 December a height of 3,750m (12,300ft) was reached in thirty-eight minutes, carrying one passenger; and in March 1915, flying from Malpensa, an Italian altitude record of 3,790m (12,435ft) was established, again with one passenger.

Nieuport-Macchi had become an important element of the Italian aircraft manufacturing industry, and by the end of 1915 the Varese factory had expanded significantly, with its workforce increasing from eighty-four in May 1915, to 625 by the end of 1915, and to 1,554 a year later. Production was further facilitated by the construction of a new factory, equipped with new machine tools, behind the old Macchi car-body plant.

Although an important aircraft in the development of Italian aviation, the performance of the Nieuport 10.000 under difficult service conditions had not been outstanding. By the end of 1915 it had been replaced in production by the Nieuport 10, of which a total of 240 were built, and this in turn was replaced by the Nieuport 11. The company continued to search for records during 1916. One feat was the altitude of 6,550m (21,490ft) reached by Goffredo Gorini in a Nieuport 11. Subsequently the Nieuport 17 and Hanriot HD 1 were also produced in large numbers, 150 of the former being built. The Hanriot was an outstanding machine compared with the earlier Nieuports, and was delivered by Nieuport-Macchi to Italian squadrons from November 1917.

Shortly after hostilities began between Italy and Austria-Hungary, an Austrian Lohner Type L flying boat suffered an engine failure and was forced to alight intact at Porto Corsini near Ravenna. In less than seven weeks Nieuport-Macchi had built an exact structural replica powered by a 150hp Isotta-Franchini engine. Flight testing was carried out by a naval pilot, Lt Giovanni Roberti, based at Schiranna on the shore of a lake near Varese, where a shed was erected specifically for this purpose. This aircraft, the L.1, totally outperformed the equipment then operated by the Italian navy, the French FBA flying boat built under licence by Savoia at nearby Sesto Calende.

In 1916, the L.1 was replaced in production by the L.2, a redesign of improved performance. This design was in turn quickly replaced by the L.3 (renamed the M.3), of similar configuration but essentially a new design by Felice Buzio. Largely due to its low weight, this design showed a significantly improved performance compared with its Loehner predecessors, and this was demonstrated on 10 October 1916 when it established a new world time-to-height record for seaplanes by reaching 5,400m (15,170ft) in forty-one minutes. A total of 200 were built, and the increased production required an extension of the manufacturing facilities on the lake. This design was used extensively by the Italian navy in the Adriatic on reconnaissance and bombing missions.

The management of the company was now restructured in recognition of the fact that production was now centred on two distinct types of aircraft. The technical manager, Enrico Amman, remained at Varese to direct work on land-based aircraft, while his former deputy, Felice Buzio, was promoted to head the seaplane department, now firmly established in much enlarged premises at Schiranna on the shores of Lake Varese.

The M.3 concept was further developed through the M.4, of which only two were built – the M.8, with a redesigned wing of greater stiffness and reduced drag, and the M.9, a scaled-up version of the M.8 used for anti-submarine patrols.

At the beginning of 1917 Buzio and Calzavara designed the M.5, a seaplane fighter used by the Italian navy in some numbers to escort flying boats. Calzavara was naval officer on assignment to Macchi from the Ufficio Vigilanza Costruzioni Aviatorie (Aircraft Manufacturing Inspectorate) in Milano. The M.5 was further developed into the M.5bis and the M.7, the latter designed by Alessandro Tonini, who had been appointed as technical manager at Varese. Two companies based in Naples, Industrie Meridionali and Construzioni Aeromarittime S.A., assisted in the production of the M.7 series, developments of which continued in service until 1928. The M.9 was a scaled-up M.8 and was produced in military and civil forms. The final seaplane produced by Macchi was the M.12, a twin-boomed machine designed by Buzio towards the end of the war.

Although some contracts were cancelled when the armistice was signed between Italy and Austria-Hungary at Villa Giusti, altogether Nieuport-Macchi produced some 2,538 aeroplanes during the war. Of these, forty-two were Parasols; fifty-six Nieuport 10,000s; fifty Maurice Farman Series 11s, with the standard 80hp Renault engines replaced by the 100hp Fiat A.10; 240 Nieuport 10s; 646 Nieuport 11s; and the remainder mainly Nieuport 17s. To these can be added the flying boats produced at Schiranna and Masnago: 139 L.1s; ten L.2s; 200 M.3s; two M.4s; 240 M.5s; a single M.6; seventeen M.7s and thirty M.8s; and sundry other types, totalling more than 640 machines.

Most military contracts were cancelled when the war ended. In the aftermath, governments had more pressing needs than to establish the infrastructure for civil aviation, and the aircraft manufacturing industry had no alternative but to consolidate. Nieuport-Macchi ended the war with four factories, those at Coquio and Malpensa building landplanes, and those at Masgano and Schiranna building seaplanes. Workers were laid off, the numbers reducing from a peak of about 2,825 employees to around 500. Nevertheless, the company made strenuous efforts to promote its aircraft for civil use, and had some success in winning orders.

The first postwar machine to appear was the M.9bis, a four-seat cabin version of the military M.9. Next came the M.18 flying boat, in both civil and military forms, followed by the M.14 military trainer and M.14bis fighter designed by Alessandro Tonini. In parallel with the M.14 came the M.15 reconnaissance biplane. Tonini also designed a diminutive single-seat light touring aircraft, which attracted domestic and overseas orders. The M.24 twin-engined seaplane was produced between 1923 and 1927, and was used by the Regia Aeronautica as a bomber, reconnaissance and torpedo aircraft. The M.24 was the last aircraft designed by Tonini, who was superseded by Mario Castoldi.

Beginning in 1924, the company built about eighty Nieuport Delage 29C fighters under licence. This aircraft was the last type produced in co-operation with Nieuport: thereafter the company was reformed as Aeronautica Macchi, a title that it retains to this day.

The Nieuport and General Aircraft Company

The British Nieuport company was formed before the outbreak of the war by Samuel Waring, to manufacture Nieuport designs under licence in the United Kingdom. Its manufacturing facilities were at Cricklewood in north London. During the war it also built several hundred Sopwith Camels, but the decision was made by the company to undertake its own design work. To this end in 1917 the company employed Major S. Heckstall-Smith as managing director, and H.P. Folland as chief engineer and designer. Both were formerly of the Royal Aircraft Factory.

The first indigenous design, the B.N.1 powered by the Bentley B.R.2 rotary engine, appeared in March 1918 but was not put into production. This was followed by the Nighthawk. This machine was ordered in large numbers, but severe problems with its engine, the A.B.C. Dragonfly, led to the collapse of the production programme. Some Nighthawks were re-engined with Bristol Jupiter engines, and some airframes were retained for conversion to Nightjars, a navalized version. Nieuport also built the prototype of a two-engined bomber, the London, but the war ended before it could be put into production.

Stocks of government war-surplus airframes, engines and components were taken over by the Aircraft Disposal Company, a syndicate formed by Frederick Handley Page using his company as a sole selling agency and for technical back-up. The Nieuport company availed itself of an offer by Airdisco to buy back its own aircraft at a fixed price in order perhaps to protect its own sales, although it was difficult to believe that there would be a significant postwar market for such aircraft. In the event the company closed down in August 1920 and was put in the hands of a receiver the following month.

The Gloucestershire Aircraft Company took over their design and used the airframe as a basis for the Mars/Bamel racers and the Sparrowhawk, which it sold in some numbers overseas. H.P. Folland joined the company shortly afterwards as chief engineer.

British Nieuport adverts. *Flight*

Mainly Nieuport 11s being built in the main assembly hall of the Duks factory in Moscow around mid-1916.
Harry Woodman

Production in Russia

Most of the aircraft produced to Nieuport designs were used for military purposes and built under licence by the Duks Company, which also manufactured its own variants. Some early Nieuports were built by the Russo-Baltic Wagon Works (R-BVZ), Anatra (Nieuport 11), Mosca (Nieuport 11), Schetinin works in Petrograd (Nieuport 11) and the Lebedev factory (Nieuport 10). Those from the Schetinin works were criticized for their poor wing construction.

The Duks company was founded in Moscow in 1894 to build bicycles and motorcycles, and changed to manufacturing aircraft in 1910, producing six machines in its first year. The managing director was Y.A. Meller, and the production manager was engineer V.V. Bortashevich. The original name was changed to Aktsionyernoye Obshchestvo Vozdukhoplavania, 'Duks' being derived from the last word. A warehouse and repair facility was also set up in St Petersburg. Its first machine was a Farman copy powered by an 80hp Gnome engine.

The Duks plant occupied an area of 50,000sq m (540,000sq ft). By 1914 it was employing about 1,025 workers, producing ten to twelve machines per month; by 1917 the firm had grown to employ over 2,400 workers, completing some sixty machines per month on an assembly line basis. During the period from 1910 to 1917 the company produced 1,733 aircraft, of which about 150 were produced before the war.

The first Nieuport design to be built by Duks was the Nieuport IVG monoplane fitted with the 70hp Gnome engine; about 300 of these were built in Russia, mostly by the Duks company. The next design to be built was the Nieuport 10. A total of about 700 of these types were built. Other Nieuport designs that were manufactured include the 11, 16, 17, 21, 23, and 24*bis*; 133 Nieuport 17s were built by 25 October 1917.

Following the Bolshevik coup d'état of 1917, the Duks company became GAZ No. 1 (State Aircraft Factory No. 1), and continued to produce Nieuport 24 aircraft. Sixty were built in 1920, and a further eighty before production ceased in 1923.

Some dozens of Nieuport 17s were built by the Anatra factory at Simferopol, all these being sent to the Kacha fighter school near Sevastopol on the Black Sea.

Seguin opened a works in Moscow for the assembly of Gnome engines, mainly from imported French components. Although V.A. Lebedev started a small factory in 1911 to build integral propellers, the infrastructure to supply aircraft and engine components was generally lacking. As a result most material had to be imported, and this led to severe difficulties, particularly during the early part of the war.

Genealogy of the Société Nieuport & Associates

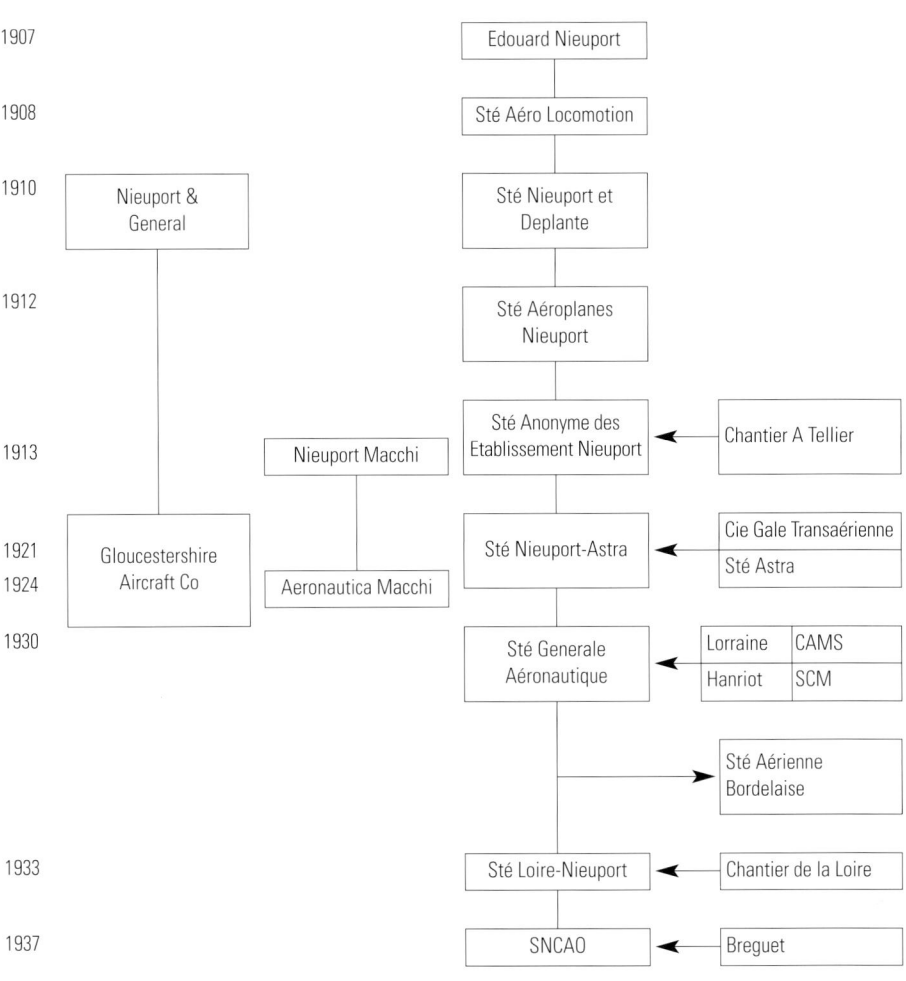

CHAPTER TWO

Nieuport Aircraft Before World War One

It is not possible to establish completely the output of aircraft by Nieuport before the war. Not only did most of the archives of the company not survive, but also the technical press was not particularly reliable in recording the activities of the many pioneer constructors of the period. Aviation in those days was not an exact science, and technical advances depended largely on trial and error. Early aviators, often working in obscure places, were only interested in making things work and in meeting the needs of potential customers; therefore details of work discarded, or modifications made, and the reasoning behind the changes, went largely unrecorded.

Considering that Nieuport himself was in the business a mere three years before his death, his output was prodigious, and the scale of development continued apace after his death. From time to time the company issued lists or catalogues of the aeroplanes available: these tended to record two or three types only, but from these and what other records survived it is possible to piece together an outline at least of the various types produced.

With one or two exceptions the output centred around two families of aircraft derived from the Type II of 1910: these comprised the Type II single-seaters, and the Type IV two- or three-seaters, with floatplane derivatives of the latter. Later developments in these families were the Types VI, X, XI and XIII, the latter three with the alternative technical designations 10.000, 11.000 and 13.000. The missing type numbers cannot be assigned with certainty, but there were plenty of modified versions to which they might have been allocated, and it may be that, due to the uncertainty, they have been included in the following narrative under other type number headings as modifications.

The 1910 Monoplane

Edouard Nieuport started to build his first aeroplane towards the end of 1908 with the help of Jacques Schneider. It is said that in his design work he derived some benefit from the work of an experimental aerodynamist, Victor Tatin, who carried out some studies by towing various shapes made of soap behind a motorboat in the Seine; but this might be speculation. It has also been written that he was further inspired by the experiences of Chalais-Mendon and his airship *La France* of 1883. Undoubtedly Nieuport's philosophy was to apply his experience from his cycling days by making the aircraft as light and as streamlined as possible, thereby obtaining the maximum performance possible from a lightweight engine of relatively low power. In this way his first aircraft was of better performance than its contemporaries, the similarly powered early Bleriot XI and the relatively heavy Voisin biplane with twice the power. In all probability he could see the commercial advantages with such a design, in that it could be made significantly more cheaply than could its competitors.

In the event, his first machine was a monoplane powered by a 20hp two-cylinder water-cooled Darracq. The fuselage consisted of a deep nacelle little longer than the root chord of the wing. The wing was very thin and of lightweight construction, the trailing edge being made of wire, which formed the characteristic scalloped shape when the linen covering was tautened. The cruxiform tail was supported by outriggers extending backwards from the wing at about mid-span and from the pair of undercarriage skids. The skids were fixed to the wings by means of vertical struts and cross-bracing from the fuselage, and supported two large, spoked wheels. A single lever operated the control surfaces for all axes.

The aeroplane made its first tentative flight on or before December 1909 at Issy-les-Moulineaux, but little else is known except that it was destroyed shortly afterwards in its hangar by a severe flooding of the Seine. It is probable that a second machine, already in an advanced state of construction, was destroyed at the same time.

The Nieuport Type II

In 1910, after gaining some flying experience in a Voisin at Mourmelon, Edouard set himself up near the military camp there, not far from the Voisin facilities. There he constructed the prototype of his second design, one that was destined to be the progenitor of a very successful family of aircraft.

This machine was generally of an advanced design, and showed a number of features that had not appeared in other aircraft of the period. The fuselage was constructed of four longerons, with spacers and cross-members of ash. The longerons were spindled out to save weight, except where

The 1910 monoplane flying at Issy-les-Moulineaux. Philip Jarrett

17

joined with the spacers by mortise joints. It was internally braced with piano wire. Unlike the first machine, the whole length of the fuselage was covered, in this case by rubberized fabric. The forward part of the fuselage, including the cockpit, was made of welded metal tubing. In front, the longerons on each side projected beyond a bulbous firewall and were joined by curved metal supports. The engine was connected to these supports by means of a curved clip surrounding each cylinder. The pressurized fuel and oil tanks were placed immediately behind the firewall. The front fuselage was deep enough for the pilot to be almost totally enclosed, with just his head protruding. Although no windscreen was fitted, the front coaming of the cockpit sloped slightly upwards, and bands of linen were also stretched around the shoulders to give the pilot some protection from the slipstream.

A flat, semicircular tailplane was mounted on top of the upper longerons. A universal joint was fitted to the vertical sternpost on which pivoted the control surfaces: these consisted of a horizontal plane, made from welded tubes covered in linen, with two fins protruding above and below at about midspan. As was common for the period, the wings were of thin section with a distinct camber, and the leading and trailing edges were slightly tapered. The wings were constructed with two parallel spars of ash, with fourteen ribs spaced equally about 30cm (1ft) apart. The spars were inserted in sleeves mounted on the fuselage sides, and the whole wing was internally braced with piano wire. Each wing was supported by two stranded cables connected to two pressed-steel brackets bolted around the front spar at about mid-span, an upper one that was supported by a cabane structure formed from four metal tubes over the cockpit, and a lower one connected to the undercarriage skid. Two further cables, attached in a similar way to the rear spar of each wing, provided both support and a means to warp the wings. The upper pair of cables from each rear spar were joined by a heavy gauge, plain wire that slid through a steel tube supported by the cabane struts, and the lower pair of cables was attached to a lever positioned below the fuselage near the rear skid support. This in turn was attached to a metal tube connected to a pair of foot pedals, which controlled each wing independently. The aeroplane was controlled in pitch and yaw by a control column. Nieuport considered that this mechanism gave some means of automatic control, as the pilot would naturally depress the pedals, in the correct sense, to counteract any deviations in flight due to gusts.

The undercarriage consisted of a single skid connected to the lower longerons by two V-struts, one from the front engine bulkhead and the other from aft of the cockpit. There was no wire bracing. Two wheels, splayed slightly outwards, were supported by a metal leaf spring mounted on top of the skid. By this design, which was a feature of his aeroplanes, Nieuport believed that as the aeroplane rested on the wheels and the rear of the skid, it reduced the loading on the rear fuselage, thereby enabling the structure to be lighter and at the same time reducing the number of times the fuselage needed to be re-rigged. The narrow track did mean, however, that the aircraft sometimes hit a wingtip on the ground whilst taxiing, and observers had also noted that it oscillated laterally when taking off.

This machine was powered by an air-cooled derivative of the earlier Darracq engine. This had a stroke of 120mm and bore of 130mm, and produced 20–24hp at 1,200rpm. It drove a Chauvière Intégrale propeller of 2m (6.5ft) diameter and 120–150cm pitch. Petrol was supplied to the carburettor, situated within the cockpit, by gravity from a tank placed in front of the pilot.

Nieuport's company, the Société Générale d'Aero Locomotion, entered three identical machines at the Semaine d'Aviation de la Champagne at Béthy, held from 3 to 10 July 1910. These aeroplanes were piloted by Nieuport, Niel and Noguès, and were given racing numbers: 48, 49 and 50. The machines averaged around 70–75km/h (44–47mph), and No. 48 recorded a speed as high as 84km/h (52mph). Nevertheless, an observer noted that, although the aeroplanes were fast, control was somewhat erratic.

Modifications were therefore put in hand to improve stability, and when the aeroplane was exhibited on the company stand at the Paris Salon in October, it was fitted with a delta-shaped tailplane and a pair of elevators with curved trailing edges. Shortly afterwards, this was replaced with a semicircular tailplane. The tail assembly

Nieuport IIN flown by Edouard Nieuport at the Grande Semaine de Champagne at Rheims in 1910. Philip Jarrett

Nieuport IIN with a more conventional empennage. Philip Jarrett

NIEUPORT AIRCRAFT BEFORE WORLD WAR ONE

Nieuport II dismantled for transportation. Philip Jarrett

was in turn replaced by a conventional rudder arrangement, the latter being more like the shape that was to be characteristic of Nieuport designs for some years to come. The wing leading-edge taper was also eliminated.

At this Paris Salon, the aeroplane was presented by the marketing director, Henri Depasse, as the Monoplane Nieuport Type II or Nieuport II. Although with its Darracq engine the type was fast, the indications were that this engine was not consistently delivering its quoted power, and at the beginning of 1911 the Type IIN appeared with a Nieuport derivative of the Darracq engine, designed by Edouard with the able assistance of an engineer by the name of Échard. The engine developed 28–32hp at about 1,300rpm when fitted with a propeller of 202cm (80in) diameter and 135cm (53in) pitch. Besides the Type IIN with the Nieuport engine and the Type IID with the 20hp Darracq (offered at 18,000Fr), the type was also made available as the Type IIA with the three-cylinder Anzani (22,000Fr for the two-seater) and the Type IIG with Gnome engines of 50hp (single-seater 24,000Fr, two-seater 26,000Fr), 70 or 100hp. Although customers could choose any engine from this range, towards the end of 1911 the company's catalogue only offered Types IIN and IIG.

With the Nieuport engine at Mourmelon, Edouard Nieuport managed to exceed a speed of 101km/h (62mph) on 6 March, and a closed circuit speed of 109.9km/h (68mph) on 9 March 1911. This same machine was shown at the Olympia Show in London in April 1911. With a Régy propeller fitted, the closed circuit speed was raised to 119.68km/h (74.37mph) on 11 May to beat the previous record held since 1910 by Alfred Leblanc in a 50hp Bleriot. It was claimed that the aeroplane had a gliding angle as high as 20:1.

Three Nieuports, of which two were Nieuport IVGs, were amongst the thirteen entrants for the 1911 Gordon Bennett Aviation Cup held at Eastchurch in June. Chevalier in a 28hp Nieuport retired with engine trouble on the twelfth lap, landing in rough pasture amongst a flock of sheep and breaking his undercarriage.

Then in the early summer of 1912, Emmanuel Helen competed in the Circuit d'Anjou in a Nieuport 'de Vitesse' single-seater powered by a Gnome rotary (given the competition number '13') and attained a speed of 163km/h (101mph). As it was painted black, it was popularly known as '*le corbeau*' ('the crow').

The Société Nieuport showed a new single-seater at the Paris Salon held in

---

Nieuport Engines

Two-cylinder, horizontally opposed air-cooled engine. Cast-iron pistons. Connecting rods and crankshaft of special steel. Cylinders screwed into an aluminium crankcase. The crankshaft was splash-lubricated, and oil was recirculated by a gear pump, worm-gear driven from the magneto driveshaft. Cam-actuated inlet and exhaust valve, timing adjustable from the cockpit. Nieuport magneto and high tension ignition. There were at least four versions, but no details are available.

28–32hp at 1,300rpm

Bore 130mm, stroke 135mm

Capacity 4.3ltr (0.9gal)

Weight 70kg (154lb)

Consumption, petrol 16ltr/h (3.5gal), oil 2ltr/h (0.4gal)

Price 5,000Fr

Nieuport engine of 1912. *The Aero*

19

November 1912 that was very different from its predecessors: it was designed for speed, and called 'Obus' (meaning 'shell' or 'bullet') by the press because of its streamlined shape. Although it retained a similar fuselage and tail assembly to earlier designs, the 50hp Gnome driving a Régy propeller was closely cowled, with the domed cowling cut away only at the bottom. The span was reduced to 7m (23ft) by removing two ribs from each wing, and the section was of noticeably less curvature and incidence. The sides of the cockpit were cut away so that the pilot could see the ground over his shoulder. The undercarriage was much simplified to save weight, and consisted of two large wheels positioned at the ends of a leafspring which was supported by a short steel skid attached directly at the rear to the fuselage and welded steel struts attached to the lower longerons at the firewall.

Nieuport entered a single-seat racer, powered by an 80hp engine and piloted by Dr Espanet, for the Coupe Gordon Bennett of 1913 held in September at Bétheny. It had the general shape of the Type II, but the Gnome engine was almost totally enclosed in a rounded cowling, with only two small cooling apertures. The wingspan was shortened by removing five of the fourteen ribs, and both the chord and the camber were reduced. The cabane struts were shortened, and the cockpit area was streamlined by adding mouldings front and rear. The undercarriage skid was shortened in front of the forward V-strut, and the spokes of the large wheels were covered with canvas. Unfortunately the Nieuport did not win the event: this honour went to Maurice Prévost in a Deperdussin, at a speed of 203km/h (126mph). To rub salt into the wound, the Ponnier that came second at a speed of almost 200km/h (124mph) was a near copy of the 1911 Nieuport. This marked the end of this line of development, and Nieuport quickly produced two new monoplanes, the Types XI and XIII.

The Type II was used by the Nieuport flying school at the beginning of the war. Argentine purchased one Type IIG, along with one Type IV, both aircraft serving with the Escuela de Aviacíon Militar. Russia acquired around fifty Type IIs and IIIs for use as trainers. Finally, Spain had one Type IIN and two Type IIGs in service with the flying school at Cuatro Vientos between 1912 and 1914.

The Nieuport Type III

A two-seater version of the Nieuport monoplane was announced as the Type IIIA, though it was not displayed at the 1910 Paris Salon. Although the choice of the engine was up to the customer, the designation would suggest that the Anzani was the preferred option. However, all known Type IIIs were fitted with REP engines. The Type III was very similar to the Type II of the period, with a similar complex tail arrangement but with a 10m wingspan. The wing area was further increased by increasing the chord through incorporating a false spar to support the elongated ribs. The front of the fuselage was longer and strengthened by a cladding of sheet metal, and the undercarriage skid was lengthened and supported by an additional V-strut.

The Nieuport Type IV

Most Type IVs were two-seaters, similar to the definitive version of the Type IIN, but larger, and powered by a Gnome engine. However, some single-seaters existed, and some were powered by Clerget engines.

Nieuport 'Obus' at the Paris Salon of 1912.

Nieuport III.

The fuselage was lengthened by 60cm (24in), and the wingspan was marginally increased by adding one more rib station. For the later two-seaters the number of bracing wires was doubled. The undercarriage wheels were mounted further back and, like on the Type III, the steel skid was supported by three V-struts made from oval-section steel.

To gain publicity for his new company, Edouard Nieuport made a series of record-breaking flights during the early part of 1911. On 5 March in a Type IVG fitted with a 50hp Gnome, with a strong following wind, he achieved an average speed of 137.125km/h (85.209mph) over 150km (93 miles). Without such a favourable wind on the following day he managed an average speed of 101km/h (63mph) over a 250km (155 mile) course. On 9 March 1911 he flew with two passengers at 102.855km/h (63.91mph), and alone at 109km/h (68mph). On 11 May, with two passengers crammed in behind him, he flew 100km (62 miles) in under an hour, setting world records over 20, 30, 40, 50 and 100km (12, 18, 24, 31 and 62 miles) flown in 11min 59.4sec, 17min 52.6sec, 22min 44.4sec, 29min 37.4sec and 59min 8sec, respectively, records that were still standing more than two years later. Later he smashed the world closed-circuit record at an average speed of 133km/h (82.7mph) with a 70hp Nieuport.

Two Nieuport IVGs were entered in the Paris to Madrid race starting at Issy on 21 May, but they did not compete because of a serious accident: in this a competitor crashed into a party of VIPs, killing the French Minister of War and injuring several others, including the French Premier Monis and the Nieuport Chairman Henri Deutsch de la Meurthe.

In June 1911, Weymann entered a Nieuport IVG powered by a 70hp Gnome in the Paris-Rome-Turin race. On the first day he got as far as Troyes after intermediate landings at Saclay and Melun to adjust his engine; but he abandoned the race on the second day after badly damaging the undercarriage of his machine on landing at Cellé-sur-Ouese. Weymann also entered the Circuit of Europe that began on 18 June, starting and finishing in Paris and consisting of nine stages around northern France, Belgium and Holland and across to London. Weymann was placed third in the first stage from Paris to Liège, and by the time he had reached Utrecht he was fourth overall, having won 6,000 francs already. But bad weather then grounded the contestants, and the next stage was not scheduled until 2 July, forcing Weymann to withdraw so that he would not miss the Gordon Bennett Cup.

Three Nieuports were amongst the thirteen entrants for the 1911 Gordon Bennett Aviation Cup held at Eastchurch in June, of which six actually started; four finished the course. Charles Weymann, in a 100hp Nieuport IV with racing number 2, flew a faultless race, completing the 151km (94 miles) in 1hr 11min 36.3secs, to win for the United States at an average speed of 127km/h (78.77mph). Edouard Nieuport, representing France in a 70hp Nieuport IV, was third in a time of 1hr, 14mins, 37.3 seconds at a speed of 123km/h (76.56mph), behind Leblanc in a Blériot. Two Nieuport IVGs were entered into the Circuit of Britain which started at Brooklands on 22 July 1911. One which was intended to be flown by Robert Lorraine crashed in France before the race. The other, piloted by Charles Weymann, completed the first leg but crash landed on the second leg between Hendon and Edinburgh.

The military version, the Type IVM, was a slightly modified Type IVG with a 100hp Gnome rotary engine, the wingspan lengthened by two ribs and the cockpit enlarged to cram in two passengers behind the pilot. It was entered into the first military competition ever to take place, the French Military Aeroplane Trials, held under poor weather conditions at Reims during October and

The 100hp Gnome Nieuport '2' piloted by Charles Weymann in the 1911 Gordon Bennett Race at Eastchurch. JMB/GLS collection

Nieuport monoplane 254 *déshabillé* at Farnborough. Philip Jarrett

November 1911. The competition was limited to French aeroplanes powered by French engines and attracted a total of thirty-five machines from fifteen manufacturers. A number of preliminary tests had to be carried out. These tests consisted of three separate flights with a landing, take-off and repeat landing made respectively on a ploughed field, stubble and a clover field. On each occasion the machine had to be dismantled and returned to the aerodrome by road. After the three landings, a flight to measure fuel consumption was required over a distance of 299km (186 miles) at a speed of not less than 60km/h (37mph). Then followed two separate flights made at full load to a height of 500m (1,640ft) within fifteen minutes. Following these preliminary qualifying tests, the winner would be the aeroplane that without landing, flew fastest with a load of 300kg (661lb) over a distance of 299km (186 miles) across country between Reims and Amiens. The Nieuport machine, powered by a 100hp Gnome driving a four-bladed propeller and flown by Charles Weymann, easily completed the qualifying tests, and completed the speed course in 2hr 33min 52sec at an average speed of 116.7km/h (72.5mph), beating the next best by over 35min. The winning machine was bought for 100,000Fr (£4,000) and ten similar machines were ordered at a price of 40,000Fr (£1,600) each. A bonus of 280,000Fr (£11,200) was also awarded to the winner for exceeding the minimum speed requirement.

Claude Graham White flew a 70hp Type IVG at the Boston meeting in the USA in November 1911. A Type IVM was exhibited at the Third Paris Salon in December 1911, alongside a Nieuport IIN. On 20 July 1912, Edouard Nieuport gained the world closed circuit record over a 5km (3mile) course with two passengers at a speed of 102.85km/h (64mph).

All the multi-seat Nieuports before 1914, with the exception of two, were derivatives of the Type IV. Only two variants featured in the catalogue of the period, but photographs show a multiplicity of modifications, most of which related to the rudder. Other modifications, arising from experience of the military, were concerned with improving the pilot's view of the ground, accomplished by reversing the position of the pilot and passenger, and making cut-outs at the wing root.

The Aero Club of France Grand Prix was held over three laps of a triangular course at Angers on 16 and 17 June 1912. It was a handicap race with time allowances given, depending on the number of passengers carried. However, because of very poor

(*Above*) **Claude Grahame White about to take off in his 70hp Nieuport IVG at the 1911 Boston meeting.** Philip Jarrett

Claude Grahame White's 70 hp Nieuport IVG '16', destined to become 282 in RFC service, in the United States in 1912, with mechanic Reginald Carr in the cockpit. Philip Jarrett

weather only six competitors started out of the twenty-eight entrants qualified to start; these included a Nieuport powered by an 80hp Gnome engine, piloted by Helen, who was quickly eliminated with a broken valve, breaking his undercarriage on landing.

The Nieuport company also entered two aeroplanes, powered by 80hp engines and piloted by Espanet and Gobé, in the Circuit d'Anjou, for four-seater aeroplanes. Each Nieuport featured a streamlined hemispherical cowling over the 80hp Gnome, especially built for the race, with the propeller mounted on an extension shaft, the undercarriage with the three V-struts, and notably a long triangular fin in front of the rudder, similar to those fitted to the floatplane derivatives. The wingspan was about

12.5m (41ft), some 40cm (16in) greater than the Type IVG. Unfortunately Espanet retired with engine trouble after achieving the best handicap time over the first lap; he did, however, win the consolation race held on the following day.

In 1913, General Bernard, head of French military aviation, expressed a requirement for an armoured aircraft, and the entrants were displayed before French and foreign dignatories in June 1913 at Villacoublay. Dr Espanet presented a modified Type IV, in which the engine was enclosed in a cylindrical cowling and protected by a shuttered plate. Nieuport had considerable reservations over the effect of the increased weight due to the armour plating on the flying characteristics; however, in the event this modification was not put to the test, as the pilots refused to fly four out of the six entrants.

Four Nieuport aeroplanes were shown at the December 1913 Paris Salon. One of these, powered by an 80hp Gnome fitted with an Integral propeller, was used by Helen to win the International Michelin Cup for that year. He completed his marathon on 2 December, by which time he had officially flown 16,096.6km (10,002.4 miles) in thirty consecutive days. Counting nine days flying lost through having to stop before reaching the official timekeeper, he had in fact completed 20,787km (12,917 miles) in thirty-nine days. He had intended to continue until the end of the year, but decided to stop because of bad weather, secure in the knowledge that his distance could not be beaten.

Although the Type IVM had won the military competition in 1911, few, if any, equipped any escadrille. As will be explained later, a single French escadrille, designated N 12, was formed in 1912 at Reims with six Type IVGs powered with the 50hp Gnome engine. Later deliveries were powered by the 80hp Le Rhônes.

Sales of the Type IVG were made to the military of Great Britain, Italy and particularly Russia. Three engine options were available, of 50, 70 and 100hp, with the 70hp version generally giving the best performance. About 300 Type IVs were built under licence in Russia in five basic versions. Early examples were powered by 50hp Gnome, 60hp Gnome or 60hp Kavalkin engines. The Schetinin plant built a Type IV '1914', featuring a longer-than-standard-span wing and powered by 80hp Gnome or Clerget rotaries. Eighty Type IV-Espanets, powered by 50hp Gnome engines, were also built by the Schetinin plant in 1915. This type was characterized by a very flexible, rectangular-shaped wing with two ribs fewer in each wing. One of these aircraft was fitted with an 80hp Gnome. The Duks plant built small numbers of the Type IV 'Duks' in 1912, powered by the 70hp Gnome. Both the Duks and Schetinin plants built large numbers of the Type IVG with 70hp Gnomes, and Type VIMs with 100hp Gnomes. As will be discussed later, Italy acquired its first Nieuports in 1911, several being assigned to the 1ª Flottiglia Aeroplani (Tripoli) with the Expeditionary Corps in Libya.

A Nieuport IVG under construction at the Duks factory. Visible are the framework for the pilot's seat, the fuel tanks and their support straps, the tubular supports for connecting the wing spars, the internal fuselage wire bracing, the engine mounts and the Gnome engine. Behind there is a glimpse of the wing spar and rib construction.
G. Petrov, via H. Woodman

		1910 Monoplane (single-seat)	Type IIN (single-seat)	Obus (single-seat)	Type IVG (two-seat)	Type IVM (two-seat)
Engine:		20hp Darracq	30hp Nieuport	50hp Gnome	50/100hp Gnome	100hp Gnome
Dimensions:	Span, m (ft)	7 (23)	8.4 (27.6)	<8.4 (27.6)	10.93 (35.9)	12.25 (40.2)
	Chord: at root, m (ft)		2.08 (6.8)			
	at tip, m (ft)		1.73 (5.7)			
	Length: m (ft)	6 (19.7)	≈7 (23)	6.95 (22.8)	8.4 (27.6)	8.5 (27.9)
	Height: m (ft)		1.52 (5)			
	Wing area, sq m (sq ft)	12 (129)	14 (150)	12.9 (138.8)	20.5 (220.5)	22.5 (242)
Weights:	Empty, kg (lb)				340 (750)	500 (1,100)
	Loaded, kg (lb)	260 (573)	224 (494)	259 (571)		
Performance:	Speed, km/h (mph)			125 (77.7)	109 (67.7)	

Type IVs saw limited service in other countries before World War One. One Type IVG (christened 'la Argentina') served with the Escuela de Aviacioíon Militar in 1912. A Type IVG, owned by E. Argyropoulos and christened 'Alkyon', was the first aeroplane flown in Greece. Five Type IVs were purchased by Spain in April 1913 and assigned to the Escuela de Peu. Sweden purchased two Nieuport IVGs, the first in 1912 and the second the following year. (The operational history of Nieuport monoplanes before and during World War One is covered in Chapters 4–7.)

The Nieuport Destroyer

During 1912, Nieuport redesigned the structure of their monoplanes in order to reduce the empty weight and improve the load-carrying capacity. The wing spars were lightened by making them hollow, accomplished by gluing two shells together. In the fuselage, the longerons were formed of T-section wood, the thickness of any part depending on the load-bearing requirements. Ash was used for the front members where the load was greatest, and pine was used for the rear sections. Cylindrical tubing replaced the oval-section tubing used for the undercarriage structure. Alternative control mechanisms for wing warping using either hands or feet were offered.

Several new designs appeared on the Nieuport stand at the 1913 Paris Salon. One of these, dubbed the 'Destroyer', was an armoured two-seater that generally resembled the IVM, but featured the new structural design. It was powered by a fourteen-cylinder 160hp Gnome engine protected at the front by an armoured plate furnished with vanes to facilitate cooling. The propeller featured a large spinner fitted with six radial cooling gills. The fuselage longerons were of ash, and the spacers of spruce. The pilot was seated at the front of a large cockpit on top of a large petrol tank, and the single gunner was placed behind, on a seat facing to the right. His machine gun could be mounted on two or three fixed spigots set around the edge of a wide U-shaped frame situated on the two sides and rear of the cockpit. However, the field of fire was severely restricted by the wings and fuselage and by the cabane struts. The engine and the front portion of the fuselage to just behind the cockpit were armoured by 2.5mm and 3mm sheet metal, respectively.

The 'Destroyer' out-performed its competitors and attracted an order that was later cancelled. Some time in 1914, the prototype was allocated to a squadron stationed on the outskirts of Paris whose duty was the interception of airships, and for this task the aircraft was modified: the complex gun mounting was removed, and the gunner, equipped with just a large-calibre rifle and some cartridges, was seated behind the pilot facing forwards. The spinner was removed to improve engine cooling.

Nieuport Type VI and Floatplanes

Before the war, Nieuport designed several single- and two-seat floatplanes closely based on landplane equivalents. A Type IVG on floats appeared in April 1912 on the Seine at Meulan, piloted by l'Enseigne de Vaisseau Gustave Delage, who designed it in co-operation with M. Chassério. The structure supporting the floats was very complicated. The central V-strut of the landplane had been removed, and the skid was deepened somewhat and strengthened with bands of linen. Four streamlined struts were splayed out from the undercarriage anchor points on the fuselage to the floats, which were also connected by cross-members attached to the central skid. The wooden floats, made of cypress, were wide but fairly short and were strengthened with sheet metal at their bows and by canvas. Each float sprouted two small hydrofoils at the front, with the dual purpose of reducing the impact of spray on the propeller and preventing the floats from nosing into the water. A third float – oval in shape, with a capacity of 150ltr (33gal) and weighing 10kg (22lb) – was placed under the rear of the fuselage. A panel of canvas had been removed from the starboard side of the fuselage under the wing, and had been replaced by a sheet metal surround screwed to the side longerons and spacers. The two-bladed propeller was replaced by a four-bladed one of smaller diameter, but this was found to give an inferior performance and a two-bladed propeller was reinstated but with its tips strengthened with copper plating as protection against the impact of spray. With subsequent models the central skid was replaced by a metal bar and an additional inverted V-strut connecting the front and rear float supports.

Three large meetings were held in 1912, but Nieuport did not compete in the first, held at Monaco at the end of March.

During August 1912, the French navy held a competition off the coast of St Malo. A sum of £1,520 was offered in prizes on the basis of speed, with allowances for passengers carried, and Nieuport entered a two/three-seater powered by a 100hp Gnome engine. On the first day, Weymann and his mechanic took off from choppy sea outside harbour, but the motor was pulling badly and they failed to gain altitude, so an emergency

Swedish Nieuport IVG. Philip Jarrett

landing was made; unfortunately one of the floats detached and the machine capsized, though the crew were picked up safely by a destroyer. On the second day Weymann carried one passenger but did not cross the finishing line, and was penalized with twelve demerit points. On the third day, however, he completed the round trip between St Malo and Jersey in a time of 1hr 41min, beating the second-placed aeroplane by over 30min, and thereby winning a special prize for the fastest time presented by the Isle of Jersey. But due to the problems on the first two days, the Nieuport came only fifth in the military competition, with a total of twenty-five demerit points earning 2,000Fr.

For the meeting in September at Tamise sur Escaut, which was effectively a trial to select seaplanes for service in the Belgian colonies in Africa, Nieuport entered two floatplanes powered by 100hp fourteen-cylinder Gnome engines and piloted by Weymann and Gobé. But these aeroplanes did not show good seaworthiness and were not particularly fast. The floats were found to be insufficiently buoyant, and these were modified by increasing the length and making them lighter by replacing the upper surfaces with varnished Willesden linen, whilst at the same time strengthening them by extending the supporting metal cross-members across the width of the floats. A floatplane was shown at the 1912 Paris Salon, without its wings due to lack of space. This had floats of 1,850ltr (407gal) capacity, and by July 1912 large fins in front of the rudder above and below the fuselage had been introduced to improve directional stability. All future Nieuport floatplanes featured these improvements with, in addition, various changes to the rudder shape.

The first seaplane to appear in the Nieuport catalogue was the floatplane derivative of the Type VI two-seater with a 100hp Gnome engine fitted with a direct drive Chauvière propeller. The Type VI had a similar structure and wings to the Type IVM, except that, although the longerons in the fuselage were still made of wood, the vertical spacers were of steel. The wings had a slight dihedral angle with washout of both camber and angle of attack. The pilot and observer were seated in tandem. The aircraft had an endurance of about three hours. One major advance pioneered by Nieuport was the provision of a starting handle for the engine within the cockpit, it being difficult if not impossible to swing the propeller of a seaplane while standing on a float in the water. The shape of the rudder was similar to a quarter sector of a circle and a cabane consisting of two inverted V-struts joined at the apices by a horizontal bar. Cruising or maximum speeds, for they were the same, were about 100km/h (60mph) in all cases. A three-seat version, with the passengers seated side by side behind the pilot, was exhibited at the 1912 Paris Salon, the Brussels Exhibition, and Olympia early in 1913.

Espanet and Weymann in Nieuports were two of seven qualifiers for the final stages of the 1913 Grand Prix d'Hydro-aeroplanes de Monaco held during April. The Nieuports had three-stepped floats fitted with eyebolts at the base of the float struts for towing purposes. The performance of these floats attracted a great deal of interest as they were the only ones in the competition with steps. The eliminating stages consisted of six tests: starting the engine without touching the propeller, climbing to 500m (1,640ft), gliding from 100m (330ft), being hoisted out of the water with a block and tackle, and navigating a 6.25km (4 mile) course on the floats. But numerous accidents before the event even got underway saw the end of many of the entrants; amongst these was Espanet (No. 6), who had to retire before the final

An early type of Nieuport floatplane. Philip Jarrett

The 100hp Nieuport VIG '6' flown by Gabriel Espanet at the 1913 Grand Prix d'Hydro-aeroplanes de Monaco. Philip Jarrett

started after he damaged his port float on a wave. Weymann managed to take off into wind after leaving the harbour, but towards the end of the first stage he suffered a serious accident as he alighted at Beaulieu half way round the course, when a squall caused his machine to somersault backwards, throwing Weymann himself out into the water. The fuselage broke in two, with the rear fuselage and float detached. As the weather had deteriorated no one completed the course and the competition was abandoned, Weymann receiving 3,000Fr as joint second prize. A consolation race was held the following day in excellent weather, with just four competitors, one of which was Espanet in No. 6. But he continued to have problems: on taking off he had to jettison some of his spare petrol cans in order to gain height, and then had trouble with his engine. He gave up after covering 190km (118 miles), coming inshore to alight, and taxiing into port. Nevertheless he still came in third, despite not completing the course.

Weymann in a Nieuport with a 160hp Gnome with the racing number '5', and Espanet in '6' with its 100hp Gnome, also took part in the Jacques Schneider Cup that followed. Espanet dropped out after about 70km (43 miles) with a failed engine. Weymann was very cautious in the seaworthiness trial, and by the time he started, Prevost in the Deperdussin was well ahead. Despite drifting wide at the turns, Weymann was nevertheless catching up fast – but his engine failed after 240km (150 miles) and Prevost finished unopposed. Garros in a Morane-Saulnier had earlier failed to start, but seeing Weymann drop out, he made a determined effort and managed to take off, and finished the course to claim second place. Weymann was awarded third place despite not finishing.

In July 1913, Julien Levasseur entered a Nieuport floatplane in the Circuit de la Mer du Nord, which covered the route Paris–London–Dunkirk–Rotterdam–Amsterdam–Emden–Ostend–Rouen–Paris. With M. Rougerie as passenger, Levasseur flew the machine, loaded with 100ltr (22gal) of fuel and 40ltr (9gal) of castor oil, from the Seine at Meulan to Blackwall Pier on the Thames in London. They followed the Seine over a bank of fog at about 1,000m (3,000ft) altitude to Le Havre, and then followed the coast to Fécamp where they stayed for about forty-five minutes before continuing to Calais where they refuelled and rested. From there they headed to Margate, and then along the Thames to Woolwich, where they descended and skimmed the river to their destination. After leaving their aeroplane in charge of the Thames River Police, who later removed the aeroplane to the safety of their riverside enclosure, they changed from their oil-soaked clothing at a hotel and then visited friends in the City. Unfortunately en route they had passed over several prohibited areas, and two days later found themselves in court at Bow Street where they were bound over and charged five guineas costs. The authorities relented to allow them to fly back up the Thames and proceed to Rotterdam via Dunkirk. They later flew to Emden and back. Their Type VI behaved faultlessly throughout.

In August 1913, Nieuport entered two floatplanes into both the Paris–Deauville race and the military competition at Deauville immediately following it. For the former race, the floatplanes had a 160hp Gnome engine and a wing similar to the standard IVM wing, with seventeen ribs. The cockpit was very cramped when seating two. The machines entered for the military competition had 100hp engines, much larger cockpits, quarter-circle rudders, and the wingspan extended by two ribs. Both had the pyramidal cabane strut structure. In the Paris–Deauville race, which followed the course of the Seine for some 330km (200 miles), Weymann crashed into a tree at Rouen and smashed a wing. Levasseur, who made two lengthy stops, one due to magneto trouble and the other to refuel, came second, although taking more than twice the time of the winner; but he was disqualified due to missing the control point at Mousseaux. The entries for the military competition were also unsuccessful.

The floatplane exhibited at the Olympia Show in February 1914 was fitted with a revised control system, with a conventional control of the wing warping by a control column replacing the foot-operated system. The engine was fitted with a primer operated from the pilot's seat, and a specially retarded magneto to assist starting, which was declutched in favour of a normally timed magneto after the engine had started. The wings were now built up from ribs with three-ply webs and ash flanges over steel tube spars. The front spar fitted into a tubular socket mounted on the fuselage, and the rear spar was hinged. The ribs had a slight amount of play, allowing them to rotate slightly round the spar to facilitate wing warping. This type of wing was also fitted to the Type XIII. The three-step floats were constructed of three-ply bottoms, two-ply sides and canvas tops.

On 12 March 1914 Cdrs l'Escaille and Destrem of the French navy, each in a Nieuport floatplane, crossed the Mediterranean from St Raphael to Ajaccio, a distance of 257km (160 miles) in 2h 45m. In April 1914, at the aviation rally at Monaco, which preceded the Schneider Cup, Nieuport entered three floatplanes piloted by Espanet, Mallard and Weymann without achieving worthwhile results. For the Cup, the aircraft had wings shortened to fifteen ribs. The most powerful was very similar to a Type IV, unlike the others powered by 80hp engines. Mallard's aeroplane was fitted with a rectangular wing and had metal spars that were very flexible, so it was easy to flex the wings. It is possible that this machine was given to the French navy, which possessed one with metal wings.

The Aviation Maritime received its first Nieuport floatplane in January 1913, and seven had been delivered by the outbreak of the war. Three Nieuport VI floatplanes with 100hp engines were bought by Japan towards the end of 1912, after two of their pilots, Lts Sawada and Nagasawa, had been trained at the Nieuport School.

The Nieuport Type X or 10.000

Although the military considered the Type IVM to be better than its competitors, it was still not satisfied with its carrying capacity. The Type X used the new structural design of the second generation of Nieuport aircraft in order to meet these more stringent requirements. One of the first Type Xs, if not the first, was shown at the 1913 Paris Salon, along with the 'Destroyer'. It was powered by an 80hp Clerget rotary in a semicircular cowling, and the leading edge of the wing was cut back at the roots to improve the pilot's view. The large diameter of the Clerget allowed a roomy front cockpit that was placed in front of the cabane structure and fitted with a full-width windscreen. An identical windscreen was fitted to the rear cockpit. Wing warping was accomplished through cables connected to the wing through two pulleys situated at the base of the rear undercarriage V-strut. Footrests were provided for the pilot.

It was not clear whether the machine exhibited at the Salon was a two- or three-seater. However, as it evolved, the Type X

(*Above*) **Nieuport-Macchi 10.000.** Giorgio Apostolo

The armoured Nieuport XI powered by an 80hp engine.

was definitely a two-seater with the occupants seated in tandem and separated by a streamlined scuttle. The engine was placed well forward, which allowed the observer, protected by a small rectangular windscreen, to be placed in front of the cabane struts with the pilot in the rear cockpit. The leading edge was cut back by some 70cm (28in) at the wing roots to improve the view of the ground. As with other Nieuports, a small locker was provided behind the pilot.

One machine (serial N 50) akin to the Type X was operated by the French military, and a small number with interchangeable floats and wheels were used by the navy in the Mediterranean before and during the war. However, the main user of the Type X or 10.000 were the Italians: Nieuport-Macchi produced some from components made in France, and others were made wholly in its factory at Varese. The first machines bought from Nieuport-Macchi by the Italian government were three 100hp Nieuports assembled from French components. Shortly afterwards the government ordered fifty-six Nieuport 10.000s, also designated Nieuport Ni.18 mq (wing area 18sq m (194sq ft)) in Italy. These were two-seat monoplanes powered by 80hp Gnome engines, and were intended for tactical reconnaissance. Although an important aircraft in the development of Italian aviation, the performance of the Nieuport 10.000 was not, however, outstanding in service.

Nieuport Types XI and XIII

The last generation of Nieuport monoplanes appeared in 1913: a single-seat Type XI or 11.000, and a two-seat Type 13 or 13.000. Nothing is known about a Type XII. The Type XI was a single-seater intended for military reconnaissance duties, and for this reason was also known as 'Cavalry'. It was smaller and lighter than the Type X and had straighter lines, having lost some of the corpulence of the earlier model. The wings were no longer tapered but rectangular, and were situated slightly lower on the fuselage thereby slightly improving the view downwards. The traditional undercarriage with three longitudinally arranged V-struts and central skid had been abandoned in favour of what was to become a more conventional arrangement, with an axle supported at each end by V-struts and the wheel spindles sprung with bungee cord. A V-strut was retained at the rear to support the wing warping cables, for which alternative control mechanisms were offered, either by a control column or pedals. A metal cone below the stern post carried a small, pivoted, rubber-sprung skid. The tailplane and rudder of the military version could be readily dismantled and attached by means of hooks to the upper longerons to ease transportation on a standard military railcar. The engine was covered by a semicircular cowling reminiscent of a Morane-Saulnier. Three versions were proposed, similar to the IIG types, with 50, 60 and 80hp engines, giving top speeds of around 110, 115 and 125km/h (68, 71 and 78mph), respectively.

On 27 December 1913 Georges Legagneux, in a Type XI fitted with an 80hp Le Rhône engine and with the span increased to 11.7m (38.4ft), beat the world altitude record with a height of 6150m (20,178ft). An armoured version of unknown designation was designed in 1914.

The Type XIII is a bit of a mystery. A postcard of an aircraft reputed to be the Type XIII shows an aircraft very similar to the Type XI but with an annular cowling,

NIEUPORT AIRCRAFT BEFORE WORLD WAR ONE

		'Destroyer' (two-seater)	Type X (two-seater)	Type XI (single-seater)
Engine:		160hp Gnome	80hp Le Rhône or Clerget	50/60/80hp rotary engines
Dimensions:	Span, m (ft)	12.3 (40.3)	12.32 (40.4)	9 (32.6)
	Length, m (ft)	8.05 (29)	8.05? (29?)	6.49 (23.5)
	Height, m (ft)	2.85 (10.3)		
	Wing area, sq m (sq ft)	24 (258)	23.1 (248.5)	14.5 (156)
Weights:	Empty, kg (lb)	645 (1,422)		270 (595)*
	Loaded, kg (lb)	1,000 (2,205)	650 (1,433)	430 (948)*
Performance:	Speed, km/h (mph)	120 (74.6)	115 (71.5)	110–120 (68–74.5)
	Initial climb, m (ft)	500 (1,640) in 7min	2–2.7 (6.6–8.8) per sec	

* Figures based on 50hp engine

but it is uncertain whether this was an armoured version of the Type XI or a development of the 'Destroyer'.

The Pusher Seaplane

In 1913 a two-seater Nieuport floatplane with a 110hp Salmson installed as a pusher, was tested on the Seine. It was a large sesquiplane with a short central fuselage for its crew. The tail assembly was carried by two semi-monocoque booms made from cardboard impregnated with Bakelite-like resin. The origin of this machine is not definitely known, but it is probable that it was designed by the Astra company at the time it was amalgamated with Nieuport under the ownership of Henri Deutsch de la Meurthe. Under his guidance the Astra company were confined to the manufacture of lighter-than-air craft. It is possible that it was intended as a lightly armoured military machine.

The Pusher Seaplane. Philip Jarrett

The Nieuport-Dunne

In the interests of producing an aircraft of inherent stability, Lt J.W. Dunne carried out experimental work, under secrecy at the Balloon Factory at Farnborough, on a series of aircraft featuring a novel flying wing with sharply swept back wings and a pusher engine. In the event the British government showed little or no interest in the concept, and instead, Dunne formed a syndicate of businessmen at Blair Athol in Scotland to promote the aeroplane. The Astra company first became interested in Dunne's D.8 design, and sent their pilot M. Montmain over to England to test it. Subsequently Nieuport sent Commander Félix to Eastchurch to evaluate it. He was impressed, and flew one back to Villacoublay and demonstrated it before the French Aeronautical Corps. At an air meeting at Deauville in August 1913, Félix thrilled the crowd by getting out and walking on the wing while flying solo. Nieuport took out a licence and built at least one machine, fitted with a much simplified landing gear, which was shown at the 1913 Paris Salon; but they could not interest the military.

The Nieuport-Dunne. Philip Jarrett

The Nieuport-Macchi Parasol

Towards the end of 1913 Macchi produced a version of the Type 10.000 with a parasol wing. Although the parent Nieuport company had little influence over the design, the idea of improving the downward view by placing the wing above the fuselage was in all probability copied from other French manufacturers such as Blériot, REP and

Nieuport-Macchi Parasol. Giorgio Apostolo

Morane-Saulnier, who had begun to use this concept at about the same time. The machine was largely developed by a test pilot named Clemente Maggiora, who arrived at Varese early in 1914.

The wing was in two halves, joined across an open centre section by the front and rear spars. The spars at the centre section were supported at shoulder height by struts connected to the upper longerons. With most Parasols, these struts consisted of a pair of inverted V-struts at the front spar, and a pair of single vertical struts at the rear. These struts also supported a pyramidal structure of struts, from the apex of which wires supported the wings at one third and two-thirds span. Flying wires were connected from the same wing points to the lower longerons at the junctions with the undercarriage V-struts. One or more airframes had a different cabane strut structure, whereby two inverted V-struts connected the centre of both the front and rear spars to the upper longerons. With this machine, the wings were supported by wires from vertical king posts situated at the apex of the V-struts. At least one such machine was also equipped with a Neri propeller with scimitar-shaped blades. Some machines were fitted with a square aerofoil of about 1m (3ft) surface area, set vertically in the direction of flight and attached at its centre point to the apex of the pyramidal wing support pylon. The skid undercarriage was replaced by a more conventional two-wheeled undercarriage, on an axle supported by V-struts and sprung with bungee cord, and a tail-skid. The aircraft were unarmed.

A total of forty-two were built. The machine was assigned to the Third Army, and was flown from the Medeuzza and Pordenone airfields in north-eastern Italy. It was withdrawn from active use in August 1915.

		Type IV Floatplane (two-seater)	Type VI (two/three-seater)	Pusher Seaplane (two-seater)
Engine:		70hp Gnome	100hp Gnome Integral prop	110hp Salmson
Dimensions:	Span, m (ft)	12.25 (40.19)	12.25 (40.19)	15–16 (49–52)
	Wing chord, m (ft)	2.3 (7.5)		
	Wing incidence	2° 2"		
	Length, m (ft)	8.5 (27.9)	8.7 (28.5)	7.8 (25.6)
	Height, m (ft)	3.6 (11.8)		
	Wing area, sq m (sq ft)	24.8 (266.8)	40 (430)	
Weights:	Empty, kg (lb)	545 (1,202)	700 (1,544)	
	Loaded, kg (lb)	600 (1,323)	795 (1,753)	1,300 (2,867)
	Fuel, ltr (gal)	120 (26)		
	Oil, ltr (gal)	36 (7.9)		
Performance:	Speed, km/h (mph)	104–115 (64–71)	105 (65)	

CHAPTER THREE

Nieuport Aircraft of World War One

The Nieuport 10

It is believed that before the outbreak of the war, Gustave Delage was working on a racing biplane design intended as an entrant for the 1914 Gordon Bennett Cup. His recall into the navy interrupted his work, but some of his colleagues that had not been enlisted adapted his design into an armed scout. A French patent application (No. 477,457 of 30 January 1915) dated before his return described in detail salient features of the design. These features included the cutout in the upper wing to allow the observer to stand up to fire a gun mounted on the wing, the design of the mounting, the design of the tail-skid, the V-shaped interplane struts, and a mechanism for adjusting the incidence of the lower wing. Sketches of the aircraft in the patent, based on a photograph of the machine, confirm that the prototype had already been built before the patent application.

As previously related, the Nieuport company favoured the monoplane layout to achieve the best speed. However, criticism of the restricted view accorded by such a layout had already caused several companies, including Nieuport-Macchi in Italy, to adopt the parasol wing. Furthermore, both the British and French ministries had clearly stated their preference for the biplane with its superior rate of climb, sturdy construction and improved manœuvrability. The sesquiplane layout – that is, a biplane with a lower wing much smaller than the upper wing – combined these advantages with a better downward view.

The new biplane, the Nieuport 10 (or Nieuport Type XB, as it was known at the time), retained the two-seat fuselage and rudder shapes of the Type X monoplane. As before, the fuselage was of approximately square section, with the lower longerons slightly more closely spaced than the upper, and was of mixed wood/metal construction with ash longerons and the framework braced with piano wire. The tail surfaces were of welded steel tube covered in varnished fabric. The undercarriage consisted of V-struts supporting a cross-axle. The monoplane wing had been replaced by a biplane configuration, with a lower wing of narrower chord than the upper. The prototype had upper and lower wings of the same span, but subsequent machines had lower wings of reduced span. The lower wing had a small amount of dihedral and was slightly swept back, this configuration giving the best downward view consistent with a

Prototype Nieuport 10 (XB) showing the position that the observer would need to adopt in combat to fire a hand-held gun. JMB/GLS collection

Detail of the fore and aft mounting of the Le Rhône engine installation fitted to early Nieuport 10s. JMB/GLS collection

(*Above and below*) One of the earliest Nieuport 10s (XBs) delivered to the RNAS. The upper wing cutout had been replaced by an overwing Lewis gun. 3165 was initially delivered to 1 Sqn RNAS at St Pol on 25 May 1915 and was with the Dover Patrol Flight by February 1916. JMB/GLS collection

biplane layout. The upper wing was well braced to the fuselage by a complex arrangement of vertical and inverted V-struts. Lateral control was achieved through ailerons on the upper wing only, which were actuated by internal span-wise torsion tubes linked to the control column by a system of cranks and connecting rods, some of which were partially visible in slots in the upper wing and passing down through the area of the cabane struts. The leading edges of the ailerons were strengthened with wood and metal.

The single spar of each lower wing was connected to the twin spars of the upper wing by single V-struts. The single point attachment of each interplane V-strut to the lower wing consisted of a split ring fitted round the spar. This enabled the entire lower wing to be rotated about the spar, permitting the incidence to be adjusted. Whereas the patent mentioned above proposed that the wing incidence could be adjusted in flight by means of a large lever on the right-hand side of the cockpit, in practice, incidence was adjusted only on the ground. This facility was abandoned in later designs, although the V-shaped struts

(*Top*) **Nieuport 10 showing the large windscreen above the deep cockpit coaming. The gun mounting is designed to pull down the Lewis gun for reloading. In this version, access to the cockpit for both pilot and observer is from the side.** JMB/GLS collection

(*Middle*) **An uncovered Nieuport 10AR showing the fuselage structure. Note the hooped support between the vertical rear centre-section struts, the aileron linkages, and also how cramped the space is for the observer.** P. Gray

(*Bottom*) **Very basic interior of the cockpit of a Nieuport 10.** JMB/GLS collection

and the split-ring attachment to the lower wing spar were retained. This arrangement remained a weakness in the design, and led to a number of structural failures in service amongst aircraft that had seen a lot of use. Presumably the purpose of the mechanism was to adjust the wing incidence to the minimum consistent with the weight of the aeroplane. For example, the single-seat Nieuport 10 with an 80hp Le Rhône had a wing incidence of 2° 15', compared with between 2° 30' and 3° for the two-seater.

The machines were powered by the 80hp Gnome rotary, of which a total of around 9,000 were built. No machine-gun was fitted, the observer being expected to make do with a hand-held rifle or carbine.

The prototype was tested by the French authorities in early February 1915, and its performance proved exceptional: thus Escadrille N. 57 was formed on 23 May 1915 to operate the type. The machine was evaluated by both the RNAS and RFC, but only the RNAS ordered any – a total of sixty, although some of these were delivered as Nieuport 11 single-seaters.

Several modifications were made to the design before the aircraft went into production. The span of the lower wing was reduced, and its leading edge was cut back to improve the observer's downward view. The rounded surfaces of the original tailplane were replaced by straight untapered leading and trailing edges with raked tips, and the chord of the rudder was increased. Production models were fitted with the 80hp Le Rhône, although export models were powered by the 80hp Gnome. The first few Le Rhônes were mounted on lateral supports, but most production machines had overhung mountings as standard.

The Nieuport 10 was originally designed as a two-seater fighter scout with the observer in the front seat. The observer had to stand up through a cutout in the centre section in order to fire his gun, which swivelled on a pillar set on the front spar. Later deliveries in French and RNAS service had the crew positions reversed with the pilot at the front, and the hole in the centre section was made much smaller. The original complex structure of inverted V-struts at the centre section was replaced by a hoop to allow access to the pilot's seat from the rear. This change was probably made because side access was blocked due to the revised position of the aileron control levers for the upper wing. It has been suggested that the original version was designated 10AV (*avant*) and the revised version 10AR (*arrière*), referring to the position of the observer. With many of the 10ARs in French service, the observers were provided with a Hotchkiss machine-gun.

This change may have been made as a result of the suggestion that the crew positions should be reversed following a trial when a Nieuport 10 was evaluated as a fighter by Esc. MS.26 in June 1915. Other criticisms related to the tailplane that was described as 'weak', the tail-skid that was thought too heavy, the undercarriage track that was considered too narrow, and the engine that vibrated excessively. Few production machines retained the cutout in the upper wing centre section. By 1916 French Nieuport 10s were fitted with an overwing gun firing forwards over the propeller arc. Many were operated as single-seaters with the front cockpit faired over.

RNAS machines stationed at Dunkerque were fitted with fixed Lewis guns mounted above the centre section, operated by a Bowden cable and firing above the airscrew arc. Others had swivel mountings enabling the gun to be tilted downwards in order to change magazines and clear stoppages. Some of the machines that were operated in the Aegean had a single Lewis gun mounted at an angle of about 45 degrees to fire upwards through a cutout in the centre section, making the breech and magazine readily accessible to the pilot. These guns were fitted with a form of tubular gunsight.

The Nieuport 10 was supplied to the Russian Imperial Air Service late in 1915. The early examples had the original crew layout with the observer in the front seat with provision to stand up through the centre section and use a rifle or carbine for defensive purposes. However, most were used as single-seaters with the front cockpit faired over and a machine-gun mounted above the upper wing. The machine-guns

Later production Nieuport 10AR. via Paul Leaman

were installed by a subcontractor in Kiev using gun mounts on the upper wing developed by Vasili Vladimirovich, commander of aviation for the 8th Army. The Russian ace Lt Alexander Alexandrovich Kosakov for a time used a Nieuport 10 with a Vickers gun mounted at an upward angle of about 24 degrees. He is believed to have achieved his first victory in a Nieuport 10 when he shot down a German aircraft near Lake Drisviaty on 24 June 1916.

The Russians manufactured several versions of the Nieuport 10 at their Duks and Lebedev factories. The Duks plant built the Nieuport 10 with 110hp or 120hp Le Rhône engines, fitted with larger cowlings than the standard 80hp version. Another version, the Nieuport 10*bis*, was fitted with either the standard 80hp Le Rhône or the 100hp Gnome Monosoupape, the latter version having five holes in the cowling to assist engine cooling. Only a small proportion of those built were two-seaters, and production of those ceased in 1917. Single-seat production extended into 1918.

Nieuport-Macchi built 240 Nieuport 10s under licence. Besides being used by French, British and Russian squadrons, the type was also operated in limited numbers by the Finnish and Belgian air forces.

The Nieuport 12, 12*bis*, 13 and 20

The Nieuport 12 prototype first flew in the summer of 1915. It was an enlarged development of the Nieuport 10, powered by the 110hp Clerget 9Z engine. Very similar in appearance to the Nieuport 10, it retained the sesquiplane layout with V-shaped interplane struts and the semicircular cowling arrangement of the earlier model. The arrangement of the crew of the later Nieuport 10 production – with the observer to the rear and the pilot seated forward under the upper mainplane – was kept, despite the very restricted view upwards for the pilot. For this reason most production aircraft had the centre section, or at least a panel, covered with transparent material. The general arrangement of centre-section struts, including the inverted-V forward struts and the semicircular hoop to the rear, was also retained. Besides the larger engine, the main distinguishing feature was the outward rake of the interplane struts and the arrangement of the armament.

With the earlier models, armament consisted of two Lewis guns, a forward gun on a flexible mounting fitted to the rear spar of the upper wing, and a rear facing gun fitted on a fixed semicircular rail above the rear coaming of the observer's cockpit. Although this rail could not rotate, the gun itself could be pivoted laterally on its spigot mounting. However, the majority of the machines were fitted with the Étévé mounting: this was conceived by Capt Albert Étévé, the *chef du service des avions* of the Service des Fabrications de l'Aviation (SFA). It initially consisted of a horizontal revolving ring, to which was attached a curved support that moved vertically through a guide on the ring, allowing the gun to be raised or lowered. The flexibility of use was later

33

Nieuport 12 (9209). An early example produced by Beardmore, with the horseshoe-shaped cowling and an Étévé gun mounting. JMB/GLS collection

improved by fitting two pillars provided with rubber cord, one on each side of the curved support, which eased its movement up and down. When the Étévé ring was fitted, the upper decking between the cockpits was removed. By mid-1917, the Étévé mounting was being replaced by the TO3 ring, which was essentially the Scarff No. 2 mount with minor alterations, and later still by the TO4 version.

Some Nieuport 12s were built by Beardmore for the RNAS, and these differed from the Nieuport-built machines in certain respects: the lower wings were of slightly greater span, a small fairing was placed over the attachment points of the flying wires to the fuselage, and a small fairing was added behind the carburettor breather pipes. Later deliveries had circular cowlings similar to those fitted to the French-built Nieuport 12*bis*, and duplicated flying wires. Later still, a fin with a curved leading edge was added, and even later, a stronger undercarriage was fitted with V-struts of broader chord. One or more were converted to single-seaters. In service, the RNAS found that the novel method of attaching the interplane strut to the lower wing spar was not strong enough to prevent flexing of the wing. When the aircraft was put into a steep dive, all the incidence of the left-hand wing-tip, normally 5 degrees, washed out to around zero. It is believed that a modification was put in hand with Beardmore production to alleviate this problem. In response to a letter from the Air Department of the Admiralty, RNAS Dunkerque reported that whereas the speeds of the Nieuport and Beardmore machines were equivalent, the Beardmore machine handled better and had a marginally better service ceiling and climbing rate at altitude.

Despite its deficiences, with its greater power, the Nieuport 12 had a much improved performance over the Nieuport 10 and was ordered in quantity by the Aviation Militaire, the Aviation Maritime and the RNAS, production aircraft being in service by early 1916.

In 1916 an improved version, the Nieuport 12*bis*, appeared fitted with a 130hp Clerget 9B engine. The cowling was circular, and the flat sides of the fuselage were faired into it. The interplane struts were also strengthened by making the chord slightly wider in the middle. One example, designated the Nieuport 12*bis* C.2, was fitted with a *cône de pénétration* and a Lewis gun above the centre section to be fired by the observer.

A later Beardmore production Nieuport 12 (9211), with the fully circular cowling faired into the fuselage sides. It was destined to spend its service with training establishments, but was nevertheless fitted with Rankine Dart containers under the fuselage. JMB/GLS collection

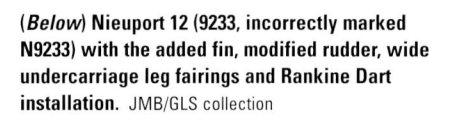

(*Below*) **Nieuport 12 (9233, incorrectly marked N9233) with the added fin, modified rudder, wide undercarriage leg fairings and Rankine Dart installation.** JMB/GLS collection

A one-off, single-seat Beardmore conversion (9241) of the Nieuport 12. JMB/GLS collection

The Nieuport 12*bis* was built in fewer numbers than the Nieuport 10 or 12 but nevertheless served in many French units, and a few may have served with the RNAS. As will be described in a later chapter, a modified machine was used by Lt Marchal in an attempt to bomb Berlin in June 1916.

Possibly there was a shortage of 130hp Clerget engines, as the RFC were persuaded to take a number of two-seaters powered by the 110hp Le Rhône. This engine was less powerful than the 110hp Clerget, but it was lighter and it had a lower fuel and oil consumption. A few were supplied to the Aviation Militaire, and were designated the 'Nieuport 20' by the SFA. On this aeroplane the cowling was semicircular, like the Nieuport 12, but it was faired into the fuselage in a similar way to the Nieuport 12*bis*. The front fuel tank was slightly larger and of a different shape, and the first vertical fuselage spacers were further aft to accommodate an engine back-plate of revised design. The pilot and observer sat back to back, and the latter was provided with a Lewis gun.

Nieuport 12*bis* with the 130hp Clerget 9B.
JMB/GLS collection

		Nieuport 10	Nieuport 12	Nieuport 12*bis*	Nieuport 20
Engine:		80hp Le Rhône 9C	110hp Clerget 9Z	130hp Clerget 9B	110hp Le Rhône 9J
Propeller:		Régy 155 or Chauvière 2219	Régy 274 or Eclair 2	Eclair 20	Régy 151 or Eclair 2
Dimensions:	Wingspan, m (ft)	7.9 (25.9)	9 (29.5)	9 (29.5)	9 (29.5)
	Length, m (ft)	7 (22.9)	7 (22.9)		7 (22.9)
	Height, m (ft)	2.85 (9.35)	2.70 (8.8)		2.70 (8.8)
	Wing area, sq m (sq ft)	18 (194)	23 (247)		23 (247)
Weights:	Empty, kg (lb)	440 (970)	520 (1,147)	550 (1,213)	453 (999)
	Loaded, kg (lb)	690 (1,520)	820 (1,808)	875 (1,929)	752 (1,658)
Performance:	Max speed, km/h (mph):				
	at sea level	140 (87)	157 (98)	149 (93)	157 (98)
	at 2,000m (6,500ft)		146 (90)	141 (87.6)	152 (95)
	at 3,000m (9,800ft)		140 (87)	136 (84.5)	
	Time to height (mins):				
	500m (1,650ft)	3	2.08		
	1,000m (3,300ft)	7	4.83	4.67	5.2
	2,000m (6,500ft)	17	10.33	10.5	12.2
	3,000m (9,800ft)		22.0	20.0	
	Service ceiling, in m	3,800 (12,470)			
	Duration (hours)	2	3	2.5	

Lewis gun on an Étévé mounting, Nieuport 12 of 2 Wing RNAS. JMB/GLS collection

A rather poor photograph of what may be the Nieuport 13 (XIIIB) fitted with a 80hp Le Rhône engine. JMB/GLS collection

Manufactured in France, Nieuport 20 (A6602) was flown to England on 8 May 1917. JMB/GLS collection

The Nieuport 13 was identical to the Nieuport 12 except that it was fitted with an 80hp Le Rhône. From what little information has been found on this model it must have been underpowered and intended as a trainer. Some were fitted with dual controls, and others were fitted with 80hp Clerget or Gnome engines. The type was a precursor of the Nieuport 80 and 81 described later.

Nieuport 11 and 16

The Nieuport 10 two-seat reconnaissance aeroplane described in the previous chapter established the mould for the generation of single-seater scouts that followed. The first was the Nieuport 11, which was smaller than the Nieuport 10 but powered by the same 80hp Le Rhône rotary engine. The Nieuport designation Nie-XIB quickly won it the nickname 'Bébé'. The type was fitted with a Lewis machine-gun above the upper wing firing over the propeller arc. The Lewis gun had a limited magazine capacity, and its position made it difficult to reload and to clear blockages. Like the Nieuport 10, the design suffered from weakness in the structure of the lower wing, which resulted in a number of accidents. However, the cause soon became known, and steps were taken to correct the problem.

The Nieuport 11 entered service at a critical time, when the Fokker E.III, with its synchronized, fixed machine-gun, had gained an ascendancy over Allied machines. Being light and agile, the design became immediately popular. The machine was operated by both the Aviation Militaire and the RNAS, but not the RFC: thus 450 were built by Nieuport-Macchi, and ninety-three by Elettro-Ferroviere in Italy as the Type 11.000. The Duks factory in Russia also built the design in quantity, and some were also allocated to the Aviation Militaire Belge. After the internment of an RNAS machine and its pilot, the design was built in the Trompenburg factory in Holland. Twenty were ordered, but only twelve were built, equipped with 80hp Thulin engines. They were delivered in 1918 and served until 1925. The aeroplane's opponents soon developed a healthy regard for the aeroplane, and at the behest of their frontline pilots, the concept was widely copied by the German manufacturers, Euler and Siemens-Schuckert – even to copying the fragile lower wing design.

(*Top*) **An unarmed and unnumbered Nieuport 11 prototype that first appeared in the summer of 1915.** JMB/GLS collection

(*Middle*) **An RNAS Nieuport 11 (3982/N594), which operated with 1 Wing at Dunkerque.** JMB/GLS collection

(*Bottom*) **A Nieuport 11 exposed, clearly showing the 80hp Le Rhône engine, and what may be an experimental installation of a stripped Lewis gun, still with its stock and with an Alkan synchronization gear.** via Paul Leaman

The Nieuport 11 was soon re-engined with the 110hp Le Rhône 9J to become the Nieuport 16. Some Nieuport 11s were re-engined by mechanics at the escadrilles, but whether these aircraft also changed their designation, or whether it just applied to new production is not known. Apart from the engine and some local strengthening of the structure, the two types were virtually identical. Due to the additional weight of the engine, the wing loading of the machines modified in the field was higher and they became seriously nose-heavy. Power was needed to hold the nose up, as the trim could not be corrected easily with the elevator alone. This made recovering from a dive, correcting a spin and landing the aeroplane in any circumstances very difficult. Nevertheless, the significant improvement in performance led to orders being placed as soon as was possible during the first quarter of 1916, and due to the similarities of the two types, production aeroplanes were almost immediately forthcoming.

Nieuport 11s were fitted with an overwing Lewis gun firing forwards over the propeller arc. The mountings varied, but an early design by Sergent Moreau was set rather low, requiring it to be angled to clear the propeller. A subsequent design used a half loop of tubing to hold the muzzle on its return from being reloaded, and this was succeeded by a higher mounting, which used a rubber cord to improve manipulation of the gun. An improved design was used on Nieuport 17s and later models.

Most Nieuport 16s were also armed with an overwing Lewis gun, but some were fitted with a Lewis gun fixed on the top decking of the fuselage and synchronized by means of a mechanism designed by Sergent Mécanicien Alkan of Escadrille MS.12. This system dispensed with the gas-operated mechanism and replaced it with an engine-driven cam contained in a heavy metal box clamped to the side of the gun.

(*Left*) **A Nieuport 11 (3978), one of the RNAS machines sent to the Aegean and from there to Rumania.** JMB/GLS collection

(*Below left*) **Nieuport 11 (3993) with a twin Lewis gun installation used by the RNAS. This machine was with 1 Wing at St Pol in June 1916.** via Paul Leaman

(*Below*) **Moreau mounting for a stripped Lewis gun on a captured Nieuport 16. The vertical mounting hinged halfway up to enable the rear of the gun to be lowered for reloading. The hinge was sprung to facilitate returning the gun to its firing position. The bead sight is between the inverted-V strut.** via Paul Leaman

French-built Nieuport 16 (5172) with the 110hp Le Rhône 9J. One of a batch transferred to the RFC from the RNAS. via Paul Leaman

Le Prieur Rockets

Le Prieur rockets were fitted on some aircraft, starting in mid-1916. These rockets were invented by Lt Y.P.G. Le Prieur of the French navy for attacking Zeppelins, observation kite balloons and aircraft. They were fitted in trial and operational installations on a number of two-seaters and scouts, including the Spad and the Sopwith Pup. However, they were fitted predominantly on Nieuport 11s and 16s for use against balloons, and for that reason are worth describing here in some detail.

The rocket itself consisted of a head, a body with an ignition device, and a stick. The head was attached to the body by means of paper or linen tape, which appears to have been varnished. The head was weighted with sand, and a pointed triangular blade was inserted into the wooden nose-cone to assist penetration of the balloon envelope. The body was filled with about 200g (7oz) of black powder, which acted as a propellant and incendiary device. This part may have been derived from a standard signal rocket, in which case it consisted of a strong cardboard tube reinforced internally with thin tinplate. The stick was about 1.5m (5ft) of square-section pine and was attached to the body by means of three lengths of white tape. The powder was ignited by a tapping key operated by the pilot, which was connected to a 2-volt battery in the fuselage and through a cable connecting all the rockets in series to a sparker inside the body of each rocket. The switch had a safety pin to prevent accidental firing.

To take the rockets, each Nieuport was fitted with four tubes on the outside of each interplane V-strut. Each tube was about 25mm (1in) in outside diameter and about 1.5m (5ft) long, and was set at an angle of about 17° 30' to the direction of flight. The struts were first covered with twenty-four-gauge sheet iron and 1.5mm (0.6in) thick asbestos extending above and below the tubes. Each group, consisting of four tubes set one above the other, was held in place by a strap on each strut secured by bolts with butterfly nuts. A twenty-six-gauge aluminium plate 650mm × 750mm (26 × 30in) was fitted to the part of the upper surface of the lower wing that was exposed to scorching. The whole installation weighed 15kg (33lb). One of the sighting systems used on Nieuports for anti-balloon patrols consisted of a sighting notch made of paper glued to the windscreen and a front ring sight with a crosswire. The line of sight was set at an angle of 14 degrees below the axis of the rocket tubes.

The diameter of the front ring sight corresponded to the diameter of a balloon at a distance of 120m (394ft). The technique required was to dive at an angle of about 45 degrees towards the side of the balloon, and fire at a range of about 100–150m (330–490ft), holding the line of flight for a short period afterwards to allow for any delay in ignition. The weapon was considered to be quite effective against balloons, a strike usually resulting in destruction of the target. However, despite using types of warhead designed for the purpose, the rockets were not so effective against airships or aircraft. In time, Vickers machine-guns provided with incendiary ammunition proved more effective.

The French were the best exponents of this weapon, and first used it to good effect during the recapture of Fort Douaumont on 22 May 1916 when Charles Nungesser and five other aces shot down all the German observation balloons over this front. Some Nieuport 16s of 1 and 11 Sqns RFC were also equipped with them, and they were used during the Battle of the Somme on 25 June when four balloons were brought down by rockets out of a total of fifteen destroyed. Several RNAS machines were so equipped, including 3987, 3988, 3991 and 3994. The Belgians and Italians also operated Nieuports fitted with Le Prieur rockets. The first recorded success was when an Austrian balloon was destroyed on 18 October on the Selo front.

The French equipped some of their Nieuport aeroplanes with cameras for high speed photographic reconnaissance. Two

French Nieuport 16 armed with Le Prieur rockets. Philip Jarrett

Nieuport 16 (N959) of *Esc*. N.65 armed with Le Prieur rockets and showing detail of the method of fixing the launch tubes to the interplane struts. via Paul Leaman

Nieuport 16s were re-engined by the Belgians and used by aces Coppens and Thieffry. The design was also built by the Duks factory in Russia under licence.

Nieuport 14, 15, 18 and 19

These machines started to appear towards the end of 1915 and were a separate line of development from previous designs. It was hoped that they would be superior to existing reconnaissance types. They were distinguished primarily by a longer wingspan and increased wing area, necessitating a two-bay wing structure. They did not attract significant orders as their performance was generally poor, and they were therefore only produced in limited numbers.

		Nieuport 11	Nieuport 16
Engine:		80hp Le Rhône 9C	110hp Le Rhône 9Ja
Dimensions:	Span, upper, m (ft)	7.52 (24.67)	7.52 (24.67)
	Span, lower, m (ft)	7.40 (24.28)	
	Length, m (ft)	5.50 (18.04)	5.64 (18.50)
	Height, m (ft)	2.40 (7.87)	2.40 (7.87)
	Wing area, sq m (sq ft)	13.3 (143.2)	13.3 (143.2)
Weights:	Empty, kg (lb)	320 (706)	375 (827)
	Loaded, kg (lb)	480 (1,058)	550 (1,213)
Performance:	Max speed, km/h (mph);		
	at sea level	165 (103)	
	at 2,000m (6,560ft)	162 (100)	156 (97)
	Time to height;		
	2,000m	8min 50sec	5min 50sec
	3,000m	15min	10min 10sec
	Service ceiling, m (ft)	5,000 (16,405)	4,800 (15,749)
	Endurance, hrs	2.5	2

The Nieuport 14

The Nieuport 14 was a two-seat reconnaissance machine based on the Nieuport 12 with a slightly longer fuselage and two-bay wings, the span being increased from 9m (29.5ft) to 11.9m (39ft) and the resultant wing area from 23sq m (247sq ft) to 30sq m (323sq ft). The outer pair of struts was canted slightly outwards.

The prototype was fitted with a Hispano engine of Spanish manufacture, which was cooled by 'Hazet' radiators of German design, six elements being fitted vertically each side of the fuselage behind the engine. In this machine, the pilot sat in the rear seat. In production examples the observer sat in the rear cockpit, and some machines were provided with a single Lewis gun on an Étévé mounting. The standard engines were Hispanos of 150hp

(*Above*) **Nieuport two-seater prototype with a 150hp Hispano Suiza engine.** JMB/GLS collection

Nieuport two-seater prototype (N2487) without a type number, powered by a 180hp Lorraine Dietrich engine. It had large cutouts in the wing roots to improve the downward view. Jean Noël, via Stuart Leslie

to 175hp. The radiators of production machines were fitted on the fuselage sides forward of the lower wing, and were canted outwards to improve cooling, which must have caused severe turbulence over the tail surfaces. The machines were fitted with a vertical tube in the observer's position for paying out the wireless aerial.

The French placed an initial order for six in November 1915. Production models began to appear in the spring of 1916, and twenty were in service before the end of that year. Single machines equipped a number of escadrilles. About twenty Nieuport Nie-14A-2s were in service in August 1917, but these were retired from frontline service during the autumn and sent to flying schools. According to a report issued by the French War Ministry, escadrilles were asked to modify the radiators to improve cooling. Furthermore the radiators had to be emptied and the filters cleaned after every flight.

It is possible that spare airframes were used as a basis for the Nieuport 14 École that appeared in the spring of 1916. The wings were identical, but the front fuselage was modified to accept an 80hp Le Rhône

A Nieuport prototype two-seater (N2354) fitted with a 200hp Hispano Suiza engine. Jean Noël, via Stuart Leslie

This is possibly the prototype Nieuport 14AR, with the pilot located in the rear seat. JMB/GLS collection

(*Below*) **A production Nieuport 14AR (N1849) with a 175hp Hispano-Suiza 8Aa and a modified cowling compared with the prototype.** JMB/GLS collection

Two Nieuport 14s under construction. JMB/GLS collection

(Middle) **A Nieuport 15 'petit Renault' with a 150hp Renault engine.** Jean Noël, via Stuart Leslie

(Above) **Nieuport 15B2 with the 220hp Renault 12F engine and an enlarged radiator.** Philip Jarrett

engine. The undercarriage was also modified to take a supplementary pair of wheels forward of the main wheels to prevent the aircraft from nosing over. After its introduction the design was converted to dual control. Another variant had the wing area reduced to 28sq m (301sq ft), and formed the basis of the Nieuport 82 trainer described later.

There were single prototypes based on the Nieuport 14. One was fitted with a 180hp Lorraine-Dietrich water-cooled engine, and the wings were modified by having the lower wings cut away at the roots to improve the downward view. A second was fitted with a 150hp Hispano Suiza water-cooled engine with the radiators placed at the sides of the fuselage. Its purpose is not known. A third was fitted with a 220hp Hispano-Suiza and a crescent-shaped upper wing.

The Nieuport 15

Appearing in November 1916, the Nieuport 15 closely resembled the Nieuport 14 and was intended for bombing missions. It may have been designed for the 1916 *concours puissant*, arranged to select a heavy bomber for the Aviation Militaire, but it was never entered for that competition. Its armament consisted of fourteen 10kg (22lb) Anilite bombs and a defensive Lewis machine-gun. The wingspan was increased by a further 5m (16ft) to 17m (56ft), and the chord and span of the lower wing were also increased to give a total wing area of 47.8sq m (514sq ft). Stagger was eliminated, and the lower and upper wings were set at the same incidence. The shape of the tailplane differed from earlier designs, being heart-shaped rather than rectangular. The aircraft was fitted with a 220hp Renault engine with enlarged radiators placed either side of the fuselage. But the performance of the Nieuport 15 was not acceptable to the Service Technique Aéronautique (STAé), and none was ordered for French units. Seventy were ordered for the RNAS – ten two-seaters and sixty single-seaters. Forty serial numbers were allocated in the range N5560 to N5599 in September 1916, and two were reported ready for tests early in December; but the serials were cancelled in February 1917 and partly re-allocated to other aircraft.

A Nieuport 15*bis*, with a 'V' painted on the rear fuselage, was tested at Cachy during July and August 1916 by pilots of Esc N.103. It was distinguished by the radiators being set further back, a door on the

Nieuport 15 with a 250hp Hispano-Suiza engine.
Philip Jarrett

starboard side for the passengers and a slightly revised engine cowling. The pilots reported that the controls were heavy, the aileron controls defective and the undercarriage too delicate. The '*bis*' nomenclature may have referred to an increase in engine output. An STAé sketch showed a Type 15A-2 described as being a 'Nieuport engine Renault 12F 220 HP Type XVA2'. In August 1916, a new variant was under test: this had a 250hp Renault with a frontal radiator, and an exhaust manifold terminating in a vertical exhaust pipe at the rear of the engine.

The Nieuport 18 and 19

Little is known of the Nieuport 18, the only twin-engined machine designed by Nieuport at the time. It was built towards the end of 1915 and was possibly conceived before the Nieuport 15; it was given the number 21.000 in the constructor's nomenclature. It had a crew of three, with the pilot sitting between the wings and with gun positions in the nose and half-way along the

A Nieuport 15 under construction.
Jean Noël, via Stuart Leslie

		Nieuport 14	Nieuport 15	Nieuport 18
Engine:		150/175hp Hispano	250hp Renault	2 × 150hp Hispano-Suiza
Dimensions:	Span, m (ft)	11.9 (39)	17 (56)	
	Length, m (ft)	7.9 (25.9)	9.6 (31.4)	
	Height, m (ft)	3.2 (10.5)		
	Wing area, sq m (sq ft)	30 (322.9)	47.82 (514.7)	51.36 (552.8)
Weights:	Empty, kg (lb)	620 (1,367)	1,332 (2,937)	1,325 (2,922)
	Useful load, kg (lb)	220 (485)	325 (717)	
	Petrol, kg (lb)	130 (287)	240 (529)	235 (518)
	Loaded, kg (lb)	970 (2,139)	1,897 (4,183)	1,850 (4,079)
Performance:	Max speed, km/h (mph):			
	at sea level	155 (96)	156 (97)	
	at 2,000m (6,560ft)	138 (86)	140 (87)	
	at 3,000m (9,850)	129 (80)		
	Time to height:			
	1,000m (3,280ft)	6min 35sec	7min 20sec	
	2,000m (6,560ft)	15min	16min 35sec	
	3,000m (9,850ft)	27min	30min 15sec	
	Endurance, hr	3 to 4		3

rear fuselage, each position equipped with a pillar-mounted machine-gun. It had a longer fuselage compared with the Nieuport 15 and an increased wingspan, giving a wing area of 51.36sq m (552.6sq ft). The wings were of a typical Nieuport configuration, with the lower wing of shorter span and narrower chord than the upper, and braced with V-struts. The undercarriage was provided with an extra pair of wheels under the nose to prevent overturning in the event of a crash landing, a formula adopted for the trainer version of the Nieuport 14. The tailplane was shaped similarly to the Nieuport 15. The armament consisted of single machineguns on spigot mountings, one in the nose and the other half-way along the rear fuselage. They were powered by two 150hp Hispano engines mounted by struts between the wings and braced to the fuselage. It is probable that the Nieuport 18 was subject to several small orders from the RNAS, which were not proceeded with. The Nieuport 19 was similar to the Nieuport 18, but was fitted with 110hp Clerget engines.

There is no record of the Nieuport 22, a type number which, if in sequence, should have been allocated in September or October 1916. There were several projects or prototypes under consideration at this time that might have been candidates. One possibility is the prototype that is described later, with a Nieuport 24-style fuselage and a twin-spar lower wing of increased chord but with 'V' interplane struts. There was also a similar type proposed with a 150hp or 180hp Hispano engine. Other candidates are the Type 'Ecole' which went into production much later as the Type 82. There were also derivatives proposed of the two-seat Nieuport 14 with the wing area increased to 35sq m (377sq ft), and Lorraine or Hispano engines for scout or army cooperation purposes.

The Nieuport 17, 17*bis*, 21 and 23

Variations of the Nieuport sesquiplane scout layout continued to appear. Some did not receive a type number, or the record of the type number has been lost. These types were not manufactured in sequence, but in many cases were produced side by side as circumstances dictated.

Nieuport 17 (N1831), captured by the Germans when Lt Santa Maria of Esc. N.86 was brought down in combat. via Paul Leaman

The Nieuport 17

The next scout produced by Nieuport was a direct development of the Nieuport 16. The standard engine was the 110hp Le Rhône 9J, but it could also be fitted with the 110hp Clerget. The wing area was increased to compensate for the weight of the more powerful engine and to improve the service ceiling, and a number of small refinements were added. The centre section was covered with transparent panels to improve the pilot's view, the line of sight being well below the level of the upper wing. Some early Nieuport 17s were fitted with a *cône de pénétration*: this was a fixed fairing that looked like a spinner, but was mounted on a forward extension of the stationary crankshaft and an additional ball-race fitted to the front of the engine.

The Germans captured several examples of the Nieuport 17, and we are indebted to their authorities for handing down for posterity a detailed description and drawings of this aeroplane. As we have described a gradual progression of development, it would be appropriate at this stage to summarize the German information in order to review the type of construction used for the Nieuport 17. Thus, the fuselage was of a rectangular section forward, tapering to a trapezoid section aft, with the bottom narrower than the top. Forward, the longerons were of ash, whilst the vertical struts, cross-members and longerons aft of the cockpit were of spruce. The fuselage was diagonally braced with wire, and had steel socket joints and wiring plates. The top decking was faired with light formers and longitudinal stringers. The engine bearer, supported by an assembly of steel tubes, was a fabricated heavy-gauge steel plate lightened by recesses and corresponding in shape to the rectangular cross-section of the fuselage. The engine was overhung from this bearer without the front support seen on the Nieuport monoplanes. The circular cowling was of aluminium, and was provided with two holes in the lower starboard side for ventilation and exhaust discharge. Curved aluminium fairings were provided to blend the cowling into the sides of the fuselage, and these featured large oval access panels on each side. A faired headrest was provided for the pilot. Plywood panels reinforced the fuselage around the sternpost, but otherwise the fuselage was fabric covered.

The sesquiplane layout and the V-shaped interplane struts of the earlier types were retained, together with the unique circular clamps joining the struts to the lower wing spar which allowed the incidence of the lower wing to be adjusted on the ground. The spars of the upper wing were widely spaced, the front spar being set close to the leading edge, and the rear set vertically above the single spar of the lower wing. The wing box-spars were of spindled spruce channels, glued along their vertical centreline with an I-section hardwood key. At junction points with struts, root attachment points and ribs, the spars were reinforced with internal wooden blocks to support the metal fittings and their attachment bolts and screws. The steel tube, centre-section struts were vertical at the front and consisted of an inverted V at the rear.

The wing ribs had ash flanges and limewood webs with lightening holes. The leading and trailing edges of the wings,

Nieuport 17 (A6644) of 1 Sqn RFC. This aircraft was shot down on 18 June 1917 and its pilot, Lt T.H. Lines, taken prisoner. JMB/GLS collection

Attachment of interplane struts to the main spar of the lower wing, showing packing pieces around the spar and locking collar. redrawn by Mick Davis

46

including the trailing edges of the ailerons, consisted of spruce strips. The ailerons were fitted to the top wing only, and increased in chord towards the tips. The ailerons were mounted on steel tubes at their leading edges, which were actuated by a system of push rods and hinges. The heart-shaped quadrants visible at the centre section were the links between the aileron shafts and vertical rods operated at the bottom ends through bell cranks and horizontal rods to the control column. The elevators and rudder were controlled by cable and pulley. The tail surfaces were fabricated from light steel tubing with pinned and brazed joints. All flying surfaces were fabric covered.

The main wheels were supported by V-struts made from streamlined steel tube, and the cross-member between the legs was an aluminium channel that held a steel tube axle sprung at either end by bungee cord shock absorbers. The tail-skid was a flat, slightly curved steel spring mounted on a wooden shoe on a streamlined projection under the fuselage.

The Russian-built Nieuports were somewhat heavier than their French-built equivalents, mainly because pine substituted the wood used in the construction of the French machines, and other materials of construction were substituted.

To begin with the Nieuport 17 was fitted with a single Lewis gun on a simple mounting above the upper wing. A field modification consisted of two pillars, upon one of which the rear of the gun was pivoted, and a front pillar that held the retaining catch. These were not universally liked, mainly because of the distance between the gun and the sight, and because the gun was not perfectly parallel to the line of flight. Later, most machines in French service were fitted with a single synchronized Vickers gun centrally mounted on top of the fuselage. This necessitated a slight modification to the rigging wires between the centre-section struts that normally met in a V at the centre of the fuselage where the gun was placed. With the advent of disintegrating-link ammunition belts, the canvas belts were stored in drums within side fairings behind the engine cowling. Some machines were fitted with the Vickers gun mounted off-centre. This change required the reshaping of the oil reservoir, fuel tank, munitions box, exhaust pipe and windscreen. Several Aviation Maritime aeroplanes of Escadrille 313 at Dunkerque were fitted with twin Lewis guns mounted above the wing as standard –

Nieuport 17 (N1424) with, unusually, a 110hp Le Rhône. This example was fitted with a *casserale d'helice* that rotated with the engine. via Paul Leaman

Cockpit and engine installation of the Nieuport 17. JMB/GLS collection

Nieuport 17 (N2091) in French service showing the fuselage-mounted Vickers gun. via Paul Leaman

and one machine had twin Lewis guns in addition to its Vickers gun; however the increased weight must have affected the performance too much, as this configuration was not adopted. As with the Nieuport 11 and 16, the Nieuport 17 could be fitted with Le Prieur rockets.

Most of the Nieuport 17s were delivered to the RFC with the French specification fittings for the fuselage-mounted Vickers gun, but the Aircraft Depots were ordered to remove these and fit single Lewis guns on Foster mountings instead. A trial was made with both guns fitted, but the performance of the aircraft proved to be inferior, the speed reduced by 5km/h (3mph) and the ceiling by 1,250m (4,100ft), and the time at 3,000m (9,850ft) and 4,575m (15,000ft) increased by 45sec and 6.5min respectively. Furthermore the Vickers gun was considered unreliable, and stoppages could not be cleared as the guns were inaccessible.

The armament of French-built Nieuports for Russia consisted of a Lewis gun, fixed on a support above the centre-section firing above the airscrew disc, and a synchronized Vickers gun mounted on the coaming in front of the cockpit. Russian-built Nieuports adopted the British system of a Foster mounting whereby the over-wing Lewis gun could be pulled down for reloading or for attacking enemy aircraft from below, and several Russian aces used their guns in this way.

Nieuports delivered from the factory did not have an instrument panel, the few instruments being attached to various parts of the airframe. After a trial this omission was soon rectified by the RFC as a field modification. Some aeroplanes in French service used for the high-speed reconnaissance role were fitted with a 260mm camera installed in the fuselage behind the pilot's seat, reached through a hinged plywood panel on the left side of the fuselage.

The Nieuport 17 was undoubtedly a great improvement over the Nieuport 16, and was built in large numbers in France, Russia and Britain. French contractors building the type included the Société pour la Construction et l'Entretien d'Avions (CEA), the Ateliers d'Aviation R. Savary et H. de la Fresnaye, and the Société Anonyme Française de Constructions Aéronautiques (SAFC). It is not possible to give the exact number, but it must have approached one thousand. The type saw extensive service with the Aviation Militaire, being used notably by Nungesser, Madon and Guynemer in the Escadrille Cigognes. One French escadrille equipped with the Nieuport 17 took part in the defence of Venice. It was also used by one unit of the Aviation Maritime. About 500 Nieuport 17s and 23s were used by the RFC; two of the British aces using it were Ball and Mannock.

The Nieuport 17 was built in Italy by Nieuport-Macchi, 150 of which were powered with the 110hp Le Rhône and given the type number 17.000. These were armed with a single Vickers machine-gun, and some were equipped for photographic reconnaissance. The aircraft was also used in Russia, Belgium and Holland; the latter country built twenty, and five were still in service in 1918 as trainers. Finland was provided with two examples, and the American Expeditionary Force was equipped with seventy-five.

By the beginning of 1917, although no failures were reported in French service, serious structural problems became apparent, which threatened to mar the service career of the aeroplane in the RFC. One of the first was reported on 16 November 1916 when the starboard lower wing of a Nieuport 16 (A216) 'slipped during combat'. This was attributed to poor fitting of the locking collar. Then on 1 February 1917 a machine was returned to 2 AD with a broken lower wing; and on 28 March, Lt C.H.F.M. Caffyn of 60 Sqn RFC was killed when the rear spar of the upper wing broke and the starboard wings sheared off. A month later 2nd Lt H.G. Ross, also of 60 Sqn, was seriously injured when all four wings of B1512 folded up when he was diving on a ground target.

On 19 April Edward Mannock of 40 Sqn was engaged in shooting practice at ground targets in the butts in Nieuport 17 (B1597) when the bottom right-hand wing broke away completely. He was only diving slowly at about 460m (1,500ft) when the incident happened. He managed to get down, but the machine turned over on landing. Inspection afterwards found that the left-hand wing had also broken away from the V-strut due to faulty welding of the strut bracket, and that the spar had broken near the middle and at the fuselage attachment. The machine had only been taken on charge the previous week and had accumulated fewer than ten hours' flying.

On 30 April Lt A.R. Penny managed to land after his Nieuport shed part of its lower port wing while diving to attack an Albatros scout, as did Lt W.M. Fry in similar circumstances.

Thus in service the design suffered from structural failures of the lower wings which could be attributed to both the unique strut attachment point and to weaknesses in the wing spar. A report received by 2 AD explained that:

> ... the locking ring on the main spar of the lower plane, which carries the bottom socket of the V-strut, is sometimes found to be not properly fitted to the wood blocks on the lower plane main spar... The result of this will be that if the machine is dived steeply, the locking ring will slip into its proper position and cause the rigging on that side of the machine to go slack.

Nieuport did not abandon the collar fitting for its V-strut single-seater fighters: instead the aeroplanes were modified in the field. Packing pieces were fitted between the spar and the locking ring, and the attachment of the packing pieces to the spar was improved. The spar at the attachment point was reinforced using an aluminium sleeve cast in two parts. The spar was strengthened by increasing the thickness of the three-ply internal reinforcement, and also by binding and gluing tape over the whole length. The wing was also strengthened by panels of 2mm three-ply top and bottom between the leading edge and the spar. This cladding on the underside was later deleted. The modifications were introduced by mid-May 1917, and all aeroplanes that were returned to depots for repair were similarly modified.

Trouble was also experienced with fatigue and corrosion of the engine cowlings. One horseshoe-shaped cowling, the so-called Morane converted type, proved to be very brittle and tended to split, especially round the apertures for the exhaust gases. The two variations of cowling designed by Nieuport, one with a central top section and the other made from two halves, had L-shaped annular ribs riveted around the front opening of the cowlings. These ribs tended to detach and fall away on the first type, though this didn't happen with the latter. This latter type was eventually adopted as standard, but even so still suffered from bimetallic corrosion at the annular reinforcing rib. There is evidence that the rib was cut at the interface points, probably to allow the cowling to be removed without removing the propeller, which would have necessitated retiming the synchronization gear if fitted with the Vickers gun.

The Nieuport 23

The Nieuport 23 began to make its appearance during November 1916. It was very similar to the Nieuport 17, and early production samples were fitted with the same engine. However, most were fitted with the 120hp Le Rhône 9Jb, which had the same bore and stroke as the 9Ja, but with cast-iron pistons replaced by aluminium ones. In any case it was not uncommon for the engine types to be interchanged between the Nieuport 17s and 23s in the field, making the two types virtually indistinguishable. The change of engine conferred a slight improvement in performance as compared with the Nieuport 17. There were also minor changes to the construction of the rear spar of the upper wing.

The Nieuport 23 also had a modified form of interrupter gear for synchronizing the Vickers gun, which resulted in the gun being positioned a few centimetres to the right of the centreline of the fuselage top decking. Because the RFC continued to fit overwing-mounted Lewis guns on Foster mountings in place of the Vickers gun, even this small difference was eliminated, although the retaining bolts for the Foster mounting plate were in a slightly different position due to the change in rear spar construction.

However, none of these changes improved the structural integrity of the wing structure, and accidents continued to occur. A notice from the *Generale chef de service aéronautique* to the *Grand Quartier Général* (GQG) dated 4 September 1917 reported that Nieuport 23s would not be allowed to continue flying unless additional cables were used to reinforce the wing. It was suggested that 150 wing sets be obtained, which gives an indication of the number of Nieuport 23s in service with the Aviation Militaire. Another GQG memo, dated 10 December 1917, called for the replacement of the tail-skids because of frequent breakages, and so a new type of skid was fitted with a rubber shock absorber.

At the end of the war, a Nieuport 23 variant appeared with an 80hp Le Rhône engine, called the Type 23 École. This appeared in Nieuport catalogues as the Type 21/23.

The Nieuport 17bis

Shortly after production of the Nieuport 17 began, the Nieuport 17*bis* appeared, powered by the 130hp Clerget 9B, although a

Nieuport 23 (N375?) of Esc. d'Athene, N.506. Jean Devaux via Stuart Leslie

Nieuport 23 with Adj Edmund Thieffry of 5ème (Comete) Escadrille via Paul Leaman

Nieuport 23 (B1617) of the RFC. JMB/GLS collection

Armament of the Nieuport 23, showing the offset Vickers gun that distinguished it externally from the Nieuport 17, and an overwing Lewis gun. via Paul Leaman

(*Below*) **Nieuport 17*bis* (N5875) with a 110hp Clerget engine. This aircraft was allocated to Chingford for home defence, and was still there on 30 March 1918.** JMB/GLS collection

(*Bottom*) **Nieuport 17*bis* (N3204) with a 130hp Clerget engine. This aircraft served with 6 (N) Sqn. It was shot down on 6 June 1917 and its pilot, Flt Lt F.P. Reeves, was killed.** JMB/GLS collection

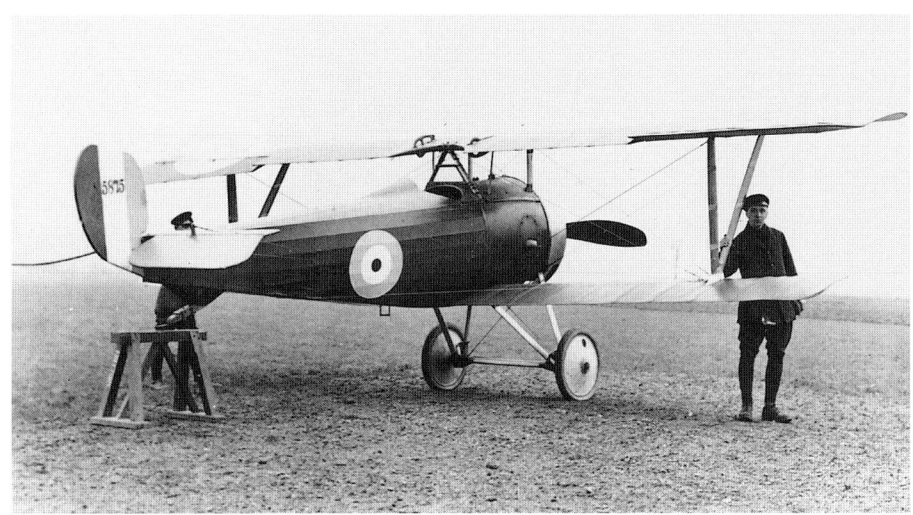

few were powered by the 110hp Clerget 9Z. As the Aviation Militaire preferred the 110hp Le Rhône for its scouts, because it was lighter and had a lower fuel and oil consumption than the Clerget of the same nominal power, it was unlikely that there would be sufficient to meet the production numbers required by the British. The 110hp Clerget was becoming obsolete, and Delage recommended to the British that they should press the French to supply the 130hp Clerget instead. Later production of the Nieuport 17*bis* also had a more streamlined appearance resulting from the addition of six stringers on each side of the fuselage extending from the rear of the flank cowlings to the fuselage spacer just in front of the tail-skid. The engine was also fitted with a relatively narrow chord cowling with a gradual rearward reduction of diameter characteristic of Clerget installations.

According to Sqn Ldr C.L. Courtney RNAS, Sous-Lt Nungesser of Escadrille N.3 had a high opinion of the Nieuport 17*bis*. He reported:

> One of the original type was given to Sous-Lt Nungesser, with whom I spoke about it, and he reports the performance as follows: speed at 3,000m (9,850ft), 186kg (410lb), climb 3,000m in 7½min. Sous-Lt Nungesser is very enthusiastic about the machine, and says it is the best he has flown for attacking an enemy machine, starting from the ground. He has had his machine fitted with a Vickers gun firing

through the propeller, and a Lewis gun on the top plane; tracers being used only in the latter, and the guns aligned so as to fire about 4ft [1m] apart (vertically) at 200yd [183m]. He stated, however, that if he was already at the required height, he would prefer to be in the Spad, owing to its superior diving performance.

Nieuport quoted a top speed of 190km/h (118mph), but this was not achieved by machines in British service. The Nieuport 17*bis* retained the armament of one synchronized Vickers gun and one wing-mounted Lewis gun, although consideration was at one time given to fitting a pair of Vickers guns for aircraft supplied to the RNAS, trials having shown that performance was unaffected by this installation.

A small number of Nieuport 17*bis* were manufactured for the Aviation Militaire, and a specially modified one was used by Nungesser between May and September 1917. Thirty were ordered by the RNAS and equipped 6(N) Sqn. Machines ordered from British Nieuport were late being delivered to the RFC due to modifications and were quickly replaced at the Front by Sopwith Camels.

The Nieuport 21

The Nieuport 21 combined the 80hp Le Rhône 9C engine and fuselage shape of the Nieuport 11 with the wings of the Nieuport 17. Intended as a trainer aircraft, there may be truth in the assertion that it was also considered as a high-altitude bomber escort. At least one Nieuport 21 was fitted with a 90hp Le Rhône 9Ga, and some may have had the 120hp Le Rhône 9J.

Some Nieuport 21s were assigned to French frontline units for use alongside

Experimental Nieuport 17*bis* fitted with a large *casserale d'helice*. JMB/GLS collection

(*Above and below*) Nieuport 17B (21), which combined the engine and fuselage of the Nieuport 11 with the wings of the Nieuport 17. via Paul Leaman and JMB/GLS

		Nieuport 17	Nieuport 23	Nieuport 17*bis*	Nieuport 21
Engine:		110hp Le Rhône 9Ja	120hp Le Rhône 9Jb or 110hp Le Rhône 9Ja 9C	110hp Clerget 9Z 130hp Clerget 9B	80hp Le Rhône 9C
Dimensions:	Span, upper, m (ft)	8.16 (26.8)	8.16 (26.8)	8.16 (26.8)	8.16 (26.8)
	Span, lower, m (ft)	7.80 (25.6)	7.80 (25.6)	7.80 (25.6)	7.80 (25.6)
	Length, m (ft)	5.80 (19)	5.80 (19)	5.80 (19)	5.80 (19)
	Height, m (ft)	2.40 (7.9)	2.40 (7.9)	2.40 (7.9)	
	Wing area, sq m (sq ft)	14.75 (158.8)	14.75 (158.8)	14.75 (158.8)	14.75 (158.8)
Weights:	Empty, kg (lb)	375 (827)	350 (772)		
	Loaded, kg (lb)	560 (1,235)	573 (1,263)	530 (1,169)	
Performance	Max speed, km/h (mph):				
	at sea level	165 (103)		175 (109)	150 (93)
	at 2,000m (6,560ft)	160 (99)			
	at 3,000m (9,850ft)	154 (96)		172 (107)	
	Time to height:				
	2,000m (6,560ft)	6min 50sec			8min 27sec
	3,000m (9,850ft)	11min 30sec			15min 42sec
	Service ceiling, m (ft)	5300 (17,400)			
	Endurance, hr	1.75			2
	Range, km (miles)				250 (155)

Nieuport 17s. There may have been as many as twenty-eight Nieuports with 80hp Le Rhône engines in use with the Aviation Militaire in August 1917, but this total may have included Nieuport 10s and 11s. The French provided Russia with Nieuport 21s whilst keeping the more powerful Nieuport 17s for their own units, and eighty-six were built there under licence. The Russian examples had the wingspan reduced slightly to 8.02m (26ft). The Ukrainian air service received two in 1918. Five were acquired by the RNAS. The USA purchased 197, and some were assigned to 31 AS. Several Nieuport 21s were acquired by the Aviation Maritime in 1920, and were used to practise take-offs from a platform on the *Bapaume* until replaced by Nieuport 32s in 1922. Brazil received twenty Nieuport 21 trainers in 1920.

The first Nieuport triplane to appear (N1118) was based on the Nieuport 10, and had the middle wing staggered back from the others. Philip Jarrett

The Nieuport Triplanes

The Sopwith Triplane made its appearance over the Western Front in February 1917, its prototype having been passed for flight testing towards the end of the previous May. Its fighting qualities, which made such an impression on friend and foe alike, led indirectly to the Fokker Dr.I following suit in August 1917. However, the triplane concept had been anticipated in a Nieuport patent application on 10 January 1916 (No. 502.709), which claimed that such a configuration would eliminate the need for cross-bracing wires and would produce 'a light aircraft of great lifting capacity and of great stability, both lateral and longitudinal'. What the patent did not anticipate was the greatly improved agility afforded by the short wingspan and the concentration of mass about the centre of gravity.

As far as can be deduced, Nieuport produced three prototype triplanes of two different basic configurations. The first to appear was similar to the aeroplane illustrated in the patent application, apart from the design of the cabane struts; it bore a French serial number of N1118. Based on the not necessarily valid assumption that it was built in sequence with the other serial numbers in the range, its date of its manufacture might be placed around April 1916. It was a two-seater with a fuselage very similar to the Nieuport 10, with the same tail and undercarriage configuration, and powered by the same 80hp Le

Rhône rotary engine. All three wings were of narrow chord and constructed with single main spars. The lower and upper wings were set conventionally, with a marked degree of stagger which placed the upper wing forward of the front cockpit. The lower wing was attached to the lower fuselage longerons, and the upper wing supported from the fuselage longerons by a pair of vertical inverted-V struts. The middle wing was staggered behind the other two and attached to the upper fuselage longerons, with its main spar in line with the rear cockpit. The root was cut away by about the distance between two ribs, thus extending the full width of the chord to improve the crew's view. Ailerons were fitted to the middle wing only, and were tapered slightly outwards towards the wingtips. A triangular arrangement of single interplane struts connected the spars of each pair of wings at about mid-span.

No flight test data have been found to establish whether the patent claims for greater stability were well founded, but the possibility exists that the reverse may have been true. In any event, the first machine was followed by another design. This appeared to be based on a single-seat Nieuport 17 fuselage, tail unit and undercarriage. The configuration of the three wings was changed, however, with the middle wing placed well forward of the lower wing, and the upper wing set well back. The aircraft was powered with a 110hp Le Rhône 9J engine fitted with a *cône de pénétration* and a stripped-down Lewis gun with Alcan synchronization. The upper wing had cutouts in both the central leading and trailing edges in order to improve the pilot's view.

The aircraft was given the designation Nie-11C (or 11.000), and was tested by the STAé; but the design was not adopted by the French authorities, and was declared obsolete in November 1916.

Despite this, examples were acquired both by the RFC and the RNAS, presumably for trial purposes. One, in an overall silver finish and bearing the French serial N1388, was flown to 2 Aircraft Depot at Candas by Adj de Courcelles on 26 January 1917. Now bearing the RFC serial A6686, it was given a preliminary test there in which it returned good climbing figures (4min 43sec to 1,500m (5,000ft) and 9min 48sec to 3,000m (10,000ft)), and was reported to be still climbing well at the higher altitude. It was then sent on 9 February to the Aeroplane Experimental Station at Martlesham Heath for a more detailed evaluation, where it is recorded as having a 110hp Le Rhône 9J engine driving a Levasseur propeller.

The official report recorded a speed of 177km/h (110mph) at 900m (3,000ft), and 155km/h (96.5mph) at 3,000m (10,000ft),

The second triplane did not bear a serial number and was based on the Nieuport 17 with a 110hp Le Rhône fitted with a *cône de pénétration*. JMB/GLS collection

A6686 (formerly N1388) sent to Martlesham Heath for testing on 9 February 1917. JMB/GLS collection

a time to 1,500m (5,000ft) of 5min 18sec, and to 3,000m of 13min 36sec; the ceiling was estimated as 5,180m (17,000ft). Its longitudinal stability was recorded as not very good, its lateral stability as fair but directionally unstable. Its controllability on all axes in the air was good, but in taxiing was poor. Landing was judged difficult, as the machine was apt to slew round. The view directly forwards and downwards was thought poor as it was obstructed by the middle wing. The report concluded that the machine was very tail heavy, and practically no improvement could be made by re-rigging. Its performance was therefore judged to be considerably below that of modern British fighting scouts, and on the basis of this report it is not surprising that the RFC showed no further interest in the machine.

The RNAS had also shown an interest in the machine. As early as November 1916, Sqn Cdr C.L. Courtney, on visiting aircraft factories in Paris, reported that a Nieuport triplane with a 130hp Clerget engine 'was nearing completion in the shops and was expected to be out for trials in under a week'. As the French authorities at this time had declared no interest in the type, it would suggest that this prototype was built with the express purpose of being tested by the RNAS. Certainly it would appear that the Admiralty had made a specific request for the type some time before 15 February 1917, and one such aircraft with a 130hp Clerget was delivered to the Dunkerque Depot on 29 March 1917. Formerly given the French serial N1946, it was allocated the RNAS serial number N521. The machine had a faired fuselage, which suggests that the machine was based on the Nieuport 17*bis* with which it had a common engine, rather than on the Nieuport 24.

N521 went to 11 Sqn RNAS where it was involved in comparative trials with a Nieuport 17*bis* (RNAS serial N3194) early in April 1917, during which it proved to be some three to four knots faster than the biplane near the ground. It was returned to the depot at Dunkerque as unserviceable by 3 May, and was deleted on 30 June.

According to Admiralty records another Nieuport triplane, this time with a 110hp Clerget engine, was transferred from the War Office and allocated the serial number N532. Another Admiralty record indicates that early in June, N532 was at Martlesham Heath without an engine. It is only an hypothesis, but it is likely that A6686, which had completed its tests at Martlesham Heath some six weeks previously, was stripped of its valuable Le Rhône engine by the RFC and passed engineless to the RNAS, which intended to fit a Clerget engine. The final fate of N532 is not known.

N521 (formerly N1946), which was based on the Nieuport 17*bis* with a 130hp Clerget engine, was sent to 11 Sqn RNAS for comparative trials against a Nieuport 17*bis*.
JMB/GLS collection

	Nieuport Triplane	
Engine:		130hp Clerget
Propeller:		Levasseur
Dimensions:	Span, upper, m (ft)	8.16 (26.8)
	Length, m (ft)	5.8 (19)
	Wing area, sq m (sq ft)	13.3 (143.2)
Weights:	Empty, kg (lb)	375 (827)
	Loaded, kg (lb)	560 (1,235)
Performance	Max speed, km/h (mph):	
	at sea level	170 (106)
	at 2,000m (6,560ft)	164 (102)
	at 3,000m (9,850ft)	159 (99)
	at 4,000m (13,125ft)	149 (93)
	Min speed, km/h (mph)	110 (68)
	Time to height:	
	at 2,000m (6,560ft)	6min 10sec
	at 3,000m (9,850ft)	11min 0sec
	at 4,000m (13,125ft)	18min 50sec
	Ceiling, m (ft)	5,100 (16,730)
	Endurance, hr	2.5

The Nieuport 24, 24*bis*, 25 and 27

Although possessing a better rate of climb and agility, the Nieuport 17*bis* was unable to match the speed of the contemporary Spad 7C.1, due mainly to the greater power of the Hispano Suiza engine fitted

Nieuport 24 (N4662) at 2 AD Candas on 28 July 1917. This became B3601 in RFC service, and served with 40 and 29 Sqns. Lt A.G. Wingate-Gray was taken prisoner when he failed to return from a mission whilst flying this machine on 7 April 1918. JMB/GLS collection

to the latter. Despite having fitted an Hispano Suiza engine to an experimental Nieuport biplane in 1915, Gustav Delage had not proceeded with such an installation in a production model, probably because all the engines produced were required for other aircraft types. As regards the operational type to succeed the Nieuport 17, the Aviation Militaire chose the 130hp Le Rhône 9Jb, which despite having the same nominal power output as the Clerget 9B, initially gave only 120hp.

Nevertheless the new type, designated the Nie-24C.1, did differ in other, more favourable respects from its predecessor, principally in the shape of its wing section – which was given a greater camber of the upper surface, thereby giving more lift – and in the elliptical shape of the fin and rudder. Tests by the Section Technique de L'Aéronautique (STAé) on 15–19 February and 17 March 1917 showed a modest improvement in performance compared with the Nieuport 17bis, and as a result the Nieuport 24 joined the 17bis on the production lines.

The Nieuport 24

Apart from the wings and tail unit, the Nieuport 24 retained most of the characteristics of the earlier Nieuport designs. The basic fuselage structure was similar, with the distance between the lower longerons being slightly less than that between the upper ones. The longerons were of spruce and were partially wrapped in linen tape. The formers supporting the spruce stringers were of 4mm ply, and were scalloped and fretted to reduce weight. The covering behind the engine was of 4mm composition board, and 2mm board covered the head fairing. The rest of the fuselage was covered in fabric. The cabane struts supporting the upper wing again consisted of a pair of vertical struts attached to the front spar and an inverted-V strut supporting the rear spar. The bungee-sprung undercarriage consisted of a cross-axle supported by streamlined V-struts of aluminium tubing, and the tail-skid was of a conventional Nieuport design.

The Le Rhône engine could be fitted with Levasseur 549, Régy 351 or Chauviere 2228 propellers; it was supported by flanges consisting of a fretted steel pressing, and was provided with a standard cowling. The petrol tank was mounted behind this support, and the oil tank was squeezed between the engine and the support. As with the Nieuport 23, the single Vickers gun was mounted slightly to starboard of the centreline. The ammunition box was placed to starboard, and the empty belt was fed into a large drum enclosed within the fuselage side panel on the port side.

The wings were given an aerofoil section designated the 'N 5', said to be derived from that of the concurrent Sopwith scouts, and most production aircraft had ailerons that curved towards the tip. The box spars were built up of two lengths of channel-section spruce and central webs of plywood (2mm for the twin spar upper wing, and 5mm for the single spar lower wing). The ribs consisted of poplar webs and 4mm ash capping strips. The leading edge consisted of a skin of 2mm ply covering the nose of the aerofoil sections' upper surfaces back to the front spar. The trailing edges consisted of oval section (6 × 12mm) steel tube. Actuation of the ailerons was by spanwise torque tubes with a bell crank at the inner ends connected to the transverse shaft of the control column by pushrods. The flying wires were of 4mm steel cable, and the landing and drag wires were of 3mm cable. The wings were not interchangeable with the earlier types, and the construction of the interplane struts and connections with the mainplane spars were also different. The gap between the wing and ailerons was filled with a fairing strip of canvas reinforced with spring strips and attached to the rear spar of the wing.

The construction of the tail surfaces differed from the canvas-covered steel tube of earlier designs. The tailplane and elevators had spruce spars, and the horn-balanced rudder had a spruce leading edge. The rest of the structure consisted of interlocking ribs and sub-spars of 4mm birch ply. The outer edges of the tailplane and rudder were of poplar, and those of the elevators were of walnut. All tail surfaces were covered with two-ply, consisting of strips of veneer 25mm wide and 0.8mm thick glued at right angles, and coated on the outer surface with fabric. These panels were glued and pinned to the tailplane structure.

An early modification of the Nieuport 24C.1 appeared with the serial number N3760. It differed from production Nieuport 24s in that the forward struts supporting the upper wing centre section were of inverted-V configuration rather than vertical. The Vickers gun could not therefore be mounted on the centreline of the upper fuselage, but instead was mounted on the port upper longeron. It was possible that this arrangement was changed in later machines because the strut arrangement proved unsatisfactory with regard to sighting the gun, and its position made the clearance of jams difficult. Also this machine differed in that the engine was provided with a longer chord cowling, the cockpit sides were higher, and the undercarriage had a split axle. Although fairing strips were fitted to the gap between the wing and the ailerons, the trailing edges of the ailerons were straight rather than curved.

The Nieuport 24bis

The definitive Nieuport 24 was produced alongside the Nieuport 24bis C.1. This model retained the earlier type of tail unit and rudder shape, constructed of fabric-covered steel tube, but was otherwise similar. This was evidently an interim type, and may indicate that there were some initial production difficulties in manufacturing the new form of tail unit.

The Nieuport 24 appeared on the Front by May 1917, but unfortunately both the Nieuport 24 and 24bis quickly acquired an unfavourable reputation. As early as the

Maybe an early Nieuport 24 (N3760), this had the split axle and sprung tail-skid of the Nieuport 27, but the straight-edged ailerons of a Nieuport 17. JMB/GLS collection

A well-worn Nieuport 24*bis* (N4359). JMB/GLS collection

beginning of June, Major J.P.C. Sewell reported to RFC HQ that: 'French squadron pilots say the climb and speed at high altitudes are good, but that it is a disagreeable machine to fly. It is an unpopular machine.' This was confirmed as more than hearsay when two French pilots delivered machines to the RFC at 2 AD Candas on 27 July. After flying Nieuport 24 N4662, Lt F. de Marmier reported: 'The aircraft's aileron control is extremely heavy, and in this respect the aeroplane's lateral controllability is deficient, so much so that in my opinion it would be dangerous to perform aerobatics near the ground.' Adj Henri de Courcelles was equally critical of Nieuport 24*bis* N4569: 'Machine very heavy on the ailerons, lacks control in turns and when landing. Precision of control very inferior to the Type 17.'

These comments were quickly confirmed by Capt F.G. Dunn, who flew one of the machines immediately on arrival at 2 AD. He reported:

> As regards the new type Nieuport that arrived today from Paris. On arrrival the pilot explained that it was extremely heavy on the lateral control, so I made a test flight with the following observations. It was very heavy laterally and needed considerable force to get it out of a bank. This makes it very dangerous to bank heavily near the ground when S-turning to enter a small aerodrome. It would also be extremely hard work to fight with, as sometimes it needs both hands to get level. This machine is very much heavier on lateral control than any previous type.

However, a solution was soon to hand. On 20 August, M. F. Legros of the Nieuport company wrote to the British Aviation Commission as follows:

> We beg to inform you of a new modification that we have introduced on some of our machines. This alteration has given excellent results as regards ease in handling the machines. Along the aileron hinge on the upper plane is a canvas band stiffened with spring blades. In time the band remains lifted, forming a sort of windscreen, and so interferes with the aileron, giving it a neutral point beyond which the movement is hard, as the aileron pushes against the band. In order to overcome this, it is only necessary to cut off the band along the rear spar of the upper plane. The planes do not look so neat, but the efficiency of the ailerons is greatly increased.

The RFC itself had already come to the same conclusion. On 8 September, 2 AD advised RFC HQ that:

> Reference Type 24 and 27 Nieuport machines: it is notable that these machines were very stiff on the lateral control, and a number of experiments have been conducted here with a view to eliminating the trouble. At last it has been found that when the piece of fabric that extends over the hinge joint between the ailerons on the top plane is cut away flush with the rear spar, the sluggishness in lateral control disappears. Nieuport machines B3631 and B6753 have been so altered, and are reported by the test pilots to behave normally, that is to say like Types 23 and 17.

This information was passed on to the affected squadrons, and on 21 September, 1 Brigade reported that the modification had been a success. It also reported that '...if the leading edge of the aileron, instead of being flush or slightly below the trailing edge of the main plane, is set about half an inch [13mm] above, it makes the machine almost as light and quick as a Sopwith Scout.'

A Soviet Nieuport 24*bis* (N4301), whose pilot defected to the Poles during the fighting following the Armistice, seen here resplendent in new Polish markings. JMB/GLS collection

Sufficient Nieuport 24*bis* machines were produced to partially equip several French escadrilles, also to send five to the RFC, and supply 140 to the United States Air Service in France. Some were also provided to Italy and Belgium.

The Nieuport 24 was produced under licence by Duks in Russia from 1917 to 1920. From 1917, France exported several dozens of Nieuport 24s and 24*bis*, which stayed in service until 1921. From 1919, Nakajima in Japan built seventy-seven Nieuport 24s, using the aeroplane as a scout and trainer under the designation K-03. Exceptionally, these replaced the Spad 13 and stayed in service until November 1926.

Two Prototypes

Two prototypes appeared during this period, although official designations have not been traced for these. One was a single-seater scout that may have preceded the Nieuport 24. It had the standard wing and strutting, with straight aileron trailing edges and the troublesome fairing strip. The fin and rudder were similar to the Nieuport 24, but without the horn balance. The main undercarriage had a single axle, and the tail-skid was of the type mounted on an inverted pyramid of struts that became standard in late 1916/early 1917. The aeroplane was unique in having a high *cône de pénétration* ahead of the propeller, with a central intake for cooling air to the engine. The type of powerplant is uncertain, but it may have been either the 140hp Clerget 9Bf or the 150hp Clerget 9Bd, which had its stroke increased from the standard 160mm to 170mm, and the compression ratio from 5.2 to 5.4.

Delage also attempted to utilize the 150hp Hispano Suiza in his classic V-strut design. This prototype was similar to that to which the *cône de pénétration* had been fitted. It is not known whether this design showed any improvement compared with the Spad 7, but it was not put into quantity production; certainly by the end of 1917 the

This machine may have been a Nieuport 17*bis* variant with a Clerget engine of unknown type fitted with a very large *cône de pénétration*. Philip Jarrett

(*Below*) **The experimental machine fitted with a 150hp Hispano Suiza engine.** Philip Jarrett

V-strut concept was obsolete, and lacked potential for further development. More advanced airframes were required to take the more powerful engines and increased armament required.

The Nieuport 25

Next in numerical sequence was the Nieuport 25. It was very similar to the Nieuport 27 except that most had a broader chord engine cowling that housed a Clerget engine. It is not certain which type of engine was fitted, but it was possibly a variant of the Clerget 9B. Nungesser's machines had broader chord undercarriage strut fairings, possibly indicating that they had a strengthened undercarriage with steel tube struts of larger section than standard. Judging by what little data has been found, its performance was little better than that of the Nieuport 24, and development was not taken further. It is uncertain how many were built, but Nungesser had two, and some were delivered to Russia.

Nieuport 25 (N5324) decorated with the personal markings of Charles Nungesser. via Stuart Leslie

The Nieuport 27

The final sesquiplane variant of this period to go into production and see service was the Nieuport 27. It was very similar to the Nieuport 24, but differed in having the split-axle undercarriage and simple tail-skid that had previously appeared on one of the prototypes discussed above. The wheels were sprung by bungee cord on either side of each V-strut, and were on individual axles pivoted at the centre joint by twin spreader bars. The prototype was fitted with straight-edged ailerons and the troublesome aileron fairing strips, but production models had tapered ailerons with the fairing strips deleted.

At first the angles of incidence of the mainplanes of the Nieuport 27 were set at less than those of earlier types. But the Nieuport company later issued an instruction to re-rig the aircraft to 2° 40' of incidence to the upper wing and 3 degrees to the lower wing, increasing to 4 degrees at the struts for the starboard lower wing only as a means of counteracting torque. One machine (B6774) was tested by 2 AD RFC with the revised incidence settings. The testing showed that the machine was marginally slower on the ailerons, but no heavier than before, and would fly hands-off with the engine on or off – and the aerobatic qualities were unchanged. As no particular advantage could be found for the change, no specific instruction was issued for a modification.

The engines of some Nieuport 27s were fitted with a device operated by the pilot, which was claimed to burn oil off sparking plugs if they became short-circuited in flight. The device was known as a *carboliseur*, and was basically a current intensifier, weighing only a few ounces. A Nieuport (N5637) fitted with one was delivered to the RFC, but the aeroplane was recalled before it could be tested.

Some Nieuports (N5618, N5622, N5623 and N5627) delivered to the RFC were fitted with 50ltr (11gal) Lanser fire-proof tanks, but these tanks were removed before the aeroplanes were issued to RFC squadrons and sent to England for testing.

The Nieuport 27 replaced the earlier Nieuport designs on the production line,

This photograph is believed to show the Nieuport 27 prototype. JMB/GLS collection

Nieuport 27 (B3650), which from September 1917 served with 1 and 29 Sqns RFC before being flown to England on 19 April 1918. JMB/GLS collection

(*Below*) **Nieuport 27 (B6827), formerly of 1 Sqn RFC, after it had been captured by the Germans on 6 November 1917.** JMB/GLS collection

and equipped some French and RFC units from the summer of 1917. However, the general concept had become outdated, and the type was relegated to less onerous duties in other theatres of operations or training units as more suitable types appeared. The USAS received 287 Nieuport 27s for training purposes. Italy used Nieuport 24 and 27 types made in France and Italy: the Nieuport 24 served in flying schools, and the Nieuport 27 began operations at the Front in October 1917 and continued until the Armistice.

		Nieuport 24	Nieuport 24*bis*	Nieuport 25	Nieuport 27
Engine:		120hp Le Rhône 9Jb	120hp Le Rhône 9Jb	150/170hp Clerget	120hp Le Rhône 9Jb
Propeller:		Régy 354			
Dimensions:	Span, upper, m (ft)	8.21 (26.9)	8.21 (26.9)	8.21 (26.9)	
	Span, lower, m (ft)	7.82 (25.7)	7.82 (25.7)	7.82 (25.7)	
	Length, m (ft)	5.87 (19.2)	5.87 (19.2)	5.87 (19.2)	
	Height, m (ft)	2.40 (7.87)	2.40 (7.87)	2.40 (7.87)	
	Wing area, m (ft)	14.75 (158.8)	14.75 (158.8)	14.75 (158.8)	
Weights:	Empty, kg (lb)	355 (783)			
	Loaded, kg (lb)	547 (1,206)	535 (1,180)		
Performance:	Max speed, km/h (mph):				
	at sea level	176 (109)	170 (105.6)	172 (107)	
	2,000m (6,560ft)	171 (106)	170 (105.6)	170 (105.6)	
	3,000m (9,850ft)	169 (105)	168 (104)	167 (103.7)	
	6,000m (19,690ft)	155 (96)			
	Time to height:				
	at 1,000m (3,280ft)	2min 40sec	2min 40sec		
	at 2,000m (6,560ft)	5min 40sec	5min 40sec	4min 40sec	5min 40sec
	at 3,000m (9,850ft)	9min 25sec	9min 40sec	8min 00sec	9min 25sec
	at 5,000m (16,400ft)	21min 30sec	21min 40sec	20min 10sec	21min 30sec
	Ceiling, m (ft)	6,900 (22,640)	6,300 (20,670)	6,850 (22,475)	
	Endurance, hr	2.25	2.25		

Gustav Delage was looking at the adoption of a twin-spar lower wing well before the Nieuport 28 appeared. This prototype, bearing a strong resemblance to the Nieuport 24/27, appeared in 1916. JMB/GLS collection

The Nieuport 28

Even before the Nieuport 24 and 27 entered service it was apparent that for a further improvement in performance a more powerful engine was needed, coupled with a stronger airframe and greater wing area to carry the increased weight. A prototype with a larger wing area, similar to the Nieuport 24 and 27, appeared in 1916 fitted with a lower wing of much greater chord, increasing the total wing area to 18sq m (194sq ft). The lower wing had twin spars, but the V interplane struts were retained. The ailerons were of the standard straight-edged type. Upper and lower wings were rigged with similar dihedral. The landing wires were unusual in that the rear cable was anchored to the upper fuselage longeron, and the front cable to the top of the rear wing-support struts. The engine was a standard 130hp Le Rhône 9J fitted with a long chord circular cowling of ample proportions. As discussed earlier, this may have been the 'missing' Nieuport 22.

A Nieuport 28 Prototype

A machine that could be considered the prototype of the Nieuport 28 was the subject of a patent application on 31 July. The wings of this machine were untapered, with elliptical tips and a cutout on the trailing edge above the cockpit. The lower wing was of reduced chord compared with the upper wing. Only the lower ones were fitted with ailerons. Each wing consisted of two spars and spruce leading and trailing edges supported by fourteen ribs on each side, of which four were compression ribs of increased strength. False ribs between the main ribs helped to support the leading edge. Each rib web was made of poplar, capped with thin strips of ash nailed to the top and bottom rib surfaces. Critically, as will be discussed later, the capping strips did not extend forward of the main spar on the top surface; instead, three-ply birch plywood extended across the top of the whole span from the main spar to the leading edge, and was rebated into the capping strips. The wing was strengthened by cross-bracing wires between the two spars and between the outer ribs and trailing edge. The wing spars were the same distance apart. This allowed the interplane struts, of hollowed spruce struts bound with linen, to be parallel, and these were joined by false ribs at their extremities, thereby eliminating the need for rigging wires between the struts and adjustments of incidence and stagger. Only the upper wing, which was joined at the centreline, had dihedral (*dièdre total*), and the stagger was 30 degrees.

An experimental version of the Nieuport 28 (N4434), with marked dihedral on the upper wing, and the centre section at eye level (*dièdre complet*). Another prototype of this version also existed. Jean Noël, via Stuart Leslie.

(*Below*) **A Nieuport 28 and its 160hp Gnome Monosoupape rotary engine stripped of fabric during a Swiss Air Force evaluation.** Greg Van Wyngarden

As with previous types, the basic fuselage structure was a wire-braced box girder with ash and spruce longerons. However, in the case of this design, fretted formers and stringers were added to give a polygonal, almost rounded cross-section that gradually tapered to a vertical knife-edge at a duralumin sternpost. Behind the circular aluminium pressed cowling, the forward fuselage and headrest were covered with 4mm compressed composition board, and to the rear of the cockpit to the sternpost the fuselage was covered with fabric. The tail unit looked identical to those of the Nieuport 24 and 27, and consisted of a series of small ribs between an outline of wood, covered by a 25mm two-ply skin of tulipwood strips glued at 90 degrees and covered by fabric and doped.

As with the Nieuport 27, the undercarriage consisted of two faired V-struts with a split axle and bungee cord shock absorbers. The legs were cross-braced with wire, and a central cable ran from the axle joint to the fuselage underside. The tail-skid was hinged on a cross-member between the lower longerons, with the shock absorber consisting of bungee cord between the top of the skid and the preceding cross-member. It was armed with a single Vickers gun mounted on the port longeron. The first machine (N4434) flew in May 1917.

Two More Prototypes

Two more prototypes appeared in October 1917 and were test flown the following month. Both dispensed with the first aeroplane's slightly swept-back wings. One of them also had the dihedral of the upper wing deleted, leaving neither wing with dihedral (*dièdre nul*). The upper and lower wings were of unequal chord and span, and together had a wing area of 20sq m (215sq ft). The fairing of the fuselage was retained, but the metal panels between the rear of the cockpit and the engine were replaced by panels of two-ply made from tulip wood; the access panels, however, were of aluminium. The landing gear was similar to the earlier prototype.

The definitive version was powered by a nine-cylinder Gnome Monosoupape (single valve) 9N rotary engine delivering 160hp at 1,400 rev/min. It was housed in a

Nieuport 28 rib and spar construction. Mick Davis

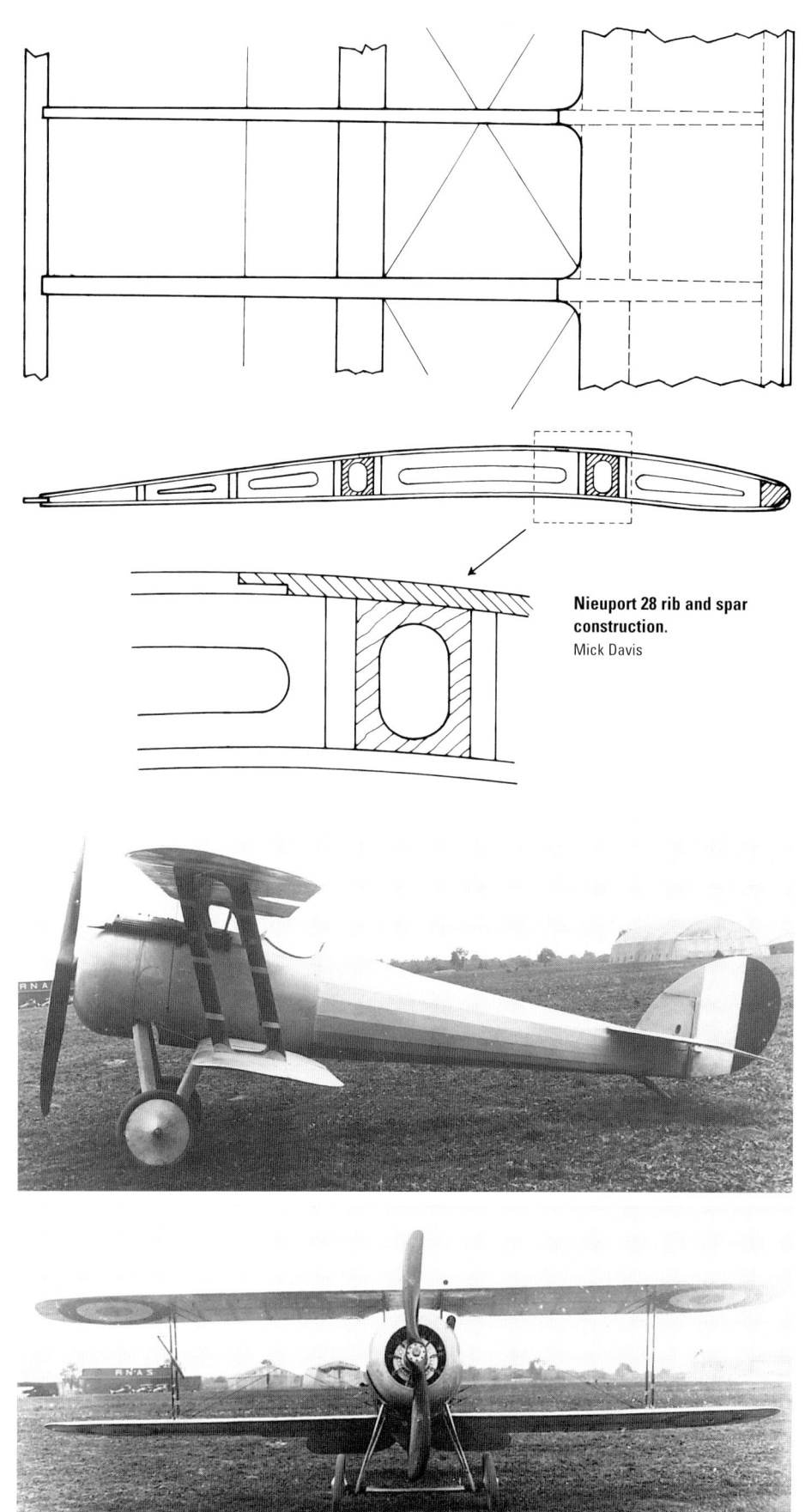

The Nieuport 28 prototype (no serial) without dihedral. Jean Noël, via Stuart Leslie

deep-chord circular aluminium cowling. The relatively small frontal opening was supplemented by vents in the sides. An annular oil tank of 25ltr (5.5gal) capacity was fitted under the cowling. Although fuel tankage varied, a typical layout was two fuel tanks, one of 85ltr (18.7gal), and a second of 45ltr (9.9gal) fitted under the fuselage. A Guer et Mansuy hand pump was available to pump fuel from the auxiliary to the main tank should the Weymann fuel pump break down.

Some of the earlier troubles experienced with Gnome engines were partially overcome later by fitting dual ignition. Replacement of the inlet valve of the earlier-model engines – situated in the crown of the piston, and which operated through the differential pressure between the cylinder and crankcase, by ports in the cylinder walls – also improved reliability. However, the Monosoupape had an unfortunate tendency to catch fire. The engine had no throttle, power being adjusted by operating a 'blip-switch' that suppressed the ignition in one, three, six or all nine of the cylinders. Rapid use of the switch could cause uneven firing and significant vibration. Furthermore, if the pilot failed to switch off the fuel supply when he cut the ignition, unburnt fuel would spill out of the exhaust valves into the cowling where it could catch fire or explode, often with disastrous results. Another source of fire came from leaking fuel lines: the copper tubing from which they were made tended to crack because it was improperly annealed, and there was no flexible coupling to offset the effects of vibration.

Following testing of the second prototype, some dihedral was incorporated, which led to the third variant (*demi-dièdre*) in which an intermediate setting of 1° 10' dihedral was adopted for the upper wing. The change was accomplished by reducing the height of the centre-section struts, leaving the interplane struts unaltered. This angle of dihedral was retained on production models, but the entire upper wing was raised by lengthening both the centre section and interplane struts by the same amount. This improved the pilot's view and also made room for a second Vickers gun mounted on the top decking inside the port centre-section struts.

The standard armament was one 0.303 calibre Vickers machine-gun to the left of the centreline; this was soon supplemented by a second on the left side of the fuselage, outboard of the centre section. In American service these were later modified to take 0.30 calibre ammunition. They would use service ammunition and special tracer, incendiary and armour-piercing ammunition. For balloon busting the additional amount of incendiary material that could be carried in 11mm (0.43in) calibre ammunition was preferred, and guns of this calibre were sometimes fitted so that every fifth cartridge was an incendiary.

This type was ordered by the Aviation Militaire and given the designation Nie-28C.1, but in the end the order was severely cut back. Despite its performance being better than the earlier Nieuport Scouts, it was still judged inferior to the new Spad 13C.1, put into production by the end of 1917. The American Expeditionary Force (AEF) had hoped to receive the Spad 13, but there were not enough, and because it was in desperate need of aircraft it was obliged to receive Nieuport 28s instead; it took a total of somewhat less than 200.

At least two variants of the Nieuport 28 airframe were built. One, a contemporary of the Nieuport 28, had a 180hp Gnome and a laminated wooden fuselage; and another, which acted as a test bed for the 200hp Clerget 11E rotary engine, had wings of increased area with revised dihedral.

Problems in Combat

Combat experience with the Nieuport 28 showed that it had outstanding manœuvrability and rate of climb compared with the Spad 13. However, it also had certain drawbacks, and these gave it a bad reputation with its pilots. The engine tended to catch fire, and it would shed fabric from its wings during its recovery from a high-speed dive, sometimes taking the leading-edge riblets with it. This occurred on at least seven occasions in American machines in service with the 94th and 95th AS.

The first official notification came in a report by Capt Du Doré, a French liaison officer serving with the American army. He reported that: '… the front wing is too weak; it gives way, the ribs between the front of the wing and the main spar break, the fabric tears off, and the upper wing, particularly the starboard one, loses its fabric completely.' Whilst Capt Du Doré's report highlighted the wing stripping as by far the most significant problem, it also listed many other faults, namely: numerous breakages of the outer tubes of the undercarriage during hard landings; the oil tank tended to leak; the engine cowlings were of poor quality and broke easily; the gasoline tanks were poorly soldered and sprang leaks due to engine vibration; larger diameter oil and petrol pipes were required; the gasoline tanks were too exposed to enemy fire; and finally the engine tended to overheat, and on average lasted only twenty-one hours.

A prototype with a strong resemblance to the Nieuport 28, but with a shorter wingspan, revised cabane structure, and a 200hp Clerget 11E eleven-cylinder rotary engine. Jean Noël, via Stuart Leslie

(*Top*) **Factory-fresh Nieuport 28 (N6215) in US service at Orly.** Greg Van Wyngarden

(*Middle*) **1st Lt Douglas Campbell with Nieuport 28 (N6179), usually flown by 1st Lt Reed Chambers.** Greg Van Wyngarden

(*Bottom*) **1st Lt Eddie Rickenbacker in the cockpit of a Nieuport 28 of 1st Flight, 94 AS, showing the arrangement of the twin Vickers guns.** Greg Van Wyngarden

The conclusions of the above report were further amplified by a report from Major A.M. Atkinson, the commander of the US First Pursuit Group, to Brig Gen B. Foulois, Chief of the Air Service to the American First Army. In it he gave an overall assessment of the Nieuport 28, but laid stress on the problem with wing failures. Concerning these he wrote:

> The weak construction in the upper wing is due to both wing spars being too close to the middle (front to rear) of the wing. In four cases in this Group, upon redressing after steep dive, the leading edge of the upper wing has collapsed, carrying away the fabric of the upper surface of the wing.

He acknowledged two advantages of the aircraft, namely that it was very manoeuvrable, and its engine started easily so that it could respond quickly to alerts. However, he listed eleven other problems associated with the aircraft, one of the more serious being that the engine vibrated too much, causing the oil and gasoline tanks to leak, and leaking gasoline could impinge on the rather exposed distributor plate and catch fire. Also the gasoline tanks were badly placed, in particular the reserve tank, which was located just to the right and forward of the pilot's seat, presenting a favourable target for enemy incendiary bullets. It was therefore recommended that the tanks be situated lower down and behind the pilot to give him a better chance of survival; this meant that a fuel pump would be required to feed the engine – though it would also allow room for another ammunition box. Atkinson also observed that the aircraft lacked sufficient speed in a dive; and concluded that it lost about 25 per cent efficiency after between fifteen to thirty-six hours' flying.

As commander of the 94th AS, Major J. Huffer had personal experience with the Nieuport 28, and in a letter to Foulois he

A refined Nieuport 28 variant with a wooden monocoque fuselage construction, revised empennage shape and construction, and a 165hp Monosoupape Gnome engine. Jean Noël, via Stuart Leslie

was equally scathing but more specific with regard to the causes of the wing failures:

> It has several times been witnessed, after a steep dive, that the entering edge of the upper wing, which is made of veneered wood, tears off from the spar. This is probably due to the fact that the plane being exposed to the sun most of the time and the veneered wood not warping in the same proportion as the spar, the joint between the veneered wood and the spar becomes loose and cannot stand the strain of the great wind pressure.

Huffer went on to address some of the other problems experienced in service. He suggested increasing the gauge of the landing wires to strengthen the undercarriage. He also suggested that the gasoline pipework and connections should be reinforced, and to place the gasoline tanks under the fuselage between the landing gear struts, and to make them detachable so as to reduce the incidence of fires when the aircraft was hit by incendiary bullets.

The mechanism by which the wing failed has been the subject of much discussion, but it would appear that, when the aircraft was pulled out of a high-speed dive, a region of strong negative pressure would form on the leading edge of the wing, and the wing structure was simply not strong enough to resist the resultant forces.

The wings were strengthened on late production Nieuports by using battens to secure the plywood surface between the leading edge and main spar to the ribs. These battens extended from the leading edge to just aft of the main spar along each rib, and were glued to the plywood and pinned through the plywood and capping strips into the rib webs. Besides securing the plywood in place, it also provided additional structural support to prevent the leading edge from collapsing. However, this modification came too late to save the reputation of the Nieuport 28, and as is recounted in a later chapter, the American military were anxious to replace the machine at the Front by the Spad 13.

Despite all these problems, in the spring of 1918 an American Nieuport 28 was forced to land in Switzerland. This machine sufficiently impressed the Swiss authorities for them to buy a further fourteen examples from French surplus stocks in 1923, and they maintained them in use until 1930.

After the war, a number of Nieuport 28s were used by the French postal authorities to carry mail between London and Paris during 1920.

Nieuport-Delage Monoplane 180hp ('Madon')

During the course of 1917, Nieuport considered returning to the monoplane configuration for its next generation of fighters. Its design office continued working on the concept, particularly the problems of wing structure and visibility. It produced a design in response to a specification issued in 1917 requiring the following performance figures:

speed at 3,000m: (9,850ft)	210km/h (130mph)
service ceiling:	7,500m (24,600ft)
strength coefficient:	6.5
wing loading:	less than 39kg/sq m (8lb/sq ft)
fuel:	for 2hr endurance
useful load:	165kg (364lb)
armament:	two machine-guns, or one machine-gun and one cannon

Rather than cut away part of the wing root in order to improve the view below, which would have a detrimental effect on the wing structure and result in a reduction in the wing area, the designers came up with a different configuration. They set the wing so that it was level with the top of the fuselage and placed the pilot above the wing in the centre to give him a perfect view forwards and upwards. To give the required downward view, transparent panels of glass or cellon were incorporated into a fairing between the lower wing roots and the fuselage sides. Another advantage of the configuration was that all the drag-inducing bracing wires would be eliminated.

The fuselage was directly derived from the Nieuport 27, although both were subject to some modifications during the course of development. The wing was of conventional construction, but to accommodate the transparent panels the leading edge sloped downwards at the junction with the fuselage. The undercarriage axle was covered by a streamlined auxiliary wing that also provided anchor points for a complex arrangement of struts. A pair of struts joined the spars at the midpoint of each wing to the extremities of the axle fairing, which in turn was supported by two N-struts from the fuselage.

(*Above*) **Nieuport-Delage monoplane with a 160hp Gnome Monosoupape rotary engine, November 1917.** Jean Noël, via Stuart Leslie

(*Right and below*) **Three views of the Nieuport-Delage 'Madon' monoplane with a 180hp Le Rhône 9N.** Jean Noël, via Stuart Leslie

A trial installation was carried out to supplement the standard armament of two machine-guns with what was called a *boîte à mitraille*. This consisted of a cannon mounted along the axis of the engine. As it would not have been possible to install the cannon through the crankshaft of a rotary engine, it must have been secured directly to the propeller boss and rotated with the engine. It was of a non-standard 16mm calibre, and loaded with a single shell weighing 500g containing thirty-six steel balls. This was expected to inflict considerable damage over a wide area of an opponent's machine, but although the concept found favour with combat pilots, and may have been suggested by Madon himself, it did not generate any interest with the General Staff. This is not surprising, as it is difficult to see what advantage a single shell could have over twin Vickers guns firing armour-piercing bullets. Also, by 1918 the French had gone a long way towards perfecting a 37mm cannon, which could be easily mounted in the Hispano-Suiza or engine of similar configuration.

The Nieuport 'Madon' was not retained by the STAé, which favoured the next generation of biplane scouts including the Ni D-29. However, the career of the design did not end with the end of the war, because one of the prototypes was converted into a racing machine for the 1919 Coupe Deutsch de la Meurthe. The wingspan was reduced to give a wing area of 12sq m (130sq ft)compared with 18sq m (194sq ft), the armament was removed, and the windscreen was sloped backwards. Piloted by Keith Jensen, a Dane formerly of the French air force, it attained a speed of 200km/h (124mph) on the first day of the race; but this was surpassed shortly afterwards by Sadi-Lecointe in the Ni D-29V.

Nieuport-Delage 31Rh. Jean Noël, via Stuart Leslie

An additional V-strut joined the fuselage to the centre of the axle fairing.

When first seen at the factory in November 1917, the first prototype was fitted with a 160hp Gnome; but this engine was replaced by a 180hp Le Rhône 9N before the aircraft first flew at the beginning of 1918. It achieved a speed of 205km/h (127mph) at 3,000m (9,850ft), and had a service ceiling of 7,000m (23,000ft). Two modifications were incorporated early in the test programme: a small cutout was made in the wing root to improve the downward view, which must have been found wanting; and the surface area of the vertical tail surfaces was increased by adding a fillet between the fin and the fuselage.

The Nieuport-Delage 31

Following the formula begun by the 180hp Nieuport monoplane described above, in 1918 Nieuport designed the Ni D-31 powered by a 170hp Le Rhône, which chronologically appeared before the Ni D-29. Having the same general appearance as the earlier monoplane, it differed in some important respects. The fuselage was of monocoque construction, similar to that of the Ni D-29. The wings were not fixed directly to the fuselage, but instead the outer panels were joined by a centre plate set on top of the fuselage. The span was 8.6m

		Nieuport 28	Madon	Ni D-31
Engine:		160hp Gnome 9N Monosoupape	180hp Le Rhône 9N	170hp Le Rhône
Dimensions:	Span, upper, m (ft)	8.0 (26)	9.40 (30.8)	8.60 (28.2)
	Length, m (ft)	6.25 (20.5)	6.40 (20.9)	6.60 (21.6)
	Wing area, sq m (sq ft)	16.0 (172)	18 (194)	18 (194)
Weights:	Empty, kg (lb)	400 (882)	500 (1,103)	
	Loaded, kg (lb)	698 (1,539)	703 (1,550)	780 (1,720)
	Fuel load, kg (lb)	120 (265)		
	Wing loading kg/sq m (lb/sq ft)	44 (9.02)		
Performance:	Max speed, km/h (mph):			
	at sea level	200 (124)	205 (127)	230 (143)
	at 2,000m (6,560ft)	202 (125)		
	at 3,000m (9,850ft)	200 (124)		
	at 4,000m (13,120ft)	196 (122)		
	Time to height:			
	1,000m (3,280ft)	2min 38sec		
	2,000m (6,560ft)	4min 6sec		
	3,000m (9,850ft)	8min 10sec		
	5,000m (16,400ft)	19min 48sec		
	Ceiling, m (ft)	7,000 (22,970)		
	Endurance, hr			2

(28ft), much shorter than the monoplane, but with a wider chord to give a similar surface area of 18sq m (194sq ft). The transparent panels in the fuselage were deleted, but a cutout was provided in the wing root instead to give sufficient downward view for racing purposes. Also the auxiliary wing supporting the undercarriage was extended beyond the wheels, which were provided with fairings. The shape of the fin and rudder were similar to those of the Ni D-29.

Two prototypes were built, and the second was tested by the STAé at the beginning of 1919. But faced with a preference of the General Staff for biplanes, further development was abandoned.

The Nieuport 80, 81, 82, 83 and 84

During 1917 and 1918, Nieuport produced derivatives of its scout and reconnaissance machines for training purposes, and these were given type numbers in the 80 to 84 range, these probably making reference to the 80hp Le Rhône engine that was commonly used to power these machines. The Nieuport 80 was evolved from the Nieuport 13 E2, a two-seater with one set of controls for the pilot in the rear seat. The Nieuport 81 was derived from the Nieuport 13 D2, which was similar to the Nieuport 80 but

The Nieuport 81E2 (N8300). Jean Noël, via Stuart Leslie

(*Above*) **Two views of a Nieuport 82E2 primary trainer (N8065).** Jean Noël, via Stuart Leslie

A Nieuport 80. Jean Noël, via Stuart Leslie

with dual controls. Some Nieuport 81 D2s were converted to single-control 81 E2s. The Nieuport 82 D2 was a derivative of the Nieuport 14 with the rotary engine. One version had the supplementary pair of wheels supported in front of the main undercarriage, and was christened the *Grosse Julie*. The Nieuport 83 E2 was a derivative of the Nieuport 10 two-seater, with controls only for the pilot in the rear cockpit.

The general course of tuition at the flying school at Pau was for *ab initio* training, to be carried out on the dual-control Nieuport 82, followed by further training on the dual-control Nieuport 81. A pupil's solo flight was carried out in a single-seat Nieuport 80, and further experience was gained up to receiving his certificate on the single-seat Nieuport 83.

In addition to production for the Aviation Militaire, Nieuport trainers were also used by the American Expeditionary Force flying school at Issoudun: a total of 147 Nieuport 80s, 173 Nieuport 81s, and 244 Nieuport 83s were delivered. The Japanese produced the Nieuport 81 and 83 under licence.

In 1920 some Nieuport 80s and 81s were converted into Nieuport 80*bis* and 81*bis* by replacing their 80hp Le Rhônes by 80hp Clerget 7Zs.

The Nieuport 84 was a very different machine from the others, only the fin shape being recognizable from earlier machines. Little is known about the machine, but it was probably a trainer or scout aircraft with new wings that gave it a strong resemblance to the Fokker D.VII.

The Nieuport 83E2. Jean Noël, via Stuart Leslie

		Nieuport 80	Nieuport 81	Nieuport 82	Nieuport 83
Engine		80hp Le Rhône	80hp Le Rhône	80hp Le Rhône	80hp Le Rhône
Dimensions	Span, m (ft)	9 (3.3)	9 (3.3)	11.9 (39)	7.9 (25.9)
	Length, m (ft)	7 (23)	7 (23)	7.9 (25.9)	7 (23)
	Height, m (ft)	2.7 (8.8)	2.7 (8.8)	2.7 (8.8)	
	Wing area, sq m (sq ft)	22 (237)	22 (237)	30 (323)	18 (194)
Weights	Empty, kg (lb)	450 (992)			
	Loaded, kg (lb)	760 (1,676)	820 (1,808)	700 (1,544)	
Performance	Max speed, km/h (mph):				
	at 2,000m (6,570ft)	110 (68)	120 (74.5)		
	Landing speed, km/h (mph)		75 (47)		
	Time to height (mins):				
	1,000m (3,280)	8			
	1,700m (5,580)	15			
	2,000m (6,560)	19			
	3,000m (9,850)	38			
	3,500m (11,480)	60			

Relationship between main Nieuport types.

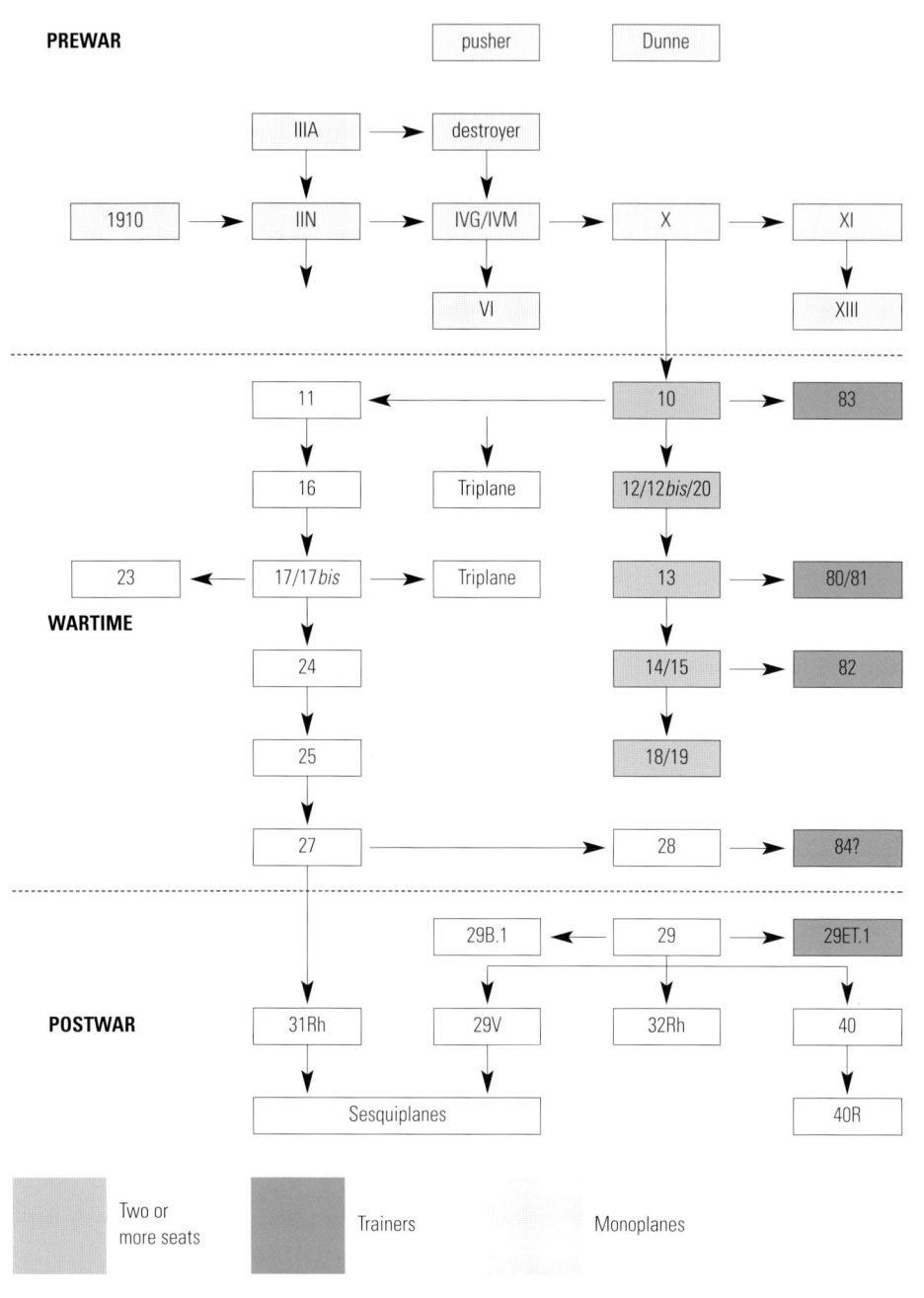

```
PREWAR                                    pusher        Dunne

                        IIIA    →    destroyer
                         ↓              ↓
         1910   →   IIN    →    IVG/IVM    →    X    →    XI
                         ↓              ↓            ↓
                                       VI           XIII

----------------------------------------------------------------

                        11    ←                10    →    83
                         ↓                      ↓
                        16         Triplane   12/12bis/20
                         ↓                      ↓
           23   ←    17/17bis  →  Triplane     13    →    80/81
                         ↓                      ↓
WARTIME                 24                    14/15    →    82
                         ↓                      ↓
                        25                    18/19
                         ↓
                        27         →           28    →    84?

----------------------------------------------------------------

                              29B.1   ←   29   →   29ET.1
                                ↓         ↓         ↓
POSTWAR                31Rh    29V      32Rh       40
                         ↓      ↓                   ↓
                         Sesquiplanes              40R
```

Legend:
- Two or more seats
- Trainers
- Monoplanes

The Designs of Società Anonima Nieuport-Macchi

The L.1 and L.2

Shortly after hostilities began between Italy and Austria-Hungary, on the night of the 27/28 June 1915 an Austrian Lohner Type L flying boat suffered an engine failure due to a damaged radiator. It was forced to alight at Porto Corsini near Ravenna, and was captured intact before the crew could destroy it. This aircraft was powered by a 150hp six-cylinder inline water-cooled Heiro engine.

In less than seven weeks Nieuport-Macchi had built an exact structural replica powered by a 150hp Isotta-Franchini engine. Flight-testing was carried out by a naval pilot, Lt Giovanni Roberti, based at Schiranna on the shore of a lake near Varese, where a shed was erected specifically for this purpose. This aircraft, the L.1, totally outperformed the equipment then operated by the Italian navy, the French FBA flying boat built under licence by Savoia at nearby Sesto Calende.

The L.1 was a biplane with three bays on either side, and with the lower wing flush with the upper longerons of the fuselage. The lower wing was of narrower chord and shorter span than the upper wing. Only the lower wing had dihedral, and only the upper wing was fitted with ailerons. Both wings were of constant chord, and were designed with 10 degrees sweepback from a rectangular centre section. Each wing had three spars, the upper wing with nineteen ribs and the lower with thirteen. The upper wing also had intermediate ribs extending from the leading edge to the rear spar. The ailerons, unlike those of the Lohner that were almost rectangular in shape, had reverse taper, giving wing-tips of wider chord. The ribs of the ailerons were shaped to confer washout at the wing-tips. The six pairs of interplane struts were vertical when viewed from the front, and were staggered forwards by about 18 degrees. A V-shaped stay connected to each of the foremost outer wing struts and further braced to the tops of both outer struts, supported the upper wing's overhang.

The hull was finely tapered, with the cross-section of the planing bottom changing from a V to a slightly concave shape backwards to a single step. The cockpit had two seats side by side in the forward fuselage, and the crew were protected from the slipstream and spray by an upward slope to the latter. One version had a glass-panelled cabin forward of the cockpit with dual controls. The uncowled engine was suspended between the wings by a complex strut system; it was fitted with a frontal radiator, and drove a pusher propeller. The fuel tank was placed above the centre section. The rectangular tailplane and trapezoid single fin and rudder were supported well clear of the water by a system of struts above the rear fuselage. The floats were set at the wing-tips and consisted of a metal, tapered cylinder fitted with a wooden flat-bottomed glove set at an angle to the water. The cockpit could be fitted with a forward-mounted machine-gun.

A total of 139 L.1s was produced.

In 1916, the L.1 was replaced in production by the L.2. This was a redesign by Nieuport-Macchi staff, substantially reduced in structural weight and aerodynamic drag, and powered by a 160hp Isotta-Franchini V4B engine. The wingspan was reduced by about 40cm (16in), and the total number of wing bays from six to four. The floats were of

Nieuport-Macchi 11. via Paul Leaman

Nieuport-Macchi 11. via Philip Jarrett   (*Below*) **Macchi L.1 copy of the Lohner flying boat.** Giorgio Apostolo

a more streamlined shape, of circular cross-section tapering to a beaver tail. The L.2 showed a better performance compared with the L.1, though only ten were produced: this was because an even better derivative, the L.3, was in the offing.

The M.3, M.4 and M.8

The L.2 was in turn quickly replaced by the L.3 (renamed the M.3), of similar configuration but essentially a new design by Felice Buzio. The outline of the fin and rudder was changed, with the leading edge curving backwards, and a scalloped curved trailing edge. A streamlined aluminium cowling that partially covered the engine was also designed for the machine, but was not always fitted. This required the frontal radiator to be replaced by twin radiators splayed at an angle either side of the engine. The floats were replaced by wooden floats of rectangular section tapering to a horizontal knife-edge front and rear. It could be armed with a machine-gun on a ring in the front cockpit, or sometimes a small cannon. Largely due to its lower weight, this design showed a significantly improved performance compared with its Lohner predecessors, and this was demonstrated on 10 October 1916 when it established a new world time-to-height record for seaplanes by reaching 5,400m (17,720ft) in 41min. Two hundred were produced, and were used extensively by the Italian navy in the Adriatic on reconnaissance and bombing missions.

After the war, several M.3s were converted to civil use. These had a cowled engine with a frontal radiator, and the fin and rudder were mounted directly on to the fuselage with a strut-braced mid-mounted tailplane. A partially enclosed cabin for two passengers was placed immediately in front of the wings, with an open cockpit on a raised decking for the pilot beneath the engine behind.

The M.3 was further developed into the M.4, designed for reconnaissance and bombing. This represented a considerable advance over the original Lohner concept. The aerodynamic design was very refined for its day, and this, along with the single-seat M.6 derivative, represented the final stage in the evolution of this series of multi-role seaplanes for the Italian navy. Unlike the earlier versions, the tail surfaces were mounted directly and cleanly to the fuselage. The design was studied as a possible platform for the Vickers cannon, intended for use against submarines caught on the surface.

At the end of 1917 Macchi, having studied the structural and aerodynamic characteristics of traditional rectangular biplanes, designed the radically new M.8. This was a heavily modified L.3, with stronger 'W' configuration interplane struts of adjustable length. It was of greater stiffness, and showed reduced drag compared with the earlier design. This gave a significant improvement in speed from 146 to 165km/h (90 to 102mph), although retaining the original 160hp engine. It was used by the Italian navy for coastal patrol duties.

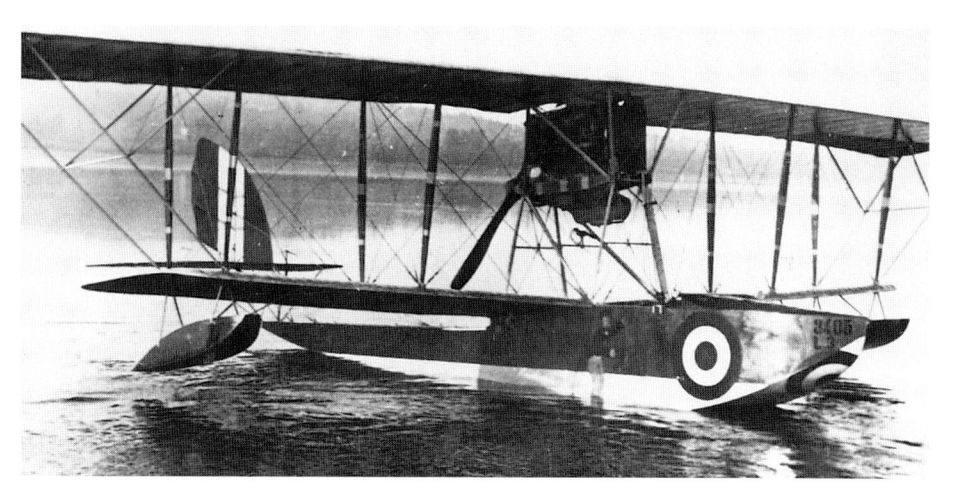

Macchi L.3 (M.3). Philip Jarrett

M.5, M.5*bis*, M.6 and M.7

The provision of both military and naval aircraft was the responsibility of Mag Gen G.B. Marieni, the director general of aeronautics. His plan for the naval air arm for 1917 saw a requirement for forty-six seaplane scouts of advanced design for escorting bombers and reconnaissance seaplanes such as the M.3 and FBA, and for patrol and scouting work. As it happened, by September 1916 Buzio, in cooperation with Calzavara, already had a single-seat seaplane fighter design on the drawing board: this was destined to be the forerunner of the Macchi M.5 variants.

Lacking a suitable engine with sufficient power, the designers decided to improve performance by reducing size and weight. Although of similar construction, the fuselage was about 20 per cent shorter than the Macchi L.1. The wings showed strong Nieuport influence, being of sesquiplane layout with a twin-spar upper wing and a single-spar lower wing joined by V-struts. The wingspan was reduced by about a quarter, giving a surface area little more than half that of the L.1. The empennage was made of steel tube, and was placed on a steel-tube framework typical of Lohner designs. The control cables were run externally. Large floats were faired into the wings near the tips. The uncowled engine was set below the upper wing and was equipped with a pair of vertical frontal radiators. Although the prototype was unarmed, it was conceived that a single machine-gun could be mounted on a pillar forward of the windscreen.

Initial flight tests showed that modifications were necessary. The step was moved forwards by about 30cm (12in), and the bow was slightly widened and the nose shortened by about 20cm (8in). A Fiat machine-gun was installed under a new sheet-metal forward decking, and a Nieuport-style windscreen was fitted, together with a metal faired headrest. The fin and rudder were also moved forwards by about 30cm (12in), and the tailplane was simplified by giving it a trapezoid plan form. The engine was fitted with an aluminium cowling with detachable side panels and a single frontal radiator. The fuel tank inside the fuselage was enlarged.

A contract for ten machines (4866 to 4875) was authorized on 17 February 1917, and experimental testing of the first began in May 1917. The reports of the tests were

		Lohner Type L	Macchi M.3
Engine		150hp Hiero	160hp Isotta-Fraschini V.4B
Propeller:		Starre	
Dimensions:	Span upper, m (ft)	16.20 (53)	15.95 (52.3)
	Span, lower, m (ft)	10.00 (32.8)	
	Chord, upper, m (ft)	2.05 (6.7)	
	Chord, lower, m (ft)	1.80 (5.9)	
	Length, m (ft)	10.85 (35.6)	10.25 (33.6)
	Height, m (ft)	3.50 (11.5)	3.20 (10.5)
	Wing area, sq m (sq ft)	45.0 (412)	45.0 (412)
Weights:	Empty, kg (lb)	895 (1,973)	895 (1,973)
	Loaded, kg (lb)	1,325 (2,922)	1350 (2,977)
	Wing loading, kg/sq m (lb/sq ft)	29.5 (7.09)	29.3 (7.22)
	Power loading kg/hp (lb/hp)	8.85 (19.5)	
Performance:	Cruising speed, km/h (mph)	127 (79)	
	Maximum speed, km/h (mph):		
	at sea level	105 (65)	145 (90)
	Time to height (min):		
	500m (1,640ft)		
	1,000m (3,280ft)	15	6
	3,000m (9,850ft)	26	
	4,000m (13,120ft)	39	
	Service ceiling, m (ft)	5,500 (18,000)	
	Range, km (miles)	650 (404)	700 (435)
	Endurance, hr	6.5	
	Petrol capacity, kg (lb)	230 (507)	
	Oil capacity, kg (lb)	15 (33)	

decidedly favourable, both speed and climb being judged clearly superior to enemy machines currently used on the Front. Eight machines of the first batch had been delivered by 30 June 1917.

On 1 July 1917 ambitious plans were made by the Ispettorato Sommergibili ed Aviazione (Submarine and Aviation Inspectorate) to expand the air arm of the Regia Marina. These plans were for the production of 102 seaplane scouts and 96 reconnaissance machines (or MMs as they were called in the plan). Although there was no indication of the type to be ordered, it was evident that the M.5 (or MM) was intended for both roles. Repeat contracts were set for two further batches of fifty machines each. At the same time, 200 Vickers guns were ordered from Britain.

Early operational experience showed that further changes were necessary. A new fin was designed that joined directly to the rear fuselage, and the shape of the stern was changed from a beaver tail to a rectangular section. The new shape allowed the control wires to be run internally, thereby affording protection from salt-water corrosion and improving directional stability. The vertical faired floats were changed to smaller units mounted on steel struts.

Further changes were made at some point during the production run of the first batch of fifty. For instance, the structure of the upper wing was completely redesigned; the number of ribs was increased from seventeen to twenty-seven; and the full-chord false ribs inherited from its Lohner origins were replaced by additional ribs running from the leading edge to the front spar. Also the steel ailerons with seven ribs were replaced by wooden units with eleven ribs. Although the overall dimensions were unchanged, the new wings were not interchangeable with the old. A vertical camera, operated by the pilot with a lever that opened a trapdoor in the bottom of the hull, was fitted to some, if not all of the machines used for photographic reconnaissance.

At least one machine (7080) was altered structurally to take a 25.4mm Fiat cannon in place of the machine-gun. The additional weight and the recoil were counteracted by fitting three spanwise steel tubes of 20mm (¾in) or 35mm (1.4in) diameter, supported by twin 20mm V-struts.

More orders were received, raising the total to 420 aircraft, including 340 from Macchi and 80 from Aeromarittima in Naples. Actual deliveries were limited – by the introduction of the more powerful M.7, and by the end of the war – to about 348. During the war, some of the machines were repaired by contractors, for instance twenty-three by Monti & Martini of Milan and four by Zari. Six were repaired by Macchi, but they were forced to relinquish this line of business in 1918 because of the pressure of production and development work.

The M.6

A variant of the M.5 appeared in 1917, designated the M.6. This had a similar fuselage to the M.5, but the sesquiplane arrangement was replaced by untapered equal span wings, both upper and lower wings having twin spars. The performance of the M.6 was very similar to the M.5, and as the latter was preferred due to its advanced stage of development, the M.6 never progressed beyond the prototype stage.

The M.5bis

The M.5 was further developed into the M.5 *modificato* or M.5*bis*. This has been variously reported to be a V-6-powered M.5, an M.5 with M.6-pattern wings or a V-4B-powered M.7. However, a Nieuport-Macchi report, dated March 1919, refers to an important order for 320 M.7s with 250hp Isotta Fraschini V6 engines, and it goes on to say that it was also agreed to transform the remainder of the M.5s under construction by fitting them with M.7-type wings. It is most probable that this is the identity of the M.5*bis*. Acceptance trials of this design began in the summer of 1918, with the twenty-first production model (13153) being tested on 19 September. It is unlikely that any served operationally, because the first to be mentioned in operational reports is 13132 with 260[a] Squadriglia in late November 1918, followed by 13153 at Brindisi in early December.

At least three M.5*bis* (13139, 13152 and 13153) were further modified by fitting long-range fuel tanks to give a duration of flight of about five hours. These were designated the M.5*as* (*autonomia speciale*) and were otherwise unchanged except for possibly being fitted with cylindrical wing floats. After the war, and as a result of the 1923–24 seaplane programme, about thirty-two M.5s were retrofitted with V-6 Isotta Fraschini engines.

Macchi M.5. Giorgio Apostolo

		Macchi M.5	Macchi M.5*bis*	Macchi M.7*bis*
Engine:		160hp Isotta-Fraschini V4B	190hp Isotta-Fraschini V4B	260hp Isotta-Fraschini V-6
Dimensions:	Span, upper, m (ft)	11.90 (39)	9.7 (32)	7.75 (25)
	Span, lower, m (ft)	8.92 (29)		
	Chord, upper, m (ft)	1.60 (5.2)		
	Chord, lower, m (ft)	8.92 (29)		
	Length, m (ft)	8.06 (26)	6.78 (22)	
	Height, m (ft)	2.85 (9.3)	2.85 (9.3)	2.97 (9.7)
	Wing area, sq m (sq ft)	28.0 (301)	26.0 (280)	
Weights:	Empty, kg (lb)	720 (1,590)	760 (1,675)	775 (1,700)
	Loaded, kg (lb)	990 (2,180)	1,030 (2,270)	1030 (2,270)
Performance:	Maximum speed, km/h (mph):			
	at sea level	181 (112)	170 (106)	257 (160)
	at 2,000m	164 (102)		
	Time to height, (mins);			
	1,000m (3,280ft)	3min 45sec	4min	
	2,000m (6,560ft)	8min	9min	
	3,000m (9,850ft)	12min	15min	
	4,000m (13,120ft)	28min	23min	
	Service ceiling, m (ft)	3,900 (12,800)		
	Range, km (miles)	500 (310)		
	Endurance	3hr 40min	3hr 40min	

The M.7

The first design by Alessandro Tonini, who had been appointed as technical manager at Varese, was the M.7. This was another direct derivative of the M.5, fitted with the 250hp Isotta-Fraschini engine and with reduced-span wings. In flight trials the M.7 recorded a speed of 210 km/h (130mph), which made it the fastest seaplane in the world at the time. However, the Italian navy required it to be modified as a longer-range escort fighter, and the added weight reduced its performance slightly. The modifications also delayed its entry into service, and only three were delivered by the end of the war, and a further fourteen afterwards.

During the early postwar period the basic M.7 design was developed into the M.7*bis*, M.7*ter* and M.7AR (*ali ripiegabli* or 'folding wings'). Two companies based in Naples, Industrie Meridionali and Construzioni Aeromarittime S.A., assisted in the production of the M.7 series, developments of which continued in service until 1928.

Macchi M.7. Philip Jarrett

CHAPTER FOUR

French Operations of Nieuport Aircraft During World War One

Nieuport IV in Aviation Militaire Service

The Aviation Militaire expressed an intention to order ten machines of the winning type in the military concours of 1911. It is not known how many were actually ordered, but some Nieuport IVGs were purchased following the success of the Nieuports in the competition. In 1912, six IVGs were formed into a single escadrille designated N.12 and based at Reims. This unit – with other aircraft now in its inventory – moved to Stenay on 8 August 1914 under the command of Capt Aubry, where, together with four other escadrilles, it was placed under the V Armée. With attrition the Nieuports, powered by either 70hp Gnomes or 60hp Clergets, were partially replaced by similar types with 80hp Clergets.

From Stenay the unit carried out reconnaissance missions, occasionally up to 50km (30 miles) behind the lines, but more commonly along the enemy's front lines at an altitude to minimize the effect of anti-aircraft fire. Esc. N.12 participated in the Battle of Guise on 29 August and the Battle of the Aisne on 15 September, flying missions over Craonne and Brimont. By 28 February 1915, the unit was based at Châlons-sur-Vesles. These machines, in common with other shoulder-wing monoplane types, were by this time not considered to be suitable for the reconnaissance role due to the wing obstructing the view. Also their carrying capacity and climbing rate were limited. The Nieuports were therefore relegated to a training role and replaced with Morane Saulnier Type L Parasols, the unit being re-designated as Esc. MS.12.

The Nieuport VI and X in Aviation Maritime Service

The Aviation Maritime was formed on 15 April 1912, and during the following month it acquired its first aircraft for evaluation: a Voisin, a Farman, a Breguet and a Nieuport VI with a 100hp engine, the Nieuport being rented from the manufacturer. During the 1912 manœuvres the authorities were impressed by the Nieuport's endurance, and the fact that its pilot could generally spot the opposing fleet successfully, and so on 26 August it was decided to purchase a second similar Nieuport.

By May 1913 the service had six machines: two Nieuports, two Farmans, a Voisin and a Breguet. In the 1913 manœuvres, a Nieuport flew from the *Foudre*, an old cruiser modified into a seaplane carrier in the summer of 1910, and made a successful attack on the fleet anchorage at Isles de Lérins. As a result, two new Nieuports were ordered, besides a replacement for one destroyed by fire. Two more flights by Nieuport floatplanes impressed the authorities: on 18 December LV (Lieutenant de Vaisseau) Reynaud, LV Fournié and EV (Enseigne de Vaisseau) Destrem flew in formation from Saint Raphaël to Nice and back; and on 13 March LV de l'Escaille and Destrem flew from Saint Raphaël to Ajaccio in Corsica in three hours.

At the outbreak of the war the Aviation Maritime had just thirty-five pilots and an assortment of machines, comprising seven Nieuports with various engines (serials N1 to N7), six Voisins, two Caudrons and two Breguets. By the end of August the number of Nieuports had increased to thirteen. Of the personnel, seventeen pilots, seven officers, two observers and two engineers were stationed at Saint Raphaël, supported by forty-two sailors and marines. The situation was slightly improved by the call-up of reservists, some of whom were experienced pilots or mechanics, such as Julien Levasseur who had been a test pilot with Nieuport. Many of the pilots had earned Aero Club de France brevets in civil flying schools, though very few had experience with seaplanes. Three pilot officers were sent to Nice, and two others to Bonifacio; two more were assigned to the *Foudre*. The remainder were stationed at a *centre d'aviation maritime* set up at Saint Raphaël.

The situation at the beginning of the war was confused. Italy was part of the Triple

Nieuport IVM during the 1912 manœuvres.

Alliance with Germany and Austria-Hungary and was expected to enter the war against France if provoked. Just prior to the outbreak of the war on 29 July 1914 an escadrille, at first with four Nieuports and later with eight, was based at Nice under the command of de l'Escaille within the range of La Spezia. A flight of four machines was sent to Bonifacio under LV de Laborde to cover Sardinia. The *Foudre* was equipped with two Nieuports. Initial sorties from Nice and Bonifacio were therefore tentative, and confined to reconnaissance sorties close to the coast. It was decided to base six Nieuport XH floatplanes – two of which had been held back from a Turkish order for fifteen machines, the freshwater lake, coupled with its high altitude, made it difficult for the aircraft to take off, and their performance was significantly affected. One ended up being destroyed on the lake, and the other was returned to Malta in the steamship *Liamone*. Disenchanted with the Nieuports' performance, these aircraft were later shipped to Port Said.

During the opening days of the war two German cruisers, the *Goeben* and *Breslau*, attacked French installations at Bône and Philippeville on the north African coast. However, they were bottled up in the Mediterranean by the British fleet based at Gibraltar, and were forced to take refuge in the eastern Mediterranean where they Dardenelles, and LV de l'Escaille was ordered to set up a base on Tenedos with two Nieuport seaplanes, one officer and eleven ratings from *Raven II* before it returned to Egypt. However, it proved impossible to control two separate establishments – the one at Tenedos and the Escadrille de Port-Said – so far apart. By 11 April the unit had been re-attached to the British forces on the island, which already had twenty aircraft, eleven pilots and 100 men under the command of Cdr Samson. They were embarked on the *Ark Royal*, but by 20 May the section had been returned to Egypt where they continued to give valuable service. Despite continual demands it proved difficult for the British to release these men and machines, and the French set up a new unit in November 1915 to operate with the troops in the Dardenelles.

After their period with the British, in April 1916 the surviving Nieuport XHs were assigned to the seaplane carrier *Campinas* and sent to Argostoli on the island of Cephalonia off the west coast of Greece, arriving on 24 May 1916. The Nieuports involved were N.18, N.19 and N.20 with 80hp Clergets, and N.21, N.23 and NB.3 with 110hp Clergets. There they carried out patrol duties off the west coast of the Peloponnese until May 1917. Two months later the unit was transferred to Mytika.

At the request of the Italian government, the *ministre de la Marine* decided to set up on 29 July 1915 an escadrille of three Nieuports and one Caudron Type R at Brindisi for the purpose of carrying out reconnaissance missions and protective patrols, and to search for enemy warships passing through the Straits of Otrante. The unit was commanded by LV Hautefeuille, and was staffed by a small contingent of Italian officers, who were trained on the spot, and some French marines. The original intention was to use Nieuport floatplanes destined for Port Said, but instead three others were delivered on 25 September; these were given fleet numbers NB.1, NB.2 and NB.3. For offensive purposes they were equipped with two bombs consisting of 105mm shells carried within the fuselage and jettisoned by the observer. On 17 December the unit was reinforced with a single Caudron Type R. By the end of the year, the Italian Naval Air Service had relegated the unit to a reconnaissance role, and the Aviation Maritime closed down the unit and transferred the machines to Port Said where there was an urgent need for more aircraft.

Nieuport XH (N.16) with the Escadrille de Port Said in the Red Sea during July 1915.
L. Morareau

and one from a British order – in Bizerte, where they would form the backbone of the Aviation Maritime during the early part of the war.

A section of two Nieuports was transferred in the *Foudre* to Antivari in Montenegro, arriving on 17 October 1914. This unit was under the command of LV Cintré, who had a civil pilot's licence but no experience of flying floatplanes, with LV Destrem and QM (Quartier-maître) Levasseur as pilots. Following an attack by Austro-Hungarian aircraft, these were moved to Lake Scutari, but this move proved unsatisfactory as the low density of joined forces with the Turks. They were therefore out of the range of aerial reconnaissance, and so it was decided to equip the *Foudre* with the six Nieuport XH seaplanes, five pilots and two observers from Saint Raphaél, and send it to Port Said. This force became known unofficially as the 'Escadrille de Port-Said', and there it was seconded to British forces for the defence of the Suez Canal. This 'Escadrille' stayed in Port Said from December 1914 to April 1916, and served with distinction – a story told elsewhere in this book.

During March 1915 it was felt necessary to maintain a permanent presence near the

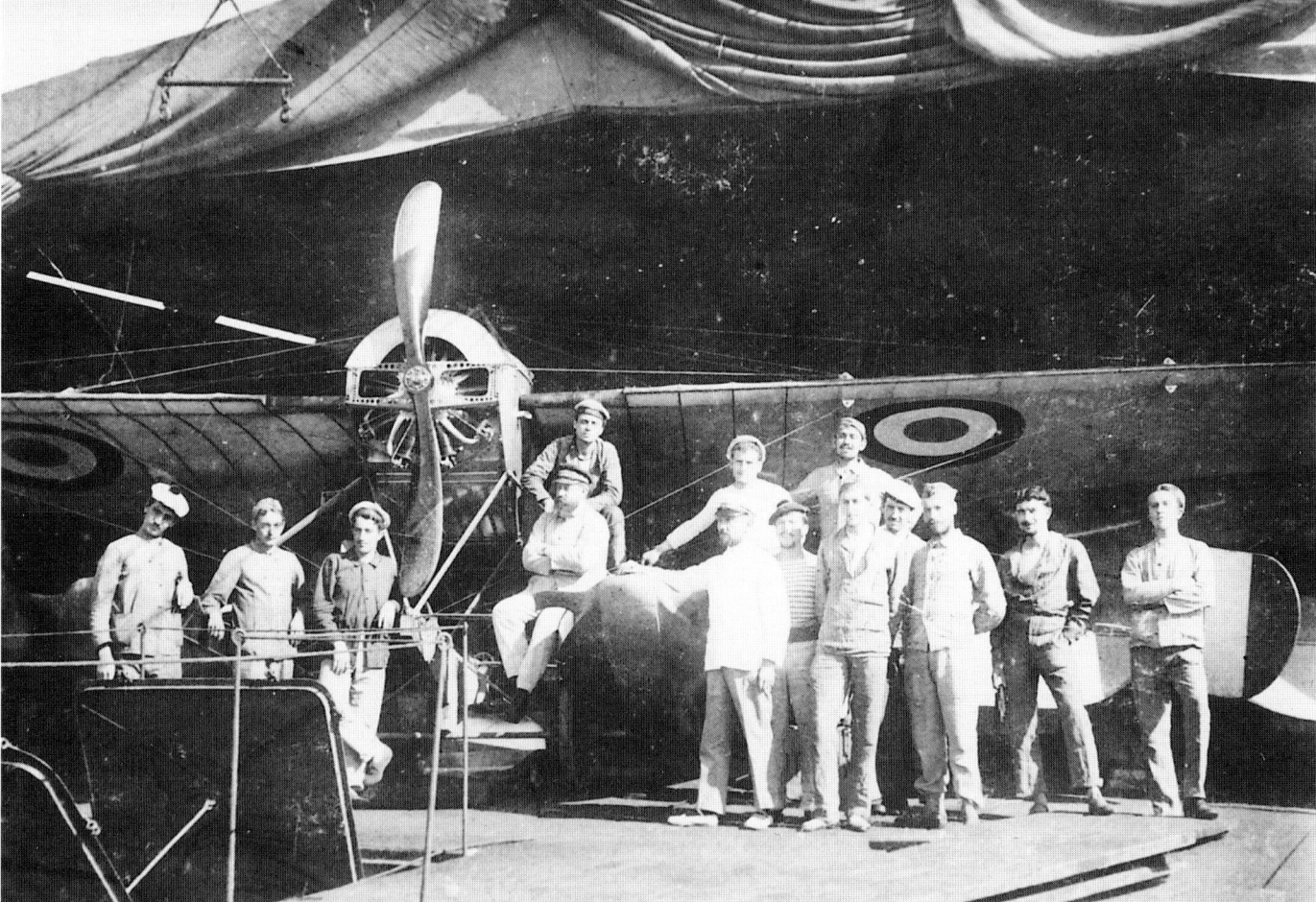

Nieuport XHs with the Escadrille de Port Said at Port Said in 1915. L. Morareau

Apart from the machines sent to Port Said, most other Nieuport floatplanes were regarded as obsolescent by 1915 and were used for training purposes only. They were replaced in operations by flying boats, the FBA powered by a 100hp Gnome and the Donnet-Denhaut with a 150hp Lorraine. Altogether some twenty-five Nieuport floatplanes were used during the war (not counting three examples that were damaged and returned to the manufacturer before the war started).

The Nieuport 10, 11 and 16 with the Aviation Militaire

The Nieuport 10

The Nieuport 10 was demonstrated to the Service Fabrication Aéronautique (SFA) early in 1915. It was accepted for scouting purposes and began to arrive at escadrilles in late April. By August there were forty-two Nieuport 10s at the Front, with another thirty-nine held in reserve, and seven in training units. These were initially supplied to units using the Morane Saulnier Type L Parasols, some of these units having previously had one or two Nieuport monoplanes on strength. By February 1916 the Aviation Militaire had 120 Nieuport 10s and Nieuport 12s on strength, for the large part Nieuport 10 single-seaters, operating in fourteen escadrilles, ten of which had been re-designated from Morane escadrilles in September 1915.

In 1915 the Allied Front occupied by French forces stretched all the way from Picardie astride the Somme via the Champagne, Verdun and Nancy to the Swiss border. Nieuport escadrilles were involved along the whole Front. As examples, N.23 was situated on the Belgian front, N.3 was assigned to the Armée de Picardie, N.37 took part in the Champagne offensive as part of Groupe de Chasse Cachy, N.15, N.23 and N.67 were at Verdun, and N.65 was part of the Groupe de Combat Malzéville. This latter Groupe was formed in August 1915, and had two Nieuport 10s in addition to its Caudron G.4s. Its function was to provide escorts for the bombers of GB.2 during daylight raids, and to provide cover for its base at Malzéville and nearby Nancy. By 25 February 1916, GC Malzéville had been

Nieuport XH (NB.2) with the Escadrille de Brindisi during 1915. L. Morareau

Nieuport XH (N.19) with CAM Argostoli during 1917. L. Morareau disbanded, and N.65 transferred to the Verdun sector.

The Nieuport 10s were primarily used for combat patrols along the front lines to prevent German aircraft from penetrating into French-held territory. The Nieuports also escorted bombers, flew reconnaissance missions, and even dropped agents behind enemy lines. The type showed adequate speed and superior manœuvrability when operated as a single-seat fighter. In this role the aircraft was equipped with a forward-firing Lewis gun fixed above the upper wing. The trigger mechanism was later modified with a Bowden cable to allow the gun to be fired from the cockpit.

The Nieuport 11

The Nieuport 10s continued to serve as scouts until they began to be replaced by Nieuport 11s at the beginning of 1916. The first Nieuport 11s arrived at the Front in December 1915, and by 1 February ninety of the type had joined the 120 Nieuport 10s in service, with more due to be delivered in April. A total of nineteen escadrilles operated the Nieuport 11 for fighting and reconnaissance alongside the other types.

Falkenhain, the German chief of staff, decided to launch a big offensive in the spring of 1916 in the important Verdun sector: any breakthrough there would threaten Paris and the British flank to the north. In order to achieve aerial superiority he assembled about 180 aircraft, including twenty-one Fokker Eindekkers. The Fokkers had been concentrated into three units, and these achieved the desired aerial superiority over the Front at the start of the offensive on 21 February 1916. The French escadrilles were too dispersed to achieve any effective opposition, with the result that the enemy could successfully conduct reconnaissances over the French lines whilst denying the same opportunity to the French.

Major Trincornot de Rose was assigned the task of re-establishing control of the skies over Verdun. This he attempted to do by concentrating escadrilles with Nieuport 11s and Morane Type Ns into a stopgap Groupe de Chasse in the Verdun area. N.65 and N.67, based at Bar-le-Duc, formed the nucleus, with N.23 in reserve at Vadelaincourt. N.15 and N.69 were also at Bar-le-Duc, but under the command of the X Armée, and N.37 was based at Brocourt. N.57 arrived later and was based at Lemmes. Selected pilots from N.3 were also used.

The French aircraft operated in flights of six or more aircraft and were assigned areas to patrol, and ordered to keep at least one aircraft in the air at any one time. This policy caused the Allies to quickly regain control, and aerial supremacy had been regained by the middle of April. N.124 also became involved after its formation.

Altogether the French units claimed sixty-seven victories during this period: six for the N.3 detachment, three for N.12, nine for N.15, seven for N.23, seven for N.31, five for N.57, thirteen for N.65, ten for N.67, four for N.69 and three for N.124.

The British had been intending to open an offensive of their own, but this was forestalled by the German offensive at Verdun; but eventually, on 1 July 1916, they launched an offensive on the Somme in order to relieve the pressure on the French. During April 1916 the Aviation Militaire had begun to build up their strength in the VI Armée sector at Cachy, at the southern end of the British sector and about 15km (9 miles) south-east of Amiens. N.103, an Escadrille d'Armée with the VI Armée was already there, and it was joined by N.3 on 16 April, N.62 on 5 May and N.26 on 5

Single-seat Nieuport 10 (N257), possibly with Esc. N.12. Castor oil from the engine exhaust has stained the taut fabric where it covers the vertical spacers. JMB/GLS collection

Nieuport 11 (N1135) of Capitaine le Comte J.L.V. de Plandes Sièyes de Veynes of Esc. N.26, brought down inside German lines between Flers and Douai on 3 July 1916, with just a broken tail-skid. via Paul Leaman

June. N.37 joined the day after the offensive began, and N.37 arrived on 22 July, followed by N.67 in August.

In order to achieve aerial superiority over selected areas of the Front to prevent enemy reconnaissance aircraft from detecting French troop movements, several Nieuport scout escadrilles were concentrated into two formations: the Groupement de Combat de la Somme, with N.3, N.26, N.73 and N.103; and the Groupement de Combat Cachy, with N.5, N.23, N.37, N.62, N.65, N.67 and N.69. Alongside the Nieuport 11s, the Nieuport 16s and the few Nieuport 17s and 21s arriving on the scene had superior performance to the enemy machines, and quickly established air superiority. And once superiority had been achieved, the scouts could begin strafing the enemy trenches, and could also escort bombers and reconnaissance machines into enemy territory.

From the time that N.3 joined the operations, until 1 November when Groupe de Combat 12 was formed at Cachy, the unit scored a total of fifty-two victories. In the same period N.26 scored ten, N.37 five, N.62 eighteen, N.65 nineteen, N.67 eight, N.73 one and N.103 five victories, for a grand total of 118.

The Nieuport 16

By mid-1916 the Nieuport 11 was being withdrawn in favour of the more powerful Nieuport 16, although it is possible that some Nieuport 11s were re-engined with

Nieuport 11 (N1317) with a French unit in the Dardenelles. JMB/GLS collection

110hp Le Rhône engines and retained at the Front to work alongside the later models. In many cases this led to escadrilles operating a mixture of types. For example, in late March 1916, Esc. N.49 had seven Nieuport 11s, five Nieuport 12s, one Nieuport 10 and one Spad A.2 on strength; two months later there were five Nieuport 11s, six Nieuport 12s and one Nieuport 16.

Towards the end of 1916 the Aviation Militaire decided to amalgamate most scout units into 'Groupes de Combat', which it was hoped would concentrate sufficient aeroplanes to achieve control over selected areas of the Front. N.31, N.38, N.48 and N.57 were assigned to GC.11 in October/November 1916, N.67 joined GC.13 in November 1916, and N.38 became part of GC.15 in April 1917.

Two special escadrilles operated the Nieuport 11: N.92, based in Venice, was formed in August 1915 as the Escadrille de Mestre operating Nieuport 10s and 12s. From July 1916 it was engaged over the Isonzo front and also over the Adriatic, where it flew escort duties for Italian torpedo boats, destroyers and other aircraft. During this activity it succeeded in forcing down three Austro-Hungarian flying boats. N.124, destined to become the famous Escadrille Lafayette, was formed on 16 April 1916 at Luxeuil, and moved to Verdun on 19 May 1916.

A return dated August 1917 showed that no Nieuport 10s remained with operational units. On 1 April 1918, the aircraft on the strength of the French training squadrons included fifteen Nieuports with 80hp Le Rhône engines, and six Nieuport trainers. Some of the former may have been Nieuport 10s. The latter may have included early deliveries of the Nieuport 80.E2, 81.E2 or 83.E2 trainer derivatives. A basic trainer version, the Nieuport 10.E2, also existed, some of these being powered by the 80hp Clerget 7Z engine. After retirement from the front line, Nieuport 11s and re-engined Nieuport 16s were used in training units, pilots having previously progressed from the MF.11, Voisin 3 and Caudron G.3.

Nieuport 16 (N959) armed with Le Prieur rockets. This machine was captured by the Germans when Adj Henri Réservat of Esc. N.65 was shot down on 22 May 1916.
via Paul Leaman

Nieuport 12 in Aviation Militaire Service

In French service, the Nieuport 12 was mainly intended as a reconnaissance aircraft, but was also employed in ground attack, barrage flights and even as a fighter for bomber escort. Nieuport 12s often made up a substantial proportion of an escadrille's strength: for example, during the Battle of the Somme, N.38 had five Nieuport 12s and five Nieuport 11s on strength. Of the fourteen aircraft on the strength of N.49 in March 1917, five were Nieuport 12s. Nieuport 12s made up the main part of N.77s strength from its formation in September 1916 until the middle of 1917. Other escadrilles using the Nieuport 12 as part of its inventory in this period were N.3, N.12, N.15, N.23, N.26, N.31, N.37, N.48, N.57, N.62, N.65, N.67, N.68, N.69, N.75, N.78–N.81, N.102, N.103 and N.124. Otherwise it was allocated in small numbers to Nieuport-equipped scout escadrilles for routine reconnaissance duties.

An RFC officer visiting the Groupe de Bombardement No.1 at Malzéville during March 1916 reported that, when the Nieuport 12 was used for bomber escort duties, the usual practice was for the bombers, in a group of thirty to forty, to rendezvous with their escorts after about an hour's flying at an agreed place. The Nieuport two-seaters, based at Bar-le-Duc, would protect their charges by providing cover above, below and at the sides of the bomber formation.

An outstanding feat was performed by a Lt Marchal on the night of 20 June 1916. He took off from Nancy in an extensively modified Nieuport 12 and dropped leaflets on Berlin. It was his intention to continue his flight to land beyond the border between Russia and Germany at Rovno, but unfortunately after travelling a distance of about 1,400km (870 miles), he came down in enemy territory at Chol and was taken prisoner. The aircraft was fitted with a 80hp Le Rhône, which although less powerful than the 110hp Clerget, had a lower fuel consumption. The wing area was marginally increased to about 24sq m (258sq ft). Tankage was increased to take 354ltr (78gal) of petrol and 88ltr (19gal) of oil, to give an endurance of more than fourteen hours. With an empty weight of 530kg (1,086lb), a useful load of 100kg (220lb), and all the petrol and oil, the all-up weight reached 1,000kg (2,200lb).

French Nieuport 12 (N883) visiting 2 Wing at Imbros in the Aegean. JMB/GLS collection

Nieuport 17, 17*bis* and 23 in Aviation Militaire Service

The Nieuport 17 partially equipped every French scout unit at some time during 1916, and many were still in service until the middle of the following year. These were supplemented by the very similar Nieuport 23, and both types served side by side in the same escadrilles. All the principal French fighter aces flew the Nieuport 17, including Guynemer, Nungesser, de Turenne, Dormé, Madon, Boyau, Deullin, Pinsard and Ambrogi. Despite receiving an official SFA designation, the 17*bis* C.1 did not appear to be regarded as a standard type in French service, although a few did see operational use with the Aviation Militaire.

Following the success of Groupe de Combat de la Somme in achieving local air superiority over the Front at crucial periods during the Battle of the Somme, five permanent *groupes de combat* were formed, the first three in November 1916 and the other two in March 1917. GC 11 was formed at Vadelaincourt from N.12, N.31, N.48 and N.57, with N.94 arriving later. This Groupe was assigned to the II Armée sector and later to the Groupe Armée de Reserve (IV, V and VI Armées). GC 12 was formed from the escadrilles that comprised the Groupe de Combat de la Somme, namely N.3, N.26, N.73 and N.103, and provided air cover for the Groupe Armée de Reserve, and the X Armée. GC 13 comprised N.65, N.67, N.112 and N.124, with N.37 joining later. This Groupe was based at Ravenel and assigned to the Groupe Armée du Nord and later to the III Armée sector. By June 1917 this Groupe had been reorganized, and comprised Escadrilles

Nieuport 17 (N3509) with the 'wasp' emblem of Esc. N.89. Jean Devaux, via Stuart Leslie

(*Top*) **Nungesser in front of his Nieuport 17*bis* (N1895) at a RNAS aerodrome.** JMB/GLS collection

(*Middle*) **Nieuport 21 in French service.** JMB/GLS collection

(*Bottom*) **Nieuport 23 (N2903) of Esc. N.561 in Venice.** JMB/GLS collection

N.15, N.65, N.84 and N.124 based at Maisonville on the Aisne front in support of the VI Armée, and later moved to the V Armée sector. All the escadrilles of this Groupe were re-equipped with Spad 7s from June 1917 onwards. All three Groupes were involved in the Battle of Chemin des Dames.

GC 14 comprised Escadrilles N.75, N.80, N.83 and N.86, and was based at Bonne-Maison in support of the Groupe Armée de Reserve. Between 16 April and 7 May 1917 it provided support for reconnaissance machines during the Battle of Chemin des Dames, and in July of that year it was assigned to the II Armée. GC 15 was formed with seven escadrilles: N.37, N.78, N.81, N.85, N.93 and N.112, with N.102 joining later. The Groupe was based at la Noblette in the IV Armée sector, where it provided support during the Battle of Champagne, which began on 17 April. By July 1917 most of the component escadrilles had been re-equipped with Nieuport 23s and 24s. One more *groupe*, the Groupe de Combat Chaux, had a brief existence, being formed in February 1917 from N.49, N.81 and N.82, and disbanded in mid-1917. It was based at Chaux in support of the VII Armée.

Although formed primarily for achieving aerial supremacy, the duties of these *groupes de combat* included escorting bombers ordered to attack enemy communications. However, the Nieuports were not suitable for this sort of work because, in common with most other single-seaters, their range was limited. Instead they flew escort for reconnaissance and artillery-spotting machines assigned to the Armées, and intercepted enemy reconnaissance machines and attacked observation balloons, activities designed to prevent the enemy from determining Allied troop movements.

However, the majority of the escadrilles equipped with the Nieuport 17, totalling some thirty-one units, did not form part of these *groupes de combat*. Instead they were assigned directly to the Armées. These escadrilles were little involved in direct combat with enemy machines but were nevertheless in almost constant action, flying escort to reconnaissance and bomber aircraft, carrying out fighter patrols and accompanying Nieuport 12s on reconnaissance sorties. They also escorted Nieuport 12s and Sopwith 1½-Strutters that were dropping agents behind enemy lines, and strafed enemy trenches.

Of the escadrilles involved in direct support of the Armées, in November 1917 N.82 went to Italy with the X Armée. It was based at San Pietro di Godego, where it escorted reconnaissance and bombing missions. On 1 January 1918 it moved to San Pietro in Gu, where it carried out reconnaissance missions over Adige, Brenta and Piave, and escorted the army cooperation machines of the 31st Corps d'Armée. In March 1918, it returned to France where it was assigned to GC 22. Esc. N.92, previously operating the Nieuport 11 in the defence of Venice, changed its designation to N.392 and switched to the Nieuport 17 in June 1916.

Two escadrilles were briefly equipped with the Nieuport 17, and were assigned to the *escadrilles de l'intérieur* of the Defense Contre Aviation. N.311 was formed in February 1917, and disbanded in June. N.312 was formed in March, and renumbered in July.

The Nieuport 12, 16, 17 and 24*bis* in Aviation Maritime Service

The Escadrille de Chasse Terrestre du Centre d'Aviation Maritime based at Saint-Pol-sur-Mer, Dunkerque, received four Nieuport 12s, delivered one at a time between January and May 1916. These were known as the Nieuport 23m in Aviation Maritime service (a reference to the wing area of 23sq m) and given the numbers NM.1 to NM.4 (NM for 'Nieuport Marine'). In August 1916 they were renumbered 11 to 14. They were assigned escort duties to protect the bombers and reconnaissance machines operated by the unit. One was converted to a single-seater but was destroyed in an accident in September. The three others served until January 1917, when they were returned to the Aviation Militaire.

A single Nieuport 16, given the serial number 1, was used at Saint Pol-sur-Mer between July 1916 and September 1917.

The Escadrille received seven Nieuport 17s in October 1916, the last of these surviving until March 1918. They were given the serial numbers 2 to 8. Each sported a black eagle emblem on the side of its fuselage. For a period they were operated side by side with Sopwith Triplanes, until these were returned to the RNAS. One of the pilots there was LV Georges Guierre.

Much of the action involved the Sopwiths, but on 25 January 1917 an enemy machine attacked over Houthulst forest escaped three Nieuport 17s piloted by Sous-Lt (Sous-Lieutenant) Delesalle, QM Le Garrec and QM Habillon. On 26 April, EV1 (Enseigne de Vaisseau de 1^{ière} Classe) G. Guierre, piloting Nieuport 17 number '5', attacked a formation of six enemy machines and claimed one and two probables. On 25 May, QM Le Garrec in Nieuport number '7' and QM Vacher in a Sopwith attacked a Gotha returning from a raid over England and forced it to land in the sea.

During March 1917, the Navy General Staff decided to form an escadrille equipped

Nieuport 16 (1354) of CAM Dunkerque at St Pol during 1916. L. Morareau

(*Above*) **Nieuport 17 (1865) of CAM Dunkerque at St Pol in July 1917, clearly showing the twin Lewis gun arrangement favoured by the Aviation Maritime.** L. Morareau

(*Left*) **Line-up of Nieuport 17s of CAM Dunkerque at St Pol during 1917.** L. Morareau

with landplanes to protect the anchorage at Corfu, as the existing flying boats were not good enough for the job. A suitable site for an airfield was found inland near the village of Potamos by 9 April, but the necessary aircraft had not been delivered in time to prevent two Austrian machines raiding the town of Corfu on 24 May. This concentrated the minds of the General Staff, and the Aviation Militaire formed Escadrille N.562, equipped with Nieuport 24*bis*, which was put under the command of an army officer, Sub-Lt Philbert. The unit was actively engaged in patrol duties to protect military and naval installations on Corfu right up to the evacuation of the Austrian forces from Albania in October 1918. After the Armistice the unit was disbanded and its equipment passed over to the Greek army.

During the autumn of 1917, consideration was being given to carrying out trials of flying landplanes from platforms on warships, a procedure that had already been tried with some success by the Royal Navy. Specifically it considered the use of a Nieuport 24*bis* from such battleships as the *Bretagne*, *Jean Bart* or *Diderot*. When the trials eventually took place the Nieuport had been replaced by an Hanriot HD.2.

Nieuport 17 of the CAM Dunkerque at St Pol during 1917 fitted with Le Prieur rocket tubes. L. Morareau

The Nieuport 24 and 27 in *Aviation Militaire* Service

The Nieuport 24, 24*bis* and 27 all operated in Aviation Militaire service. These types supplemented and replaced the Nieuport 17 and 23 in the escadrilles operating these types, both those in the *groupes de combat* and those directly involved in close support for the Armées. The Nieuport 24*bis* entered service in early 1917: for example in March 1917, N.84 was equipped with this type, apart from a few Spad 7s. The standard Nieuport 24 equipped Nieuport escadrilles between its introduction in April and its withdrawal before January 1918. These types also equipped around a dozen new escadrilles formed in the second half of 1917, many of which converted to the Nieuport 27. However, in October 1917, Général Petain wrote to the French Minister of War setting out the requirements for the Aviation Militaire for the spring of 1918; in his report he said:

> The Nieuport is inferior to all enemy aircraft. It is essential that it be withdrawn very soon from all the escadrilles at the front. In my view it is vital to have by early spring 1918 an Aviation de Chasse composed wholly of Spad single-seaters or Nieuport Gnome Monosoupape, if the trials of the latter are satisfactory.

Nieuport 24 (N3961) of Esc. N.91. JMB/GLS collection

The Nieuports at this time were being progressively replaced in the escadrilles of the *groupes de combat* by the much superior and better armed Spad 13C.1. However, there were production problems with the Spad, and there was a massive shortfall in the number required; so the army escadrilles retained their Nieuports while waiting for the Nieuport 28 or Morane A1. The Nieuports therefore continued in service well into 1918. On 1 February 1918 Général Duval, head of the French aeronautical services, wrote to the Under Secretary of State for Aeronautics:

> These deficits have made impossible the re-equipment of the escadrilles of Nieuports, aircraft recognized several months ago as useless for fighting

duties ... If the production forecasts for February and March are not realized in full, it can only be expected that about ten fighter escadrilles will still have Nieuports at 1 April 1918.

In fact the situation was not as bad as Général Duval feared. The returns for 1 April 1918 showed that the fighter escadrilles had 372 Spad 7s, 290 Spad 13s and five Spad 12s. However, although not officially listed, several escadrilles were still wholly equipped with Nieuports. At the same time the French training units had a total of fifty-six Nieuports of various types with 120hp Le Rhône engines.

L'Escadrille Lafayette and American Volunteers in the Aviation Militaire

Another unit that has achieved renown is *l'Escadrille Lafayette*, largely because the exploits of its American volunteer pilots were publicized throughout the USA before that country entered the war. However, this should not detract from acknowledging the heroism of its pilots in risking their lives in the cause of a foreign country.

L'Escadrille Lafayette, or *l'Escadrille Americaine* as it was more commonly known at first, was formed as N.124 on 20 April 1916 at Luxeuil-les-Bains about 65km (40 miles) from the Front and some 55km (35 miles) from the Swiss border. Capt Georges Thénault was appointed as commanding officer, and Lt Alfred de Laage de Meux as his executive officer. To start with there were just seven American flyers allocated. The unit was given a full complement of workshop equipment and groundcrew at the outset, but had to wait until the first week in May before it received its first six Nieuport 11s.

The Escadrille carried out its first patrol on 13 May, and just five days later achieved its first victory when Sub-Lt K.Y. Rockwell crossed the lines north of Mulhouse and attacked a German two-seater reconnaissance machine from close range, killing the crew and watching the aircraft sideslip and crash vertically into the ground just behind the enemy lines.

This was the only victory before the Escadrille moved to Behonne on 20 May, some 30km (10 miles) from the Front, to become involved in the air war over Verdun, a battle that had started a few weeks before, on 21 February 1916. Just two days later, Adj W.B. Hall scored his first victory when, having left two colleagues guarding French observation balloons, he shot down an Aviatik two-seater over Malancourt, after killing the pilot with a long burst.

The escadrilles in the area combined to form continuous patrols over the Front, at three heights between 1,000m (3,280ft) and 4,000m (13,120ft), each unit contributing two patrols each day. Voluntary patrols were allowed, provided that the official needs were met. It was on one of these, at about dawn on 24 May, that Lt W. Thaw, accompanied by Rockwell, surprised and shot down a Fokker E.III. However, the tables were turned later that morning when, against Thénault's orders, five Nieuports dived onto twelve German two-seaters flying at low altitude. The enemy machines formed a circle to defend each other's tails, and drove off the Nieuports, injuring Thaw, Rockwell and Sgt V.E. Chapman. On 1 June, Sub-Lt N. Prince was injured when unsuccessfully trying to prevent an air-raid on Bar-le-Duc. Chapman was again injured on 17 June when jumped on by five Fokkers, and six days later he was killed when in a brand new Nieuport he engaged three Fokkers. Masson borrowed a Nieuport 12 from Capt Happe of GB.4 to fly Rockwell's brother over the battle zone to commemorate his death.

Despite constant activity, the Escadrille did not achieve another confirmed victory

Line-up of Nieuport 11s of the Escadrille Americaine at Behonne near Bar-le-Duc. JMB/GLS collection

A closer view of Sgt Lawrence Rumsey's Nieuport 11 of the Escadrille Americaine at Behonne, near Bar-le-Duc. JMB/GLS collection

for some weeks; but the bad run was broken when Nungesser, on a spell of leave to recover from wounds, briefly joined the unit and promptly shot down an Aviatik for his tenth victory on 21 July. The bad spell broken, a string of victories followed, Hall shooting down a Fokker two days later, and de Laage getting a two-seater four days after that.

Gervais Raoul Lufbery joined the Escadrille on 24 May. Unlike many newcomers he was meticulous in his preparations before a patrol. He would carefully check every round of ammunition before loading them into his magazines, thus minimizing stoppages, and he would inspect or supervise every aspect of the maintenance of his aircraft and engine. He also practised his flying until he was completely at home with his machine, a luxury rarely afforded to newcomers before they were committed to the fray. It was therefore some weeks before his preparations paid off, and it was not until 31 July that he scored his first victory, shooting down a two-seater that burst into flames on hitting the ground. On 3 August he shot down two more in quick succession, and five days later, while escorting some reconnaissance machines, he shot down an Aviatik.

S/Lt N. Prince fitted Le Prieur rockets to his machine and, after some days' search, found a German observation balloon, which he shot down. He unfortunately ground-looped his machine on landing. Both Sgt J.R. McConnell and Sgt P. Pavelka were badly hurt in accidents before this. On 23 August, Prince scored a victory over a German two-seater, which he escorted back to Allied lines after killing the observer. On 9 September, just before the unit was sent on a well-earned leave, Rockwell shot down a two-seater and Prince shot down one of three Fokker Eindekkers, upon which he had launched a surprise attack.

The American pilots returned to Luxeuil from leave to find that they were now sharing the airfield with the Sopwith 1½-Strutters of 3 Wing RNAS. Unfortunately the Nieuport 17s that they were expecting as replacement aircraft had not yet arrived. However, five appeared on 20 September, and two of these were ready for use three days later. On this day Rockwell and Lufbery, on patrol, attacked several Fokker scouts. Lufbery's Vickers gun jammed almost immediately, but both pilots managed to extricate themselves from the fight. Rockwell continued with the patrol, while Lufbery landed to clear the stoppage, and dived onto an Aviatik. Unfortunately Rockwell was killed when hit by enemy fire, and the Nieuport continued its dive to earth, shedding its wings in the process.

Due to a shortage of ammunition, the unit was unable to avenge this loss for several weeks; but finally that time came, and Prince managed to surprise a Fokker that was returning to its aerodrome at Habsheim and shoot it down.

The RNAS lost one of its Sopwiths when it collided with a Nieuport 12 of GB.4, the wings of both aircraft collapsing under the impact. And there were further losses: on the afternoon of 12 October 1916, the Farmans and Breguet-Michelin IVs of GB.4, and the Sopwiths of the RNAS, set off to bomb the Mauser factory at Oberndorf, a 720km (450-mile) round trip, most of which was over enemy territory. The formation was escorted by four Nieuports of N.124 as far as the Rhine, where the Nieuports had to turn back; thus far they had not seen an enemy aircraft. However, several bombers were lost to groundfire on the way out, and on the way back the remainder were attacked by enemy aircraft, initiating an aerial battle that continued until the four Nieuports, now refuelled, arrived to help. More bombers were lost, but Lufbery shot down a Roland C.II, and Prince a Fokker E.III, and both Adj D. Masson and De Laage forced down two E.IIIs. Masson himself crash-landed on the French side of the lines with a holed fuel tank; Prince died of his injuries having struck power lines when trying to land in the dark on his return.

On 19 October l'Escadrille Américaine was transferred to the airfield at Cachy Wood in the Somme valley where, along with N.15, N.84 and N.65, it became part of Groupe de Combat 13 under Commandant Philippe Féquant. The airfield was shared with the escadrilles of GC.12. There the establishment was reinforced by several more American pilots, including Adj F.H. Prince, the late N. Prince's brother, R. Soubiran and W. Haviland. By 30 October the unit had received twelve new Nieuport 17s, now emblazoned with the unit's new emblem, the head of an Indian chief.

There was little opportunity for action as the enemy only flew at night, and this fact encouraged Pavelka to install lighting in his cockpit to illuminate his instruments. But this installation was found wanting when enemy aircraft bombed the airfield. Pavelka took off in pursuit of the raiders by the light of a burning hangar, but his cockpit lights failed, leaving him to navigate in the pitch dark until he ran out of fuel. Luckily dawn was breaking as his engine failed, and he was able to make a dead-stick landing just inside the British lines. By this time severe winter weather had set in, making flying patrols an infrequent event. However, Lufbery scored his seventh victory when he rescued Sub-Lt E.C. Parsons from the attentions of three German two-seaters

A civil Nieuport 27: F-AIB, c/n N5748. Jean Devaux, via Stuart Leslie

after he had strayed over the lines on his first patrol after joining the unit.

Shortly afterwards, on 26 January 1917, the Groupe left the ramshackle billets of Cachy for an even more inhospitable airfield at Ravenel near St Just-en-Chaussée: here the accommodation was for a time non-existent. The weather was extremely cold during March, and in one snowstorm a patrol became separated; the pilots managed to land, but were scattered along the Front. On 19 March, J.R. McConnell, who had rejoined the unit a few days previously, was killed, and Sgt E.C.C. Genêt was injured by very accurate fire from two German two-seaters.

The United States entered the war on 6 April, and although this did not affect the status of the L'Escadrille Américaine, it did improve morale. GC.13 was strengthened by one more Nieuport escadrille, N.88, and assigned to a reconnaissance role with the French V and X Armées, a change that involved a move from Ravenel to Eppeville on the outskirts of Ham. It was intended that N.124 would carry out a familiarization flight along the Front on 8 April, but it was called off after a series of accidents reduced the unit's strength by a third. Sgt E.F. Hinkle completed a circuit of the airfield but landed heavily, shearing off his right wheel and demolishing his lower right wing. Sgt H.B. Willis shot off his own propeller when the synchronization gear failed when he was ground-testing his Vickers gun. Adj W. Lovell's engine seized on starting, and Genêt's sheared a piston rod. Sgt K. Marr completed the havoc by hitting a pile of railway sleepers when landing after completing a circuit. Laage retrieved the day a little by taking off on a lone patrol and managing to shoot down two enemy aircraft harassing a lone Nieuport that had been attempting to protect an observation balloon.

To support the impending Nivelle offensive, the Groupe were carrying out sorties to intercept enemy observation planes over their own lines, to carry out sweeps into enemy territory to gain air superiority, and finally to carry out ground attack duties in order to neutralize the enemy defences and gather information regarding potential targets for the artillery. The artillery bombardment started on 16 April, and on this day Genêt was shot down and killed by groundfire, becoming the first American citizen to be killed after the declaration of war. Sgt R.W. Hoskier was shot down whilst flying a borrowed Morane Parasol on 23 April, but he was doubly avenged when Lufbery shot

A civil Nieuport 27: F-ADCB. Philip Jarrett

A civil Nieuport 28 operated by the Compagnie Générale Transaérienne. via Paul Leaman

down an enemy aircraft on the following day, and two days later when Adj C.C. Johnson and Haviland each shot down an Albatros D.III without loss during a melée involving two opposing patrols. Two days later Lt W. Thaw and Haviland combined to shoot down an enemy two-seater. The Nivelle offensive petered out with an appalling loss of life and the air battle subsided. However, it was not the end of the Escadrille's losses, as de Laage was killed in an accident while trying out a Morane Bullet.

The Groupe was transferred from Ravenel to Chaudun. By this time the Nieuports were gradually being replaced by Spad 7s; however, there was one more incident involving a Nieuport that is worth recording. Sgt A.C. Campbell always flew his aircraft to the limit, and on one occasion exceeded it. He was beating up the airfield when on about his fourth climbing zoom his lower port wing snapped off at the root and was left dangling by its V-strut and bracing wires. Miraculously Campbell managed to bring his crippled machine down for a perfect landing.

Once fully equipped with Spads, the Escadrille moved to St Pol-sur-Mer on 18 July 1917 and took part in the Battle of Ypres. It then moved to Senard in time for the Pétain offensive at Verdun that began on 13 August 1917, and then back to Chaudun to support limited activity in the Chemin-des-Dames area. During the summer of 1917, there was an attempt to transfer Americans serving with the Escadrille Lafayette, and with other escadrilles, to the fledgling United States Air Service. Some pilots returned to the USA as instructors, but most elected to stay with the Escadrille in France. The Escadrille then moved to its last base, a disused airfield at Noblette Farm, and its personnel were gradually dispersed during January 1918. Those remaining became the nucleus of the new 103rd Aero Squadron under the command of W. Thaw – and thus on 18 February 1918, the Escadrille Lafayette had disappeared from the order of battle. During its twenty-two months at the Front its pilots had shot down thirty-nine German aircraft for the loss of six pilots killed in combat, one due to anti-aircraft fire and two due to accidents, with another five badly wounded.

Brief Histories of French Nieuport Escadrilles (Victories refer to those of aces in the particular unit)

N.3 Beginning as B.13 with Blériots during July 1912, it became MS.3 with MS Type Ls in 3.1915. It was equipped with Nieuport scouts by 20.9.15 and became N.3 on 16.4.16. It was first assigned to the Armée de Picardie. Moved to Vadelincourt in the Verdun sector in 2.16, and joined GC de la Somme at Cachy on 16.4.16 and GC.12 on 1.11.16. Credited with thirty-eight aircraft and three balloons between 18.3 and 18.8.16, and thirty-six aircraft from 19.8 to 19.11.16. Mixed Nieuport/Spad unit from autumn 1916, and became Spa.3 equipped with Spads in early 1917. Credited victories: Capt A.V.R. Auger, two; Adj A.J. Chainat, ten; Lt A.L. Deullin, nine (one); S/Lt R.P.M. Dorme, twenty-three; S/Lt J.-H. Guiguet, three; Lt G.M.L.J. Guynemer, fourteen; S/Lt C.M. Haegelen, two; Lt A.M.J. Heurtaux, four; Lt M.M.J.A. Tenant de la Tour, six (one).

N.12 Formed with ten Nieuport monoplanes in 1912 at Reims. Moved to Stenay with the V Armée on 8.8.14. Re-designated MS.12 when re-equipped with Morane Saulnier Type Ls on 28.2.15. Again N.12 on 9.15 with Nieuport 10s and later Nieuport 11s, 12s and 17s and assigned to the V Armée. With the II Armée during the second half of 1916. Moved to the Verdun sector with II Armée on 5.10.16. Part of GC 11 from 1.11.16 with the V/I/VI Armées. Became Spa.12 in 12.17. Credited victories: Capt J.M.X. de Sevin, six; Lt P.H.E. Dufaur de Gavardie, six; S/Lt H.F. Languedoc, seven; S/Lt M.J.M. Nogues, two; S/Lt P.Y.R. Waddington, one.

N.15 Began as REP.15 equipped with REP monoplanes on 22.8.12, and became MS.15 with Morane Saulnier Type Ls on 30.3.15. Became N.15 in autumn 1915. Part of Groupe de Chasse et Reconnaissance in 10.15 with X Armée, except 3.16 to 4.16 with Groupe de Chasse at Verdun and Battle of the Somme in 7.16. Joined GC.13 in 3.17 and variously assigned to VI/I/II Armées. Became Spa.15 on 17.10.17. Credited victories: S/Lt B. Antigau, twelve; S/Lt L.J. Jailler, eleven (one).

N.23 Began as MS.23 on 4.8.14, and became N.23 on 20.9.15 assigned to IV/VII Armées and finally II Armée. Cited on 5.11.16 as having destroyed seventeen aircraft and four balloons, and twenty-three more by 19.3.18. Equipped with Spads for some time before becoming Spa.23 in 8.18. Credited victories: S/Lt J.P.H.P.J. Casale, eight (one); Adj A.M. Lenoir, ten (one).

N.26 Formed as MS.26 on 26.8.14, and became N.23 by 5.16, equipped with Nieuport 11s and later 17s. Initially based on the Belgian front, it was assigned to GC de la Somme in 6.16, then GC.12 on 1.11.16. With X/V/I/VI Armées while progressively equipped with Spads to become Spa.26. Credited victories: S/Lt N.H.A.L. de Rochefort, six (one); Adj G. Naudin, one; Capt A. Pinsard, one; Sgt C.F. Soulier, five (one); Capt M.M.J.A. Tenant de la Tour, one.

N.31 Formed as MS.31 with Morane Type L on 24.9.14. With I Armée, received Nieuport 10s by 4.15, and had ten Nieuport and some Nieuport 11s by 1.16. Moved to II Armée as part GC 11 in 11.16. Received first Spads from 7.1.17 to add to Nieuports, Sopwith 1½-Strutters and Morane Parasols. Moved to V then II Armée in Flanders in 2.17. Became Spa.31 on 17.9.17. Credited victories: Capt A.V.R. Auger, two; Adj G.P. Blanc, two; S/Lt J.C. Covin, two; Lt J.F.T. Ortoli, one.

N.37 Formed as MS.37 with Morane two-seaters in 1.15 with the II Armée. During 7.15 it received some Nieuport 10s, and became N.37 on 20.9.15. Moved to Lisle-en-Barrois and took part in the Champagne offensive in 9.15. Based at Sainte-Menehould from late 1915 to early 1916, and converted to Nieuport 11s during the spring of 1916. At Verdun in 2.16, then part of Groupement de Chasse de Cachy with the VI Armée in 7.16. Moved to III Armée in 1.17, and IV Armée in 3.17. Part of GC.15, then began to re-equip with Spads, and became Spa.37.

N.38 Formed as MS.38 with Morane Parasols at Chateaufort, then re-equipped with Nieuport 11/12s to become N.38 on 20.9.15. Assigned to the IV Armée, and took part in the Champagne offensive that month, and the Battle of the Somme. Became part of GC.15 on 19.3.17, and on 14.6.17 was cited for twenty-eight victories in ten months. Became Spa.38 with Spad 7s and 13s in the autumn of 1917. Credited victories: S/Lt A.J. Delorme, three; Adj G. Douchy, eight; Capt G.F. Madon, seventeen; Adj C.A. Revol-Tissot, one; Sgt P.J. Sauvage, two.

N.48 Formed as MS.48 with Morane Type Ls on 29.3.15, then N.48 on 20.9.15 with Nieuport 10/11/12s and based at Froidos. Moved to II Armée in 10.15, and joined GC.11 in 10.15 with some Nieuport 17s and Spads. With V, IV and again V Armées, and became Spa.48 in the latter half of 1917. Credited victories: S/Lt G.M. de Guingand, four; Capt A.J.G.J. de Turenne, six; Capt J.G.F. Matton, seven (one); Adj R. Montmon, seven.

N.49 Formed as MS.49 on 18.4.15, then N.49 with Nieuport scouts on 20.9.15 and assigned to VII Armée. Based at Fontaine in May 1916. Became Spa.49 with Spad 7s and 13s in 12.17. Credited victories: S/Lt M. Arnoux, one; S/Lt J.G. Bouyer, five; Capt P.A. Gastin, five.

N.57 Formed as N.57 on 10.5.15, and assigned to the Arras front with the X Armée. Served on the Verdun front from 16.3.16, and joined GC.11 on 1.11.16. Moved to V Armée sector on 8.4.17, and cited for claims of twenty aircraft and six balloons on 24.5.17. With I and V Armées, then became Spa.57 late in 1917. Credited victories: Lt J. Chaput, five; S/Lt A.P.J. Cordonnier (one); Lt L.F. Coudouret, one; Asp J.C. Dubois de Gennes, one; S/Lt M.R. Hasdenteufel, one; Sgt M. Hauss, five; Capt G.M. Lachmann, two (one); Capt J.G.F. Matton, one; Capt M.M.J.A. Tenant de la Tour, one; Adj V.L.G. Sayoret, five; Adj P.A.F. Violet-Marty, five.

N.62 Formed on 11.8.15 as MF.62 at Lyon-Bron, and joined GC de la Somme at Cachy on 5.5.16, and became N.62 on 25.5.16. Assigned to the VI Armée, then to GC de la Somme, and then as an Escadrille d'Armée back to VI Armée based at Fismes in January 1917. Claimed fifteen aircraft and six balloons by 13.1.17, and a further fifteen aircraft by 16.11.17. Became Spa.62 with Spad 7s and 13s in November 1917. Credited victories: S/Lt M.R.L. Bloch (six); Lt P.A.P. Tarascon, eight.

N.65 Formed on 2.8.15 at Lyon-Bron as a Provisoire de chasse as a component of the GC Malzéville with two Nieuport 11s, three Nieuport 12s and three Caudron G4s, assigned to the VII Armée near Nancy. Became N.65, totally equipped with Nieuports, on 24.10.15, and moved to Behonnes near Bar-le-Duc. Joined GC de Cachy in 6.17 for the Battle of the Somme. Assigned to GC 13 on 1.11.17. In the beginning of 1917 equipped with Spad 7s and Nieuport 17s, and on 17.3.17 assigned to VI Armée for the Second Battle of the Ainse. Became Spa.65. Credited victories: S/Lt J.D.B.R. de Bonnefoy, five; S/Lt E.J.E. Camplon, three; Adj M.L. Henriot, one; Lt C.E.J.M. Nungesser, eighteen (three); Sgt P.J. Sauvage, six.

N.67 Formed in 17.9.15 at Lyon-Bron and assigned to IV Armée. Based at La Cheppe, initially with Nieuport 10s, under Region Fortified de Verdun from 10.15 until joined GC.13 on 1.11.16 and re-equipped with Nieuport scouts. Carried out many reconnaissance and bombing missions, and cited on 7.16 for claiming eleven aircraft in 257 combats. With X/VI Armées until 24.3.17, when it moved to III Armée sector. Groupe assigned to Groupe Provisoire de Bonneuil on 1.6.17, and became Spa.67 on 1.8.17. Credited victories: Capt J.M.E. Derode, two; S/Lt G.C.M.F. Flachaire, eight; S/Lt J.M.D. Navarre, nine; S/Lt M.P. Viallet, seven; Adj M.G.F.L. Vitalis, one.

N.68 Originally an Escadrille de Cavalerie unit, re-designated N.68 in 9.15. Assigned to VIII Armée with Nieuport 12/24/27s. Equipped with Spads and Nieuport 22/24 from 3.17. In August had Spads and Nieuport 24/24*bis*. It became Spa.68 with Spad 7s in 11.17. Credited victories: S/Lt P.G. Gaudermen, one; Lt M.C.M. Lecoq de Kerland, one.

N.69 Formed from Bleriot XI Esc BLC.5 in September 1915, and assigned to X Armée as a scout unit at the beginning of 1916. Moved to the Verdun sector in 2.16, but reassigned to X Armée in 7.16. Moved to Italy with X Armée in 10.17 after being cited for twenty victories. Became Spa.69 with Spad 7s and 13s in 12.17. Credited victories: Capt P.L. Malavialle, five; Capt R.L.H. Massenet-Royer de Marancour, three; Capt G. Pettettier d'Oisy, two; S/Lt P. Pendomes, three; Sgt P.G. Rodde, three.

N.73 Became N.73 shortly after being formed as the Detachment Nieuport de Corcieux in VII Armée sector in 4.16. Assigned to GC de la Somme in 11.16, and to GC.12 on 1.11.16 with Nieuport 24s. The first Spads arrived in January 1917, and it became Spa.73 shortly afterwards.

N.75 Formed in 7.16 with Nieuport 12s and assigned to VIII Armée. With Division Armée Lorraine in the latter half of 1916. Became part of GC 14 on 12.4.17, and became equipped with Spad 7s as Spa.75.

N.76 Formed in 8.16 to fly Caudron R.Ivs, but re-equipped with Nieuport scouts and became N.76 in early 1917. Based at Muizon and assigned to the V Armée. Became Spa.76 with Spad 7s and 13s late in 1917. Credited victories: Lt H.M.J.L.G. de Bonald, five; Capt R. Doumer, five.

N.77 Formed in 9.16 at Lyon-Bron equipped with Nieuport 12*bis*/17s. Assigned to VIII Armée on the Lorraine front. Equipped with Nieuport 17/22s, with Spad 7s from 4.17 and Nieuport 24s in 6.17. Became Spa.77 in 9.17. Credited victories: Lt M.J-P. Boyan, four; Lt M.A. Hugues, one; Lt A.P.L.M. Marty, five; Lt J.T.F. Ortoli, nine.

N.78 Formed on 12.12.16 at St Étienne-au-Temple with a variety of Nieuport scouts. Joined GC.15 and assigned to IV Armée in March 1917. Soon became Spa.78. Credited victories: Capt A. Pinsard, fifteen.

N.79 Formed on 20.11.16 with Nieuport and Sopwith two-seaters, and assigned as an Escadrille d'Armée to III Armée. The first Spads arrived on 9.6.17 and were assigned to the Groupe Provisoire de Combat at Bonneuil on 24.7.17. Became Spa.79 with Spad 7s and 13s in 1.18.

N.80 Formed on 13.12.16 at Lyon-Bron with Nieuport 17s, and assigned to V Armée. Moved to Bonne-Maison in January 1917. Joined GC.14 on 17 March 1917 with X Armée, then II Armée on 5.7.17. Moved to VI Armée 11.10.17, and became Spa.80.

N.81 Formed at Villacoublay on 26.12.15 with Nieuport 12/17s, and assigned to VI Armée at Sacy-le-Grand on 5.1.17, and then to VII Armée at Fontaine on 29.1.17. Moved to IV Armée sector on 17.4.17, and joined GC.15. The Groupe moved to the II Armée sector on 25.7.17. Became Spa.81. Credited victories: S/Lt P.F.P. de Cazenove de Pradines, five; Sub-Lt M.M. Dhome, five; S/Lt A.R.C. Herbelin, five; Lt M.A. Hugues, seven; Capt A.L.J. Leps, five.

N.82 Formed in January 1917, based at Sacy-le-Grand and assigned to VII Armée with Nieuports and Spads. Subsequently moved to Fontaine, Chaux and Bonne-Maison, and briefly joined GC.14 in 4.17. Variously assigned to VII and III Armées before going to Italy with X Armée in 11.17 where it was based at San Pietro di Godego, and on 1.1.18 to San Pietro in Gu. Returned to France in 3.18, and was assigned to GC.22, and became Spa.82 with Spad 7s and 13s. Credited victories: Lt F.E.M.A. de Boigne, four; Capt R.C.R. Echard, four; Adj E.J. Pillon, four.

N.83 Formed at Lyon-Bron in 1.17, equipped with Nieuport 12/17s and assigned to V Armée. Moved to VI Armée sector in early 1917, based at Rosnay. Participated in the Battle of Chemin de Dames. Moved to Bonne-Maison on 24.3.17, and joined GC.14. Received first Spads shortly afterwards, and became Spa.83.

N.84 Formed on 6.1.17 at Ravenel, equipped mainly with Nieuport 24*bis* and some Spad 7s. Joined GC.13 on 22.3.17, and assigned to III Armée, then to II Armée on 9.8.17, and to VI in 9.17, and to IV Armée in 12.17. Became Spa.84 with Spad 13s in 2.18.

N.85 Formed at Lyon-Bron on 7.3.17 with Nieuport 23/24s and assigned II Armée, except with GC.15 between 22.4 and 7.6. Formed the nucleus of N.98 and became Spa.85 in early 2.18. Credited victories: Capt A. Achard, one.

N.86 Formed at Villacoublay on 6 April 1917, and assigned to GC.14 equipped with Nieuport 23s and some Spads. Spent time with X, II, VI and III Armées. Became Spa.86 early in 1918. Credited victories: Capt H.J.M. Hay de Slade, five.

N.87 Formed in 3.17 at Lyon-Bron and assigned to VIII Armée. On 1.1.18 had two Spad 7s, three Nieuport 24s, one Nieuport 24*bis* and three Nieuport 27s. Became Spa.87 with Spad 7s and 13s on 4.5.18. Credited victories: Adj L.B. Ruamps, one.

N.88 Formed as an Escadrille de Chasse at the end of 3.17, and assigned to VII Armée. Moved to the VI Armée sector at Chemin de Dames on 30.6.17. Became Spa.88 on 30.9.17. Credited victories: S/Lt C.E. Plessis, two; Adj A.J.E. Rousseaux, one.

N.89 Formed in late 3.17 at Villacoublay as an Escadrille de Chasse for the VIII Armée with Nieuport 24/24*bis*/27s. The first Spad 7s arrived in 8.17, and became Spa.89 in 2.18.

N.90 Formed in early 1917 from Detachments de Chasse N.504 and N.507 and assigned to VIII Armée. On 3.3.17 it had three Spad 11s, three Nieuport 24s, two Nieuport 24*bis* and seven Nieuport 27s. It became Spa.90 with Spad 7s and 13s on 27.4.18. Credited victories: S/Lt M.J.-P. Ambrogi, two; Adj M. Bizot, two; Lt M.C.M. Lecoq de Kerland, one.

N.91 Formed in 4.17 from Detachments de Chasse N.505 and N.507 and assigned to the VIII Armée based in Lorraine. Completely re-equipped with Spad 7s and 13s, and became Spa.91 in 1.18.

N.92 The designation was briefly applied to a unit at Venice (see N.392). Reformed on 2.5.17 at Chaux from Detachment de Chasse N.502 and N.503 with the VII Armée. Moved to the II Armée sector on 27.7.17. Became Spa.92 on 14.5.18 as part of GC.22. Credited victories: Adj M.J.E. Robert, five.

N.93 Formed 26.4.17 at Corcieux from Detachments de Chasse N.501 and N.506 of the VII Armée in the Vosges sector. It joined GC.15 on 27.7.17. Spad 7s and 13s began to arrive in 11.17, and became Spa.93. Credited victories: Lt G.V. Dalalier, four; S/Lt F.E. Guyou, one.

N.94 Formed on 14.5.17 at Melette from Detachments de Chasse N.512, N.513 and N.514, and assigned to the IV Armée equipped with Nieuport 24/27. Joined GC.18 on 30.1.18 at Villeneuve, which became part of Escadre de Combat 1. Became Spa.94 at the beginning of 2.18. Credited victories: S/Lt A.H. Martenot de Cordou, one.

N.95 Detachments de Chasse N.517 and N.519 at Vadelaincourt became Escadrille NF on 15.5.17, N.106 on 16.5.17, and N.95 on 20.5.17, equipped with Nieuport 23/24. Initially assigned to II Armée, it moved to the VI Armée sector on 7.7.17, then back to II Armée in 9.17. Joined GC.19 in 2.18, and as Spa.95 became part of Escadre de Combat 1 on 24.2.18. Credited victories: S/Lt J.-H. Guignet, one.

Brief Histories of French Nieuport Escadrilles *continued*

N.96 Formed from Detachment de Chasse N.510 of II Armée in 6.17. Moved to IV Armée sector on 9 July, and V Armée sector on 22.7.17. Joined GC.19 in 2.18, and became SPA.96. Credited victories: Capt A. Archard, one (when N.510).

N.97 Formed from Detachments de Chasse N.511 and N.519 of II Armée in 6.17. Moved to IV Armée sector in 7.17, and II Armée sector in 9.17. Became Spa 97 by 8.12.17, and joined GC.15. Credited victories: Lt M.A. Hugues, two.

N.98 Formed from elements of N.85 in 11.17 and assigned to II Armée. Joined GC.21 on 1.3.18, and became Spa.98 in 4.18.

N.99 Formed in 11.17 from elements of N.87, and assigned to VIII Armée. Joined GC.20 at the end of February 1918. Became Spa.99 in April with Spad 7/13s.

N.100 Formed from elements of N.89 on 16.1.18, and assigned to VII Armée with Nieuport 24/24*bis*/27s. Joined GC.17 at the beginning of 2.18, and became Spa.100 on 15.3.18.

N.102 Formed as Breguet Escadrille 17 during 1913, became Voisin Escadrille VB.2 on 18.10.14, and VB.102 at St Cyr in 11.14. Became N.102 at Malzéville, and assigned to II Armée. It moved to I Armée sector in the Marne area on 27.1.17, then to IV Armée between 4.17 and 12.17. Moved to I Armée on 14.1.18, and became Spa.102 in 2.18, although it had Spad 7s and 13s on strength long before then. Credited victories: Lt L.F. Coudouret, one; Capt J.M.E. Derode, four; S/Lt A.R.C. Herbelin, three; Adj E.J. Pillon, one.

N.103 Formed at Longvic on 2.8.14, then became VB.3 on 23.11.14 and VB.103 on 4.3.15, and N103 on 19.2.16, when it became an Escadrille de Chasse with the VI Armée. Assigned to the Groupement de Combat de la Somme at Cachy in 4.16. Part of GC.12 on 1.11.16. Re-equipped with Spads, and became Spa.103.

N.112 Created as Voisin 29 on 1.9.14 and changed to VB.112 in GB.4 on 15 May 1915. Reformed as VB.112 in GB.1 on 20 November 1915 then to F.112 and N.112 on 11 June 1916. Assigned to the IV Armée on 14 February 1917 and to GC.15 in March 1917, and with II Armée on 27 July. Became Spa.112 in December 1917. Credited victories: S/Lt V.F.M.A. Regnier, five.

N.124 Formed on 20.4.15 at Luxeuil-les-Bains with American volunteers as the Lafayette Escadrille. Moved to the Front on 20 April, and to the Verdun sector on 19.5.16, and back to the VII Armée at Luxeuil on 14.9.16. Received Spad 7s in 6.17, and was assigned to the VI Armée sector at Verdun in August, and to the the Ainse sector in September. Moved to the IV Armée sector in 12.17, and was disbanded in 2.18 to become the 103rd USAS.

N.150 Formed in 7.17 and assigned to the VII Armée. Re-designated Spa.150 with Spad 7s in 12.17.

N.151 Formed at Chaux in 7.17 with Nieuport 24/24*bis*/27, and assigned to the VII Armée. Became Spa.151 in 12.17.

N.152 Formed at Lyon-Bron on 9.7.17 with the VII Armée, and became Spa.152 with Spad 7s in 5.17. Credited victories: Capt C.E.J.M. Lefevre Zeppelin.

N.153 Formed at Etampes-Montdesir on 1.7.17 with Nieuport 24s. Assigned to Groupe de Combat Provisoire at Bonneuil a week later in the III Armée sector. Equipped with Nieuport 24*bis* and Spad 7/13s, and became Spa.153 in 11.17.

N.154 Formed on 11.7.17 at Martigny, with III Armée. Assigned to GC Provisoire on 17.7.17. Disbanded on 1.8.17 and re-assigned to Groupe d'Escadrilles de la III Armée as Spa.154.

N.155 Formed on 12.7.17 at Montdésir with Nieuport 24*bis*, but these soon replaced by Nieuport 27s and assigned to VI Armée. Became Spa.155 in 12.17.

N.156 Formed in January 1918, and assigned to IV Armée. It was re-designated MS.156 a month later, when it received Morane-Saulnier Type AIs.

N.157 Formed on 20.12.17 at Chaux with the VII Armée, and on 1.3.18 assigned to GC.21 with IV Armée. Became Spa.157.

N.158 Formed on 1.1.18 at Bonneuil and assigned first to the III, then to IV, and back to III Armée on 21 February with Groupe Escadrilles d'Armée. Briefly became MS.158 with Morane A.I, then Spa.158 with Spad 7s in 3.18.

N.159 Formed on 16 .1.18 from elements of N.90, and was based in Lorraine assigned as an Escadrille with the VIII Armée. Became part of GC.20 the following month as Spa.159.

N.160 Formed on 25.1.18, and was based at Brabant-le-Roi and assigned to the II Armée. Became Spa.160 equipped with Spad 7s and 13s in 5.18.

N.161 Formed on 14 December 1917, based at Lhéry and assigned to the V Armée. Briefly became MS.161 with Morane A.Is, then Spa.161 with Spad 7s and 13s in May 1918.

N.162 Formed on 28.1.18 at Concieux from elements of N.152, and assigned to VII Armée. Became part of GC.20 on 7.3.18, and became Spa.162.

N.311 Equipped with some Nieuport 23s, beginning early 1917.

N.312 Formed in 3.17, but reformed as N.313 on 7.7.17 for the defence of Dunkerque.

N.313 Formed in 7.17 from personnel of the disbanded N.312. Assigned to provide cover for naval aircraft operating out of Dunkerque. Subsequently re-designated Escadrille de Dunkerque ou St Pol. It also had Sopwith 1½-Strutters on charge when equipped with Nieuport 27s. Became Spa.313 with Spad 7s and 13s on 13.7.18.

N.314 Assigned to protect the city of Nancy in 8.17. On 9.7.18 it became Spa.314 with Spad 7 and 13s.

N.315 Formed in 2.18 from N.311, and assigned to the Defense Conte Aviation to defend the city of Belfort. Became Spa.315 with Spad 7s and 13s in 7.18. Credited victories: Lt A.R. Chabrier, two.

N.387 Combined Franco-Serbian unit, part of the Army Forces Oriental.

N.391 Based in Serbia, and equipped with Nieuport 11s as part of the Army Forces Oriental.

N.392 Six aircraft were stationed at Mestre from 15 August 1915 for the defence of Venice, and designated the Escadrille de Mestre. In December the unit was moved to the Lido to be nearer Venice. Re-designated N.92, then N.392 in 6.16, it was also active over the Isonzo front. In 7.17 it was re-designated N.561.

N.523 Formed from H.387 in 7.17. Assigned to the Army Forces Oriental in Serbia. It was later re-equipped with Spad 7s and 13s, and became Spa.523.

N.531 Formed on 13.3.18 as a Franco-Hellenic unit with Nieuport 27s. Later re-equipped with Spad 7s and 13s as Spa.531. Credited victories: S/Lt B.F. Saune, five.

N.561 Re-designated from N.392 on 1.7.17, and used for the defence of Venice for the rest of the war. In 4.18 it had ten Nieuports on strength. It was credited with the destruction of twelve aircraft and four balloons. Later it became Spa.561, with Spad 7s and 13s. Credited victories: Sgt A.R. Levy, five.

N.562 Created in Corfu in 7.17 to protect the city of Potamos. Disbanded in 12.18.

N.581 Formed in 2.17 with eight Nieuport 17s and 23s and seven Spad 7s, and began operations with the Seventh Russian Army in 5.17 at Boutchatch, Galicia. Transferred to Buzcacz in 7.17, and re-assigned to the Third Corps on the Rumanian front in August. Re-designated Spa.581, the 'Escadrille de Kiev', by 2.18 when it re-equipped with Spad 7s. Repatriated to France in 3.18. Credited victories: Capt G.M. Lachmann, six.

CHAPTER FIVE

British Operations of Nieuport Aircraft During World War One

Nieuport Monoplanes in Prewar Service

On 8 September 1911, Capt J.D.B. Fulton, the Commandant of the Air Battalion, Royal Engineers, sent a memorandum to the Director of Fortifications and Works, setting out the guidelines for the provision of aircraft for 1912. He recommended four aircraft, all of which were French: a Breguet biplane, and the Nieuport, Deperdussin and Sommer monoplanes. Examples of the first three were purchased.

Before the end of September 1911, a Nieuport monoplane with a 50hp Gnome engine had been bought and allocated to the Aeroplane Company of the Air Battalion with the serial number B4. On 14 February 1912, Lt Barrington-Kennett, with Cpl Ridd as passenger, flew this machine on a round trip from Larkhill for a world record distance of 393km (244 miles) to win the Army Section of the Mortimer Singer Prize of £500. 'B4' became '253' following the assimilation of the Air Battalion into the Royal Flying Corps in May 1912. It flew most months until August 1912, and had completed 40hr 29min in the air by the time the monoplane ban was imposed on 14 September. It was reported on 23 November 1912 that the wings of this Nieuport were in need of re-covering, but it was declared serviceable on 28 December at Larkhill. In January 1913 it was again considered necessary to re-cover the wings, and by 14 March the Nieuport had been packed for despatch to Farnborough.

Another Nieuport – a Type IVG monoplane with a 50hp Gnome – was purchased by Lt C.R. Samson in January 1912 at a cost of £1,040. After a period on loan to the Eastchurch Naval Flying School (as M3), where it was probably never used, it was purchased by the RNAS, given the serial number 409, and sent to the CFS at Upavon. It was flown by Capt E.L. Gerrard in the Royal Navy Review off Portland in May 1912. This aircraft, again piloted by Capt Gerrard, was due to take part in the 1912 RFC and army manœuvres at Thetford. But after leaving Upavon on 13 September, its engine failed with a loud bang somewhere between Port Meadow near Oxford and Thetford, and Capt Gerrard had to glide from about 300m (1,000ft) at an increasing angle to effect a forced landing. A connecting rod had broken in two places, and the gudgeon pin and its bush were also damaged. The failure was attributed to insufficient hardening of the big-end bearing, and while no blame could be attached to the aeroplane itself, this was just one of a number of monoplane accidents; as a consequence of all this, on the following day the War Office imposed a ban on any further flying of monoplanes by the Military Wing.

One of these accidents involved a Nieuport IVG powered by a 70hp Gnome over

Nieuport monoplane of the Air Battalion at Larkhill, almost certainly B4 that was later to become 253. JMB/GLS collection

70hp Nieuport IVG (B4). M.H. Goodall, via Paul Leaman

93

Salisbury Plain on 5 July 1912. This machine had originally belonged to Robert Loraine, and had not received a serial number as it was still undergoing acceptance trials. At about 4.50am Robert Loraine's brother, Capt Eustace Loraine, took off with Cpl Ridd as passenger. He climbed to about 320m (1,000ft) towards Shrewton, and then began a steep left-hand turn; but the aircraft then started to side-slip and lost a considerable amount of height. He managed to recover, but the engine began to misfire, and he flew back to Larkhill immediately. The engine was quickly looked at, and Loraine again took off at about 5.30am, this time with S/Sgt

Nieuport monoplane, possibly 254 or 255. JMB/GLS collection

Nieuport monoplane '282', powered by a 70hp Gnome, donated to the RFC by Claude Grahame-White. JMB/GLS collection

Wilson as passenger, the latter being a pilot and also an expert on the Gnome engine. As before, Loraine gained height flying towards Shrewton, and began to turn back towards Larkhill. At about 100m (300ft) over Fargo Bottom he began another steep left turn – but the Nieuport's nose dropped sharply and the aircraft dived into the ground. Lt Fox in a BE3 landed nearby, but Wilson had died instantly, and Loraine also died within a few minutes of reaching Bulford Hospital.

Two more Nieuport monoplanes were taken on charge in June 1912, one with a 70hp Gnome and the other with a 100hp Gnome. They were given the serial numbers 254 and 255 respectively, and allocated to 3 Sqn at Larkhill. The first was flown to Larkhill by Lt B.H. Barrington-Kennett on 2 August 1912, where he and Capt D.G. Conner took turns to fly it. It was damaged in a landing mishap on 14 August, but was again in evidence there after being sent to Farnborough for repair. On 6 September, piloted by Maj C.J. Burke, it landed at Hatfield and then at Baldock on its way to Thetford for the RFC and Army Manœuvres. But the monoplane ban was enforced a few days later, and it was returned to Farnborough; its total flying time was about two and a half hours. There is no record of 255 having flown with 3 Sqn. Although it was reported as lacking flying wires in November, it was again serviceable by December at Larkhill, although it would not have done any flying there, following the ban. By 15 February it was at Farnborough.

A single-seat Nieuport IIN with a 28hp Nieuport engine was taken on charge by the RFC on 22 October 1912 and given the serial 264. Why an aircraft with such little military potential was obtained, particularly when the monoplane ban was already in force, cannot be explained. It was allocated to 3 Sqn, and although its engine was being overhauled in November, it is unlikely that it ever flew again. It was at Farnborough by 1 February 1913 and, despite twisting of the fuselage under load, had passed a structural test some time before mid-April. This was a considerable feat, since up to that time no other monoplane had passed such a test.

All four Nieuport monoplanes were on the strength of the Flying Depot at Farnborough on 14 April 1913, and it is probable that they remained there without ever flying again. At this time there was another Nieuport monoplane at Farnborough waiting to be allocated to the Military Wing of the RFC: it had the serial number 282, and was one of several aircraft sold to the War Office by Claude Grahame-White in March 1913 at a time when every effort was being made to increase the strength of the Military Wing. Grahame-White had originally taken delivery of the aeroplane at Cherbourg in August 1912 on his way to the USA: there he won many prizes at the Boston and Nassau Boulevard flying meetings. However, although the aeroplane flew at least once at Farnborough, it was never sent to a squadron.

None of the aeroplanes survived until the war. No. 255 was written off on 5 August, followed by 253 on 13 August after 40hr 29min flying; also 282 on 20 August, 254 on 1 September, and 264 on 15 October 1913.

Nieuport Floatplanes for RNAS Training

Twelve Nieuport floatplanes with 100hp Gnome engines were ordered from Nieuport in France and given serial numbers 3187–3198. These were fitted with the revised control system, and were actually supplied powered with 110hp Clergets. Most were erected at Calshot during November 1915 after being delivered to the Central Supply Depots at Wormwood Scrubs or White City. One (3187) was wrecked at Calshot when flown by FSL C.B. Gasson on 13 November 1915. Another (3190), flown from Bembridge by FSL T.G.M. Stephens with L.M. Kent as crew, force-landed in the sea on 8 February 1916. The aircraft was put under tow by the hospital ship *St Andrew*, but broke adrift; it was too badly damaged for repair, and was written off. A third (3198) capsized off Westgate on 16 March 1916 whilst piloted by S/Cdr R.P. Ross, and was completely wrecked. Four of these floatplanes (3191, 3193, 3194 and 3197) were sent to the Northern Aircraft Flying School at Windermere. 3191 was not re-erected and was probably used for spares. The other three were withdrawn a couple of months after the Flying School was taken over by the RNAS and re-designated RNAS Windermere on 29 June 1916.

Nieuport Type XH Floatplanes On Board RN Ships in the Eastern Mediterranean

It is necessary to make a brief introduction in order to understand the importance of the activities of the RFC and RNAS in the eastern Mediterranean. When Turkey entered the war on the side of the Central Powers in November 1914, it immediately threatened the links between Britain and France with Russia through the Mediterranean, with the British Empire through the Suez Canal, and with supplies of oil from the Middle East, particularly Abadan. In order to support Russia, it was felt necessary to force the Dardenelles by sea, with a supporting landing on the Gallipoli Peninsular. In support of these operations the Franco-British fleet used the port at Mudros on the island of Lemnos as its main base, and an airfield at Tenedos. An RNAS advance party arrived at Tenedos on 24 March 1915 prior to the arrival of 3 Sqn, later designated 3 Wing. Operations were to continue from Tenedos and other aerodromes at Mudros and Imbros throughout the war. When Allied forces later drew back from Gallipoli during December 1915 and January 1916, their withdrawal released Turkish reinforcements for their forces threatening the Suez Canal, leading to RN operations off the coasts of Palestine and Turkey in support of army operations. The failure at Gallipoli also encouraged the Central Powers, with Bulgarian support, to attempt to crush Serbia and open up links with Turkey through the Balkans. To thwart this campaign Britain and France landed in Greece on 5 October 1915 to establish a base in Salonika.

Nieuport floatplane in service with the RNAS at Windermere. JMB/GLS collection

Nieuport floatplanes were first involved with British operations in the eastern Mediterranean when the French seaplane carrier *Foudre* arrived in Port Said on 30 November 1914 and was placed at the disposal of Lt Gen Sir John G. Maxwell, commander of the British forces in Suez. This vessel was equipped with five Nieuport XH floatplanes (N.7, N.11, N.12, N.13 and N.14), which, together with their French crews, were transferred to British vessels and gave invaluable service. The French pilots were LV A. Delage, QM J. Levasseur and QM H. Grall, who were accompanied by two observers, LV L. Barthélémy de Saizieu and LV A. Cintre, thirty-eight ratings and two petty officers. The observers had pilot's brevets but did not have experience in flying seaplanes. Three more Nieuports (N.15, N.16 and N.17), fitted with 80hp Clerget engines instead of le Rhônes, arrived on a cargo boat on 3 January, along with two *quartier maître* (QM) pilots – equivalent to leading seamen – and a large supply of munitions, including bombs and anti-personnel fléchettes.

Also available to the British were two improvised seaplane carriers converted from former German freighters *Aenne Rickmers* and *Rabenfels*, seized at Port Said in August 1914. These at first retained their German names and were operated under the British mercantile flag, but ten months later they were commissioned into the Royal Navy and re-christened *Anne* and *Raven II*. Neither of the vessels was structurally modified in any way, the Nieuports merely stowed on hatch covers under rudimentary canvas hangars, and handled by standard cargo derricks. Most of the early operations were carried out by *Anne* under the expert guidance of Capt L.B. Waldon of the Dublin Fusiliers who had previously spent fourteen years with the Egyptian Survey Department and had expert, first-hand knowledge of the Egyptian landscape. The crew of the *Anne* were mainly Greek, though there were also Royal Navy and Royal Marine personnel on board.

Besides the Nieuports transferred from the *Foudre*, British vessels operated a further eight (N.18–N.23, NB.1 and NB.2) supplied by the French, two of which were put into service just a few days before the Nieuports were returned to the French at Malta during May 1916. The Nieuports were operated with French pilots and mainly with British observers, some of whom were from the Egyptian Survey Department. All the Nieuports bore French camouflage and markings.

The likelihood of an attack on the Suez Canal by Turkish forces was apparent shortly after the British declaration of war on Turkey on 5 November 1914. It was essential that the enemy's intentions should be established by means of air reconnaissance of the Turkish bases and lines of communication. Aircraft sent by the RFC from Britain commenced operations on 27 November, but Turkish staging posts across the Sinai Peninsular were beyond the range of these aircraft operating from Suez.

The first operations by Nieuport XH floatplanes in the Suez campaign were carried out from the cruiser *Doris* lying off the

Nieuport XH NB2 operating with HMS *Anne*. JMB/GLS collection

Nieuport XH being hoisted aboard HMS *Anne*. JMB/GLS collection

Sinai Peninsular on 10 December 1914, and from the cruisers *Diana* and *Minerva* in the Gulf of Aqaba during the same month. The aircraft from all three cruisers assisted in attacks against the hostile forces along the coasts, but their most important function involved aerial observations of the location and movements of the Turkish forces being concentrated inland for the attack on the Canal. As an example of these operations, on 11 December a Nieuport piloted by Delage, with Capt T.R. Herbert as observer, carried out a patrol near Beersheba. Returning with a faulty engine and the wings and floats peppered with bullet holes, Delage managed to land the seaplane near to the *Doris* and it was picked up before the floats filled with water. The Nieuport was repaired, and was again in service within four days. On 31 December, Grall, with Capt Stirling as observer in N.13, were carrying out a reconnaissance near Aqaba when they force-landed about 30km (20 miles) behind enemy lines. Stirling was hurt in the crash, and Grall left him and made his own way to the coast where he was picked up. A subsequent search for Stirling proved unsuccessful.

Nieuport XH aboard HMS *Doris*. JMB/GLS collection

These initial operations were replaced by more concerted efforts from the two seaplane carriers, beginning on 18 January 1915. Some of the activity involved landing and communicating with sometimes rather unwilling Arab agents along the coast, but most of the worthwhile information was obtained by sustained reconnaissance missions by the aircraft, which enabled an accurate assessment of the strength and movements of the Turkish forces. When the Turkish assault on the Suez Canal came on 3 February, the British troops, aided by bombardment from the fleet and bombing attacks from the air, were well positioned to repulse the attack.

These operations were not carried out without loss: on 27 January, Nieuport N.14 – crewed by Lt Partridge of the Ceylon Rifles, and a French naval rating, Le Gall – took off from Port Said to make a reconnaissance of Bir El Abd. After flying as far as Kantara the crew ran into fog and decided to return to Port Said; but they had to land on Lake Bardawil due to engine trouble. Having located the source of the trouble, they took off again, only to be forced to land off the coast. They waded ashore with the intention of getting back to Port Said on foot, and reached the British lines without mishap – but because they were unable to give the correct password, they were shot dead by understandably trigger-happy Gurkha soldiers at an outpost. The Nieuport was later recovered by *Anne*.

In addition to Le Gall's loss, Delage and Levasseur were repatriated to France on 7 February and 25 March respectively, and this led to a shortage of pilots; however, the situation was alleviated by the arrival of LV Cintré and EV Berthélémy de Saizieu, which restored the establishment to six pilots.

For the rest of the year *Anne* and *Raven II* continued to carry out similar operations along the Palestinian coast in support of the British advance and against Turkish installations. But a major setback occurred on the night of 10/11 March 1915, when at about two o'clock in the morning, *Anne* was torpedoed by the Turkish TBD *Demir Hissar* during an operation to neutralize the harbour at Smyrna. *Anne* was successfully beached despite the Greek crew panicking and deserting the ship. *Euryalus* sent a working party that rigged a collision mat over the hole, and despite headwinds and a heavy sea, *Anne* was able to reach Mudros harbour. After several weeks' delay, she was again patched up, this time by a working party from the repair ship *Reliance*, before sailing to Alexandria for permanent repairs in the dry dock there. Meanwhile *Raven II* had transferred *Anne's* two Nieuports at Mudros by means of a line strung between the two vessels, and had resumed her duties in the eastern Mediterranean.

Raven II was sent to support the Gallipoli landings on 26 March, with three Nieuports and de Saizieu and Trouillet as pilots; and eight days later a reconnaissance found the *Demir Hissar* in the harbour at Smyrna. On 27 March the two surviving Nieuports with 80hp le Rhône engines – which by this time were completely worn out – were replaced by three new machines fitted with 80hp Clerget engines.

RIMS *Hardinge* carried out reconnaissance duties along the Red Sea coast between 9 and 27 June 1915 with four Nieuports (N.16–N.19) on board, one or more of which had been transferred from the armoured cruiser *Montcalm* of the French Indian Ocean Fleet.

Three Nieuports were lost during *Anne's* operations, in each case with *Anne* off the coast at Wadi Gaza. First, on 10 October 1915, N.14, crewed by Trouillet and Paul, was obliged to touch down with engine trouble near Beersheba; they made a perfect landing, although both floats were smashed. After being surrounded by Arabs and robbed, the crew were taken into custody by mounted Turkish officers. Then on 22 December, de Saizieu and Ledger were lost in N.17 whilst attempting a reconnaissance of Beersheba; an enemy wireless message confirmed their fate. It appears that they force-landed with engine trouble, and de Saizieu was made prisoner, whilst Ledger was shot dead when resisting arrest. On the third occasion, N.22 capsized and sank after hitting a wave when attempting to take off in a heavy swell; the crew on this occasion were saved. By 3 January 1916, the engine of N.11 was completely worn out, and the aircraft was reduced to spares. The last flights by Nieuports from *Anne* were in April 1916.

In late January 1916, the Royal Navy established the East Indies and Egypt Seaplane Squadron comprising four seaplane carriers: *Anne* and *Raven II*, with their complement of Nieuport VI floatplanes, and *Ben-my-Chree* and *Empress*, with other types of aircraft on board; the squadron's base was at Port Said. Their objective was to range around the eastern Mediterranean and the Red Sea spotting gunfire for the fleet, anti-submarine patrols, also mine spotting, carrying out reconnaissance missions inland, and attacking port installations, enemy vessels, troop encampments and supply lines, including warehouses, bridges and the railway system.

On 7 April 1916, four Nieuports (two 80hp and two 110hp) were put aboard the French seaplane carrier *Campinas*, accompanied by three pilots, including Destrem. On 18 April, the remaining Nieuports were dismantled and loaded in packing cases on board *Anne*, which then sailed for Malta. *Anne* arrived at Valetta on 9 May where all the personnel of the French squadron and the Nieuports were transferred to the *Campinas*, which sailed for Cephalonia on 12 May. *Anne* and *Raven II* continued to serve until August 1917, when they were decommissioned as naval vessels and reassigned to mercantile service.

By the time the Nieuport operations had come to an end, these aircraft had carried out 1,072 sorties, including some 500 hours over enemy-held territory. Their operations were not carried out without difficulty: the strong winds sometimes experienced in the Mediterranean would cause planned sorties to be cancelled, bearing in mind that the maximum speed of the Nieuports was at best around 110km/h (70mph); and poor engine performance often prevented aircraft from taking off. When they did so, operating heights were commonly restricted to around 600–700m (2,000–2,500ft), and many sorties were aborted because of engine trouble.

The Nieuport 10 in Service with the RNAS in France and the Aegean

The Nieuport 10 was evaluated by both the RNAS and the RFC. As early as 21 February 1915, Nieuport sent a letter to Lt D. Ware of 5 Sqn RFC outlining the aircraft's performance and explaining that, subject to agreement by the French authorities, two machines a month could be supplied from thirty days after receipt of an order. Although Lt Ware's favourable report of his flight test in the aircraft had been forwarded to RFC Headquarters by 24 March, no order from the RFC ensued. However, the RNAS ordered an initial batch of twenty-four machines, acting on the advice of Lt Dollfus, their French technical adviser. This batch was given RNAS serials 3163–3186. A further batch of thirty-six was ordered as 'Nieuport two-seaters (80hp Le Rhône)' and allocated serials 3962–3997. However, it is unlikely that more than thirty-eight in total were delivered as two-seaters, known in the field as 'Standard' Nieuports, the remainder from 3974 onwards being delivered as Nieuport 11s. Some, including 3965 and 3966, were converted to single-seaters. The aeroplanes of the second batch had more angular and perhaps larger tailplanes.

The first three Nieuport 10s (serials 3163 to 3165) were delivered to the RNAS at 1 Sqn at Dunkerque by 24 May 1915, the last being delivered on that day from Paris by Lt S.V. Sippé. Also with the unit at this time were three more awaiting their RNAS serial numbers but identified as 104, 114 and 120, these numbers being derived from their original French serials. The serial numbers of Nieuport 10s allocated to the Dunkerque squadrons included 3163–3168, 3173, 3176–3178, 3180–3186, 3962, 3963 and 3965–3973. Two more 'Standard' Nieuports, serials 8516 and 8517, were delivered to 1 Wing RNAS at Dunkerque early in September 1915 after a brief stay with 4 Wing RNAS at Eastchurch. However, the former machine – 8516 – was soon lost, on 26 September.

The role of 1 Wing covered a number of operations: anti-Zeppelin duties, anti-submarine patrols, artillery spotting for monitors, coastal and shipping reconnaissance, and aerial photography. By November 1915 the operations at both Dover and Dunkerque were controlled from the headquarters at St Pol under the command of Wg Cdr A.M. Longmore RN. Single- and two-seat Nieuport 10s, along with other types of aircraft, were participating more or less daily in these activities, and some of the highlights – and disasters – are given below.

FSL R.H. Mulock of Eastchurch Group in 3177 claimed to have sunk a U-boat 30km (20 miles) off Nieuport when he attacked it with five 9kg (20lb) bombs on 6 September 1915. On 18 October 1915, 3177 was lost when FSL J.T. Bone was killed when he force-landed on the sands near Bray Dunes after suffering engine failure following an attack on the airship sheds at Berchem Ste Agathe near Brussels. Then on 14 December 1915, 3971 of 1 Wing, crewed by FSL C.W. Graham and FSL A.S. Ince, shot down a large German seaplane in flames when north-east of Le Panne, before they were obliged themselves to force-land in the sea, when they overturned and sank. Luckily the crew were picked up by the *Balmoral Castle*.

On 12 December 1915, FSL H.R. Simms of B Group in 3973, after chasing a number of enemy machines off La Panne, was blown over in strong winds on landing and his machine was badly damaged. After action in other types of machine, including a Nieuport 11, he was again in combat in a Nieuport 10 (3963) on 23 January 1916. On that day he dived to about 150m (500ft) above a U-boat as it crash-dived 16 to 20km (10 to

Nieuport 10 of the RNAS at Imbros. via Paul Leaman

12 miles) west of Ostende, and dropped four 7kg (16lb) bombs. FSL E.W. Norton of B Group in 3182 also contributed a 7kg (16lb) bomb. A couple of days later FSL Keeble of HQ Sqn in 3178 forced down a seaplane 11km (7 miles) off Nieuport.

Whilst on hostile aircraft patrol from Detling on 19 March 1916, Flt Cdr R.J. Bone in 3964 chased a Freidrichshafen FF33 (No. 537), which had been bombing Margate, and forced it to alight on the sea off Zeebrugge. On 23 April 1916, Nieuport 3173 was damaged beyond repair when FSL J.D. Marvin, of the War Flight, Dover, side-slipped from 50–60m (about 200ft) on attempting a night landing. On 1 June 1916, 3176 survived damage in a fight with an enemy aircraft near Abeele; the pilot, FSL I. de B. Daly of A Sqn 4 Wing,

H.G. Travers of C Sqn 1 Wing. Whilst with the Dover Defence Flight, FSL S.J. Goble in Nieuport 10 8517 was twice in action: during the evening of 27 July 1916 he sent a two-seater down out of control from 3,000m (10,000ft) when 5km (3 miles) east of Dixmude; and on the morning of 15 August 1916 he destroyed a two-seater seaplane when the left wing collapsed during a combat 8km (5 miles) off the coast at Ostende.

Most of the Nieuports serving with 1 Wing survived until struck off charge in the early spring of 1917, the last remaining in service until 30 June. Before then, four Nieuport 10s – 3176, 3185, 3964 and 3965 – were briefly attached to 29 Sqn RFC at Abeele for special duties late in March 1916, 3185 being returned to Dunkerque

December 1915, later appeared with 2 Wing at Mudros; it was finally shot down by Oblt von Lyncker of Jasta 25 on 18 February 1917. 3172 also had an eventful career: arriving at 3 Wing Tenedos by August 1915, it was the mount of Flt Cdr R. Bell-Davis when he won a VC for rescuing FSL G.F. Smylie from his stricken Henri Farman on 19 November 1915. It was later damaged beyond repair when, on 24 June 1916, FSL K.V. Hooper dived in from 60m (200ft) whilst on detachment with B Sqn 2 Wing at Mitylene.

The Nieuport 12 and Nieuport 20 in RNAS and RFC Service

Tracking the orders and serials of Nieuport 12 deliveries to the RNAS is difficult due to deliveries out of sequence, and reallocations of serials to and from other aircraft. Initial orders totalled sixty-eight, of which fourteen had been delivered by 25 February 1916, thirty by 23 March, and the remainder by 11 September. However, at this point some eighty-four serial numbers had been allocated: 3920–3931, 8510–8515, 8524–8529, 8708–8713, 8726–8744 and 8902–8920. The initial batch of twelve aircraft, with serials in the range 3920–3931, was apparently obtained by reducing by twelve an order for thirty-eight Caudron G.IVs that had been allocated serials in the range 3894–3931; and the second and third batches were reallocations of serials originally intended for Voisin twin-engined pushers. A further batch of aircraft was ordered from Nieuport. Some of the orders were converted to Nieuport 17s, the surviving Nieuport 12s being allocated serials N3170–N3171, N3174–N3183 and N3188. Of these, only the first four were definitely Nieuport 12s; the rest, powered by the 130hp Clerget, were probably Nieuport 12*bis* C.2s. Overall it would appear that a total of eighty-nine Nieuport 12 and 12*bis* aeroplanes were obtained from French sources.

In addition to the Nieuport-built machines, the RNAS ordered fifty Nieuport 12s from Sir William Beardmore & Co Ltd at Dalmuir under Contract No. C.P.150907/15; these were allocated serial numbers 9201–9250. The first of these was test-flown by A. Dukinfield-Jones on 10 May 1916, and a further two were accepted during the next ten days. Deliveries were slow thereafter, the rest being gradually delivered over the ensuing year. A contributory factor to the delays was the

Nieuport 10 (8517) of 1 Wing RNAS, serving at Dunkerque and Eastchurch and with the Dover Patrol. FSL S.J. Goble scored two victories in this machine, which was eventually taken off charge in January 1917. via Paul Leaman

was injured. On 29 June 1916, 3968 was completely wrecked when it suffered an engine failure on take-off and stalled when trying to return to the airfield at Dover. The pilot, Flt Lt G.R.H. Talbot, was killed, and AM1 A. Hampson died of his injuries. On 8 July 1916, 3962 was badly damaged when it collided with Caudron 9125 during a dusk landing whilst being piloted by FSL Wyllie of A Sqn 4 Wing. It survived this mishap, but was finally struck off charge, worn out after extensive service. On 18 July 1916, 3181 sank at sea following a forced landing when piloted by FSL

for repair on 2 April, and the others to 1 Wing by the middle of April.

Some Nieuport 10s went to 2 Wing in the Aegean, including 3167–3172, 3174, 3175 and 3179, and experienced varied fortunes. Stationed at Imbros, 3168 went missing in the Anzac/Suvia/Imbros area on 20 December 1915; the pilot FSL F. Besson was killed and the observer wounded. Presumably this aircraft was recovered, as it later saw service with 2 Wing at Long Island and Marsh, before being damaged beyond repair on 2 October 1917. 3167, withdrawn from service with 1 Wing at Dunkerque by

large number of modifications made to the design in the interim, the later aircraft having modified engine cowlings, fuselage flank fairings, interplane struts and bracing and undercarriage. Some even had a new vertical tail assembly with a fixed fin and plain rudder.

Of the machines manufactured by Nieuport, thirty-eight were shipped to the Aegean, five of which (8513, 8514, 8524, 8525 and 8731) were handed over to the Rumanian authorities. Except for one retained by the French Government (8903), the remainder were delivered to the ADD at Dunkerque. Most were written off there after varying degrees of service, although around seventeen found their way to the UK. Apart from those transferred to the RFC – one of which went to the Aegean and six to Dunkerque – the remainder of the Beardmore-produced machines remained in the UK. Of these, some went into store and the remainder went to training units.

Several RNAS machines in the Aegean were involved in incidents. For example 3921, operating from Imbros, was badly shot up by a Fokker during a reconnaissance over Gallipoli on 17 March 1916, but managed to return to base; one of the crew, FSL H.K. Thorold, was unhurt, whilst Sub-Lt R.H. Portal was wounded.

Later in the year, on 23 October 1916, FSL G.K. Bands and Lt R.G. Blakesley were both taken prisoner when their Nieuport, 8913, was shot down near Drama whilst carrying out a reconnaissance towards Buk. On 11 February 1917, Flt Lt C.E. Wood and 2nd Lt E.P. Hyde in N3175 of D Sqn 2 Wing were shot down by an Albatros near Angista. On 13 February, Flt Lt H.E. Morgan and Sub-Lt A.E.H. Roberts, whilst serving with B Sqn at Thermi, survived a burst petrol tank, managing to land in the water near the aerodrome. On 20 February, 3929 – known as the 'Gun Machine' – allocated to D Sqn of 2 Wing at Stavros, made a forced landing behind enemy lines, but was successfully recovered undamaged under the cover of darkness. On 22 March 1917, Flt Lt S.G. Beare and Lt E.P. Hyde, in N3182, became prisoners of war when shot down by a Halberstadt scout piloted by von Eschwege over the Drama–Mavala road. Less fortunate were Flt Lt J.E. Morgan and Sub-Lt A. Sandell, who were both killed when shot down in 9203 by a Fokker near Smyrna on 30 March.

Likewise several RNAS machines with 1 Wing at Dunkerque were also involved in action. On 24 April 1916, FSL H.R. Simms and FSL H.A. Furniss, during a fleet patrol in 8904, engaged a Freidrichshafen FF33E seaplane at 3,000m (10,000ft) while it was attacking British ships 8km (5 miles) off the coast at Zeebrugge. The pilot was seen to slump forwards and one crew member jumped out at 1,000m (3,000ft), and their machine then dived into the sea, its bombs exploding on hitting the water; Ltn z S Kurt Faber and Flugmeister Paul Reutter were both killed. Shortly afterwards FSL H.R. Simms lost his own life, as did Sub-Lt C.J.A. Mullens RNVR, when shot down at sea on 5 May 1916 by a Freidrichshafen 33H piloted by Oblt Reinhart with Bönisch as observer. According to a German report, the Nieuport was hit during a head-on attack at a range of 100m (300ft), and with its engine stopped, it hit the water, overturned and sank. The bodies of the crew were picked up by a British destroyer. The German aircraft was slightly damaged from fire from a German TBD that it was flying to protect.

Twenty Nieuport 12s were transferred to the RFC by the Admiralty in response to a plea by Trenchard for reinforcements during the period preceding the Battle of the Somme in 1916. An official document dated 28 June requested that between two and three Beardmore Nieuport two-seaters

Nieuport 12 – RNAS 9214, renumbered A/3270 on transfer to RFC – allocated to 46 Sqn RFC in France. via Paul Leaman

Nieuport 12 (3923) in the Old Workshops, St Pol. JMB/GLS collection

Beardmore-built Nieuport 12 with a 110hp Clerget engine at RNAS Chingford.
Philip Jarrett

Nieuport 20s with 28RS at Castle Bromwich. JMB/GLS collection

without guns should be transferred each week from 1 July. In the event these aircraft were delivered directly from Beardmore during the last three weeks of September. The aircraft were fitted with a fixed Vickers gun and the Scarff-Dibovsky interrupter gear. The aircraft concerned were serials 9213–9232, which were given alternative serial numbers in RFC service, namely A3270–A3275 and A3281– A3294. A3288 (ex-9226) received a very unfavourable report when evaluated by the CFS test flight at Upavon on 3 and 7 October 1916:

> Pilot's view not good on account of the high fairing round his cockpit.
> When carrying full reconnaissance load it is so heavily loaded as to be not only useless in the matter of performance but dangerous to fly, while in any case it is much too bad in climb to be any use as a fighter.
> Vibrates badly.
> Tiring to fly owing to cramped position.
> Landing very difficult in a confined space as there is not sufficient elevator control to get the tail properly down.
> Remarks
> (a) Pilot's position very cramped, the rudder bar being much too close.
> (b) Switch is awkward to reach; it would be better placed on the instrument board. Fine adjustment is controlled at carburettor and is difficult to reach and operate. Throttle is placed too near pilot.
> (c) Tailplane is much too small. Machine tends to stall with engine, and dive with engine off.
> Improvements in Design
> Owing to the very bad performance of this machine, it appears that no alterations practicable would render it fit for service overseas.

This report did not save 46 Sqn RFC from receiving the type. In fact the first (A3282) had already been delivered to 1 AD St Omer, destined for this squadron on 5 October 1916 before the trials had been completed. On 26 October 1916 the squadron arrived at Droglandt with its full complement of aeroplanes, and operations with Nieuports continued until they were replaced in April 1917, some, if not all in service by then being Nieuport 20s.

A further twenty Beardmore-built Nieuport 12s, numbered A5183–A5205, were allocated to RFC squadrons during November and December 1916, some of them being fitted with the 100hp Gnome Monosoupape engine. They went to training units or squadrons working up to operational status.

Thirty Nieuport 20 machines were allotted to the RFC during the week ending 5 August 1916, and these were due to be delivered during the third quarter of the year. They were given French serial numbers, although this marque was not adopted by the French. Two were under test at Villacoublay in mid-September 1916, and were subsequently flown to 2 AD at Candas on 15 September, N1816 by E. Guillaux, and N1829 by Sgt Elliot Cowdin, formerly of Escadrille Lafayette and recently attached to the British Aviation Mission in Paris. These were given RFC serials, A258 and A259 respectively. These had been preceded by some others, for example A154 and A156, which were in the hands of 1 Sqn RFC in June and July respectively. A154 differed in some respects from the others in the batch, and may have been an early production machine identical to the Nieuport 12 except for the engine. Two others, A185 and A188, are known to have been delivered to 1 Sqn RFC at this time. The former was fitted with the 'Arsiad' interrupter gear, designed by Major A. Vere-Bettington of the Aeroplane Repair Section, No.1 Aircraft Depot (hence 'ARS1AD').

Twelve Nieuport 20s were due to equip 1 Sqn RFC by December, together with six Morane-Saulnier Type BB biplanes. However, deliveries of the batch continued only slowly, and by mid-October 1916, at Trenchard's request, steps were taken to obtain the much more desirable Nieuport 17. By 28 October, Capt Lord Robert Innes-Kerr was able to report that 'I have definitely arranged for the outstanding order for twenty-three double-seater machines to be converted to one of ten single-seater and thirteen double-seater machines'. In the event, as far as can be ascertained, only twenty-one of the original order of thirty Nieuport 20s were delivered.

At least five Nieuport 20s served with 1 Sqn RFC. One of these (A258) had an overwing gun fitted in mid-October 1916. With the exception of one that was lost on 17 October, these were transferred to 46 Sqn RFC, together with another seven. When 46 Sqn was re-equipped with Sopwith Pups in April 1917, the Nieuport two-seaters were relegated to training units, and remained in service with these for several months. Two of these were briefly allocated to 39 Sqn at Woodford for Home Defence duties, though one was reallocated to Training Brigade, and the other was found unfit for service. This type of aircraft was also operated by 45 Sqn RFC, which received six in lieu of Sopwith 1½-Strutters that had been held up by an industrial dispute in Britain. The squadron's opinion of the aeroplane is illustrated by the following quote from Wg Cdr N. Macmillan's book, *Into the Blue*:

> The 1½-Strutter was already obsolescent, but the Nieuport was obsolete ...The Nieuport had two closely coupled cockpits, its 110hp Le Rhône rotary engine was superior to the Clerget, and it had a strong steel undercarriage. These were the only good points. Cockpit view was bad, its controls were heavy as lead, its performance dud. I measured a top speed of 80mph at full 1,225rpm. Ceiling with war load was only 8,000ft. The fixed tailplane was not adjustable; fore and aft trim was supposed to be obtained by altering the incidence of the small lower wing about the base of their interplane struts. These wings were behind the centre of gravity, but even at their maximum incidence I found the two Nieuports I flew were always tail-heavy when carrying an observer with gun and ammunition ... It was therefore impossible for Nieuports to do the work of 1½-Strutters. (Major) Read posted two Nieuports to each Flight and restricted their use to line patrols.
>
> I learned to spin the defective Nieuport by accident. One day when the sky was full of heavy clouds, McArthur and I went off on two Nieuports to make a north line patrol. He led the way upward through a narrow gap. Following him, but to one side, I flew into cloud. Tail heaviness increased, the airspeed indicator needle swung back, speed swiftly rose and I fell, completely out of control, earthward, through the cloud. When I came out of the cloud, and by the earth's horizon below I saw that I was spinning, I moved the controls and came out into the resulting dive. Three times I tried to follow McArthur through the clouds, but every time my badly rigged Nieuport stalled, spun and redelivered me into the clear sky below the bottom of the cloud bank.

The Nieuport 11 and 21 in RNAS Service in France and the Aegean

The RNAS, which already operated the Nieuport 10, was immediately interested in the smaller and more agile Nieuport 11, to the extent that deliveries were switched to the later type in mid-contract, resulting in the aeroplane being operated by the RNAS at about the same time as the Aviation Militaire. Some served with 2 Wing in the Aegean (3974, 3975, 3979, 3984) and the rest – in the range 3976 to 3994 – with 1 Wing in France. Two early examples (3975 and 3978) were despatched to Rumania from the Aegean. Two others (3976 and 3977) were deleted by mid-1916. Of the remainder, some were lost in accidents and combat, and the survivors carried on until April to June 1917 when they were retired, worn out from continual use.

The RFC never operated the Nieuport 11. It had been intended to transfer six RNAS machines (including 3956–8 and 8750–1) to the RFC, and serials A8738–A8743 were allocated for this purpose; but the transfer never took place. Of these six RNAS machines, one Nieuport 11 (3986) served with 9 Sqn RNAS at a time when it was supposed to be on the strength of the BEF. The other machines were similar to the Nieuport 21 (known as the Nieuport 17B), being Nieuport 11s with Nieuport 17 wings. Of these five, 3957 had been lost on 8 December 1916 when FSL The Hon A.C. Corbett of 8 Sqn RNAS was shot down and killed. 8750 and 8751 were on the strength of the RNAS Detached Squadron, subsequently known as 8(N) Sqn, that was formed at the end of October 1916 to join 22 Wing RFC. 8750 returned to Dunkerque on 15 January 1917, and both 8750 and 8751 joined 9(N) Sqn and later 11(N) Sqn on 27 March 1917 before being struck off charge on 30 June 1917. 3956 and 3958 were SOC on 16 May 1917.

On 15 January, FSL H.R. Simms piloted 3981 to attack a German TBD off Ostende; two days later he emptied a drum into a German machine over the coast at Ostende, though without apparent effect. On 20 February 1916, FSL R.S. Dallas of A Sqn 1 Wing used the same machine to shoot down an enemy aircraft; and nine days later it was used again by FSL H.R. Simms first to attack an LVG over Ypres, and then on the same day to shoot down an LVG in flames in front of the Belgian trenches near Dixmude. FSL R.S. Dallas was again in action with this same aircraft on 23 April, when he destroyed a two-seater – though damaging his own machine in the process.

Some time before 11 May 1916, 3992 was fitted with a 13m (42.6ft) wing and sent to the Experimental Flight; whilst here, it was used on 21 May by FSL Mulock to send two two-seaters down out of control. On the 20, FSL R.S. Dallas – still with A Sqn – had used 3993 to shoot down a seaplane, causing it to sink 7km (4 miles) off Blankenberge; and the following day, in 3989, he shot down a two-seater in flames north of Westende. Then on 8 July 1916, Flt Lt T.F.N. Gerrard used the same 3989 to send a Fokker Eindekker out of control 3km (2 miles) off Ostende.

Flt Lt R.G.A. Baudry was killed when his Nieuport 11 (3990) was hit by AA fire 6km (4 miles) north of Ypres on 2 August 1916. During the week ending 17 August, FSL D.M.B. Galbraith in 3992, with B Sqn 1 Wing, sent down a seaplane out of control 16km (10 miles) off Calais, though his own machine was damaged in the process. In the afternoon of 9 July, FSL R.H. Dallas had been flying 3994 and had shot down a Fokker E.III, killing the pilot, over the aerodrome at Mariakerke; and in the morning of 20 October in the same year, Flt Lt E.W. Williams used the same aircraft to shoot down a kite balloon with Le Prier rockets at 250m (800ft) near Ostende. Two days later, on 22 October, FSL D.M.B. Galbraith of B Sqn, 1 Wing, was in 3986 when he caused an enemy seaplane to dive into the sea 4km (2.5 miles) off Blankenberge.

On being transferred to 6(N) Sqn at Petit Synthe, 3981 failed to return from a raid on Zeebrugge on 26 February 1917, force-landing at Cadzand in Holland after its fuel tank had been holed by groundfire. Its pilot, FSL G.P. Powles, was interned in Holland, and his machine became LA40, then N213, and finally N230 in the Dutch air force. FSL D.H. Masson was killed on 20 April 1917 when 3991 crashed.

Locker-Lampson had been in Russia for some time supporting the southern flank against the Turks and Kurdish dissidents. Then, it was concentrated in Odessa, but after Rumania came in it operated on the Galician Front and in Rumania itself, giving support to the inexperienced Rumanian army that was having a torrid time against the Bulgarian and Austrian forces. To give support to the division, and to give some protection to Bucharest from German bombing attacks, the RNAS sent two groups of aircraft from 2 Wing at Imbros to Bucharest: these comprised three Henri Farmans and seven Nieuports, and they were designated 'S' Squadron. The Nieuports

Russia by mistake. He eventually reached Bucharest on the 30 November.

Known to the Rumanians as the 'English Squadron', its activities had little influence on the outcome of the war on this front; but it did give valuable instruction to the fledgling Rumanian aircrew. The two-seaters were generally flown by British pilots with Rumanian observers. A few combats were recorded, and one enemy aircraft was shot down by Flt Lt A.F.F. Jacobs on 23 December. When Bucharest fell, late in 1916, S Squadron left its aircraft behind, and Locker-Lampson evacuated its personnel, along with some British volunteer nurses.

The Nieuport 16, 17, 17*bis* and 23 in RFC Service

The Nieuport 16

The RFC received its early Nieuport 16s from an order originally intended for the RNAS; the latter service in fact never operated the type. This transfer occurred some two months before the plea from Trenchard, communicated to the Secretary of the Admiralty on 23 June 1916, for assistance prior to the Somme offensive. Whatever the background, the type was destined to equip some RFC squadrons for the following two years. The transfer represented a considerable loss to the RNAS, and denied that service an effective single-seater fighter until the introduction of the Sopwith Pup and Triplane.

The first three (5171–3) were delivered from the RNAS at Dunkerque to 1 AD St Omer, and were then allocated to 1 Sqn RFC. The first arrived with the squadron on 24 March 1916. Test reports from the latter suggest that this aeroplane were equipped with the fuselage-mounted gun and Alkan synchronization gear. About two weeks later it was tested against a DH2, and it was found that the Nieuport could reach 3,000m (10,000ft) in a little more than half the time taken by the DH2, and that it was faster by 15–20km/h (9–12mph) at 2,400m (8,000ft). It is believed that a further fourteen Nieuport 16s of the RNAS order were delivered directly to 1 AD from the manufacturer, together with three Nieuport 17s. The early allocations to squadrons came at a time when single-seater scouts were sent in ones and twos to squadrons equipped with two-seaters. The initial allocations went to 1 and 11 Sqns, but later two went

Three Nieuport 12s – 8514 Read, 8524 Cox and 8525 Jacob – of 2 Wing RNAS at Imbros on 25 October 1916, just prior to flying to Rumania. JMB/GLS collection

Fortunes were not so good in the Aegean. On 18 November 1916, with 2 Wing at Mudros, FSL A.J. Whetnall was killed in 3979 when he was forced down over Bojran by von Eschwege during a bombing attack on Drama aerodrome. Then at the turn of the year, on 14 January 1917, Flt Lt W.H. Peberdy, with A Sqn 2 Wing at Thasos, was killed in 3983 when he suffered engine failure and failed to return from a scouting flight. While based at Imbros, 3984 was captured by the Germans and exhibited as a war trophy during 1917.

Nieuport 11 and 12 with the RNAS in Rumania

Rumania joined the war on the Allied side in the autumn of 1916, and at that point a British armoured car division under Oliver

consisted of two Nieuport 11s – 3975 and 3978 – and five Nieuport 12s – 8513, 8514, 8524, 8525 and 8731. It was also intended to send a squadron of Sopwith 1½-Strutters, but this idea was abandoned.

Some of the Nieuports arrived in Bucharest without incident, but others were not so fortunate. Flt Lt G.A. Cox left Imbros in 8524 on the 25 October 1916, but force-landed at Dragnaeuusti 65km (40 miles) south-west of Bucharest. He must have completed the journey safely, however, because his aircraft was reported as being under test in Bucharest on 3 November. Flt Cdr S. Adams flew 3978 from Imbros a month later. He force-landed 26km (16 miles) south-south-west of Bucharest due to engine failure, and had to complete the journey by lorry. Flt Lt A.F.F. Jacob took off from Imbros in 8525 on the same day, but got lost and landed in

Nieuport 16 (5172) at 1 AD St Omer on 26 April 1916, with Lt W.J.C. Kennedy-Cochran-Patrick at the controls. It saw service with 1 and 60 Sqns RFC before being written off in an accident on 30 September 1916. P.S. Leaman

fired successfully during the flight, but evidently something went seriously wrong while he was firing the second because there was a sudden discharge of oil accompanied by serious engine vibration, indicating that the propeller had been badly damaged. The cockpit floor was ripped out, the petrol tank was pierced, and the fuselage was swinging on the wings owing to the slackness of the centre-section wires that were hanging in festoons. He landed as quickly as possible on the beach near Dunkerque.

Probably the last reference on Nieuport 16s in active service is when A131 was transferred from 60 Sqn to 29 Sqn on 11 March 1917. It was struck off charge on 7 April on being returned to 2 AD for repair. On 14 May 1917 an instruction was issued for 2 AD to pass all remaining Nieuport 16s in its hands to join those at 1 AD to be used in the Scout School there. Presumably this use did not last long as on 25 October 1 AD was instructed to return all Nieuport 16 spares to the UK.

The Nieuport 17

Favourable reports of the Nieuport 17 as compared with the Nieuport 16 soon reached the notice of Maj Gen Trenchard, and under his instructions British orders were converted to this type in July 1916. The first three Nieuport 17s to enter RFC service were those transferred from the RNAS in mid-July; these were used briefly by 1 Sqn RFC before being passed on to 60 Sqn RFC. By the end of that month the first two of an order for ten machines from Nieuport for the RFC had been delivered, but a shortage of engines held up the rest for some

to 3 Sqn, and more of the original batch went to 60 Sqn when it began to re-equip. At least eleven more went directly to 60 Sqn in the summer, so it must have been almost completely equipped with the type by mid-October 1916.

It was quite evident that the three Nieuport 17s delivered with the second batch were significantly better in performance than the Nieuport 16, and this led to a request on 2 July 1916 for all future deliveries to the RFC to be of this type, and indeed most future deliveries were Nieuport 17s and its derivatives. Unfortunately no spares came with the aircraft, so the Aircraft Depots were instructed to use any spare time that their carpenters and sailmakers might have to manufacture complete sets of wings, rudders, tailplanes and elevators for the Nieuport. To this end all damaged surfaces, regardless of their condition, were to be sent by the squadrons to the depots to act as patterns and components.

It was very difficult to change drums on the Lewis gun with the over-wing mountings originally fitted to the Nieuport 16. Although the gun could be tilted downwards for this purpose, the drum was still out of easy reach. But by the end of April, a Sgt Foster of 11 Sqn RFC had designed a curved rail mounting that enabled the drum to be brought down within reach of even the shortest pilot. These mountings were adopted officially, and by the middle of June enough of them had been made to equip all the Nieuports; indeed, this mounting remained the standard for all subsequent Nieuport types in RFC service.

The change to the over-wing Lewis gun on a Foster mounting was hastened by the experience of Capt C.J.K. Cochran-Patrick. He carried out a test at 1 AD St Omer on 19 May 1916 on one of the few Nieuport 16s supplied to the RFC with a fuselage-mounted Lewis gun fitted with the Alkan synchronization mechanism. The first drum was

Another Nieuport 16 (A126) of 11 Sqn used by Albert Ball. JMB/GLS collection

104

time. By mid-October the RFC had ordered a further sixty machines, and by the end of the year some thirty-nine of these had been delivered. Another order for fifty was made in January, and it is probable that all of these were subsequently delivered.

By early November, the RFC were concerned that its stocks of spares and replacement aircraft were dangerously low. It attempted to order 160 Nieuport 17s during the first quarter of 1917, but this request was blocked by the French authorities who were themselves in desperate need for additional aircraft. A review of these stocks made on 4 February 1917 showed that there were twelve at 1 AD and sixteen at 2 AD, with one on its way from the manufacturer, and fifty-five still to be delivered. Compared with this total of eighty-four, it was estimated that the wastage of those already in service with 1 Sqn and 60 Sqn would be eighty-one by the end of June. Thankfully the French relented, no doubt in recognition that the support of the RFC was essential, and released a further sixty scouts to the RFC at Le Bourget during the week ending 17 March 1917, in exchange for thirty Sopwith 1½-Strutters. Part of this consignment was Nieuport 23s.

In the event, losses occurred at a greater rate than predicted. In just the first three weeks of April the wastage of Nieuport Scouts totalled fifty-five, and a week later no fewer than forty-three were under repair at the depots. As a result, two further batches of fifty each were allotted to the RFC by the French, and all of these were handed over at Buc during the week ending 12 May 1917. Most of these were Nieuport 17s, but some were later Nieuport types. Despite these reinforcements, the situation continued to deteriorate and stocks became dangerously low. On 17 July the Aircraft Depots were told to give Nieuport reconstructions priority over all machines except DH4s and SE5s.

The Nieuport 17 could be considered obsolescent by the end of July 1917, but its anticipated successors, the Nieuport 24 and 24bis, had proved to be disappointing and had been relegated to school work. The type therefore continued to be employed on the front along with Nieuport 23s and 27s. The RFC squadrons equipped with Nieuport scouts were 1, 29, 40 and 60 Sqns, together with 6(N) Sqn RNAS, which was for a period attached to the RFC. Of these, 40 Sqn had been completely re-equipped during July and August with SE5as. Otherwise the intention was to re-equip 1 and 29 Sqns with Nieuport 24s and 27s, with 40 Sqn destined to retain the Nieuport 17 for longer than the other squadrons.

Nieuport 17s of 'C' Flt 29 Sqn RFC. JMB/GLS collection

As far as can be established, the RFC had at least eighty Nieuport 23s. Certainly thirty Nieuport 23s were allotted to the RFC during the week ending 18 August 1917, and a further eighteen were handed

2nd Lt L.B. Blaxland in a Nieuport 23 (A6733) of 40 Sqn RFC in the summer of 1917. JMB/GLS collection

---

No.1 Squadron RFC

This squadron was originally formed as an 'Airship Company', and came under RFC control in May 1914. It was re-formed as an aeroplane unit equipped with a variety of machines and sent to Bailleul, France, in March 1915, where it stayed until March 1918. It received its first Nieuports 16, 20 and 17 in March, June and July 1916 respectively, and Nieuports 23, 24 and 27 in May, August and September 1917 respectively. It began re-equipment with SE5/5as in January 1918.

Pilots making claims whilst flying Nieuports include: P.F. Fullard, forty (Nieuport 17 B1553, B3486, B1666, B3459, Nieuport 23 B1559, Nieuport 27 B6789); W.C. Campbell, twenty-three (Nieuport 17 B1635, A6670, B1700, B3466, Nieuport 23 B3474); L.F. Jenkin, twenty-two (Nieuport 17 B1554, B1638, B1690, B1547, B1649, B1681, Nieuport 23 B3474, Nieuport 27 B3635); T.F. Hazell, twenty (Nieuport 17 A6604, A6738, B1649, B3455, Nieuport 20 B1632); H.G. Reeves, thirteen (Nieuport 17 B1630, B1650, B1672, B3558, B3630, B6774); G.P. Olley, ten (Nieuport 17 B1691, B1681, Nieuport 27 B3628); R.A. Birkbeck, ten (Nieuport 17 B1582, Nieuport 27 B6753, B6826); C.C. Clarke, three (Nieuport 17 A6672); G.B. Moore, seven (Nieuport 17 B1508, Nieuport 27 B3629); W.W. Rogers, nine (Nieuport 23 B3463, Nieuport 27 B6754, B3629, B6789, B6827); C.S.I. Lavers, five (Nieuport 17 3495, B3485, Nieuport 23 B1692); W.V.T. Rooper, eight (Nieuport 23 B1675, Nieuport 27 B3632, B6767); E.S.T. Cole (Nieuport 17 A6619, A6603, B1508, A6690, Nieuport 23 A6790); W.D. Patrick, four (Nieuport 27 B6768, B6830); C.J. Quintin-Brand, seven (Nieuport 17 A6668); E.O. Grenfell, two (Nieuport 16 A208, Nieuport 17 A278); L. Cummings, five (Nieuport 27 B3631, B6790, B6815); F. Sharpe, five (Nieuport 17 B1550, B3481).

> **No. 60 Squadron RFC**
>
> No. 60 Squadron was formed from No. 1 Reserve Aeroplane Squadron at Gosport on 1 May 1916 under Major F. Waldron. It was initially equipped with Morane monoplanes and biplanes, but was withdrawn from the line to re-equip and retrain between 3 and 27 August 1916. Its new aircraft were Nieuport 16s and 17s, although some Morane 'Bullets' were retained. Nieuport 23s appeared in the squadron's inventory at the end of March 1917. Its last victory using a Nieuport occurred on 23 July 1917, and during the following week it was completely re-equipped with the SE5/5a.
> During the time it was equipped with Nieuports, the squadron's pilots made 216 claims, of which seventy-seven were definitely destroyed, at the cost of thirty-one officers killed or died of wounds, ten wounded and fourteen taken prisoner. Famous aces that scored with 60 Sqn whilst flying Nieuports include W.A. Bishop with thirty-six claims (Nieuport 17 A306 and B1566, Nieuport 23 A6769); A.C. Ball with twenty-nine (Nieuport 17 A200, A201 and A213 and Nieuport 16 A212); H. Meintjes with fourteen (Nieuport 17 A274, A279, A311); W.E. Jenkins with twelve (Nieuport 17 B1503 and B1566 and Nieuport 23 B1629); A.J.L. Scott with ten (Nieuport 17 A306 and A6647 and Nieuport 23 B1575); K.L. Caldwell with ten (Nieuport 23 B1618 and B1654); W.E. Molesworth with eight (Nieuport 17 A200 and Nieuport 23 A6763, B1569 and B1652); W.M. Fry with eight (Nieuport 17 A274, B1503, B1597 and B1602, and Nieuport 23 B1619); and A.D. Bell-Irving with six (Nieuport 17 A203). Others with claims included G.L. Lloyd with four (Nieuport 23 A6776, B1606, Nieuport 17 B1645, B1693 and Nieuport 24 B3612); D.R.C. Lloyd with four (Nieuport 23 B1610) and E.S.T. Cole, one (A174?).

over the following week, together with one aircraft described as a Nieuport 23*bis*. Deliveries were complete by the end of October, the balance consisting of three Nieuport 23*bis* and one Nieuport 27.

Except for those of 29 Sqn, which was not completely re-equipped until April 1918, Nieuports had virtually disappeared from the Western Front by the end of 1917. Its service career was by no means over, however, as some were sent to Egypt, sixteen Nieuport 17s and four Nieuport 23s being ordered for despatch in January, along with fourteen damaged airframes to act as spares. Other Nieuports found their way to the Middle East later, including a Nieuport 23*bis*. In the Middle East, the RAF's Nieuports remained in service until the end of the war. On 19 September, 14 Sqn and 113 Sqn had three and five respectively, which were used to protect their RE 8s. During the final Palestine offensive, the Nieuports were used as courier aircraft bringing messages back from the Front.

Nieuport 17*bis* RNAS Service

Thirty Nieuport 17*bis* (allocated serials N3180–N3209) were ordered for the RNAS some time before 25 November 1916. Why the RNAS ordered these aircraft having rejected the earlier version is not clear, but there may not have been any alternatives in view of the pressing demands of the RFC. It was anticipated that ten of these would be supplied before the end of the year and the remainder by the end of January 1917. However, deliveries to the RNAS were slow, and only four had been completed by 8 February 1917. The remainder had been held up by a lack of engines at the works, although an allocation had been made for the RNAS. Following prompting from the British Aviation Commission, the missing engines were found, and all but five of the batch had been delivered by 8 March, and the rest followed shortly after. The first four machines (N3180–N3183), and possibly one other (N3188), were delivered as Nieuport 12 two-seaters. One Nieuport 17*bis* (N3185) was delivered to Nieuport & General Aircraft Company at Cricklewood on 31 March 1917, where it stayed for about a year, presumably to act as a pattern and for trial work. The remainder of the batch were allocated to 6(N) Sqn at Petite Synthe. Their armament normally consisted of a synchronized Vickers gun and an over-wing Lewis gun.

The first of the batch (N3184) received by 6(N) Sqn was tested by Flt Cdr J. Petre, and he reported on 12 February 1917 that:

> This machine is very heavy on all controls, but can be manœuvred quickly by a pilot who will use brute force to swing it about. The position, even for a pilot of average height, is very cramped and for a tall pilot it becomes unbearable after flying for some time. It is suggested that the rudder bar be moved forward five inches.

Sad to relate, two months later, on 13 April 1917, J.J. Petre, by that time promoted to squadron commander, was killed when the Nieuport 17*bis* N3206 that he was piloting, crashed.

Before any of the French production had been delivered, a further batch of fifty (N5860–N5909) was ordered from the British Nieuport company. The first five or six were built to the French manufacturer's standard, but to comply with an instruction from the Admiralty, the rest had redesigned fittings, and the cable bracing was replaced by streamlined RAF wires. This requirement added to the delays already being experienced. The latter machines were also to be fitted with twin Vickers guns synchronized with the Sopwith-Kauper mechanism. In the event, only four of the British-built machines were delivered to 6(N) Sqn. Some eighteen either went to UK defence or training squadrons, and the remainder went directly into store at Hendon. At least fourteen of the British production were fitted with the 110hp Clerget 9Z in place of the 130hp Clerget 9B. By 19 October these machines were being cannabalized, with instruments being removed and sent to the RFC as spares. Six machines were allocated to Handley Page so that female staff could practise assembling aircraft. In fact it is unlikely that all were sent, but certainly one (N5904) and possibly a second (N5905) did go.

It did not take long for the naval squadrons to become disillusioned with the performance of the Nieuports, and to call into question the future types that were to be manufactured by British Nieuport. On 9 May 1917, the senior officer at Dover reported to the director of Air Services:

> The existing 130hp Clerget Nieuport machines are rather disappointing on active service, none of the machines giving the same performance as the type of machine that was sent by the Nieuport company from Paris, and they reach a ceiling at 17,000ft (5,185m) which is not high enough for the future. In addition, the casualties of this type of machine are much higher than either the Sopwith Scouts or Triplanes, and there is no doubt that they are rather more difficult to fly. Further, the pilots who have to fly this type of machine on active service have to be specially trained on Nieuports before they can fly them with any ease. This is due to the fact that they are heavier loaded, with a faster landing speed, and far heavier to manœuvre in the air.

As a result of such unfavourable reports, two more batches of fifty machines (N6030–N6079 and N6530–N6579) ordered from the British manufacturer were subsequently cancelled.

6(N) Sqn was probably unique in being equipped solely with the Nieuport 17*bis*C.1 for a while; however, four were lost to enemy action, and most of the others were written off between 24 March and 30 June 1917. The only other RNAS unit to use the Nieuport 17*bis* was 11(N) Sqn, though only six – N3100, N3101, N3191, N3205, N5860, N5861 – all transferred from 6(N) Sqn, are known to have been used, and some only briefly. Otherwise 11(N) Sqn used an assortment of Pups and Triplanes, and by mid-July was equipped solely with the Pup. Camels began to arrive in July and August shortly before the unit was disbanded on 27 August.

One of the machines at the Gunnery School flight at Eastchurch (N5863) became involved in defence duties on 12 August, when it spent about an hour and a half on a defensive sortie against a force of Gotha bombers that bombed Southend.

The Nieuport 24 and 27 in RFC Service

At the time the Nieuport 24 was entering service, the RFC were anxious to obtain as many Nieuports as possible in order to keep up the inventory of this marque. A calculation made on 15 July 1917 showed that the number of deliveries of Nieuports by the end of that month would be eighty-six, compared with an estimated wastage of seventy-two. If this rate of attrition actually occurred, then the Nieuport units could only be kept up to strength until the beginning of August. The number of Nieuport 24s and 24*bis* actually received by the end of July was fifteen (given serials B3601–B3614 and B3617). The Le Rhône engines were in short supply, and the RFC had to pay back engines from its stock at Villacoublay in exchange for those fitted to the aircraft.

Despite the problems that had arisen over the heaviness of the controls due to the aileron fairing strip, RFC HQ had been forced to issue instructions to 2 AD on 2 August to the effect that if supplies of Nieuport 17s, 23s or 27s were insufficient, then Nieuport 24s should be issued to operational squadrons, these in preference to the Nieuport 24*bis* that was to be retained for school work. In the event, several Nieuport 24s and one or two Nieuport 24*bis* were issued to front line squadrons, namely 1, 29 and 40 Sqns.

From 15 August, 40 Sqn received six or more of the type, some directly from 2 AD and others from other squadrons. At various times, 1 and 29 Sqns also operated four each, some of these being reallocated from 40 Sqn. 40 Sqn retained B3610 after it

> ### 6 (N) Squadron
>
> This squadron was formed in December 1916 at Petite Synthe, and was seconded to the RFC in March 1917. Its Nieuport scouts were replaced by Sopwith Camels, starting in June 1917, but it was disbanded in August.
>
> Pilots making claims while flying Nieuports include the following: E.W. Norton, ten (3994, N3184, N3187 and N3208); B.P.H. de Roeper, one in N3209; J. de C. Paynter, one in N3184; C. Draper, two in N3101; A.L. Thorne, two in N3205; A.H.V. Fletcher, one in N3192; O.J. Gagnier, one in N3189; C.L. Bailey, one in N3199; A. McB. Walton, one in N3199; G.G. MacLennan, one in N5860; R.F. Redpath, one in N5861; and G.E. Stevens, two in N5865. All were Nieuport 17*bis* except 3994 (Nieuport 11).

> ### No.40 Squadron RFC
>
> This squadron was formed in February 1916 at Gosport with FE8s, and was despatched to France in August. Its FE8s were replaced by Nieuport 17s in March 1917, and these were themselves replaced in October by SE5as.
>
> Pilots claiming victories flying Nieuports include the following: E. Mannock, fifteen (Nieuport 17 B1552, B1682; Nieuport 17/23 A6733, B3554 , B3541; Nieuport 24 B3607); A.E. Godfrey, thirteen (Nieuport 17 B1684; Nieuport 24 B3601); A.W. Keen (Nieuport 17 B1633, B1686, B3465; Nieuport 23 B6771); I.P.R. Napier, two (Nieuport 23 A6778); W.L. Harrison, one (Nieuport 17 A6674); J.H. Tudhope, two (Nieuport 24 B3617); H.E.O. Ellis, seven (Nieuport 23 A6780; Nieuport 17 B1519, B1545); W. Maclanachan, six (Nieuport 17 B1693; Nieuport 24*bis* B3608); J.L. Barlow, (Nieuport 23 A6789, A6771; Nieuport 17 B1670); W.A. Bond, five (Nieuport 17 B1545); G.B. Crole, five (Nieuport 17 B1552; Nieuport 23 A6793); R.N. Hall, five (Nieuport 17 B1542; Nieuport 17/23 A6733).

Nieuport 24*bis* of 113 Sqn RFC at Sarona, near Jaffa, Palestine. JMB/GLS collection

converted to the SE5a in mid-October 1917. This aeroplane was occasionally flown by Brig Gen Gordon Shephard; but on 19 January 1918 he spun it in at Auchel and subsequently died of his injuries. Three Nieuport 24*bis* and one Nieuport 24 went directly to the Scout School, and as late as 3 May 1918, one was flown to England from 1 ASD presumably for use as a training aircraft. The last Nieuport to remain in operational use (B3601) was allocated to 29 Sqn on 30 March 1918. This aeroplane was lost on 7 April whilst being flown by Lt A.G. Wingate-Grey on a special mission. One Nieuport 24 and three Nieuport 24*bis* went to the Middle East, one of the latter serving with 113 Sqn at Sarona in Palestine.

Provision for deliveries of the Nieuport 27 began in June 1917, and it was hoped to obtain 120 aeroplanes of this type. The need was urgent, as the reserves of Nieuport scouts were diminishing. By 27 July, authorization had been given by the French SFA for 100 Nieuport 27s to be delivered to the RFC in August and September from the factories of the Société Anonyme Française de Constructions Aéronautique (SCAF), or Les Ateliers d'Aviation R. Savary et H. de la Fresnaye, along with spares equivalent to thirty more aircraft. However, the French were unable to meet this commitment, and offered the same quantity of Nieuport 24*bis* instead. This offer was declined, and a compromise was reached of thirty Nieuport 23s to be delivered in August, followed by twenty Nieuport 27s in September, and fifty more in October. In the event, seven Nieuport 23s and sixteen Nieuport 27s were delivered for the RFC in mid-August, and the total allocation was delivered by 20 October 1917, consisting of twenty-nine Nieuport 23s and seventy-one Nieuport 27s.

It was originally the intention that only 40 Sqn RFC would receive Nieuport 24s and 27s, but in the event, although this squadron briefly operated six Nieuport 24s and two Nieuport 24*bis*, it received Nieuport 17s and 23s as replacements, and no Nieuport 27s. This squadron started to re-equip with the SE5a on 10 October 1917, and returned its last Nieuports to 2 AD five days later.

The Nieuport 24s and 27s went to make good the wastage at 1 and 29 Sqns instead. By the beginning of February 1918, 1 Sqn had also re-equipped with the SE5a, leaving just one Nieuport 27 with the squadron. On the other hand, 29 Sqn still had nineteen Nieuport 27s and only one SE5a at that time – and this squadron was the last to operate Nieuports on the Western Front, finally parting with its remaining Nieuport Scouts on 19 and 20 April.

It was the intention to send many of the Nieuport Scouts withdrawn from use in France to the Middle East. In January 1918, fourteen Nieuports, including three Nieuport 24s and four Nieuport 27s, were sent to Egypt, some without engines to act as spares. It was also the intention to send one Nieuport 23*bis* and three Nieuport 24*bis* from the Scout School when it closed in March 1918. The retreat and subsequent movements of the Aircraft Depots threatened by the German Spring Offensive in 1918 prevented many of the remaining Nieuport 27s, made surplus by the re-equipment of 29 Sqn, from being sent to Egypt, and many of these went to England instead. However, 1 ASD managed to send eleven Nieuports, including at least one Nieuport 27, to X AD at Abukir on 3 May 1918. Besides the Nieuport 24*bis* with 113 Sqn at Sarona, another later-type Nieuport found its way to 111 Sqn in 1918.

Probably most of the Nieuports that returned to England went to training units. However, two (B3637 and B6818) went to Farnborough, where both still resided in the spring of 1919. By March the former had been fitted with auxiliary struts between the leading edge of the lower wing and the forward interplane strut, probably in an attempt to stabilize any vibration or twisting of the lower wing.

---

29 Squadron RFC

This squadron was formed in November 1915: first equipped with DH2s, it received Nieuport 17s in March 1917, and Nieuports 24 and 27 later.

Pilots making claims while flying Nieuports include the following: W.B. Wood, thirteen (Nieuport 23 A6721, B1609, B1665; Nieuport 17 B1646, B1553); F.J. Davies, one (Nieuport 27 B6815); W.E. Molesworth, twelve (Nieuport 27 B6812, B6820, B6797); R.H. Rusby, three (Nieuport 27 B3622); A.S. Shepherd, ten (Nieuport 23 A6787; Nieuport 17 B1504); J.G. Coombe, (Nieuport 27 B6821, B6832, B6836, B6820, B6786); D'A.F. Hilton, six (Nieuport 17 B3494); A.G. Jones-Williams (Nieuport 23 A6721; Nieuport 17 B1577; Nieuport 27 B3656, B3647); E.S. Meek, seven (Nieuport 17 B1551, Nieuport 27 B6807, B6812, B3637); A.W.B. Miller, six (Nieuport 17 B1506); P.A. de Fontenay (Nieuport 23 B1618; Nieuport 17 B3578; Nieuport 27 B3625, B6826); F.J. Williams (Nieuport 27 B6826; Nieuport 24*bis* B3605).

Serials of Nieuport Aircraft in British Service

Nieuport IIN	264
Nieuport IIG	253 (B4), 254, 255, 282, 409 (M3 & 13)
Nieuport VI	3187–3198
Nieuport 10	3162–3186, 3962–3973, 8516, 8517
Nieuport 11	3974–3994
Nieuport 11 or 17*bis*	8745–8751
Nieuport 12	3920–3931, 8510–8515, 8524–8529, 8708–8713, 8726–8744, 8902–8920, 9201–9212, 9233–9250, A3270–A3294, A3270–A3275, A3281–A3294, A5183–A5202, A8967, N3170–N3183, N3188
Nieuport 16	5171, 5172, 5173, A116–A118, A121, A125–6, A130, A133–6, A164–5, A184, A187, A208, A210–2, A214, A216, A223–5
Nieuport 17	A200–1, A203, A213, A215, A271–6, A278–9, A281, A305–7, A311, A313, A6603–5, A6609–11, A6613–24, A6644–7, A6657–8, A6664–5, A6667–80, A6684, A6689, A6691–4, A6701, A6706, A6718, A6726, A6751–2, A6754–6, A6773, B1501–11, B1513, B1515–7, B1519–20, B1522–3, B1539–56, B1558, B1566, B1568, B1570, B1577, B1582, B1584–5, B1590, B1595, B1597–8, B1600–2, B1621, B1630–40, B1624–3, B1645–51, B1656–9, B1666, B1670–2 B1674, B1676–8, B1680–91, B1693, B1699–1700, B3452, B3454–6, B3458–9, B3461–2, B3465–9, B3473, B3481, B3483–5 B3487, B3494–7, B3500, B3540, B3561, B3577–8, B3583, B3585–7, B3589, B3593–5, B3597, B3643
Nieuport 17 or 23	A6726, A6733, A6734, A6738–9, A6744–5, B3540–1, B3554–5
Nieuport 17*bis*	N3100–N3104, N3184–N3187, N3189–N3209, N5860–N5909
Nieuport Triplanes	A6686, N532
Nieuport 20	A154 (N1169), A156 (N1175), A185 (N1196), A188 (N1198), A228 (N1824), A229 (N1817), A258, A259 (1829), A285 (N1818), A291 (N1823), A292 (N1819), A309 (N2290), A314 (N2296), A6602 (N2296), A6625, A6707 (N1836), A6725, A6731–2, A6735–7, A6740–3
Nieuport 17B (21)	3956–3958
Nieuport 23/23*bis*	A6720–1, A6761–72, A6774–98, B1512, B1514, B1518, B1557, B1559, B1567, B1569, B1571–2, B1574–6, B1578–9, B1583, B1603, B1605, B1607–10, B1613, B1616–9, B1624–6, B1629, B1641, B1644, B 1652, B1654–5, B1662, B1665, B1675, B1679, B1692, B3453, B3463, B3470, B3474, B3478, B3482, B3486, B3581, B3584, B3598, B3644, B6799
Nieuport 24/24*bis*	B3582, B3584, B3591–2, B3601–14, B3617
Nieuport 27	B1606, B1694, B3600, B3621–37, B3647–50, B6751–6, B6765–70, B6774, B6778–9, B6784–93, B6797–8, B6800, B6803–4, B6807, B6809–10, B6812–15, B6818–32, B6836–7
Nieuports (unspecified)	3149, A151, A6690, A6733–4, A6738–9, A6744–5, B1663, B3540–1, B 3554–5, B3580, B3618, B6761, N521

108

CHAPTER SIX

Nieuport Aircraft in Russia and on the Eastern Front

Prewar Service in Imperial Russia

In 1885, the military set up a special school for aeronauts at Volkov Field near St Petersburg. The experience gained was put to good use in the Russo-Japanese war of 1904–5 when a balloon company proved useful in providing aerial observation for the army. Although at the time mainly interested in airships, the War Ministry used some of its funds to order five Wright biplanes in 1908/9. The Grand Duke Alexander Mikhailovich was quick to appreciate the significance of Blériot's flight across the Channel in 1909, and under his influence the Imperial Navy was one of the first to organize and train its own air service. By 1911 the balloonists' school at Volkov Field had been expanded by the army to include aeroplanes, the first being a Blériot imported from France. Shortly after, the Gatchina military flying school was set up just outside St Petersburg, and this was soon followed by the Sevastopol School of Aeronautics, set up at the well appointed Kacha field, where both army and navy officers trained. This became the base for the Volunteer Air Fleet (VHF), an organization financed by monies raised by voluntary public subscription. To recruit pilots, the army set up a Siberian Aeronautics Battalion on December 1911, and followed this with a second recruitment battalion, the Seventh Aeronautics Company in Kiev in June 1912. On 30 July a separate aeronautics department was formed and linked to the General Staff to coordinate the growing aviation programme.

The Second Aeronautical Exhibition was held in 1912, following an unsuccessful attempt to arrange one the previous year. It was held at the military aviation training ground and aviation depot some 3km (2 miles) south of St Petersburg. A competition was organized that was advertised throughout Europe, and which awarded

A training Nieuport II in the foreground with a Nieuport IVG flying overhead, probably at the training school of the Imperial Moscow Aeronautical Society (IMPV) at Khodynka Field in 1912. G. Petrov, via H. Woodman

An upended Nieuport II; note that the trainee's seat is no more than a minimal wooden support fixed immediately behind the pilot's seat. G. Petrov, via H. Woodman

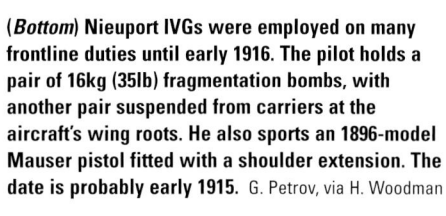

(*Top*) **A Nieuport IVG fitted with triple skis.** G. Petrov, via H. Woodman

(*Middle*) **A line-up of Nieuport IVGs of the XVIII Corps Section of the St Petersburg Military District 1913.** Harry Woodman

(*Bottom*) **Nieuport IVGs were employed on many frontline duties until early 1916. The pilot holds a pair of 16kg (35lb) fragmentation bombs, with another pair suspended from carriers at the aircraft's wing roots. He also sports an 1896-model Mauser pistol fitted with a shoulder extension. The date is probably early 1915.** G. Petrov, via H. Woodman

first, second and third prizes of 30,000, 15,000 and 10,000 roubles respectively, the first prize being equivalent to about £3,000 in 1912. The competing aircraft were required to carry two passengers and all equipment and supplies for a 3hr flight. With this load the aircraft were expected to be able to reach a height of 500m (1,600ft) in 15min, and achieve a speed of 80km/h (50mph). In addition a flight of 1½hr duration was to be completed.

Of the eleven machines that actually reached the competition, two were from Germany and the remainder were entered by Russian companies, some of these being imported foreign machines. Irrespective of the terms of the competition, what was really wanted were reliable machines of rugged construction that would survive rough treatment during transportation and in the hands of trainee pilots. It was preferred that the machines were either of Russian design and construction, or foreign machines built in Russia under licence. The winner of the competition was the Sikorsky S6B, with the Duks versions of the Farman VII and Nieuport IVG coming second and third, the latter piloted by E. Boutmi.

On 30 July 1912 the Army Air Service was reorganized, with Major General Shishkevich placed in charge of the aviation section of the chief administration of the General Staff. Plans were formulated to set up sixty-three sections of six aircraft, one for each army corps and Fortress. In October 1912, some experience in aerial reconnaissance was gained when a group of volunteer officers and civilians supported the Bulgarian forces fighting the Turks. By 4 March 1913, plans had been approved to expand the eight air sections available at the beginning of that year to thirty-seven field sections, one further

A Russian Nieuport IVG captured intact by the Austro-Hungarians, probably during the winter of 1914/15.
G. Petrov, via H. Woodman

section allocated to each of the ten armies, eight fortification sections, and eight others for special assignments. However, many of these units were undermanned in August 1914.

The domestic aircraft industry lacked the expertise to supply adequate numbers of suitable aircraft for the Service. As a result, the Duks company were unsuccessful in selling their version of the Farman, the Russian army preferring to buy Frenchbuilt examples instead. The Nieuport special competition model was sold only in small numbers. However, several Nieuport II and III models were bought from France, and the standard Nieuport IVG, mainly powered by the 70hp Gnome engine, were built by the Schetinin firm in St Petersburg and the Duks factory in Moscow. A few were also built by the Russo-Baltic Wagon Works (R-BVZ). It became a standard aircraft of the early Corps Aviation Sections, and was used for reconnaissance purposes well into 1915.

Two sections of the First Aviation Company took part in the manœuvres held in September 1913 at Krasnoe-Selo, the first comprising four Nieuport IVs and two Farmans, and the second operating five Nieuports and one Wright biplane.

Wartime Service with the Imperial and Provisional Governments

By the outbreak of the war, the Army Aviation Corps was numerically larger than the air forces of the other major belligerents, but the number of useful aircraft was much lower. It was equipped with a large variety of aeroplanes mainly of foreign origin. In total some 248 aircraft were available, most of which were Nieuport IVGs and Farman XVIs and XXIIs. The early Nieuports were gradually replaced by Morane monoplanes in the scout role.

Russia's allies were sympathetic to Russia's needs for more and better aircraft. Deliveries were made by ship, arriving in Murmansk and Archangel. Inevitably there were losses en route: for example, the *King David* was sunk by a U-boat on its way to Archangel with forty-six Nieuports and Farmans on board. From the docks the aircraft were despatched by rail, still in their packing cases, to be reassembled at depots in Moscow and Petrograd. However, the capacity of the railway was very limited and much of the consignments remained at the docks.

The situation gradually improved during 1915, and the majority of the air units had returned to the Front by the spring. By the autumn there were some 553 aircraft split between fifty-eight army air sections: these units included the 1st–13th Army Air Sections, the 1st–37th Corps Air Sections, the 1st–5th Siberian Air Sections, the 1st and 2nd Guards Air Sections, and the 1st Turkistan Air Section. Altogether a further 910 aircraft were made available between August 1914 and the end of 1915, to give a total of 1,158. Of these, 139 were lost to enemy action, twenty-five were forced down behind enemy lines, and thirty-nine were burnt and abandoned during a retreat. A further 450 had been written off as worn out or obsolete, leaving 505 machines available, of which 328 were in working order.

By the middle of January 1916 the number of aircraft in working order had fallen to 311, with 76 held in reserve and 118 under repair. Virtually all of these were aircraft of French origin, with Voisins and Morane Parasols predominating. However, fifty-eight were Nieuports, twenty-five being at the Front with twenty-five in reserve and eight under repair. Some success was achieved in training pilots, however, with twelve military flying schools in operation by early 1916. Between April and August 1916, with the arrival of fighter aircraft including Nieuports from France, forces were concentrated into four air combat groups in opposition to similar German fighter units.

By the end of 1916 the Army Aviation Corps had an estimated seventy-four units equipped with about 800 aircraft, including 1st–12th Fighter Air Sections, 1st–13th Army Air Sections, 1st–37th Corps Air Sections and 1st–4th Artillery Air Sections, 1st–5th Siberian Air Sections, and the 1st Turkistan Air Section. Nieuport 10s were in service with the 2nd, 3rd, 5th and 12th Fighter Air Sections in 1916. By 1 March

(*Above*) **A brand new, Duks-built single-seat version of the Nieuport 10 at the Duks airfield at Moscow in mid-1916. Note the Duks design of head-rest, also seen on Nieuport 11s, and the characteristic Duks cockade.** Kopanski, via H. Woodman

One of the many gun arrangements devised by V.V. Iordan. This shows a Russian standard 1910 Maxim fixed rigidly to the centre section of a Nieuport 10. The plywood cover contained the ammunition belt, and the pulley wheel on the right was activated by a cable operated by the pilot, which cocked the gun and helped to clear jams. The standard sight is shown raised, for no apparent purpose, as a duplicate sight was fitted below the wing where the firing lever was also fitted. When pulled, it pressed the firing button between the hand-grips. The Russians frequently employed this system, but it was rarely seen elsewhere. Harry Woodman

(*Below*) **F.P. Shishkovsky in a Duks-built Nieuport 11, probably taken at the Duks airfield in 1916, with a French-built Voisin III LAS in the background.** Harry Woodman

1917 a total of twenty-nine were in service on four fronts, and a similar number were still in service in June. Most Nieuport 10s were used for reconnaissance, with the two-seater versions acting mainly as a trainer.

An offensive by Russian troops on the south-west front had caused the Germans to considerably reinforce their ground and air forces on this front, using forces withdrawn from the west, mainly from the Verdun sector. By the summer of 1916 the Central Powers had established mastery of the air over many parts of the Front. The Russians decided to concentrate their fighter aircraft in certain sectors at decisive moments, particularly to protect reconnaissance machines. For this reason it was decided to form aviation army groups, each comprising several fighter

(*Top*) **Two Duks-built Nieuport 11s with a Morane Saulnier Type I of an unknown section, in the winter of 1916/17.** G. Petrov, via H. Woodman

(*Middle*) **A Nieuport 17 (1963), with a Nieuport 10 in the background, showing the style of Russian markings applied to Nieuport-built aircraft. The gun is a Vickers, fitted with the Alkan-Hamy synchronization system.** G. Petrov, via H. Woodman

(*Bottom*) **A French-built Nieuport 21 (1875) fitted with an over-wing French Hotchkiss portative modéle 1909 machine-gun. The egg-shaped canister was a Russian-designed container for the ammunition belt. By 1916 the French had abandoned this infantry weapon for the handier Lewis gun.** G. Petrov, via H. Woodman

sections, and put them under the control of the field armies. However, because of a lack of trained pilots and suitable aircraft, this reorganization took place only slowly. The first fighter section appeared on the Front in June 1916, and twelve more had been formed by the end of that year.

A small number of Nieuport 12 and 12*bis* aeroplanes were imported from France, and there was also an 80hp Le Rhône version used for training, designated the Nieuport 13E. The number of Nieuport 12s in service increased from four on 1 April 1917 to ten by June. Four were on the Russian western front and six on the south-western/Rumanian front.

The Nieuport 17 joined the Russian military arsenal towards the end of 1916. The pilots of the Fourth and Tenth Fighter Air Sections of the Sixth Aviation Division were the first to receive it, three examples made in France (serials 1911, 1912 and 1917) being delivered in December 1916. But further deliveries were very slow, and only twenty-six more Nieuports were in service by 1 June 1917. These were allocated to experienced pilots who could make best use of them, such as Staff Capt Alexander Kozakov (serial 1910), Staff Capt Pavel Argeev (serial 1908) and Capt Evgraf Kruten (serial 2232). By the end of the year the number of Nieuports – 17s and 23s – had increased to around fifty, most of which were to be found in aircraft parks and depots.

A provisional government under Kerensky was formed in early March 1917 following the overthrow of Tsar Nicholas II at the end of February. Imports of aircraft from the Allies continued, particularly in

A French-built Nieuport 21 (1970) fitted with rocket tubes photographed during the winter of 1916/17. G. Petrov, via H. Woodman

the first half of the year when a large batch of Nieuport 17s and some Spad A2s and A4s were delivered. Forty-three Spad 7s were also received in the late spring, and these were used to replace or supplement obsolescent Nieuports with the new First Air Division under Kozakov. By mid-July there were an estimated 461 aircraft at the Front, with a further 106 planes at the aircraft parks, and numerous aircraft still in their packing cases in various aviation stores. The exact number of Nieuport 17s and 23s imported from France during this period is not known, but at least 400 were sent in 1917. Russian archives mention the presence of 144 French-built Nieuport 17s and 23s between December 1916 and November 1917.

Following a short production run of Nieuport 16s, the Duks factory produced 133 Nieuport 17s and 23s during this period, though only forty of these reached the Front. It is possible that the Anatra factory at Simferopol may have produced a dozen, all of which were delivered to the flying school at Kacha. Many of the imported aircraft never reached the Front. At the warehouse in Archangel it was reported that there were a further 142 crates of British and French planes, and 182 cases of aero-engines. At the central aircraft stores there were many unused aircraft, including twenty-three Nieuport 17s, seventy Nieuport 23s and ninety-nine other types.

The total of 400 aircraft mentioned above included twenty or thirty Nieuport 24s, and this type remained in service until 1921. The Nieuport 24*bis* was built in Russia at the Duks factory from 1917 to 1920, and was used operationally during that period.

Estimates of the total domestic production of aircraft before the revolution vary significantly, though it was likely to be well below that of the Central Powers or the other Allies. There was also a serious lack of engines and other spare parts, and maintenance standards fell well below those of other countries. Nevertheless the army air units remained reasonably intact, and continued to fight while most of the ground forces around them disintegrated.

The organization of the Russian air forces was split between the directorate of the air fleet and the directorate of naval aviation, and the service of Nieuport aircraft in each of these directorates is summarized below.

Nieuport Scouts in the Army Aviation Corps

It would not be possible to cover all the activities of units employing Nieuport aircraft. However, as explained earlier, the more experienced flyers were allocated the best aircraft and the newly delivered Nieuports fell into this category. Thus it happened that Nieuport aircraft featured prominently in the exploits of the Russian aces. The large majority of the enemy aircraft destroyed by the aces were two-seaters, many of them Brandenburg C.Is, engaged in artillery spotting or reconnaissance. Very few were single-seat scouts.

A pilot became an 'ace' when he scored five confirmed victories, and the Russian authorities were very strict in assessing combat successes, normally requiring confirmation from ground observers or from established flying officers of repute. On the other hand, each pilot of what might have been a number involved in any one particular combat, was given credit for a victory for every enemy aircraft destroyed. Therefore commanders' leading flights tended to get inflated scores, whereas pilots on lone patrols were sometimes not given their due credit, particularly in cases where their opponents crashed unseen behind enemy lines.

The First Air Division

Staff Capt A. Kosakov, who became commander of the First Air Division, was earlier in charge of the Fourth Air Section, where he became famous for his unconventional methods of bringing down enemy aircraft; these included ramming and the use of explosive charges attached to trailing cables. He first flew Moranes with his new unit, until he obtained a Nieuport 10 (serial 222). To this machine he had fitted a Maxim machine-gun extending from the cockpit at an angle of 24 degrees, so that the barrel went up through the front edge of the top wing. Nearly 700 rounds of belt-fed ammunition were stowed in the forward fuselage. Kozakov began to use this machine on 5 February 1916, two days after the modifications were complete. Aiming the angled gun proved difficult, however, and numerous enemy aircraft escaped before he finally achieved success on the 27 June when he shot down an enemy aircraft near Lake Drisviaty.

Kosakov joined the Nineteenth Air Section on 1 October 1915, but this section was withdrawn from the Front in August 1916 as part of a reorganization to amalgamate smaller units into larger groups. On 22 August Kozakov was promoted to command the First Air Division, comprising the Second, Fourth and Nineteenth Air Sections, and on 2 September returned to the southern front near Lutsk, an important railway junction. There he was joined by Smirnov, Argeyev and Leman, all of whom became aces. The division was equipped with Nieuport 11s and Spad A.2s, whilst retaining some Nieuport 10s. The Fourth Air Section was sent to defend the town of Luzk, located north of Tarnopol, from air attack; with this section was Ensign Kokorin, also destined to become an ace.

In early February 1917, the First Air Division was transferred by train to the Rumanian front, and the division was re-equipped with Nieuport 17s and 21s, Spad 7s and Morane Saulnier monoplanes. Due to lack of action, the division moved from its first base near Jassy to an airfield near the town of Stanislav to the north, with the Fourth Air Section positioned near the town of Monastyresko. The division was occasionally engaged in bombing missions. For example, on 30 May, Argeyev in a Nieuport two-seater with Starskii as observer carried out a night raid on a railway siding and troop concentrations near Stanislav. And on 26 September Leman brought down an enemy two-seater near Gusiatina; this was his fifth victory, but he was seriously injured in the process and took no further part in the war.

A French escadrille, N581, equipped with eight Nieuport 17s and seven Spad 7s, was formed in February 1917. It was assigned to the Russian Seventh Army, and began operations in May 1917 based at Boutchatch Galicia in support of the First Air Division. In response to the German offensive of 19 July on the Sixth Army front, the unit was transferred to Buzcacz. In August it moved to the Rumanian front where it was assigned to the Third Corps. By February 1918 it became equipped with Spad 7s and was re-designated Spa 581.

The Second Air Division

On 20 May 1916, Lt Evgraf Kruten was appointed in command of the newly formed Second Air Division, comprising the Third, Seventh and Eighth Air Sections. However, there was the usual shortage of pilots and aircraft, and the unit did not reach the Front until late July. On 8 August it was established at Nesbizh in the Smolensk area, partially equipped with Nieuport 11 scouts; Kruten obtained his first victory in a Nieuport 11 on 12 August. He then spent a spell in France and did not return to Russia until 24 March 1917, whereupon he again took command, in early April, of the Second Air Division, now equipped with Nieuport 17s and 21s. The division moved to Plotych, 10km (6 miles) north of Tarnopol, where it was involved in protecting its own airfield, spotting for artillery, escorting reconnaissance machines and carrying out combat patrols. After scoring further victories, on 19 June Kruten was returning from a patrol over his own airfield when his Nieuport 17 suddenly went into a spin and crashed; he died of his injuries.

Another pilot who scored combat victories with the Second Air Division was Lt Boris Sergievsky, an experienced pilot who had formerly flown Voisins with the Twenty-Fifth Air Section. He joined the Second Fighter Air Section, as part of the Second

The gun arrangement devised by V.V. Iordan and fitted to A.A. Kazakov's Nieuport 10 in 1916. According to Russian sources the gun was a captured MG 08. Note that the circular centre-section aperture has been plated over, also the cockpit instrumentation and the ammunition belt feed. The gun was sighted by a crude system fitted on top of the centre section. Harry Woodman

Air Division, on 1 June 1917; it was equipped with ten aircraft, namely one Morane and five different Nieuport types, of which two were two-seaters and five Nieuport 21s. Sergievsky took over when the unit commander Baftalovsky was seriously injured. Sergievsky tried to train inexperienced pilots by accompanying them on patrols, though this was not always successful. Returning from leave as a staff captain, Sergievsky had time for one more victory in a Nieuport before the armistice between Russia and the Central Powers was signed.

On 5 April 1916 the Seventh Fighter Air Section, one of the components of the Second Air Division, was given its first location, at an airfield near the village of Tarnopol in Galicia; it was equipped with the Nieuport 11. It had been formed a few months earlier under the command of 2nd Lt Ivan Orlov, who had previously gained experience with the Nieuport at the Odessa aviation school. The air section was soon involved in daily combats in support of the Russian offensive, which started on 1 May under General Brusilov. Also assigned to this air section was Ensign Vasili Yanchenkow, who arrived on 7 April after service elsewhere, and a refresher course at the Moscow Air School. To begin with he made nearly forty combat patrols without any success.

Another pilot who became an ace was 2nd Lt D. Makeenok, who joined the air section in December 1916. This was not his first introduction to Nieuport aircraft: he had graduated from the Sevastopol School on 7 March 1914 after initial training on a Nieuport IVG, and after a spell with the Third Corps, was sent to Odessa for advanced training on the Nieuport 11. Yanchenko and Makeenok together discussed how to revise their tactics, and this re-direction of policy was soon put to good effect when on 7 March 1917 they shot down an enemy aircraft, thus recording Yanchenko's fourth and Makeenok's first victory.

After a period training in France with Esc. N.3, Orlov returned to the air section on 17 March 1917, and he scored his fifth victory just four days later (or his fourth if his victory with Esc. N.3 is discounted). During most of May and June the section carried out a large number of combat patrols. On 1 July 1917, General Brusilov launched Russia's last offensive of the war, resulting in fierce air battles in which the section were involved several times a day. The war-weary Nieuport 11s lacked proper maintenance and should have been withdrawn, but there were no replacements available and they continued to be used. Unfortunately on 4 July, whilst in combat with four enemy machines, the lower starboard wing of Orlov's machine collapsed and his machine fell from 3,000m (10,000ft) and he was killed.

2nd Lt J.V. Gilsher assumed command of the air section, but his period in office did not last long. By 20 July the Russian army was in retreat, and enemy aircraft appeared in force over the section's airfield at Tarnopol. Yanchenko, Makeenok and Gilsher took off to intercept this force, but Makeenok became separated whist fighting his own lone battle, leaving the other two attempting to fight off more than fifteen enemy planes. One of these was shot down, but the observer of another managed to rake Gilsher's Nieuport with machine-gun fire: as a result the engine tore away, the wings folded, and the machine fell to the ground, killing Gilsher.

On 5 August, Yanchenko and Makeenok spotted an enemy two-seater attacking a Russian reconnaissance machine trying to photograph the enemy trench system. The enemy machine fought back and seriously wounded Makeenok before it was shot down, and as a result Makeenok took no further part in the war.

Yanchenko became seriously depressed following the loss of several of his comrades and because of the precarious state of the war, and on 20 September 1917 he was transferred to another unit, the Thirty-Second Corps Air Section on the Rumanian front. Whilst with that unit he scored his last three victories of the war, still using a Nieuport machine, to bring his total to sixteen. Later Yanchenko went to Novocherkassk, and early in 1918 joined the Volunteer Army under generals Denikin and Wrangel; from August 1918 he commanded the Second Air Section, a post he occupied for two years. Makeenok recovered from his injuries and eventually joined the 3rd Polish Section, just before the outbreak of the Russo-Polish War of 1920–1. After Poland gained independence, Makeenok remained with the 3rd Section until the end of 1921.

Other Fighter Air Sections

The First Fighter Air Section was equipped with Morane Parasols and Nieuport 10s in the spring of 1916, and early in July the section received its first Nieuport 11s. Lt K. Vakulovsky was appointed commander of the section on 16 July 1916, and gained his first victory whilst flying a Nieuport 11 (serial 1295) on 7 September. There was plenty of action through August and September. As examples, Ensign P.M. Tomson, who had been with the section since 16 May 1915 and was destined to become an ace, used Nieuport 10 (serial 160) to carry out twenty-five reconnaissance, bombing and escort missions during this period, and on 1 September 1917 flying a Nieuport 23 (3747). And Vakulovsky had sixteen air battles in one day, culminating in two victories.

The Ninth Fighter Air Section was organized under the command of Ivan Loiko in August 1916. Another pilot who would become an ace, W/O Grigory Suk, joined this section on 19 August, and he was joined on the 24th by another experienced flyer, W/O (later Ensign) Vladimir Strizhevsky. The unit was sent to the Rumanian front, mainly equipped with Nieuport 11 scouts, and by early October 1916 it was located near Okna, north of Focsani. The section continued to support the Rumanian army while it was trying to link up with the Russians to the north-east following a heavy defeat. Very bad weather curtailed aerial activity during the winter months, but nevertheless the unit managed to score a number of victories.

The section continued to be active during the following months. For example, Strizhevsky made twelve combat flights during April, during which he scored three confirmed victories, two of these in Nieuports. On 8 August Suk scored his third and last victory in a Nieuport when he shot down an Oeffag C.II engaged in artillery spotting. Thereafter Suk recorded another six victories flying Vickers FB.19 and Spad 7 aircraft. Loiko achieved his sixth and last victory (his fifth in Nieuports) when he and Sapozhnikov shot down an enemy two-seater.

The Tenth Fighter Air Section was formed in the summer of 1916 as part of the Tenth Russian Army in Rumania, under Cossack Captain Belofastov; it was based at Gnidava airfield. A pilot who would become an ace, W/O Alexander Pishvanov, joined the section on 2 October 1916 – though it would be more than five months before he saw his first enemy aircraft. After more than fifty patrols totalling more than eighty hours, on 21 March 1917, whilst flying a Nieuport 21 (1890) – a type he used in all his victories – he came across a two-seater and forced it to crash-land in its own territory. He scored his fifth and last victory on 7 July, but was shot in the leg during this encounter; furthermore, four days later he lost two fingers of his right hand in another combat. By the time he had recovered, hostilities were at an end. In December he flew to Novocherkassk and joined the volunteer army under generals Denikin and Wrangle.

Naval Nieuports in Wartime Service

Before the outbreak of the war, Russia had two strong naval formations in Europe: the Black Sea Fleet and the Baltic Fleet. Each of these fleets had an aviation section, which late in 1916 became separate divisions, the Black Sea Air Division and the Baltic Air Division, within the respective fleets. As early as 1915, a need for aircraft to protect both the fleet and shore bases was evident, and this need became acute towards the end of 1916 when the Russian forces found themselves having to give assistance to Rumania, which had come into the war on the side of the *entente*. Both air fleets supported a plan put forward in the spring of 1917 to form a land-based air division, elements of which could be used to protect shore bases or beachheads, and carry out limited reconnaissance and ground attack roles. This plan was approved, and in early April, Vice-Admiral A.V. Kolchak, Commander of the Black Sea Fleet, put in an order for an army unit or at least some Nieuport 11s, without pilots – and even without engines, as there were surplus 110hp Le Rhônes available in store at Sevastopol.

Similar assistance was also required by the Baltic Fleet, but such help was not forthcoming in time to prevent German forces from attacking the Russian naval stations at Tserel and Arensburg on Oezel Island in mid-June 1917, in which two sheds and two flying boats were destroyed and four more flying boats badly damaged. Nine days later, the Baltic Fleet staff requested two detachments of land-based fighters, as flying boat fighters had been incapable of making a worthwhile contribution either in defence or attack. This request was re-emphasized a week later when it was pointed out to the naval general staff that carrying out aerial reconnaissance in the Irben and Domesnes areas would be difficult, if not impossible without escorts.

Russian Aces: Victories with Nieuport Aircraft

Pilot	Total victories	Nieuport victories	Squadron(s)
P.V. Argeyev	13 + 2 n/c	6 + 1 n/c	19th
L. Coudouret	6	2	N.57/N.102
J.V. Gilsher	5	5	7th
M.R. Gond	5	4	N.3
N.K. Kohorin	5	4	4th
A.A. Kozakov	20 + 3 n/c	19 + 3 n/c	19th
Y.N. Kruten	7	5	2nd
G.M. Lachmann	8 + 2 n/c	3 + 2 n/c	N.57
E.K. Leman	5	5	19th
I.A. Loiko	6 + 4 n/c	5 + 4 n/c	9th
J.M. Mahlapuu	2 + 1 n/c	2 + 1 n/c	12th
D.A. Makeenok	8 + 1 n/c	8 + 1 n/c	7th
I.A. Orlov	5	4	7th
A.M. Pishvanov	5 + 1 n/c	5 + 1 n/c	10th
E.M. Pulpe	5	3	N.23/10th
C.A. Revol-Tisset	5	2	N.3
M.I. Safonov	5	3	Glacol
B.V. Sergievski	2 + 1 n/c	2 + 1 n/c	2nd
A.N.P. de Seversky	6	2	2 Baltic
I.V. Smirnov	11	3	19th
V.I. Strizhevsky	7 + 3 n/c	4 + 2 n/c	9th
G.E. Suk	9 + 1 n/c	3	9th
A.N. Sveshnikov	2 + 1 n/c	1 n/c	7th Corps
P.M. Tomson	1 + 4 n/c	1 + 4 n/c	1st
K.K. Vakulovski	6	5	1st
V.I. Yanchenko	16	14	7th/32nd

It was evident to the command of the Naval Air Service that a supply of trained fighter pilots would be necessary if an effective fighter force were to be established. To this end, early in 1917 a project was launched to establish a class of aerial combat within the naval aviation school at Taganrog by the Sea of Azov. Later, at the end of May, it was decided that such a school should be set up as a special air combat school located at Krasnoe Selo, 28km (17 miles) south-west of Petrograd, where a large military field and cavalry training area was already established.

Negotiations had already begun in February 1917 with the Duks company in Moscow to provide fighters. An initial requirement made by the deputy naval minister on 19 March for forty single- and two-seat Nieuport 10 machines was amended on 5 April to twenty-five Nieuport 17s and fifty Nieuport 10s, of which twenty were to be single-seaters, fifteen two-seaters and fifteen dual-control trainers. Alternative similar types could be substituted by the manufacturer without objection from the customer. The cost of each airframe without engine, armament and dual control gear was 13,000 roubles. However, within a week the price had risen by 10 per cent due to 'disturbances taking place within the state' (in fact the uprising leading to the abdication of the Tsar). The order was officially confirmed on 19 May, to be fulfilled in the period 14 July 1917 to 14 January 1918. All the aircraft were to be built and accepted in Moscow, crated and despatched to SS Schetinin in Petrograd where they would be re-assembled and tested and then flown to the air combat school. It was not clear how the operational units were to be supplied with Nieuport fighters; however, by August the Baltic and Black Sea Fleets had received sixteen and eleven Nieuport 17s respectively, and by November the air combat school had received twenty-three Nieuport 10s, twelve Nieuport 17s and at least three Nieuport 21s.

The contract discussed above was evidently just a preliminary exercise, as the navy envisaged a much more comprehensive use of fighters. The plans called for every air division to operate four units of land planes in 1918, with each of the four units equipped with twelve aircraft – six operational and six in reserve – amounting to a total of 145 aircraft including spares. It seems that an even greater expansion of air power was envisaged, because by late 1917, the Duks company in Moscow had orders for seventy-six fighters, and the Meltser company in Petrograd for fifty-five. Furthermore, on 18 September a Russian naval aviation purchasing commission in Paris was instructed to obtain a set of manufacturing drawings of the Nieuport 24bis for the use of the Duks company. Although it is known that the Nieuport company were preparing a set of these drawings by 6 October, the manufacturer had advised the Russians that the model had been superseded by a better design, for which a licence for manufacture would be necessary.

Steps were also taken to secure production from French sources. By early October an order had already been placed for 100 airframes from the Nieuport factory. These were to be supplied without their 130hp Clerget engines, at a cost of 15,650FF each. Two airframes were shipped to Russia on board a steamer at the beginning of October, but deliveries were stopped in late 1917 with the contract only half completed for fear that the machines might fall into enemy hands. Records also show that forty-two Nieuport 17s, to be fitted with 125hp Le Rhône engines, had been ordered from an unknown source on 25 September 1917.

The only modification requested by naval pilots was for the provision of a collimater gunsight. One manufactured by Duks was considered, but on 11 October a contract was signed by the Naval Aviation Board for the military-technical workshop at Rur to manufacture fifty sights, designed by Jnr Lt (Army) Musinyants, at a cost of 10,000 roubles.

The Air Combat School

The air combat school at Krasnoe Selo was set up by 2nd Lt A.A. Nelidov for the purpose of training pilots for naval land-based fighter units. He had obtained his wings with the Royal Naval Air Service in England, and had also qualified at the School of Aerial Gunnery at Cazeaux in France. The school was declared operational on 7 August 1917, with a two-phase programme involving instruction in Lebed 12 two-seaters, followed by solo experience in Nieuport 17s or 23s. The first twelve Duks-built Nieuports were accepted between 4 October and 1 December. By 14 November the school possessed a total of twenty-two operational aircraft. There were nine instructors and nineteen pupils, with six having completed the second phase of training. A total of 132 flights had been made, totalling eighty-four hours. In addition to the pilots trained at Krasnoe Selo, the initial intake of pupils for the Baltic Air Division were trained in Moscow. Several prominent leaders of Soviet units mentioned later were trained at the air combat school, including N.A. Yakovitsky, B.A. Schepotiev and N.N. Evampliev.

Nieuports in the Baltic Air Division

Ten Nieuport fighters were allocated to the Baltic First Air Brigade at Arensburg and Tserel by 16 August 1917, with six at Arensburg and four at Tserel. There was a seaplane base and aerodrome near each town, and the Nieuports were intended to protect both areas, which had been constantly bombed, from further attack. The Nieuports were given fleet code numbers NR-1 to NR-10 (N = Nieuport, R = Le Rhône) and were allocated as follows: NR-1 to Sub-Lt M.I. Safonov, NR-2 to Jnr Lt (Army) Zherebtsov, NR-4 to Capt (Cavalry) V.M. Nadezhdin, NR-5 to Capt (Army) Galyshev, NR-9 to Lt (Admiralty) V.V. Petrov, with NR-10 non-operational at Arensburg and NR-3 to Jnr Lt (Army) V.L. Yakovlev, NR-6 to Lt A.N. Prokofiev (later known as Seversky), NR-7 to Sub-Lt V.M. Okhremenko and NR-8 to Jun Lt (Army) V.N. Filippov at Tserel.

The machines were fitted with a variety of armament, most of it very poorly maintained and in an extremely dirty condition. When visited on 22 August, four of the Nieuports at Arensburg were reported to have synchronized Vickers guns, three of British and one of Russian calibre. Of the four machines at Tserel, two were fitted with British Vickers guns, one with a synchronized Vickers and a wing-mounted Lewis, and the last with just a wing-mounted Lewis gun.

The first successful action involving Nieuports took place on 7 September when three Nieuports, together with two flying boats, took off from Tserel to intercept two German aircraft. One of these was shot down 6km (4 miles) from Arensburg, probably by the combined efforts of one of the flying boats and Lt Safonov in Nieuport NR-1. This was followed on 10 October by further successes when two Nieuports forced down two German seaplanes. On 12 October, three Nieuports piloted by Seversky, Filippov and Petrov forced a German seaplane to land on the sea, and shortly afterwards Seversky and Petrov forced down another, at the expense of damage to Seversky's engine.

Safonov had three more successes within a couple of days. On 15 October he forced down an enemy machine after taking off from Kuivast on Moon Island. The following day he shot down a Freidrichshafen FF33L that crashed on Moon Island, killing the crew of two. The next day, whilst flying over a German section of two battleships and two cruisers with escorts, he opened fire on a twin-engined bomber from a range of 20m (65ft). Plywood and fabric splinters flew off the target and the machine started to burn and fall away.

But with the Russian forces in retreat, the Russian pilots' luck began to run out. Seversky, making his way to Kuivast on 14 October, was obliged to force-land near Orissar Dam due to engine failure, and had to destroy his Nieuport, able to salvage only his machine-gun. On the same day Petrov, also making his way to Moon, survived a crash; but Filippov became a prisoner of war after landing on enemy-held territory. On 17 October Galyshev crash-landed after a Lewis gun magazine jammed in his rudder pedals; and on the same day 2nd Lt (Admiralty) D.I. Shteven damaged a Nieuport beyond repair during a landing at Hapsal. The following day Zherebstov survived a crash in his Nieuport after suffering engine failure. Yakovlev's and Okhremenko's Nieuports were abandoned at Arensburg, and one was lost in Oezel Island and possibly one at Verder. Therefore within the space of a few days the Baltic Air Division had lost most, if not all, of its Nieuports.

Alexander Nikolaivich Prokofiev de Seversky had experienced a varied career, amongst other things enjoying four confirmed victories whilst operating Grigorovitch M.9 flying boats in the Baltic, but also sustaining several injuries, and including latterly a period as technical adviser to the Shchetinin aircraft factory: in late July 1917 he was appointed commander of the Second Baltic Fighter Air Section stationed on Oesel Island, to defend its fortifications from aerial attack. The main Russian army had withdrawn behind the Dvina in anticipation of an overwhelming German attack, leaving rearguard units to defend the islands in the Baltic. The section was given four Nieuport 21s, one Grigorovitch M.9 and six Grigorovitch M.15 flying boats to achieve this task. Seversky's section stayed on the island during the German assault, during which he claimed several victories that were not confirmed. However, two victories over a scout and bomber on 10 October 1917 in a Nieuport were confirmed by groundforces. The section was evacuated four days later after its aerodrome and hangars had been destroyed by gunfire from the German fleet. During the evacuation, Seversky's Nieuport developed engine trouble and he was forced to land behind enemy lines; but in the general confusion he was able to return through his own lines. He eventually made his way to the United States where he set up his own aircraft manufacturing business.

Safonov returned to the Front on 14 November 1917 after getting married, and assumed command of the Second Fighter Air Section now located at Kuivastoin. From there he flew his Nieuport to intercept an enemy aircraft that crashed on Moon Island. The next day Safonov intercepted a twin-engined bomber that had been dropping bombs on Russian ships at Moon Island. After an exchange of fire the enemy aircraft began to smoke and crashed into the sea: this was Safonov's fifth and last victory, and his third in a Nieuport. Following the revolution, Safonov escaped to Finland with his wife and three other pilots in two Nieuport 10s and two Nieuport 17s. In 1919 Safonov was briefly with Denikin's White Army near Novocherkassk.

Nieuports in the Black Sea

Due to a lack of engines and armament, the Duks factory were unable to fulfil a request by the Naval General Staff Aeronautical Department made on 14 July 1917 to supply the Black Sea Air Division with four Nieuport 17s fitted with 120hp le Rhônes, and two Nieuport 21s with 80hp le Rhônes. Instead the navy had to rely on the army, resulting in its 6th Corps Aviation Unit being attached to the naval formation operating from a base near the town of Izmail on the Danube estuary. Although normally equipped with Farman F.30s, this unit had five Nieuports at its disposal, all fitted with 80hp Le Rhône engines: two Nieuport 10s (707 and 726), one Nieuport 11 (846) and two Nieuport 21s (1821 and 1906).

The unit carried out regular reconnaissance sorties in this area, which was relatively quiet. There were, however, one or two incidents. The Nieuport 11, piloted by Jnr Lt Morozov, crashed on landing on 30 July. On 10 October Nieuport 10 (726), piloted by Jnr Lt Kim with Lt Fedoseev as observer, were flying over the Kataloi–Tulca road when they were subjected to groundfire. A splinter hit a cylinder valve, resulting in a broken connecting rod and piston. The engine stopped and Klim glided a long way to reach a rear trench area. The crew and aircraft survived, despite being subjected to shellfire.

Meanwhile the authorities had made some headway in their attempt to set up the four fighter units in the Black Sea area, with the 13th Air Section being the first to become operational. On 7 October 1917 this air section possessed two fighters that had been assembled at Sulina, with a number of others in crates at Kiliya, and by the end of the year this number at Sulina had been increased to six operational and two non-operational Nieuport 17s. It is not known for certain whether this unit was involved in combat, but by the middle of February 1918 it left for Odessa, where it survived the enemy invasion. On 29 September 1918 the unit took off for the Don region and disappeared, its ultimate fate not being recorded.

Nieuports in the Balkans with Rumania and Serbia

Rumania

As a result of French diplomatic pressure, Rumania came in on the side of the Allies: on the night of 27 August 1916 the Rumanian army entered Transylvania, previously an ancient province of Rumania, and sparked off hostilities against Austria-Hungary.

At the beginning of the war, the Rumanian Military Aviation had at its disposal some ninety-seven pilots, forty observers and forty-four aeroplanes of French origin, including Caudrons, Maurice Farmans, Voisins, Blériots and Nieuport 11s. Organized into four squadrons, F.1 Sqn was attached to the First Army based at Talmaci in Transylvania, F.2 Sqn was with the Second Army at Brasov, and F.3 Sqn with the Northern Army in the Piatra Neamt. A reserve squadron, with the rest of the aircraft including the Nieuports, was situated near Bucharest. A second reserve squadron was also formed with four aircraft on 30 August 1916, to cover the Bulgarian front.

Within a couple of months the situation on the Rumanian front had deteriorated, and it became necessary for the French to send in a military mission under the direction of Gen H. Berthelot; this arrived in Bucharest on 15 October. The mission was accompanied by much needed reinforcements, comprising forty-one Nieuport 11s, thirty-eight Farman 40s, eighteen Breguet-Michelins and four Henri Farmans. Its aeronautical part was commanded by Lt Col de Vergnette de la Motte, who played a major role in the reorganization of the Rumanian military aviation. Under his direction, the strength of the Rumanian squadrons was bolstered by French personnel, although three squadrons, including one of Nieuports, remained essentially Rumanian. The British, for their part, sent two Nieuport 11s and five Nieuport 12s, which arrived in Bucharest towards the end of October 1916.

During December 1916, the Rumanian air force, now comprising fifty-three operational aircraft including eighteen Nieuport

Rumanian Nieuport 11 over the front at Marasesti. Valeriu Avram

Captured French Nieuport 17*bis* (N4487) in service with the Bulgarian forces.

Rumanian Air Force Nieuport 17 on a visit to Lwow airfield in Poland in 1919.
T. Kopanski

11s and 17s, was withdrawn for retraining and regrouping. The Rumanian government purchased a further twenty-five Nieuport 17s during 1917. The air force was reformed into three groups, one for each of the armies, with a total of nine squadrons, increasing to twelve by May 1917. Each of these squadrons was equipped with a single aircraft type, namely Nieuport scout squadrons, Caudron squadrons for reconnaissance, and Breguet-Michelin bomber squadrons. The four Nieuport squadrons were as follows: N.1 Sqn commanded by Capt R. Chambe coming under First Grupul at Borzesti in the Second Rumanian Army sector; N.3 Sqn commanded by Capt M. Gonde and assigned to the Second Grupul at Cioara in the First Rumanian Army sector; N.11 Sqn, commanded by Capt S. Protopopescu at Tecuci, and N.10 Sqn commanded by Capt P. Bléry at Borzesti in Galatia, both under the Third Grupul, assigned to the Sixth Russian Army. Each squadron was equipped with seven Nieuport 11s or 17s each. By the beginning of 1918, these units had received a further eighty-eight machines – thirty-six Nieuport 23s and 28s, some Nieuport 24s, and fifty-two Sopwith 1½-Strutters – giving a total of 322 machines received from abroad.

After the reorganization at the beginning of 1917, the Rumanian air force took part in many activities during the winter and spring, particularly reconnaissance over the enemy lines. The Nieuport squadrons were also engaged in many combat missions. On 4 March, Lt G. Mihail of 1 Sqn shot down a Brandenburg C.I that fell into the enemy lines killing both crew. Two Austro-Hungarian two-seaters were damaged a few days later by the same squadron. Lt V. Craiu, now commander of N.10 Sqn, managed to damage one of a flight of three Fokker E.IIIs on 21 April 1917, and on 21 May shot down a seaplane near Barbosi.

The reorganization was complete by July 1917, and on 24 July the Rumanian Second Army started a major offensive along the Marasesti-Oituz front, after initial difficulties managing to advance a considerable distance. The operation was supported by six squadrons, two of which were N.3 and N.11 engaged in escorting reconnaissance machines. On 28 July a two-seater was destroyed by one of the scouts of First Aviation Group, and on 9 August a Brandenburg, which crashed in the Rumanian lines, was damaged. Lt V. Craiu and Sub-Lt E. Nasta between them carried out sixty-four combat missions whilst spending about 100 hours in the air. Sub-Lts Muntenescu and M. Popescu carried out fifty-two missions in twenty-five hours. During the offensive N.11 alone claimed eleven victories.

On 13 September 1917, Sub-Lt M. Dragusanu of N.11 Sqn shot down an enemy aircraft over Milcov, and on 25 October Sub-Lt Muntenescu forced down two Fokker E.IIIs. Lt Craiu and Sub-Lts Nasta, Magalea and Pauckert also scored victories. These were the last victories reported, and action had virtually ceased by December 1917. Overall aerial activity was not as great as on the Western Front, and there were only thirty-one victories claimed during the whole war, Third Fighter Squadron claiming seven of these.

However, hostilities renewed in 1918, this time against Bolshevik and communist Ukrainian forces. On 1 May 1918, the Soviets gave an ultimatum demanding that Rumania withdraw its forces in Bessarabia and Bucovini, and on 27 May Bolshevik forces crossed the Nistra in considerable force. Against them were ranged the Rumanian Fifth Corps, comprising three divisions, supported in the air mainly by the Sopwith 1½-Strutters of S.2, S.4 and S.6 squadrons, escorted by the Nieuports of N.10 Sqn. The fighting gradually petered out, and by the end of 1918 Rumania had become an independent country. Some surviving Nieuport 17s were used against an incursion by the Hungarian Red Army Airborne Corps in 1919. Some Nieuport 24s were used by a Rumanian aerobatic team in 1925.

Serbia

The Serbs received extensive support from the Aviation Militaire, and three French escadrilles, equipped with Nieuport 10s and 11s, were active in Serbia in 1916. These were N.387 (a combined Franco-Serb unit), N.391 (an all-French unit) and a Nieuport escadrille under the control of the Serbian High Command. The latter unit was used for reconnaissance and to transport spies behind the enemy lines. N.387 was later assigned to the Serbian Second Army and performed reconnaissance duties over the right bank of the River Erna and the left bank of the River Vardar. It also provided escorts for Esc. MF.382.

By March 1917, four Nieuport 11s and 12s were assigned to the First Serbian Army, and a section of Nieuports was also assigned to the Second Serbian Army. N.387 by this time was under the direct command of the Serbian High Command and was based at Vertekop. By mid-1917, Spad 7s had replaced the Nieuports on the Serbian Front.

A Nieuport 11 of the First Serbian Army.

The Civil War and Foreign Intervention 1918–20

Following the Bolshevik uprisings of October 1917 and January 1918, the provisional government and constituent assembly ceased to exist. The old Russian empire dissolved into civil war, with the Bolsheviks opposed by various factions, collectively known as White Russians, the latter supported by the former Allies including French and US forces but principally the British.

The Russian air forces were in chaos following the seizure of power by the Bolsheviks after the revolution of October 1917. Many aviation specialists left the country, and most unit officers were suspected of collusion with opponents of the regime: many were driven away, and the less fortunate were imprisoned or executed. Many pilots and mechanics, disillusioned with the war, unpaid and underfed, deserted and returned to their homes. Others joined the White Russian forces, fled to the Allies or gave themselves up to the Germans. The production of aircraft and repair work virtually ceased, and many aircraft were abandoned or destroyed. However, the Bolsheviks were in possession of most of central Russia, and because they controlled the factories and depots within the country – and despite shortages of engines and raw materials – they were able to supply some new aircraft to the various areas of conflict during the civil war.

On 28 October, three days after the Bolshevik coup, a Bureau of Commissars for Aviation and Aeronautics was appointed, and instructed to take over control of aviation assets in the Petrograd area; similar organizations were formed in Moscow and elsewhere. Efforts were made to salvage and collect usable aircraft, engines and components, put the factories back to work, and vet former Army Aviation Corps personnel for their loyalty to the new regime. By November the framework had been set up to reorganize the air force into eight aviation units, with a nominal strength of twelve aircraft, to be based in the Ukraine, Mogilev, Sheremetev, Vologda, Kronstadt, Petrograd and Archangel, with one in reserve. This became the Workers' and Peasants' Red Military Air Fleet on 28 January 1918.

The renewal of the German offensive against Russia in February 1918 led to the collapse of the Russian front and the loss of much military equipment and aircraft. The new Soviet government bowed to the inevitable and signed the Treaty of Brest-Litovsk on 3 March, in which they gave up their interest in the Baltic States, Poland, Ukraine, Belorussia and some southern republics, in exchange for the opportunity to establish a Communist state in peace.

In the summer of 1918, Soviet military aviation was formalized under the Commissar for National Defence, and unit officers came under the direction of political commissars. The units were reorganized into three Area Boards, for Petrograd, Moscow and the south, with seven, thirty and twenty-two units respectively, with a nominal strength of twelve machines each. These came under the formal direction of a directorate for the Field Army on 22 September 1918. A return made in February 1919 showed that there were 1,102 machines available. However, only 349 were on active service, while a further thirty-four were allotted to military units to the rear. Of the remaining 753, 167 lacked engines, 363 were damaged or incomplete and awaiting repair, while 142 were too worn out ever to become serviceable. A large percentage of these machines were Nieuports.

At the beginning of the civil war, Bolshevik air forces supported their armies fighting in areas as far apart as southern Russia, the Ukraine, Belorussia, the Baltic States, Siberia and the Far East. The Red Army also succeeded in stopping a Polish offensive and in turn invaded Poland. But by October 1920, all this fighting, apart from a few local uprisings, had petered out in favour of the Bolsheviks.

Red naval aviation operated in the Gulf of Finland, lakes Ladoga and Onega, the Northern Dvina, the Volga and Kama rivers, the Caspian Sea, and the Dnepr and Pripyat rivers. In 1920 their units reached the Enisei and Selenga rivers in Siberia, the Sea of Azov and the Black Sea. The aircraft were moved about mainly by large, adapted river barges, towed or pushed by river steamers, which also acted as accommodation and provided rudimentary workshop facilities.

The first Red fighter unit appeared in the Baltic on 2 May 1918, led by Lt N.A. Yakovitsky, formerly of the navy. It was then transformed into the First Northern Fighter Unit and was sent to the Northern Front on 17 August. Between 5/6 September its three Nieuport 23s (1758, 1886 and 1902) carried out their first missions from an airfield near the village of Verkhnyaya Toima; but the unit made many moves subsequently dictated by changing circumstances. On 31 August 1918 it received four French-built Nieuport 24bis, which replaced the worn out Duks-built machines and were used extensively while it was on the Northern Dvina river. The unit's main activity was reconnaissance, but there were several events worthy of note. On 8 June 1919, N.S. Meinikov in a Nieuport 25 (4090, named 'Meri') attacked an enemy flying boat, but failed to destroy it. Nine days later Meinikov was again in action against two enemy aircraft, though this finished without loss to either side. However, a substantial amount of the unit's equipment and stores was damaged in an air raid on 17 June.

The Second Northern Fighter Unit, commanded by a former naval 2nd Lt, B.A. Schepotiev, arrived at the Front on 23 August 1918. It was based at an airfield near the railway station at Plesetskaya, and operated four French-built Nieuport 24bis (5101, 5115, 5116 and 5130) and two other Nieuport types; these were listed as Nieuport 23s, but one may have been a Nieuport 17 (1854). During September 1918, three Nieuport 23s and two other Nieuports (probably Nieuport 25s) were sent to the Volga fighter half-unit based at Nizhny Novgorod, and two Nieuport 25s to the Caspian Hydroaviation battalion fighter unit at Astrakhan. These units later received new aircraft and eventually reached the Black Sea and the Sea of Azov. After the retreat from Kiev in 1919, the Dnepr Hydroaviation unit remained at Gomel in Belorussia; in the autumn it acquired two Nieuport 21s, and then joined the Volga-Caspian aviation group to the south.

By 31 December 1918, a 'special purpose' unit, with up to four Nieuports and under the command of N.N. Evampliev, was based in the Narva area. Another Baltic unit was at Novyi Peterhof near Petrograd and fought against British aircraft that operated over the approaches of the Baltic Fleet anchorages in the Gulf of Finland, and specifically Kronstadt. By 1 December 1919 this unit had lost one Nieuport 10, four Nieuport 23s, one Nieuport 23bis and one Nieuport 25. The latter was lost when it spun into the sea following a reconnaissance mission over Koporie Bay. A possible cause of the accident was structural failure due to the poor state of the airframe after being left in its crate for over two years before being assembled. Its pilot S.D. Nikolsky was killed.

Another naval unit, the Northern Hydroaviation Battalion, was formed in January 1919 from the Byelomorsky (White Sea) and the Kamsky (Kama River) flying boat detachments and the First and Second Fighter Air Squadrons. In the summer of 1919, the First Fighter Air Squadron, equipped with a motley selection of aircraft including Spad 7s and Nieuports, was engaged against White Russian and British forces in the Northern Dvina area. One day – believed to be 18 June 1919 – 2 Slavo-British Squadron led by Capt Carr, and including A.A. Kazakov amongst its number – attacked the air squadron's airfield some 50km (30 miles) behind the Front at Verkhnaya Toima, 350km (220 miles) south-east of Archangel. Some of the air squadron's aircraft, including a brand new Nieuport, were out in the open being refuelled. Several of these aircraft suffered in the attack, including Nieuport 25 4090 'Meri', which was damaged, and Nieuport 24bis 5132 'Kisa', which was written off after being set on fire by an incendiary bullet. The Nieuport 25 was subsequently repaired using parts from Nieuport 25 4081 'Nata', which was considered to be an 'unlucky' aircraft. The following day Nieuport 10 1536 'Lyusa' was badly damaged in a crash and written off, and on 12 July Nieuport 24bis 'Mika', which had been previously assembled from three cannibalized machines (5106, 5132 and 5133), was written off after crashing on take-off. By 28 August 1919 the air squadron had just three operational aircraft, two Spad 7s and Nieuport 10 1524, with two Nieuport 25s (4081 and 4090) under repair. Two Nieuport 10s (1536 and 1543) had been written off, and Nieuport 23 1758 was too worn out to fly.

Possibly the last action involving Russian Nieuports occurred when the Communist authorities suppressed a mutiny of the Kronstadt garrison, dockyard workers and sailors of the Baltic fleet, including the crews of the battleships *Petrapavlovsk* and *Sevastopol*, all of whom had been objecting to the harsh economic regime being imposed. On 7 March 1921, the first day of the mutiny, four Nieuport 23s (291, 303, 338 and 343) were ordered from their base at Novyi Peterhof to fly to the airfield at Kommendantsky, north of Petrograd. Only one arrived safely, however, the others making force-landings on the way. The mutiny was suppressed after two weeks of bloody fighting by ground troops assisted by bombing attacks by Grigorovich flying boats.

The Allied Intervention

The Allies were naturally concerned that collapse of the Russian forces would release more German reinforcements for the Western Front, and would take the pressure off the Turks in the Middle East. They were also worried that their investments in Russia would be lost, and that the Communist revolution would spread. Allied intervention began in the summer of 1918, with Britain, France and the United States landing the Northern Russian Expeditionary Force at Murmansk, and with Japanese assistance another force at Vladivostok.

In June 1918 a British force with French support, the North Russian Expeditionary Force, landed in Murmansk, supported by an RAF flight of eight DH.4s. The following month the seaplane carrier *Nairana* arrived with five Fairey IIICs, two Sopwith Babys and a Sopwith Camel. These RAF units helped in the occupation of Archangel on 2 August. The original objective of the force was to push southwards along the Dvina river from its base at Archangel, to link up with White Russian forces coming from the east along the Trans-Siberian Railway. In this way it was hoped to stabilize an eastern front against the Central Powers, which had collapsed following the treaty signed between the Germans and Bolsheviks. But this objective was never achieved, and instead the British forces were confined to an area around its base.

The British were supported by a number of ex-Tsarist fliers, led by Alexander Kazakov, who were incorporated into two Slavo-British squadrons established before the British forces left Murmansk for Archangel. These were equipped with eight French-built Sopwith 1½-Strutters and two Nieuports – one Type 17 or 23, and one Type 24 (4251 and 4263) – which had been found in crates at Archangel, together with a large number of 120hp Le Rhône engines and other spares, left over from an earlier consignment intended for Rumania. These were assembled by RAF mechanics and supplemented by the Sopwith Camel from the *Nairana*. Reconnaissance and bombing operations with these aircraft began in late September 1918. More Sopwith Camels were added to these squadrons in January 1919, and D.H.9s and D.H.9As followed in June.

But by July 1919, after an ineffectual campaign lacking in both purpose and direction, the British had decided to withdraw, an operation completed by September. Kozakov was very upset by this decision and became very morose. On 3 August he took off in a Sopwith Snipe, made no attempt to gain altitude, stalled off the top of a loop and crashed into the ground, killing himself. On August 22, one of the Nieuports, considered to be unsuitable for further use, was deliberately destroyed by tying the controls in position and pulling the throttle open by a length of string. It took off pilotless in a climbing turn and spun into the aerodrome from 60m (200ft). A few of the aircraft were captured by the Red Army during the fighting, and some 250 Sopwiths, Nieuports and Farmans were later found abandoned at Archangel and Murmansk.

In November and December 1918, British and French forces landed at Novorossiisk and Odessa on the Black Sea, and remained in southern Russia until 1920. General Denikin's Volunteer Army, together with other White Russian forces operating in the same area, was sent large numbers of British-built aircraft in support to supplement the few Nieuports and other machines already in its possession.

Czechoslovakia

A Czech aviation unit, the First Aviation Detachment, was formed between the end of February and early March 1918. It initially received nine aircraft from the French aviation park at Lubny, including four Sopwiths, one Morane Parasol and at least one Nieuport, probably a Nieuport 17 or 23. But shortly after their acquisition, the Czech Army Corps began to evacuate the Ukraine, and all this material was loaded on railcars for the journey of several thousand kilometres to Vladivostok. But by then the passage of the Czechs on Russian soil was subject to conditions by which their weapons had to be handed over to the Bolshevik authorities, and the detachment gradually lost its aircraft. However, the first five aircraft, including any Nieuports, had already returned to Serdobsk by the end of March and luckily avoided the embargo. These aircraft were dispersed after arriving at Vladivostok in June 1918.

A lack of trust between the Czechs and Bolsheviks caused a confrontation at the end of May 1918, and fighting broke out along a line between Penza and Vladivostok; at this time the greater part of the Czech forces were spread out along the length of the Trans-Siberian railway. Before long the two sides were employing aircraft: the Czechs formed two aviation detachments, one on the Volga and the other in the Urals. They mainly carried out reconnaissance and bombing missions, for which Farman 30s and Voisin LA/LASs were used. Nieuport scouts were also employed on some missions, carrying out 17 per cent of the flights.

At the beginning of August 1918, the Samarian First Detachment of the White

Alexander Dedulin and Viktor Knopp by Nieuport 21 (1940). Zdenek Cwjka collection

Russian Popular Army became the Independent Aviation Detachment of the First Hussite Division of Fusiliers. It took part in combats on the Volga front from 9 June to 13 September 1918. Out of its total of eight aircraft, of which only three were available at any one time, three were Nieuports. The first of these (2415) was acquired, together with a Farman 30, when Simbirsk was captured at the end of July 1918, and the two aircraft were taken on charge at the beginning of August, replacing a worn-out Farman 30. Nieuport 2415 was little used while the unit was at the front at Kazan. On 3 to 9 August, Ensign Dedulin and 2nd Lt Melc between them flew four times – a test flight, two reconnaissance missions and a transfer flight – totalling 4hr 40min.

The career of the second Nieuport, a Nieuport 10 two-seater, was very brief, ending on its first mission: Dedulin, with 2nd Lt Arbuzov as observer, left Kazan on 3 September 1918 for a field near Kindyakouka, but two days later side-slipped on take-off in a high wind, and crashed. Both were fortunate, Dedulin himself escaping uninjured, and Arbuzov suffering just light wounds to his face and hands when he was thrown out on impact.

Less than a week later, on the evening of 10 September, the detachment acquired a Nieuport 21 (1940) when Lt Gusev defected from the 7th Soviet Fighter Air Flight, landing near Cherdakhy station. Dedulin flew the aircraft the same day to a field near Kindyakovka station. The Czech front on the Volga was crumbling, Kazan was taken by the Bolsheviks, and they were approaching Simbirsk. As a result the detachment quickly left Kindyakovka during the morning of 1 September. Dedulin rescued the Nieuport by flying to Verkhnaya Chasouina and landing near the station, carrying out a reconnaissance on the way. The detachment had in the meantime arrived there by rail, but having left behind a Farman 30 and a Voisin that had not been loaded on railcars in time and had fallen into Soviet hands. On 12 and 13 September Dedulin carried out more reconnaissances from this station, though on the second flight he ran out of fuel and was forced to land near Chelna station. The next day the aircraft was loaded onto a railcar and returned to the detachment, which in the meantime had reached Bugulma. Aerial activity had now ceased due to lack of fuel and because of the distance from the Front. Altogether during its time at the Volga front, Nieuport 21 (1940) had carried out four flights, totalling 4hr 15mn.

The second aviation unit of the Czech forces to fight the Soviets was the 33rd Hussite Aviation Detachment. It entered the fighting in mid-July 1918 at the beginning of the Ekaterinbourg offensive on the Urals front. Out of the total of nine aircraft with which it was equipped, three were Nieuports: a Nieuport 17 (N4214), a Nieuport 27 (N4000) of French origin, and a Nieuport 10 (1136) constructed at the Duks factory. These were off-loaded from their railway wagons and reassembled. Operations began on 14 July with a reconnaissance by Ensign P. Vladimirov in Nieuport 17 (N4214). Four days later, Vladimirov carried out a patrol in the same aircraft and dropped a bomb on the station at Mikhailovskaya. Following this the Bolsheviks evacuated the town, and the Czechs moved in the following day. Vladimirov carried out a reconnaissance on 5 August in the Nieuport 17, which merely served to confirm the fact that the Nieuport was unsuited for the task due to its poor downward view. By August the unit had moved to a new base near Uktus station, with two Farmans, a Voisin and the Nieuport.

Activities on the Ural front began again in the autumn, and scout missions were carried out in addition to reconnaissance and bombing; but the extent of these operations was not recorded. Vladimirov flew in the Nieuport 17 a few times during the beginning of October, and he was flying this machine on 15 October 1918 when he attacked a Soviet Sopwith of the First Detachment of Irkovtsk. But his machine-gun jammed after firing forty-three bullets, and the enemy aircraft escaped. Nevertheless, his aim must have been good, as some forty bullet holes were counted in the Soviet plane after it had landed – though despite this the crew were unhurt. The following day Vladimirov was killed when he attacked a Sopwith two-seater of the First Aviation Group of Tvessk near Shamary station, this being the first Soviet aerial victory. When the Czechs left the northern Urals front in April 1919, the 33rd Hussite Aviation Detachment was incorporated into the White Russian Army under Admiral Kolchak.

Nieuport 21 (1940) at Omsk, probably in May/June 1919. NTM Prague

Nieuport 23 (3598), probably at Prague in 1919. Zdenek Cejka collection

Meanwhile, after the collapse of the Volga front, the Aviation Detachment of the Hussite Fusiliers was withdrawn, with just one Duks-built Nieuport 21 (1359). In mid-November 1918 it was given two other aircraft, a Farman 30 from the 33rd Detachment and a Nieuport 21 (1359) from the First Russian Aircraft Park at Tcheliabinsk. The unit gradually retreated along the Trans-Siberian railway over the next six months, ending at Omsk in March 1919, where a pilot school was set up. It was placed under the orders of the general staff of the Czech forces in Russia as an aviation detachment of the Czech army. Aerial activity began there on 27 April 1919 when Dedulin carried out a test flight in a Duks-built Nieuport 21 (1940). On 3 May he tested two other aircraft, and the pilot school became operational three days later. To start with, the Farman 30 was used for training, and the Nieuport 21 (1940) was used by Dedulin as his personal mount in which he performed aerobatics.

In the second half of May, Sgt F. Hánek was transferred from the pilot school to the Third Czech Division of Fusiliers on the Krasnoyarsk front, with a second Nieuport 21 (1359). Against expert advice he was ordered to take off in a strong wind, and crashed. Thereupon aerial activities ceased, and the unserviceable Nieuport was dismantled for repatriation. Between the end of May and early June, the pilot school was reinforced by the arrival of a Czech squadron from Vladivostock. It was equipped with five LWF Type V two-seaters supplied by the United States, which were used for elementary training and practice. The Nieuport 21 (1359) and the Farman 30 were written off on 24 May.

At the beginning of August 1919, the unit left Omsk and continued on the railway to the east; two weeks later it arrived at Nikovsk Ussuryisk, and the pilot school was re-established here on 19 September 1919. The two remaining Nieuports were declared fit for service during the second half of October following the repair of Nieuport 21 (1940), but this aircraft crashed at the beginning of November during its first flight after repair. Although it was again repaired, it did not fly again. Altogether Nieuport 21 (1940) was credited with twenty-six flights with a total duration of 18hr 59min, of which twenty-two flights with the pilot school contributed 14hr 44min. Nieuport 21 (1359) was accredited with six flights lasting 3hr 50min. At the beginning of December, the training flights ceased because of bad weather. One month later, on 10 January 1920, the unit left Vladivostok by ship and began its return to Czechoslovakia. The Nieuport 21 and the Farman 30 were abandoned in Russia, but the LWFs were shipped back later.

The only Nieuport that ever served in the Czech Military Aviation arrived in Czechoslovakia on 27 May 1919, when a Ukrainian pilot Rudorfer flew to Kosice in eastern Slovakia. The Nieuport 23 was adopted by the Second Aviation Company, and was sent in combat against the Soviet Hungarian Republic. By 3 June it had returned from the Front to Uheerske Hradiste. On 8 July 1919 it was transferred to the aviation depot in Prague, and was given the number 3598, which was painted under the wings. The machine was badly damaged in an accident when the undercarriage collapsed in a crash. After a wrangle over ownership, the Nieuport was bought by Ukrainian authorities, along with two LVGs and a Lloyd. The aircraft was repaired at the Main Aircraft Works at Olomouc in November 1922. It was eventually written off on 19 February 1925 and its engine retained for spares – even though there were no aircraft on the inventory to which it could be fitted. This Nieuport had flown just 6hr 34min in Czechoslovakia.

Nieuports were part of an order for 318 aircraft from French war surplus stocks, and in the spring of 1920 the Czechs expected to receive ten 80hp Nieuports for training purposes; however the order was cancelled.

Latvia

Following Latvia's declaration of independence on 18 November 1918, the country was immediately invaded by Bolshevik forces intent on restoring Russian dominance. Getting no help from their ethnic Germans, the provisional government was forced to relocate from Riga to Liepaja, and then to flee to safety on board an RN ship in Liepaja harbour. The German forces still in Latvia at that time formed a puppet government in Liepaja, and with the aid of Latvian military forces managed to evict the Bolsheviks from Riga and into the northern area of Vidzerne, from where they were removed by a joint Latvian and Estonian force. Having removed the Russians, a combined Latvian and Estonian force, with the backing of the Royal Navy and under the orders of the Allied Military Commission, then turned on the Germans and forced them to withdraw, thereby restoring the legitimate Latvian government.

A Latvian armed force was formed shortly after the declaration of independence, and on 7 June 1919 Lt A. Valleika was instructed to organize a Latvian Army Aviation Group. Within two weeks a group of fourteen officers and ninety-five other ranks had been got together awaiting aircraft. The group were joined by three Latvian pilots who had defected from the Soviets with their Nieuports during May – though unfortunately the aircraft had been seized by German forces when they landed at the Peterfelde airstrip. Nevertheless the Latvians managed to seize these back, together with some former Bolshevik Sopwith 1½-Strutters whilst they were in transit to the Narva front. As the Germans were still fighting the Bolsheviks, the Allied Military Mission intervened and ruled that the Latvians could only retain one of each. In this way one Strutter and one Nieuport 24*bis* (formerly 4300) became the first aircraft in Latvian service, the latter being given the Latvian serial No. 1. This aircraft carried out its first mission against its former owners when Sgt J. Prieditis, who had defected from the Bolsheviks, carried out a mission on 27 August 1919, dropping seven bombs on a railway station. Eventually eleven Nieuport 24/24*bis* fighters served with the Latvian air force.

Estonia

Seizing the chance offered by the Bolshevik revolution, Estonia declared independence from Russia on 24 February 1918. However, the country was still occupied by German forces intent on retaining some influence in the area, and when peace negotiations with the Bolsheviks stalled, the Germans took control in Latvia and southern Estonia. The Armistice on 11 November 1918 led to the formation of a provisional Estonian government, and immediate steps were taken to form an army, including an Aviation Company. The latter was first commanded by Lt A. Roose, but Ensign J. Ots, a former Russian naval pilot, succeeded him in December 1918. Attempts at negotiating for equipment with the Germans prior to their withdrawal proved unsuccessful. The Estonians did, however, find the remains of fourteen wrecked aircraft of German and Russian origin at Tallinin and Haapsalu.

A Bolshevik offensive launched on 22 November 1918 led to much of the country being occupied. Over the following fifteen months fighting occurred between the various factions occupying the country, including Germans, Bolsheviks, White Russians and renegade ethnic Germans. During this time the Aviation Company operated a motley collection of aircraft that had been found, captured, or supplied by the Allies, including Britain and Finland. By the time

Estonian Nieuport 11, probably Duks-built. Philip Jarrett

the peace treaty was signed on 2 February 1920, there was a total of forty aircraft on the inventory, of which twelve were operational. Amongst these were two captured Nieuport 24*bis* (4287 and 4306), which were allocated Estonian serials 42 and 43. Several other Nieuports were acquired in 1919 from stocks intended for the White Russian North-West Army. These consisted of a Nieuport 23 (44), two Nieuport 17s (45 and 46) a Nieuport 21 (51) and a Nieuport 12 (52).

Poland

After the Armistice, Polish patriots confronted Bolshevik troops in a conflict that lasted nearly four years. The Soviet forces at first gained the ascendancy, but when the fighting had finally come to an end, Poland had achieved its independence. Polish air forces during this time relied almost exclusively on captured material, some of which were Nieuport aircraft of various types. Altogether the Poles operated at least eighteen Nieuports, of which six were Nieuport 24/24*bis*, three were Nieuport 23s, and six were Nieuport 17/17*bis*/21s.

The first Nieuport to fall into Polish hands was a Nieuport 24 (5424). It was captured at Vilnius station on 19 April 1919, having served with the Bolshevik Third Artillery Air Squadron, after the unit's commander, a Pole by the name of Lt J. Gilewicz, intentionally abandoned the greater part of its equipment there. This Nieuport was unarmed when it was found, and was distinguished from other machines by a large devil painted on the starboard side of the fuselage. After overhaul it was allotted to Fourth Aviation Squadron. During May and June 1919, the unit commander Lt A. Jurkiewicz and Lt W. Willman carried out more than ten missions in this machine, involving reconnaissance and bombing railway communications and military targets. Following this activity, during which the aircraft was damaged by gunfire and suffered engine failure, the use of the machine was of necessity conserved. In July 1919 it was stationed at Lida, and the following month at Minsk. On 13 September, the new commander of the Fourth Aviation Squadron, Lt W. Komorowski, made what was probably the last combat mission of this machine. On 24 October, following a reorganization, the Nieuport was allocated to the Staff Headquarters of the First Aviation Group; but early in 1920 it was again allocated to Fourth Aviation Squadron. Due to engine failure over Vilnius on 24 March 1920 it crashed and slightly damaged its undercarriage. It was sent to the First Regiment at Vilnius and was last reported there on 25 June 1920.

Two Nieuport 17 or 23s (6176 and 4233) were captured on the Lvov front and flown to the aviation depot at Varsovie on 8 July 1919, where they were given Polish serials 11.01 and 11.05 respectively. The first had a varied career before being written off in an accident on 26 February 1920, when Lt J. Matecki of the Fourth Aviation Group misjudged a take-off and crashed, though without injuring himself. The second machine is thought to have flown only one combat mission, in the hands of Lt S. Pawluc on 28 July, and was believed to be the only aircraft available to the First Air Wing at Mlodeczno.

Nieuport 24*bis* 5086 was acquired on 7 July 1919 through the desertion of Lt J. Gilewicz, the Polish commander of the Third Bolshevik Squadron, who flew it to Nowo-Swieciany. He had intended to desert with his whole unit, but the plot was discovered and he was obliged to flee alone. The Nieuport was dismantled and sent to the First Aviation Squadron at Vilnius, where it stayed until August without taking any active part in the fighting. By 31 August the ancient machine had been reunited with Lt Gilewicz at the Sixth Aviation Squadron, and went with him to the Fifth Aviation Squadron on 7 January 1920. On 9 February, its tail-skid was slightly damaged during a forced landing following engine failure due to a lack of lubrication. It was not then repaired, as a replacement engine was not available. It was last heard of in May 1921 at Third Regiment, where the engine was replaced.

Nieuport 24*bis* 4301 was captured on 5 May 1919 when 2nd Lt Popov deserted and landed his brand new Nieuport 24*bis*, carrying single Vickers and Lewis machineguns, at the aerodrome of Fourth Aviation Squadron at Minsk. By the following day it was sporting the Polish insignia, and it proceeded to have a varied career. Thus, on 1 April 1920 it was at the Staff Headquarters of the First Aviation Group, armed with a single Vickers gun, where it was used to conduct combat missions. Then at some time in the middle of June 1920 it was dismantled and sent to the First Regiment, and by the following November or December it was with the Fifth Aviation Squadron at Przemysl with a new 120hp Le Rhône engine. After a brief test flight it left the unit, but returned later, and was still there during the spring of 1921.

A Nieuport 17 captured by the First Company of Polish Fuseliers on the Lithuanian-Belorussian front. T. Kopanski

Nieuport 24 (5424) captured at Vilnius, seen at Lida on 15 June 1919. T. Kopanski

Two Nieuport 24*bis* (4301 and 9252) in service with the 5th Squadron at Prezemysl airfield in 1921. T. Kopanski

(*Top*) Nieuport 24*bis* (4301), seen with Lt Ivan Popov at the controls after he defected to Minsk airfield. T. Kopanski

(*Middle*) Nieuport 24*bis* (5086) of 6th Squadron taken at Tarnopol airfield in 1919. T. Kopanski

(*Bottom*) Nieuport 24*bis* (5086), now in civilian guise with the Cracow Aero Club in 1929. The pilot is Jan Soktykowski. T. Kopanski

A Nieuport 24*bis* armed with a Spandau machine-gun was captured on 1 May 1920. It was piloted by 2nd Lt P. Abakanowicz, previously commander of the First Polish Aviation Corps, being one of four aircraft of the Szyrinkin Squadron based near Pryjamino and detailed to drop leaflets on the Polish positions. Shortly after take-off he had hidden in cloud, and eventually crash-landed at the airfield of the Polish Fourteenth Aviation Squadron near Zodzin, damaging its upper wing. It was sent to the central aircraft depot at Varsovie for repair, but its fate after that is unknown. Two further Nieuport 24*bis* and a Nieuport 17*bis* (1756) captured at Wolyn were sent by the Second Regiment to Varsovie for repair during September and October 1920. One Nieuport 24*bis* (9252) was then allotted to Fifth Aviation Squadron at Przemysl at the beginning of December, where it was reassembled in early February 1921. It was still there in an airworthy condition four months later.

Nieuport 23 serial 3191, armed with a Vickers machine-gun, was captured during the first days of September 1919 on the Lithuanian-Belorussian front as a result of the desertion of Lt P. Baklanov from a Bolshevik unit at Polock. It was operational with the First Aviation Squadron by 20 September 1919. In March 1920 it was flown to the aviation depot at Varsovie for essential repairs, and renumbered 11.04. A flight test was carried out on 12 May, and it was transferred on 27 May to the Mechanics School at Varsovie. Another Nieuport 23, serial 3751, was acquired at Wolyn in 1919. It sent to the Second Air Regiment at Luck where it was reported to be in excellent condition apart from a missing elevator. It left that unit during February 1920, and is probably the Nieuport 23 reported to be at the Pilots' School at Krakow between March and May 1920.

A Nieuport 17*bis* was captured in August 1920. It stayed with the Second Air Regiment until January 1921, when it was despatched to the Third Regiment, where it was still on the inventory on 1 July 1921. Another Nieuport was captured in the second half of 1920 and sent to the depot at Varsovie where it was given the serial 11.06. Afterwards it was sent to the Aviation Command. Yet another Nieuport 17*bis* was acquired by the Fifth Aviation Squadron at Przemsyl from the Second Regiment before 10 June 1920. It crashed and was wrecked sometime between 10 and 20 May 1921, and by June had been deleted from the unit's records. A Nieuport 21 was taken from the First Ukraine Air Squadron near Koziatyn during April 1920, but its fate is unknown. Another Nieuport was shot down on 1 May 1920 by Sgt C. Lagoda and Obs K. Szczepanski of the Fourteenth Air Squadron. It was sent to the depot at Varsovie for repair. Finally, a Nieuport 23 (4227) was used sometime during 1920 by the Advanced School of Pilots at Grudziadz. It was equipped with an engine cowling similar to that of a Nieuport 11.

Ukraine

Two Nieuport 10s (725 and 1046) and a Nieuport 11 (1057) were obtained by the Ukrainian People's Republic Air Force in 1918. That same year the Ukrainians also obtained three Nieuport 17s (one of which was 1437), two Nieuport 21s (380 and 1317) and seven Nieuport 23s (3224, 3226, 3240, 3241, 3246, 3247 and 3731). One Nieuport 17 was used by the Don Cossack squadron. In 1919 a defecting Czech pilot supplied Ukraine with yet another Nieuport 23. However, the Ukrainian AF ceased to exist in 1919 when the Ukraine was occupied by the Red Army.

Service in the Soviet Air Force

After the fighting had ceased, some 500 stored aircraft, in addition to those found at Murmansk and Archangel, were taken over by the Soviet Air Force. Other aircraft were found at railway stations and aerodromes. About 300 aircraft were captured from German intervention forces and from the various White Russian armies, including a large number taken from General Denikin at Rostov and Novocherkassk. The majority of these aircraft were various Nieuport, Farman, Morane and Voisin models.

Licensed production of aircraft continued in Moscow after 1917. Amongst these was a total of some 140 Nieuport 24s delivered from the former Duks factory during the period 1920–23. At the end of 1920, the Red Air Force had at its disposal, in various states of operational readiness and decay, about ten Il'ya Muromets bombers, about 500 fighters (of which 189 were Nieuport 17s, sixty-seven were Nieuport 24s and twenty-six were Nieuport 24*bis* types, the majority of the rest being Nieuport 21s, 23s and Spad 7s), and about 500 reconnaissance and light bombing aircraft, a few of which were Nieuport 10s.

Demobilization began in 1921 following the end of the civil war. One unit to go that was partially equipped with Nieuports was the Second Flight based in the Eastern Military District. By the end of 1921 a new organization was in place. Two new units, the Second Fighter Squadron in Moscow and the Second Fighter Squadron in Kiev, were equipped with Nieuport 24s and Spads. The surviving twenty-one detached flights were equipped with a variety of aircraft including early Nieuports, Nieuport 23s and 24s. Three naval fighter units at Leningrad, Odessa and Sevastopol were similarly equipped. At least eighty different

(*Top*) **A Duks-built Nieuport 21 fitted with a single Mk I Lewis gun in 1917. The clean-doped and varnished fabric and multiple cockades of the Duks' finish are clearly shown.** G. Petrov, via H. Woodman

(*Above*) **Three French-built Nieuport 24*bis* of the Red Army Second Northern Fighter Unit at Plesetskaya in October 1918. The one on the right (serial 5116) was flown by B.A. Schepotiev and is armed with a Vickers. The central machine is armed with a Lewis gun, whilst the one on the left (serial 5130), flown by N. Filatiev, is unarmed. The latter still has its French markings.** Harry Woodman

A Nieuport 17 or 23 of a unit of the Volga and Caspian Divizion in 1919. The extension to the exhaust system is a silencer system devised by the pilot Shuikov, who is sitting on the wheel. G. Petrov, via H. Woodman

types were in service during the 1920–21 period, including Nieuport 10, 11, 12, 17, 21, 23, 24, 24*bis* and 25 models.

A total of forty Nieuport 10s were still in service with the Soviet Air Force in 1921, and some of these were still being used by front-line units – the Fourth, Fourteenth, Nineteenth and Twentieth Flights and the Second Naval Flight – in 1922. They remained in service as trainers until 1925.

Eighteen Nieuport 11s were still in service with the Soviet Air Force as trainers at the end of 1921. By June 1923 one was known to be at the Second Military School of Pilots, and two at the First Higher School of Military Pilots. The last was written off in 1925. Only two Nieuport 12s are definitely known; one of these was with the First Military School of Pilots until it was written off in April 1925.

The Nieuport 17 fighter was the most numerous taken over by the Soviet Air Force, and in December 1920 there were still 189 in service as fighters. They were used on all fronts, but the majority were at Leningrad and in the Ukraine. After the civil war the Nieuport 17 was quickly relegated to the fighter-trainer role. Of the sixty-nine remaining examples in January 1922, single examples were with the Second, Third, Fourth and Fourteenth Flights and the Second Squadron, while the rest were distributed to schools. The last twenty-nine were written off in April 1925.

In December 1920 there were fifty-two Nieuport 21 fighters in all the military districts of the Soviet Air Force; but one year later only twenty-seven remained, and the following year examples were being relegated to training duties at schools for both pilots and observers. The last – around ten in number – were written off in April 1925.

There were seventy-two Nieuport 23s in active service with flights in all military districts. At the beginning of 1922 there were still sixty in service, with the Eighth Flight being solely equipped with the type; but by the end of the year most had been handed over to schools. At least twenty were written off in April 1925, and by the following year only one remained.

The Nieuport 24 was used by the Fighter Squadron in Moscow and by the First Flight at Kiev until 1922. The type was retired from the Second Flight at Kiev, and from the Fourth, Fourteenth and Eighteenth Flights and the Second Naval Flight at Odessa in 1923. However, by September 1923 there were still 125 Nieuport 24s in service. Nieuports served until 1924 as reconnaissance machines with the Twelfth and Seventeenth Aviation Reconnaissance Sections at Pervomaisk and Chita, respectively. The end of the Nieuport 24 with the Fourth Fighter Squadron at Minsk came in 1925, and by then the number had been reduced to sixty-nine. The Nieuport 24 was then relegated to the fighter training role with the First High School of Military Pilots in Moscow, the Strel'bom school at Serpukhov, and the training squadron in Moscow. Small numbers were given to local ODVF sections in 1924–25 for instructional purposes. Fifty-six Nieuport 24s were written off in April 1925, though a few soldiered on until 1926. The last retirements were from the Fourth and Fifth Flights, and the First Light Bomber Squadron.

In December 1920, seven Nieuport 25s served with units in the Ukraine and several were stationed in Kiev and Moscow in 1922. All were scrapped in 1925 except one that survived until 1928.

A Nieuport 27 in Soviet service, taken in May 1919. G. Petrov, via H. Woodman

130

CHAPTER SEVEN

Nieuport Aircraft in Italian Service

Nieuport IVG flown by Capt Maizo on 23 October 1911.

Italy acquired its first Nieuports in 1911, several being assigned to the 1st Flottiglia Aeroplani (Tripoli) with the Expeditionary Corps in Libya. It was on board a Nieuport Type IVG that the first use of an aircraft in the history of warfare was made, when Capt Maizo of the Italian army made an aerial reconnaissance of the Turkish forces on 23 October 1911. Capt Maizo was shot down five weeks before the war ended by Aziz al-Masri, an Egyptian officer serving with the Ottoman army, using an old Austrian cannon.

The Squadriglie Nieuport

During the first days following the declaration of war between Italy and Austria-Hungary in December 1914, Italian troops had advanced to take Gradisca and Monfalcone and establish a bridgehead across the River Isonzo at Piava. At the same time, alpine units of 2 Armata had captured Monte Nero.

At this time Italy had fifteen *squadriglie*, of which six were equipped with Nieuports, the remainder being equipped with Blériots and Farmans. The Nieuport *squadriglie* were 1ª Squadriglia at Venaria Reale with the Battaglione Squadriglie Aviatori at Torino, 5ª, 6ª and 8ª Squadriglie of II Gruppo at Pordenone, and 7ª Squadriglia as part of III Gruppo at Padova.

By May 1915, 1ª Squadriglia Nieuport had been reformed as a 1ª Squadriglia Blériot in I Gruppo. On the other hand, 2ª Squadriglia Blériot, which had been assigned to the Comando Supremo for the defence of Udine on 23 August 1915, had been reinforced with two Nieuport biplanes from 8ª Squadriglia Nieuport along with their pilots. More Nieuports with their pilots arrived later, and on 19 November five Farmans and four Nieuports were used to repulse an attack by five enemy aircraft on Udine. On 1 December 1915, 2ª Squadriglia Blériot was converted to a reconnaissance and bomber *squadriglia*, and its Sezione Nieuport were transferred two weeks later.

The remaining four Squadriglie Nieuport had been moved to Campoformido, with 5ª put at the disposal of the Comando Supremo and the rest assigned to the 2ª Armata. The four Squadriglie Nieuport were equipped with a total of twenty-seven aircraft. Shortly afterwards, 6ª Squadriglia was absorbed by III Gruppo, although the unit remained at Campoformido.

In May 1915, 5ª Squadriglia was based at Campoformido as part of III Gruppo, with five 80hp Nieuport monoplanes (116, 118, 122, 126 and 260) and one 100hp Nieuport (93). On 25 May the unit carried out its first bombing sortie, and by 5 June ten raids had been carried out, using 90mm and 162mm projectiles launched through a hole in the floor of the fuselage. On 11 June the unit moved from Campoformido to Santa Maria la Longa in order to carry out a bombing campaign against Nabresina. Three missions had been carried out by 23 June, and more followed on successive days. The first night reconnaissance mission was carried out on 8 July. However, the Nieuport monoplanes were obsolete and had been disposed of by 31 July 1915. In sixty days at the Front, the unit had taken part in 112 reconnaissance and bombing sorties. The unit was reformed as the 3ª Squadriglia da Offesa and re-equipped with new Capronis.

On the outbreak of the war, 6ª Squadriglia Nieuport was based at Campoformido as part of II Gruppo, and was soon transferred to III Gruppo. The unit was equipped with five Nieuport monoplanes (108, 111, 112, 259 and 291). On 25 May 1915, three Nieuports carried out the first bombing sortie, and for the next nine days the unit carried out other reconnaissance and bombing missions. On 11 June it was moved to S. Maria la Longa.

7ª Squadriglia Nieuport of II Gruppo was commanded by Armani and was equipped with five Nieuports (125, 223, 226, 227, 254 and 292), and a sixth (119) that came later. On 25 May it carried out its first operation with a reconnaissance of Venanzi su Salzano, and continued with reconnaissance and bombing missions over the next two months. From the beginning of the war to 31 July, the unit carried out twenty-seven reconnaissance

Nieuport monoplanes built by Macchi at Varese. Giorgio Apostolo

missions, a number of attacks with both bombs and flechettes, and was occasionally involved in combats. The unit was disbanded on 17 August 1915, and was reformed with Voisins.

At the beginning of the war, 8ª Squadriglia Nieuport was a part of II Gruppo at Campoformido with three Nieuports (133, 222 and 257). The first mission took place on 24 May 1916 when the three aircraft went on a reconnaissance mission, and by the end of July the unit had carried out forty-nine reconnaissance missions, dropped twenty-five bombs and 3,000 flechettes, and taken seventy-one photographs. The unit was disbanded at Clauriano on 27 August after carrying out a total of ninety-five sorties, fifty-two of which were combat missions.

The First Battle of the Isonzo raged between 23 June and 7 July 1916, during which the Italian armies made a frontal attack on the Austrian positions at Carso without obtaining any territorial advantage. Similarly the Second Battle of the Isonzo, between 18 July and 4 August, also did not lead to an improvement in the Italian positions.

After its move to S. Maria la Longa on 11 July, 6ª Squadriglia Nieuport took an active part in the Second Battle of the Isonzo, carrying out artillery spotting and bombing missions. On 20 June Comazzi experienced engine trouble while in Nieuport 112 and crashed; luckily he was unhurt, but his observer Giovine was injured. On 23 June, De Rossi di Santa Rosa also experienced engine trouble in Nieuport 108, and crashed it into a marsh. On 6 July two Nieuports, piloted by Comazzi and Rocchi with Zoppi and Giammarco as observers, dropped incendiary bombs on hangars at Aisovizza. On 10 July the unit was placed under the direction of the artillery commander of the VII Corps d'Armata. On 27 July it suffered its first casualties due to enemy action when Rocchi and his observer Cipriani in a Nieuport were forced down in the neighbourhood of Lago di Pietra Rossa; the crew were all killed. On 6 August, Andriani and Giovine were observers for the first firing of a 305mm howitzer on Isola Morosini. Shortly afterwards, on 27 August, 6ª Squadriglia Nieuport was disbanded, and later reformed as a Farman *squadriglia* based at Pordenone.

During 1915, aircraft of improved design such as Caudron G.IIIs, Voisins and Capronis began to replace obsolete machines. First of all the Blériots were replaced, and these were followed during July by the Nieuport monoplanes of 5ª Squadriglia, with those of 8ª Squadriglia being placed in reserve at Campoformido. About 500 Nieuport 10s were delivered to the Front, of which 240 were produced by Nieuport-Macchi, and the remainder were obtained directly from France. These machines were used as fighters in Italian service, with the front cockpit faired over and with a Lewis gun fitted to the top wing.

8ª Squadriglia was reconstituted as the 8ª Squadriglia Nieuport Biplani at Mirafione on 26 July, and equipped with five Macchi-built Nieuport 10s (384, 387, 388, 595 and 596), each equipped with two machine-guns, and went into training. It was placed under the command of Tacchini and transferred on 21 August to Campoformido, for the purpose of protecting Udine from aerial attack; it carried out its first mission on 25 August. On 9 September it was transferred to Santa Caterina to be nearer Udine, and on the same day had its first encounter with an enemy machine. During the second half of October, the unit received ten more Nieuport 10s (including 1035, 1037 and 1039), this time of French manufacture. On 19 November six enemy machines were intercepted over Udine by four Nieuports – 385, 386, 1035 and 1037 – piloted by Bolognesi, Tacchini, Baracca and Scarpis, respectively. One enemy machine, an Albatros B.I from Flik 14, was shot down into its own lines and its pilot injured. On 1 December, 8ª Squadriglia was reclassified as 1ª Squadriglia da Caccia and with 1ª Squadriglia da Ricognizione e Combattimento formed the Gruppo delle Squadriglia per la difesa di Udine.

The Nieuport-Macchi Parasol in the Squadriglie Artiglieria

By 1 November two Squadriglie Artiglieria, equipped with new Nieuport-Macchi Parasols, had been sent to Medeuzza to join 1ª Gruppo Squadriglia di Artiglieria; 2ª Squadriglia per l'Artiglieria was formed on 26 May 1915 at Pordenone, and placed at the disposal of 3ª Armata at Medeuzza on 2 July. It was commanded by Santi, and was equipped with six Nieuport-Macchi Parasol monoplanes (393, 397, 399, 405, 406 and 408). These were replaced by Caudrons by the middle of November after completing 206 reconnaissance sorties and thirty-three artillery spotting missions. 3ª Squadriglia per l'Artiglieria, which was formed at Taliedo on 22 September 1915, also moved to Medeuzza to join X Corpo d'Armata of the 3ª Armata under the command of Maurel. It was equipped with four Nieuport-Macchi Parasols (including 413). Despite the use of experienced crews, the Macchi Parasol was found to be difficult to manœuvre, and easily went into a spin from which it was difficult to recover; by the end of December it had been replaced by Caudron G.IIIs in all the Artiglieria Gruppo.

The Third Battle of the Isonzo took place between 18 October and 4 November 1915, and at the beginning of December, following the success of Austrian forces in Serbia, Italian troops were disembarked in Albania to open up a new front; this proved difficult, however, and the enemy captured Durazzo.

The Squadriglie di Caccia

There was a change of nomenclature on 1 December 1915 in which *squadriglie* were classified in terms of their functions: Offesa (offence), Ricognizione e Combattimento (reconnaissance and bombing), da Artiglieria (artillery support) and da Caccia (scout). Units not equipped with Nieuports consisted of five *squadriglie* under the battalion commander, four in I Gruppo, two in II Gruppo, five and a *sezione* in III Gruppo, attached to 3ª, 2ª and 1ª Armata respectively, and five in Gruppo Aviazione per Artiglieria.

Under these new classifications, on 1 December 1915 the aircraft and crew members of 8ª Squadriglia Nieuport at Santa Caterina became 1ª Squadriglia Caccia and was placed under the Gruppo Squadriglia per Difesa di Udine, along with a Farman *squadriglia*. It became independent at the beginning of 1916, and in February received its first Nieuport 11; by 31 March it had eleven Nieuports with 80hp Le Rhône engines. On 7 April 1916, Baracca in a Nieuport 11 (1451) and Tacchini in a Nieuport 10 forced down a Brandenburg C.I 61.57 of Flik 19. A second Brandenburg 61.59 of Flik 2 was brought down by Bolognesi and Tacchini, and the crew were taken prisoner. Although further combats took place between the unit's Farmans and the enemy, the Nieuports gained no further victories before 15 April when the unit was reclassified as 70ª Squadriglia.

Preparations began at Mirafiore towards the end of 1915 to form the 2ª Squadriglia Caccia, which officially came into existence on 31 January 1916 and was ready for active service on 9 February. Commanded by Chiaperotti, it was equipped with two 80hp Nieuport monoplanes (658 and 679), a Nieuport 18m^2 monoplane (1040) and five Nieuport 10s (1263 to 1267). Its first mission took place on 18 February, when three Nieuports, including 1263, escorted Caproni bombers on the famous bombing raid on Lubiana, and during the mission were successful in driving off three Aviatiks that tried to attack the formation.

Nieuport-Macchi Parasol as used by 1ª and 2ª Squadriglia per l'Artiglieria at Medeuzza and Pordenone. Giorgio Apostolo

Nieuport-Macchi 10 of 1ª Squadriglia Caccia at Aviano. Philip Jarrett

On 2 March 1916, 2ª Squadriglia Caccia was transferred to Cascina Farello under I Gruppo to help protect the coastline from enemy incursions; but aerial activity was severely curtailed by bad weather. However, S. Amico did manage to test a Nieuport monoplane (1452) in a flight to the airfield at Pordenone. The Squadriglia carried out a number of scouting patrols during March and April; also, on 2 April Barattini and Moretto attacked an enemy machine, probably Brandenburg C.I 26.02 of Flik 12, and forced it to crash and catch fire near the monastery of Cascina Bianca, killing the crew. On 6 April, three of the Squadriglia's Nieuports were in combat with two Austrian seaplanes (L47 and L73), which were attacking an Italian destroyer off the Trieste Station. By the end of April the unit had an inventory of six 80hp Nieuports, and on 8 June the unit was renamed 71ª Squadriglia.

Between 1 and 30 March 1916 the Fifth Battle of the Isonzo took place, motivated by an attempt by the Italians to cause a diversion to prevent the Austrians from reinforcing the Germans in the fighting around Verdun. The offensive was carried out by 3ª Armata, but ended after eighteen days without any significant advantage having been gained by either side. The *armata* was supported by eight Nieuports of 2ª Squadriglia Caccia based at Cascina Farello.

The eleven Nieuports of 1ª Squadriglia Caccia were held in reserve at Campoformido and took no part in this campaign. Baracca, who became Italy's leading fighter pilot, achieved the first Italian victory on 7 April 1916 when he destroyed a Brandenburg C.I over Medeuzza.

The *Squadriglie* Reorganization

A radical change in the system of numbering *squadriglie* became effective on 8 April 1916. Numbers 1 to 24 were allocated to bombing *squadriglie*, 25 to 40 to reconnaissance, 41 to 60 to artillery support, and 70 onwards to scout. The five existing scout *squadriglie* were given numbers 70ª to 74ª in sequence, the only two *squadriglie* equipped with Nieuports at this date, 1ª Squadriglia Caccia at Campoformido and 2ª Squadriglia Caccia at Cascina Farello becoming 70ª and 71ª respectively on 15 April.

70ª Squadriglia was formed from 1ª Squadriglia Caccia at Santa Caterina airfield near Udine under the command of Tacchini, and initially it had eight Nieuport 10s. But on 9 May, a severe storm blew the wooden roofs off three hangars, blowing the wreckage some 200m, and it badly damaged eight aircraft, four of which had to be sent away for repair. On 16 May, twelve Austrian aircraft attacked Udine and Cormons, and Olivari shot down a Lloyd C.III 43.65 of Flik 2 north-east of Gorizia. Barraca sent Lohner B.VII 17.42 of Flik 12 down out of control, but didn't see where it crashed. On 8 June Nieuport 10 (1480) was damaged and had to be repaired. Another victory was obtained on 9 July when Olivari shot down an enemy aircraft behind the Austrian lines near Salcano.

71ª Squadriglia was formed from 2ª Squadriglia Caccia and stationed at Cascina Farello near Aquileia. It was assigned to I Gruppo under the command of Chiaperotti with three Nieuport 11s (including 658, 1249) and five Nieuport 10s (including 1040, 1263 and 1264), the latter pair being two-seaters. During this period the unit was ordered to cover the Italian front against Austrian aircraft penetrating the line.

Two more Nieuport *Squadriglie* are Formed

On 14 May 1916, Austria began a surprise attack in the Trentino, with the objective of invading the Asiago plain to reach Vicenza, and eventually to roll back the main Italian front. The Austrian attack was supported by intense artillery fire and forced the Italian 1ª Amarta to withdraw in the Lagarina and Sugana valleys; and on 28 May, the Austrians captured Asiago. In response to this dangerous attack, the Italians transferred forces, including a *squadriglia* of aircraft, from the Isonzo front, and finally on 1 June brought the Austrian offensive to a halt. Moreover, a counter-attack was quickly implemented, which regained nearly all the lost territory. At the beginning of August, Italy regained the initiative with the Sixth Battle of the Isonzo when it captured Sabatino and Mt San Michele, and finally Gorizia. This victory bolstered morale, but did little to alter the overall strategic position, the Austrian defences remaining a formidable obstacle. Besides their scouting and patrol duties, the Nieuport 10s also acted as escorts for Caproni bombers in their sequence of attacks beginning in August 1916 on installations and communications at Fiume, Opcina, Gorizia, Trieste, Proscini and Dornberg.

An inventory on the 19 August showed that 70ª had twelve Nieuports on strength, eight Nieuport 11s and four Nieuport 10s, the latter in particular showing their age. Despite the frailty of their mounts,

Nieuport-Macchi 11s in 1916. Philip Jarrett

Baracca and Ruffo managed to damage another Brandenburg, 61.61 of Flik 19; however, it escaped to make a perfect landing, despite the observer being injured.

On 23 May, 71ª Squadriglia with seven Nieuports (1047, 1263, 1264, 1265, 1266, 1449 and 1766) was transferred to Villaverla and put at the disposal of XIV Corps d'Armata. There were several encounters with the enemy, but without concrete results. The first death in the unit occurred on 7 June when Ghelfi took off for a patrol over the plateau on an unauthorized sortie. When he did not appear for a training exercise, Chiaperotti went in search of him and found the remains of his aircraft spread over some 100m (300ft). On 8 August the unit became part of III Gruppo, at a time when there was intense Austrian aerial activity in the sector, resulting in numerous encounters, with the Squadriglie attempting to secure the skies over Vicenza. The problem was that the Austrian aircraft came over at an altitude of some 4,000m (13,000ft), and it took the scouts about twenty minutes to attain that altitude, by which time the Austrian aircraft had reached their target.

75ª Squadriglia was also involved during this period: on 20 June, an Austrian aircraft dropped a bomb on its airfield at Tombette, but it missed the hangar by 50m (150ft), wounding just a horse. But De Bernardi, Consonni and Nannini had their revenge the same morning when they forced a Brandenburg C.I 26.11 to land in Italian territory near Arpignano.

Two new Nieuport *squadriglie* were to appear at this time: 76ª and 77ª. 76ª Squadriglia was formed at Comina near Pordenone on 25 May 1916, with four Nieuports (1042, 1043, 1805 and 1806) under the command of de Carolis. Four days later it was transferred to S. Maria la Longa, assigned to I Gruppo where it was heavily involved in the escort of reconnaissance machines and bombers. At the end of June, the unit had seven Nieuports (1042, 1464, 1606, 1806, 3438, 2182 and 2206). On 6 August, Stoppani forced down an enemy aircraft while escorting a Caproni. On 24 August, Giori in Nieuport 1615 attacked an observation balloon, but his petrol tank was holed and he was taken prisoner when forced to land behind Austrian lines. His aircraft was repaired by the Austrians, given the number 00.27 and used for training at their airfield at Wiener Neustadt.

77ª Squadriglia was formed on 31 May 1916 at Cormina airfield, and assigned to the Comando Supremo based at Istrana; by 18 June it had been equipped with Nieuport 10s. Its first combat sortie took place in July, by which time it had been equipped with Nieuport 11s. During this month it carried out twenty-two missions and was involved in two combats, one of which resulted in an Albatros being brought down in Italian territory. In August the unit was transferred to Cascina Farello, and was involved in thirty-eight flights, mainly to protect naval seaplanes.

The Nieuport 10 Replaced by Nieuport 11s and 17s

By 1 September 1916, Nieuport 10s were being progressively replaced by Nieuport 11s and 17s in the fighter role. However, they remained in front-line service as reconnaissance machines with 70ª, 71ª, 75ª, 76ª, 77ª and 78ª Squadriglie until well into 1917, when they were gradually relegated to training duties. For these duties, the Nieuports were converted to dual control, and in this form the type survived until well after the cessation of hostilities. Of the 328 front-line aircraft available in September, sixty-three were Nieuports. Fourteen of these were with 77ª Squadriglia of I Gruppo at Cascina Farello under Capt Piccio assigned to 3ª Armata; fourteen were with 76ª Squadriglia of II Gruppo at S. Maria la Longa under Capt de Carolis assigned to 2ª Armata; and twelve were with 71ª Squadriglia and eleven with 75ª Squadriglia of III Gruppo under Chiaperotti and Scarpis respectively, assigned to 1ª Armata. In addition there were fifteen Nieuports with 70ª Squadriglia and thirteen with 78ª Squadriglia under Tacchini and Bolognesi held in reserve.

During the autumn between 14 September and 4 November there were three brief campaigns, called the Seventh, Eighth and Ninth Battles of the Isonzo. These had only limited objectives, and were mainly intended as diversions to take pressure off the Rumanian forces.

By the end of 1916, 70ª Squadriglia had been on 600 sorties and had been involved in fifty-two combats with seven recorded victories, of which here a brief record. On 13 September Baracca, although his own aircraft was hit, forced Brandenburg C.I 64.07 of Flik 28 to make an emergency landing near Prosecco. The pilot and observer were both wounded, and the latter died shortly afterwards. Three days later, Baracca in his favourite mount 1451, together with Ruffo and Olivera, were able to climb above a 180hp Lohner 43.74, and the enemy machine crashed and caught fire, killing both occupants. During the rest of September the unit was involved in patrol and escort work. On 21 September the first of the new Nieuport 17s (2614) arrived from France, and this was quickly commandeered by Baracca. The following month the unit received its first Le Prieur rockets, to be used for balloon-busting work. On 31 October two more victories were secured: the first was by Caselli and Rossi with the assistance of Stoppani and Tesei from 77ª over a Brandenburg C.I 68.25. The second was by Olivari, when he attacked another Brandenburg 68.14 of Flik 16: it crashed at Dobrova, and although the crew escaped from the wreckage, the pilot eventually died of his wounds. On the down side, on 11 November the unit sustained its first loss when Ghizzoni crashed after take-off on a training flight at S. Caterina. But on 25 November, Baracca scored again when he attacked the rearmost of three enemy two-seaters: this aircraft was Brandenburg C.I 68.03 of Flik 16, and it crashed in the area of the Chiarzo valley 8km (5 miles) behind Italian lines. The pilot died, but the observer recovered from his injuries.

Meanwhile on 26 September, 71ª Squadriglia was ordered to have four aircraft constantly available and on patrol between dawn and sunset to prevent Austrian aircraft from directing their heavy calibre guns onto the Italian front along the line Vallarsa–Dolomiti–Monte Maggio. Also the unit, along with elements from 75ª, 32ª and 35ª Squadriglie, was ordered to cover the Italian offensive on Pasubio. On 30 October the unit received its first Nieuport 17. On 4 December, 71ª replaced 78ª in preventing the movement of enemy cavalry over the plateau near Valsugana, in collaboration with 75ª and 1ª Idrovolanti.

At the year end, 75ª Squadriglia had seven Nieuport 11s (1646, 1647, 1649, 1654, 1688, 1690 and 1695). During the year the unit had carried out 361 sorties, and had been involved in twenty-four combats with a single confirmed victory. Although still at S. Maria la Lunga, 76ª Squadriglia was transferred to II Gruppo on 29 September, and put at the disposal of II Armata. By the end of 1916, the unit had carried out 624 sorties and been involved in thirty-nine combats, writing off six Nieuports (1650, 1683, 1699, 2111, 3128 and 3133) in the process.

In September 1916, 77ª Squadriglia, still based at Cascina Farello, flew 124 sorties resulting in eleven combats. On 13 September the unit took part in a large operation over Trieste involving twenty Caproni bombers, sixteen seaplanes from Venezia and Grado, and fourteen scouts. Later, during an Austrian counterattack, the unit scored two victories over Austrian seaplanes. On 5 September 1916 the unit was reassigned to I Gruppo. In October the unit carried out 109 sorties involving nine combats, during which it shot down an observation balloon with Le Prieur rockets on 18 October at Selo, and scored a victory on 31 October. The following month, despite having its airfield bombed, the unit carried out 156 sorties, with four combats. In one of these, on 25 November, Ranza forced down an Albatros. In December the unit carried out seventy-seven sorties and had five combats, but without victories or losses. Altogether during the whole of 1916, the unit carried out 526 sorties with thirty combats, resulting in the destruction of two aircraft and a balloon.

On 29 June a new squadriglia, 78ª, was formed, and mobilized at Comina airfield on 15 August 1916 with Nieuport 11s. It was transferred on 3 September under Bolognesi to the airfield at Istrana, initially with seven Nieuport 11s and one Nieuport 10. Its first sortie occurred on 9 September, and by the end of 1916 the unit had carried out 211 sorties and had been involved in eleven combats, but without any conclusive results.

As can be seen, for most of the year the Italian air force had of necessity to depend on obsolescent aircraft – the early French Nieuport scouts and Caudrons, Voisins and Farmans for reconnaissance and bombing duties, and French and enemy designs of engines and equipment. It was only with the introduction of the Savoia Pomilio reconnaissance machine and the Nieuport-Macchi L.3 seaplane that the Italians were able to achieve any sort of parity.

Nieuports in the Spring and Summer of 1917

At the beginning of 1917, Squadriglie 77ª and 76ª, with I and II Gruppo respectively, and 71ª and 75ª with III Gruppo, were equipped with Nieuports, the latter having swapped in its Aviatiks. In Albania, 73ª in VII Gruppo had a flight of Nieuports in addition to two squadriglie equipped with Capronis and Farmans, while two Nieuport Squadriglie, 70ª and 78ª, were unattached. Early in 1917, Nieuport 11s were serving with 70ª to 82ª in Italy, 83ª in Macedonia and 85ª in Albania, and some were beginning to receive Nieuport 17s. There was a hiatus on 26 January when all Macchi-built Nieuport 11s across all squadriglie were grounded for inspection following structural failures.

On 19 January 1917 new numbers were allocated to specialist squadriglie: 100 to 199 for home defence and colonial units, and numbers in the 200 series for Regia Marina units. During April there was also a total reorganization and reinforcement of the squadriglie under the control of the army. Not only had numbers of aircraft increased, but these were of improved performance and included Nieuport 17 and Spad scouts. This increase in strength was beginning to show some benefit: although little was gained during the Tenth Battle of Isonzo in May despite a great many casualties on the ground, nevertheless the Austrians no longer had complete mastery in the air.

The Tenth Battle of the Isonzo took place in May. The Italian objective was to take the well fortified enemy positions on Mt Kuk and Mt Vodice, but the Italian troops suffered heavy losses without achieving any significant gain. There were also hard fought aerial clashes during this battle, and again, the Italians could achieve little in the face of superior numbers. Also at this time – between 10 and 25 June – was the Battle of Ortigara, in which the Italians attempted to regain ground taken by the enemy in their offensive of May 1916. In this, too, they were unsuccessful and suffered heavy losses.

By August 1917, none of the thirty-one squadriglie with III, IV, V and XI Gruppo were equipped with Nieuports. However, of the eighteen *squadriglie* with VI, XI and X Gruppo, 70ª and 82ª at Udine, 71ª at Villaverla, 75ª at Verona, and III/83ª at Cavazzo Carnico were all equipped with Nieuports. In addition, VI Gruppo had 76ª and 78ª, which were equipped with Nieuports and Spads. Of the eight *squadriglie* with I Gruppo, 84ª at S. Maria la Longa and 77ª and 80ª at Aiello had Nieuports and some Spads on strength. Finally, of the total of twelve units with VII, VIII and XII Gruppos, Nieuports equipped II/83ª at Belluno, 79ª at Istrana, I/83ª at Salonika in Macedonia, and a flight at Tahyraqua in Albania.

The Eleventh Battle of Isonzo took place between 18 August and 15th September 1917, during which significant gains were consolidated in the Bainsizza plain; but despite massive air support by some 200 aircraft each day, heavy casualties meant that the offensive again petered out.

Looking at the unit records in more detail, on 1 January 1917, 70ª had at its disposal ten Nieuport 11s (including 1609, 1639, 1641, 1659, 1662, 1685, 1698, 1764, 2127), two Nieuport 17s (2614 and 3127) and one other that could have been a Nieuport 11 (1451). The unit continued to be in regular action during the early months of the year. Baracca, in his new Nieuport 17, attacked a two-seater over Castagnevizza, and after a long battle the Austrian was forced to land inside the Italian lines. On the down side, the unit had a casualty when on 17 January Gentili lost his life when his scout went into a spin and crashed.

During February, Austrian aerial activity intensified in the II and III Armata sectors, and 70ª was deeply involved. Four of the unit's aircraft intercepted Brandenburg C.I 27.74 of Flik 35 that was carrying out a photographic sortie in the direction of Udine around midday on 11 February. Casali had to return to base to refuel, but Baracca shot it down for his fifth victory: the pilot was taken prisoner, and the observer was seriously wounded. On 28 February, Ruffo in a Nieuport 17 (3139) attacked two Austrian aircraft between Gradisca and Cevignano, and forced one, Brandenburg C.I 27.56, to make an emergency landing in the lines. On 15 March the unit was reinforced by two Spads, and on 16 March Oliveri continued his series of successes by shooting down Brandenburg C.I 29.53 of Flik 23 near Canziano: the pilot was taken prisoner and the observer was killed. Two days later, Gorini forced down Brandenburg 129.04 of Flik 12: it landed to the east of the home airfield.

On 4 April 1917, 70ª Squadriglia became part of X Gruppo and was used to escort Caproni bombers, along with 78ª and 79ª. Photographic equipment was also installed in the French scouts for reconnaissance purposes. On 26 April Baracca, with the help of Gorini and di Imolesi of 79ª Squadriglia near San Martino del Carso, shot down Brandenburg C.I 129.17; the crew was killed. At the beginning of May, new personnel came in from other *squadriglie* and the unit was used as the nucleus to form 91ª Squadriglia. 70ª Squadriglia was left with a few obsolete Nieuport 11s and 17s (1451, 1658, 2173, 2175, 2239, 2614 and 2775), and was put into reserve until it was transferred from Santa Caterina to Comina on 28 October 1917. After carrying out some Caproni escort duties, the unit was transferred to Arcade on 9 November. Shortly afterwards the Nieuports were replaced by Hanriot HD.1s.

An inventory dated 1 January 1917 showed that 71ª Squadriglia was equipped with eight Nieuport 11s; inevitably they had mixed fortunes. On 21 January Menegoni was killed when the right-hand wings of his Nieuport collapsed in the air and he crashed to the ground near the airfield. The cause was blamed on slack bracing wires on his Macchi-built aircraft. Bad weather permitted only fifty-one days flying between January and April, during which time the unit was employed in escorting bombers and reconnaissance machines. On 19 June, Macchi forced Brandenburg 129.25 of Flik 15 to effect an emergency landing. In June 1917 the unit received its first Spad, and in August a *sezione* of SAMLs: these were escorted on their missions by the remaining Nieuports, which by now were obsolete. On 16 December 1917 the unit was transferred to XVI Gruppo, when it was equipped with twelve Spads and no Nieuports.

During the spring of 1917, 75ª Squadriglia carried out escort and patrol duties. On 10 April 1917 the unit was transferred from III to IX Gruppo. On 24 April, Macchi in Nieuport serial no. 1646 attacked three enemy machines over Levico, but without achieving a claim. Finally, on 11 July Ghidotti was fortunate to be unhurt when he made a mistake on take-off and smashed his Nieuport (2148).

By 1 February 1917, 76ª Squadriglia had an assortment of Nieuport 11s and 17s. On 25 February the unit was transferred to

Italian Nieuport 11s and 17s. Philip Jarrett

Italian-built Nieuport 17s. Giorgio Apostolo

Borgnano airfield where, due to its proximity to the lines, it was occasionally subjected to heavy shelling from Austrian artillery. Despite the obsolescence of its mounts, the unit continued to achieve successes. On 13 April, Arrigoni forced down a Brandenburg C.I between Tivoli and Skompass, and three days later Arrigoni scored his fourth confirmed victory since 13 February, this time over Brandenburg C.I 129.13. On the down side, on 14 May the unit suffered its first casualty when Broili was shot down in combat and killed near Ciprianisca. On 1 June 1917 the unit was equipped with Nieuport 11s and 17s, but from this date it began to be equipped with Spads, and from then on it is unclear which types of aircraft were involved in the many incidents recorded.

On 1 January 1917, 77ª Squadriglia was still at Cascino Farello with I Gruppo attached to 3 Armata. It was equipped with Nieuport 11s and 17s, and during that month carried out 103 flights with two combats. Two Brandenburg C.Is were shot down in February: 29.63 by Piaggio on 16 February, and 27.60 by Rizzotto on 28 February. During March the unit was transferred to Aiello airfield and received its first Spad. By May the unit had four Nieuport 11s (1627, 1680, 2113 and 2132), four Nieuport 17s (2613, 3135, 3136 and 3137) and three Spads, and was involved in numerous combats during that month although the type of aircraft involved was not recorded. On 25 May Marazzani and Cucchetti were killed in a Nieuport (2117) during a take-off incident. The unit scored one victory in June and two in July, although again the aircraft involved are not known. In August during the Eleventh Battle of Isonzo, 77ª carried out 398 sorties and was involved in twenty combats resulting in three victories. One of these was obtained by Leggiadri over Berg 38.01 in the vicinity of Vizovlia.

On 1 January 1917, 78ª Squadriglia had thirteen Nieuport 11s and 17s of French manufacture (1655, 1658, 1666, 1667, 1669, 2109, 2153, 2156, 2158, 2184, 2619, 3122 and 3126). On 22 January the unit lost one of these when Vola was killed when his Nieuport broke up. One *sezione* of 78ª was moved temporarily to Borganano under Rudini. On 19 March, Chiri shot down Brandenburg 27.55 of Flik 21 at Gallio, and the crew were taken prisoner. On 10 April, 78ª came under the newly formed X Gruppo. The unit had another success on 19 May when Bolognesi in Nieuport 17 (2619) forced down Brandenburg 29.70, which landed at Busche: the observer was killed, but the enemy pilot was taken prisoner. The unit then took part in the Ortigara offensive. On 3 June Bolognesi claimed another victory, though it was not confirmed. On 14 June Nardini in Nieuport 3213 shot down an enemy machine in flames over Val d'Assa, and three days later Magistrini in Nieuport 3126 forced down an enemy machine over Forte Luserna. But tragedy occurred on 27 June 1917 when Fornagiare had engine trouble in Nieuport 1664 and landed near Fossalunga. He made a temporary repair, but stalled on take-off and crashed into a vineyard, killing two women on the ground. The unit was assigned to VI Gruppo on 9 July, but remained just one month before returning to X Gruppo. On 18 July Nardini claimed another victory, although much of the credit should have gone to Magistrini.

79ª Squadriglia was formed during November 1916 as the Centro Formazione Squadriglie di Arcadia, and became operational on 12 January 1917, equipped with 80hp Nieuports. It was transferred to the airfield at Istrana in order to carry out patrol and scouting duties over the Asiago plateau, and was put at the disposal of the commander of the II Armata. Weather conditions did not allow the first operational sorties until 20 January. The unit was involved in many organizational changes. On 28 March, 3ª Sezione was detailed for the defence of Padova, and on 10 April the unit was passed to X Gruppo and later to VII Gruppo under the VI Armata. One *sezione* was detached to Bolzano near Udine and participated in the Tenth Battle of Isonzo. On 5 May 1917, Nieuport 3142 was completely destroyed when Attili crashed on landing at the airfield. During the first half of June, the unit took part in the Battle of Ortigara.

The same month Reafi in Nieuport 2110 claimed an enemy two-seater near Borgo Roncegno, but the victory was not confirmed. On 14 June, Cerutti scored the unit's first confirmed victory when in Nieuport 2269 he shot down a Brandenburg D.I 28.35 near Monte Verena. Several other victories were scored during the following days, but the type of aircraft involved are uncertain.

80ª Squadriglia was formed towards the end of 1916 as part of the Centro Formazione Squadriglie di Arcade; it was mobilized on 28 February 1917, and transferred to the airfield at S. Maria la Longa with five aircraft. It was assigned to I Gruppo at the disposal of III Armata under Gordesco. The unit had become an effective fighting force by 12 March 1917, when it was equipped with ten Nieuport 11s (2060, 2125, 2139, 2140, 2142, 2147, 2152, 2157, 2172 and 2174). Two pilots flew to Cascina Farello near Aquileia and were delegated to the defence of Cervignano on 15 March. On 24 April Keller shot down a Brandenburg C.I 129.04 of Flik 12: the pilot was killed and the observer taken prisoner.

On 30 April the unit was transferred to Aiello airfield. On 24 May the crew of an Austrian Lohner flying boat (L.136) were taken prisoner when Leonardi forced it to land on the water. On 16 July the unit was transferred to Comina, where its ancient Nieuport 11s were replaced by Nieuport 17s. On 10 August Esposti shot down a Brandenburg C.I (69.92), and on the same day Allasia shared a victory with a pilot from 91ª near Monte Stol. On 17 August the Eleventh Battle of the Isonzo started and Italian artillery fire carved up the Austrian offensive. The unit was heavily involved in scouting, patrols and ground attack work during this attack and the subsequent fighting at Caporetto.

81ª Squadriglia was formed as part of the Centro Formazione Squadriglie di Arcade on 20 March 1917, and was transferred to Langoris, also called Borgnano, west of Gorizia on 20 April as part of II Gruppo of II Armata under Calori, with twelve Nieuport 11s. During the transfer on 23 April, Ciotti hit telephone wires whilst attempting to land following an engine failure, and died of his injuries. The first combat took place on 24 April, but there were no successes until Sorrentino shot down a Brandenburg C.I (27.64) of Flik 2 over Vippacco on 1 May. Between the end of May and early June, Baracchini chalked up an impressive series of victories, claiming an Albatros and three Brandenburg C.Is of FLG1. During the rest of June the unit carried out 253 missions and was involved in thirty-two combats with two claims during intense fighting. On the down side, on 14 June Guglielmi was killed when on taking off in the afternoon for a patrol he suddenly side-slipped and crashed under full power just outside the airfield perimeter. But his death was avenged when on 22 June, Baracchini and Novelli, with the aid of Piaggio from 77ª Squadriglia, shot down a Brandenburg C.I (229.65) of Flik 35 near Staragora. On 9 July the unit passed to VI Gruppo and was put at the disposal of IV Armata. In July the unit re-equipped with Nieuport 17s, and on 31 July Buzio shot down a Brandenburg C.I (229.03) of Flik 32.

83ª Squadriglia was formed on 5 May 1917 as a special unit, with its *sezione* operating separately. 1ª Sezione embarked for Macedonia, and 2ª and 3ª Sezione formed part of the Centro Formazione Squadriglie di Arcade at S. Pietro in Campo at Belluno and Cavazzo Carnico, respectively. 2ª Sezione was assigned to XII Gruppo, equipped with four Nieuport 11s (2209, 2233, 2245 and 2262), and by 10 May it was escorting Caudron G.IVs. 3ª Sezione was assigned to VI Gruppo with just two pilots. On 1 September Dell'Oro shot down an enemy aircraft.

91ª Squadriglia was formed on 1 May 1917 at S. Caterina di Udine from pilots of 70ª Squadriglia in X Gruppo, with four Spads and three Nieuport 17s (2614, 3127 and 3138). On 1 May, Baracca engaged an Austrian two-seater 4,500m (15,000ft) over Punta Sdobba, and drove it off with the observer dead or wounded. In exchange, Baracca had three bullet holes in his rudder. On 7 May a *sezione* was detached to Aiello to join 77ª Squadriglia during the Tenth Battle of Isonzo. During May, the unit received another ten Spads. Nieuports are not again mentioned in combat reports, although a unit return for 1 September included one 80hp Nieuport along with seventeen Spads and two SVAs. On 4 January 1918, the unit was re-equipped with Spad XIIIs, but retained one Nieuport 27 and one Hanriot on strength.

Nieuports in Decline

In the late summer and autumn of 1917, the Front had stabilized. The Italian troops had established strong defensive positions, and the opposing Austria-Hungarian forces had become weaker over a period of time, certainly more so than had been assumed by the Allies.

On 17 September the Comando d'Aeronautica had again amended the *squadriglie* numbering system, though as 70ª to 85ª were allocated to Nieuport and Hanriot *squadriglie*, this made no practical difference to the Nieuport allocation. The changed situation at the Front meant that of the Nieuport *squadriglie*, 78ª was moved from VI Gruppo to X Gruppo at Udine, and 79ª from VII Gruppo to Truppe degli Altipiani at Istrana. As a temporary measure on 25 October, 70ª, 82ª and 90ª Squadriglie of the Comande Supremo, 76ª, 78ª and 81ª Squadriglie of Sottogruppo di Cavazzo, and 77ª, 80ª and 84ª Squadriglie of Sottogruppo di Aiello were brought under the administration of X Gruppo. By 20

Nieuport 11s of 83ª Squadriglia 2ª Sezione at Belluno in 1917. Philip Jarrett

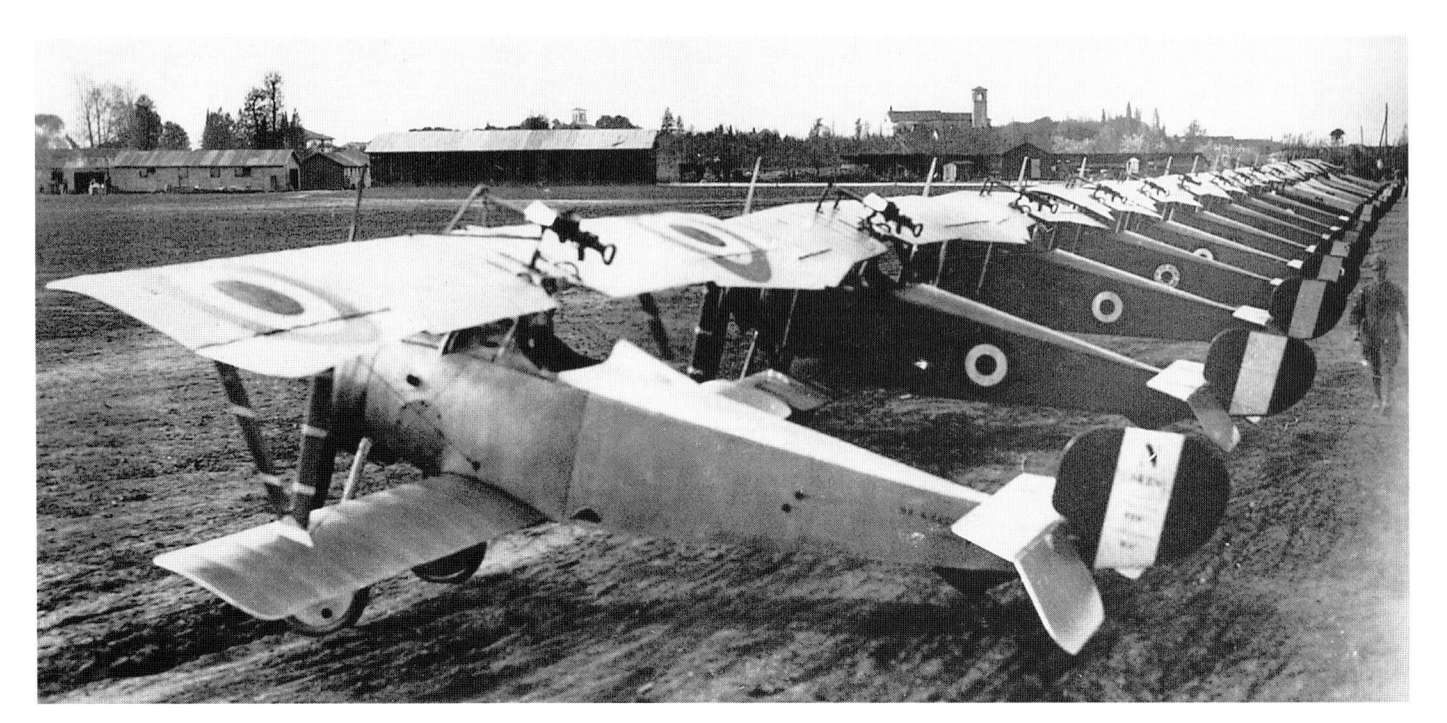

(*Above*) **Italian and French-built Nieuport 11s and 17s of 91ª Squadriglia at S. Caterina in 1917.** Philip Jarrett

Nieuport 17 (3127) of 91ª Squadriglia at S. Caterina in 1917. Georgio Apostolo

November, fifty-nine *squadriglie* and two *sezione* were available with a total of 378 aircraft, of which thirty-one were Nieuport 11s. Only 79ª Squadriglia on the Italian Front, 85ª Squadriglie in Albania and 86ª Squadriglie in Macedonia were equipped with Nieuports.

On 4 December 1917, the Austrians launched a new attack towards Trentino in search of a breakthrough, and at first achieved a sweeping success; but they came to a stop when confronted by the defences at Piave and Monte Grappa. The presence of French and British troops and two British squadrons of aircraft stiffened the Italian resistance – though despite the delivery of new aircraft, the Italians still suffered considerable losses. However, although Nieuport aircraft were not involved, British and Italian scouts won a considerable aerial victory when the Germans made a retaliatory attack on the Italian base at Istrana on 26 December 1917.

It was quiet over the whole front at the beginning of 1918, and this, together with the help of large quantities of munitions from the Italian industry, allowed time for another reorganization of the air force. The reinforcements included a large number of Hanriot and Nieuport 27 scouts supplied urgently from France. Some thirty or forty Nieuport 27s were issued to operational squadrons including 73ª, 74ª, 75ª, 79ª, 81ª, 83ª and 91ª Squadriglia and in the Defence Flight at Padua. Also Nieuport 24s were supplied mainly for training purposes. M.5 seaplanes built by Nieuport-Macchi were also received by the Regia Marina. To balance the despatch to Italy from Britain of two squadrons of scouts and reconnaissance aircraft, three *squadriglie* of Caproni bombers were transferred to the Western Front. Also some aircraft, including a flight of SVA scouts, were sent to Russia.

The Nieuport 27s were assigned to 75ª Squadriglia (which included a flight of Farmans) at Verona as part of III Gruppo with 1ª Armata, 79ª at S. Luca under XV Gruppo with 2ª Armata, and 81ª at Casoni with VI Gruppo. With an Austrian attack imminent at Caporetto, scout Squadriglie 70ª, 72ª, 75ª, 76ª, 79ª, 80ª, 82ª and 91ª were combined into a Masse da Caccia. A great deal of reconnaissance of the Austrian positions revealed the extent and direction of the expected attack, and defensive positions on the Piave were strengthened. The Italian scout *squadriglie* shot down a large number of enemy aircraft, and the reconnaissance and bomber machines continually hammered the bridges, footbridges and boats by which the Austrian troops were attempting to cross the western reaches of the Piave. As a result the enemy offensive was halted on 21 June 1918 just six days after it began. This signalled the end of the enemy war effort in the region, and victory over Austria-Hungary and its German allies. After the battle the Masse da Caccia was disbanded, and the *squadriglie* returned to their *gruppo*.

After the Battle of Piave, the Aeronautica in all zones had a force of 647 machines in sixty-five *squadriglie*. From these, 74ª, 75ª, 79ª, 81ª and 83ª Squadriglie were equipped with a mixture of Nieuport 27s and Hanriots, having fifteen, sixteen, twenty, twenty and seventeen machines respectively. There were also sixteen Nieuport 17s and Hanriots with 85ª Squadriglie at Piskupi in Albania, and eleven Nieuports and Spads with 73ª Squadriglie at Salonika. On 8 July 1918, XXIII Gruppo was formed with two Squadriglie – 78ª equipped with Hanriots, and 79ª equipped with Nieuport 27s – and was assigned to 8ª Armata at San Luca. It was disbanded on 1 August 1919. On 21 October, the *commandante superiore d'Aeronautica* reorganized the bomber, reconnaissance and scout *squadriglie* for the final battle of the war, in which six scout *squadriglie* were again brought together in a Masse di Caccia under the command of Piccio. However, none of these were equipped with Nieuports, and no further action took place.

By the end of the war the *aviazione italiana* had eighty-four *squadriglie* and sixty-four *sezioni* equipped with 1,055 aircraft; this included those overseas, and the twenty *squadriglie* and six *sezione* involved in home defence. Of the total of sixteen scout *squadriglie*, only 75ª at Ganfardine, 85ª at Piskapi and 73ª in Salonika were equipped with Nieuports.

We will now look at the histories of the Nieuport *squadriglie* in more detail. 72ª Squadriglia was reformed on 22 October 1917 at Castenedolo from a *sezione* of 75ª Squadriglia under the command of G. Rigone, and assigned to III Gruppo. Its equipment consisted of Nieuport 17s. Its first mission on 26 October was against the Austrian offensive at Caporetto. On 1 December it passed from III to IX Gruppo, and during the same month received its first Hanriot HD.1. By 1 January 1918, it was equipped with eleven Hanriots, five Nieuport 11s and two Farmans. The Squadriglia was involved in many operational flights and combats over the front, but the aircraft types involved were not recorded. On 1 April 1918 the Farmans went to 37ª Squadriglia, and by 15 May 1918, 72ª Squadriglia had eighteen Hanriots, one Nieuport and one Spad.

On 31 August 1917, 3ª Sezione of 75ª Squadriglia was re-equipped with Spads. On 22 October, two *sezione* of the unit were detached to form a new 72ª Squadriglia, while at the same time 75ª returned to III Gruppo. On 30 October the unit was reinforced by a *sezione* of SVAs, but due to bad weather, the unit was unable to discover the true extent of the Austrian preparations for the attack at Caporetto. On 3 November, Mancini in a Nieuport 17 (3685) sent an Austrian aircraft down out of control over Lago di Caldonazzo, having either wounded or killed the pilot. Encouraged by his success, Mancini returned to attack two more enemy machines, but had to retire when his gun jammed. On 16 December Campanaro was wounded in a fight over Vall d'Assa whilst escorting an SVA, and on 30 December Palpacelli badly damaged his Nieuport (3567) during an emergency landing when his engine failed.

At the end of 1917, 75ª Squadriglia had five Nieuports (probably Nieuport 17s), two SVAs and a *sezione* of Farmans borrowed from 50ª Squadriglia. At the beginning of 1918, the unit received its first Nieuport 27s imported from France. On the evening of 25 January, tired after a long flight, Mele wrecked his Nieuport 17 (3698) in a heavy landing. In February the unit received nine Nieuport 27s and a Maurice Farman. On 18 March, Consonni in Nieuport 5750 and Mancini in Nieuport 5838 were both thwarted when their guns jammed during combats with enemy aircraft. On 19 March the unit transferred to S. Luca. Meanwhile the unit, which had consisted of Nieuport 17s and 27s, was reinforced by nine Hanriot HD.1s.

By 1 April 1918, 75ª Squadriglia had handed over its Farman Sezione and two SP.2s to 61ª Squadriglia, leaving the unit with three HD.1s and ten Nieuport 27s (including 11326 and 11372) on strength. By 1 June the number of Hanriots had been increased to twelve, and the Nieuport 27s reduced to eight (including 11289). By 15 June the unit had been transferred to Buriago in preparation for the final Italian offensive at Grappa and Piave. The unit was fully engaged in patrols and many combats occurred, but the aircraft employed were unidentified. On 28 August a *sezione* of Hanriots with seven pilots was detached to reinforce 71ª Squadriglia. On 29 October the unit lost Sgt Bellina in a Nieuport 27 when he failed to return from a combat mission. On the cessation of hostilities the unit had eleven Nieuport 27s at Ganfardine (including 11318, 11327, 19748, 19758, 19762, 19763, 19769, 19812, 19815) and ten Hanriot HD.1s. During the last year of the war the unit had carried out 946 sorties and had been engaged in thirty combats. The unit stayed at Ganfardine until March 1919.

Squadriglia 77ª was involved in the fighting that continued through September, and on the 29th, Tesio was killed in a fight with three enemy scouts from Flik 55 at Medana. No further mention is made of Nieuports except that Ancillotto shot down three observation balloons between 30 November and 3 December during eight sorties made in an old Nieuport 11 equipped with Le Prieur rockets. By then the unit was probably equipped almost entirely by Spads.

Imolesi of 79ª shot down a Brandenburg in flames on 26 September, and Cerutti claimed another enemy machine on 26 October. Between the end of October and the beginning of November the unit received new Nieuport 27 scouts from France; on 2 November it was transferred to Nove di Bassano. On 7 November Nicelli forced down Brandenburg C.I 29.71 of Flik 24 near Fonzaso, and the crew were taken prisoner. However, Nicelli's aircraft was also damaged during the incident, and he was forced to land with a dead engine. On 24 November Cerutti, whilst escorting an SAML, attacked an Austrian reconnaissance machine, which was itself being escorted by an enemy scout, and after a brief skirmish the Austrian aircraft caught fire and crashed in flames north of Monte Grappa. The unit passed to XV Gruppo at the disposal of the troops on the plateau, and the *sezione* at Padova was restored to the unit. During 1917 the unit carried out 1,500 sorties and was involved in sixty-nine aerial combats.

In January and February 1917, 79ª Squadriglia was involved in the reconquest of Tre Monti on the plateau. During this period the unit received Hanriot HD.1s, and in March was transferred to the airfield at S. Luca di Treviso. On 10 March Imolesi was badly wounded while flying a Nieuport 27 and died three days later. The unit continued to score victories, although the aircraft involved were not always recorded. However, on 4 May Nicelli in a Nieuport was involved in combat with seven enemy scouts, and with the aid of a Camel from 66 Sqn RFC, shot down two Albatros D.IIIs. These were his last victories, as on the following day he was killed near Porcellengo when his Nieuport 27 (11353) broke up in the air and fell 700m (2,000ft) to the ground. During the second half of June, 79ª was incorporated in the Masse di Caccia in order to counter the last desperate Austrian attack on the Piave. On 17 June, during a low-level machine-gun attack, Olivieri's Nieuport (11363) was hit by groundfire and was destroyed when it crashed in the Italian lines.

On 19 June, 79ª Squadriglia had twelve Hanriots and five Nieuport 27s in its inventory. On 29 June, the Masse di Caccia was disbanded, and the unit returned to XV Gruppo; a week later it was transferred to the recently formed XXII Gruppo. On 10 September the unit had twelve Nieuport 27s and five Hanriots, and it was involved in intensive operations during the final Italian offensive. On 4 October Reali had his eleventh and final victory when in collaboration with Lucentini he shot down an Albatros D.III 253.51 of Flik 56/J south of Di Moriago, killing the pilot. But four days later the unit suffered another loss when Omizzolo was killed in a combat with an Austrian aircraft near S. Stephano di Valdobbiadene. Its last victory was scored by Cerutti whilst flying Nieuport 27 (19775) in collaboration with Chiri of 78ª Squadriglia. At the Armistice the unit was still assigned to VIII Armata, equipped with eighteen Nieuport 27s and three Hanriots. During 1918 it carried out nearly 3,000 sorties and was involved in 158 combats.

On 26 October, Leonardi of 80ª Squadriglia shot down an Austrian seaplane (K.212) over Lago di Doberdò. But on the following day the unit's airfield was overrun, and it moved as much material as it could and destroyed the rest. Four unserviceable aircraft were destroyed by fire before the airfield was abandoned. The unit had moved to Arcade by 1 November. On 6 November, Leonardi in a Nieuport 17, in cooperation with Rizzotto of 77ª Squadriglia, attacked a Brandenburg C.I (229.24) of Flik 12 that crashed near San Michele di Conegliano inside the Italian lines. The pilot was taken prisoner but the observer did not survive. On 8 November 1917 the unit became part of XIII Groupo and transferred ten Nieuport 17s by air to Marcon airfield where they joined with 77ª Squadriglia. At the end of that month, it had received the first of its Hanriot HD.1s, and Nieuports are not mentioned afterwards. During 1917 the unit had been involved in more than 2,000 sorties and 128 combats.

82ª Squadriglia was formed in March 1917 as part of the Centro Formazione Squadriglie di Arcade, and was mobilized on 11 April under X Gruppo with nine Nieuport 11s (1704, 2189, 2198, 2208, 2211, 2219, 2221, 2235 and 2236). On 25 May, 1ª Sezione was transferred to S. Caterina near Udine with seven Nieuports, and a day later Aliperta was in action over Trieste. By 9 June the unit had completed ninety-six sorties and had been involved in four combats. It was then involved in escorting Caproni bombers, right through until at least the end of August. On 1 October Aliperta, emboldened by earlier successes, courageously attacked seven or eight enemy aircraft near Tolmino in the direction of Udine. But the Italian pilot was badly injured by two bullets in the leg and had to land at Oleis airfield, from where he was rushed to hospital. On 28 October the unit was transferred, despite bad weather, to Pordenone with eight Nieuport 11s and one Nieuport 17, and due to Austrian pressure moved again to Arcade on 5 November. The unit began to receive Hanriots on 6 November, and had received more by the time it moved to Istrana on the 10th. Nieuports were not mentioned again.

During the Battle of Caporetto, 83ª Squadriglia transferred three aircraft to Feltre. On 6 November, Giannotti scored a victory. On 11 November, 2ª Sezione was transferred to Marcon, while 3ª Sezione stayed at Cavazzo Carnico; the two *sezione* were reunited under XIII Gruppo under the command of Bonomi. On 5 December, Carabelli shot down an observation balloon, and later in the day, with pilots of 77ª Squadriglia, participated in shooting down Brandenburg C.I (67.17) of Flik 32. On 8 December, Gianotti shot down an observation balloon at Grisolera using a Nieuport 11 with Le Prieur rockets. On 28 December the unit received its first Nieuport 27. 3ª became 1ª Sezione when 1ª Sezione in Macedonia achieved full *squadriglia* status as 77ª Squadriglia. In March the unit had eight Nieuport 27s (5826, 5900, 5851, 5913, 5906, 5889, 5917 and 5854) and one Nieuport 17 (3707). The unit was briefly unified at Marcon with XIII Gruppo before 1ª Sezione was transferred on 18 March to S. Pietro at Gù under VII Gruppo; 2ª was under IX Gruppo at Nelli with nine Nieuport 27s (5820, 5685, 5842, 5894, 5892, 5814, 5893, 5883 and 5821). On 23 April, Gadda of 1ª Sezione was killed in an incident when returning from a sortie in Nieuport 27 (5889). On 23 May three pilots of 1ª Sezione attacked a patrol of six enemy aircraft on reconnaissance over Val Seren and shot down Phoenix C.I (121.82) of Flik 11, the crew surviving. 2ª Sezione was later reformed, becoming the nucleus of 74ª Squadriglia, and was transferred to Pojanella.

During the Battle of Piave on 16 June, two pilots of 83ª Squadriglia shot down an enemy machine at Riva Grassa. Overall the unit carried out 262 combat sorties and 122 escort missions, during which it fired 63,800 bullets and dropped forty-two 100mm bombs. The unit then became equipped with Nieuport 27 and Hanriots and had a number of successes. On 1 August, Rossi and Galassi had a victory over Val d'Assa, and on 21 August three pilots shot down a biplane. On 14 September four pilots shot down an Albatros scout over Arsiè, and on 16 September Fougier claimed a two-seater over Feltre. Altogether by 18 September the unit had shot down seven enemy aircraft. On 4 October the unit became part of XXIV Gruppo united with 74ª at S. Pietro in Gù at Poianella. During the last days of the war the unit carried out patrols over the Trento and reconnaissance missions over enemy airfields. On 22 October Masala and Donadio shot down an enemy aircraft over Monte Veren. On 4 October 83ª Squadriglia was assigned to 6ª Armata with fourteen Nieuports. In total during 1918, 83ª was involved in 2,500 flights. By February 1919, the unit was under VII Gruppo with three Nieuport 27s and fourteen Hanriots at Pojanella. The unit was disbanded on 25 March 1919.

84ª Squadriglia was formed in June 1917 at Arcade, and on 2 July went to S. Maria la Longa and was assigned to I Gruppo with seven Nieuport 11s (3209, 2294, 2296, 2129, 2191, 2308 and 3244). It carried out numerous escort and patrol missions and combats, the first in mid-July being an escort of Voisins from 25ª Squadriglia and Caudrons of I Gruppo. On 22 July Fancello was killed in an incident, crashing into the airfield at high speed during a test flight. On 6 August Cabruna crashed but was miraculously unhurt, although his aircraft was destroyed. On 26 September the unit was transferred to Aiello under I

Gruppo, and a month later was temporarily assigned to X Gruppo at Comina. During the Battle of Caporetto, the unit was equipped with eleven Nieuport 11s, and harassed the advancing enemy despite its inferior equipment. Shortly afterwards, nine of the Nieuport 11s were written off and were replaced by nine Nieuport 17s and one Spad. However, the unit was disbanded on 11 November 1917 due to a shortage of equipment and pilots.

Sottogruppo Aeroplani di Borgnani

On 11 August 1917, 76ª, 78ª and 81ª Squadriglie were grouped together under the Sottogruppo Aeroplani di Borgnani. At this time 76ª Squadriglia received its first Hanriots, and by 13 August its equipment consisted of six Hanriots, six Nieuport 11s and three Spads. During the Battle of Caporetto the unit was involved in scouting and interdiction sorties. On 1 November 1917 the unit came under the direction of VI Gruppo at the airfield at Arcade, and on 10 November a *sezione* of four Hanriots was withdrawn to an airfield at Treviso. Nieuports are not specifically mentioned in unit combats from then on, but the Hanriots took part in the Battle of Istrana. One Nieuport 27 (5846) was reported as being wrecked on landing on 24 January 1918, which showed that the unit had at least one on its charge, but by 1 March 1918 the unit had nineteen Hanriots and only one Nieuport single-seater. From then on until the end of the war the unit was equipped with Hanriots.

On 10 August 1917, 78ª Squadriglia transferred to Cormon airfield to take part in the massive offensive on the Isonzo in an attempt to capture Bainsizza. This was unsuccessful, largely because the unit was having to use old Nieuport 11s, despite their commander repeatedly asking for new ones. On 7 August Buffa was killed in an accident during take-off in Nieuport 2303. However, three more victories followed: Costantini on the 14th at Assling, Fornagiari near Bainsizza on the 22nd, and Chiri at Loque on the 26th. Four days later Aquilino's Nieuport was badly damaged, and he just managed to get back to his lines. On 6 September Nardini claimed one victory during a combat with two enemy machines bombing Gorizia; and on 2 October Fornagiari shot down an enemy machine at Podmelec. On 25 October Veronesi was killed when he crashed into a hill near Jdersko whilst flying at low altitude in heavy rain. With the Italian withdrawal, the unit spent 28 October at the Comina airfield waiting for twelve new Hanriots, but their transfer was delayed due to the bad weather. Prior to the withdrawal, the unit had carried out 512 scouting missions, 456 patrols and 215 escorts, with 106 combats resulting in the destruction of eighteen enemy aircraft. Following their re-equipment with Hanriots, the unit joined VI Gruppo Cassia and were assigned to the sector of 4ª Armata.

81ª Squadriglia became part of Sottogruppo Aeroplani di Borgnano on 10 August 1917. In an inventory taken on 13 August, the unit had twelve Nieuport 17s, of which seven were serviceable. But the unit lost Pellanda in the early morning of 28 August: he took off for a patrol along with Sorrentino, but had to turn back with an engine problem, and tragically the engine failed before he reached the airfield at Blanchis, and he was killed in the resultant crash. On a more positive note, during the Battle of Caporetto the unit collaborated with ground forces, and successfully machine-gunned the enemy's columns and trenches. On 27 October, under pressure from the advancing Austrian forces, the unit left Borgnai for Aviano, transferring all serviceable aircraft by air. Following a series of orders, and then counter orders resulting from the general confusion, the unit was moved to Arcade on 31 October. During the retreat a Nieuport 17 (3625) was captured intact by the Austrians, and was renumbered (00.59). On 9 November the unit left Arcade for Istrana; the following day it received seven new Nieuport 27s.

By the end of 1917, 81ª Squadriglia had completed 1,650 sorties and been involved in 150 combats, with fifteen confirmed victories. On 15 January Rettori took off in Nieuport 27 (5802) for a patrol in the Alano-Rononi area, but was taken prisoner when he landed in error on the enemy airfield at S. Fior di Sopra. On 2 February, the unit transferred to Isola di Carturo, and then on to Casoni on 17 February, where they started to be equipped with Hanriots. On 19 March, Giacomelli was docked a month's pay when he smashed a second Nieuport 27 in the space of two days. On 1 April, the unit was equipped with twelve Hanriots and five Nieuport 27s. On 1 May 1918, Mellone was taken prisoner when he ran out of fuel and found himself obliged to land on the enemy's airfield at S. Pietro. In an inventory on 30 June, the unit's equipment consisted of fourteen Hanriots and five Nieuport 27s; after that there is no further mention of Nieuports.

Sezione and *Squadriglia da Difesa*

Of the twenty-seven *sezione da difesa*, only three were at any time equipped with Nieuports. One of these, 5ª Sezione, was formed towards the end of 1917. Following a fire on 8 January 1918, in which five Nieuport 11s (3234, 3237, 3240, 3247 and 3276) were destroyed, the unit was re-equipped with Nieuport 27s (including 5822, 5824 and 3276). Nieuport 5824 was lost on 22 January when Nelli, on transfer from 70ª Squadriglia, was killed in a crash. In March the unit was placed under the administration of I Gruppo; by May it had five Nieuport 27s, two Nieuport 11s and four Hanriots, and by July it had a motley collection of aircraft including two Nieuport 27s (11322 and 11342), three Nieuport 11s (1683, 1686 and 2149), three Nieuport 17s (3588, 3648 and 3659) and ten Hanriots. In August the Sezione was assigned to Gruppo Difesa Aerea Veneto-Emilia, whose duties included the protection of Padova. By September the unit had twelve Hanriots and four Spads in addition to its complement of Nieuports. The unit was disbanded on 21 December 1918.

The Sezione Difesa Bologna was formed on 15 June 1917, and was equipped with SP2s and SP3s. It was also given a section of three Nieuport 80s (2154, 2186 and 3206) for the purpose of carrying out night patrols, and at some stage it also acquired some Nieuport 11s. On 25 July, Sgt R. Gigli was killed in an incident involving Nieuport 1694. The SP2/3s were decommissioned on 14 September, and the Nieuport 11s were replaced with SVAs in October; however the Sezione was finally disbanded on 19 November 1918.

The Sezione Difesa di Brindisi was formed on 10 July 1916, but nine days later it was transferred for the defence of Rimini-Riccione. Originally equipped with Farmans, the unit was re-equipped during 1918 with Nieuport 11s (including 2130, 2235, 2253 and 2272). The only notable event that occurred before the unit was disbanded on 18 November 1918 happened on 8 July, when Natale attempted to intercept an enemy airship over Pesaro.

32ª Squadriglia Farman was formed on 15 April 1916 and equipped with Farmans and Caudrons; it was based at Villaverla. In July or August 1916 it briefly had a *sezione* of three Nieuports (1045, 1049 and 1051). 75ª Squadriglia was formed at Tombette on 1 May 1916 under the command of Scappis and assigned to III Gruppo and for the defence of Verona. It was equipped with five Nieuports (1455 to 1459). On 3 May a *sezione* was detached and sent to Villaverla with three pilots. The first combat mission took place on 11 May, when two pilots intercepted an Austrian aircraft attempting to bomb Verona; five days later an Austrian two-seater attempting to take photographs was also driven away.

On 19 January 1917 new numbers were issued to units with a special function; among these were the defence *squadriglie* that were allocated the range 100 to 199. Some of these new *squadriglia di difesa* were partially equipped with Nieuports at different periods. For instance, following the transfer of the Sezione Difesa di Brindisi for the defence of Rimini-Riccione, 103ª Squadriglia was formed for the defence of Brindisi: it received Voisins late in 1916, then SP2s in May 1917, and Nieuport 11s and SP3s equipped with Le Prieur rockets in August. By September 1917 the unit had one SP2, two SP3s and two Nieuport 11s, and at the beginning of 1918 it had three SP3s and three Nieuport 11s. By 16 May 1918 this had changed to seven SP3s and five Nieuport 11s. An inventory showed that on 30 June 1918 there were eight SP3s and five Nieuport 11s (3274, 2203, 3296, 3225 and 2214); but by the autumn of 1918 this had changed to fourteen SVAs, six SP3s and three Nieuport 11s. Very little activity took place; on 9 June 1918, one of the Nieuports is reported as pursuing an Austrian seaplane, one of thirteen attacking Brindisi, back to the coast.

108ª Squadriglia Nieuport was formed on 18 January 1918 for the defence of Milano, in cooperation with 122ª Squadriglia SAML; it was based at Trenno. 108ª was equipped with twelve Nieuport 11s, and 122ª received Nieuport 17s for night patrols. In March, 108ª received some Nieuport 27s, and by June was totally re-equipped with Nieuport 27s and Hanriots. It was demobilized on 30 November 1918. 110ª Squadriglia was formed in March 1918 for the defence of Napoli, and based at Capodichino. It was equipped with two Nieuport 17s and a *sezione* of SP2s. This unit was formed as the result of an incursion by Zeppelin L.59, which attacked the city from a base in Bulgaria. In the middle of March it received four Nieuport 11s (1451, 3228, 1675 and 2123): one of these, 2123, had been Baracca's personal mount at Udine two years previously. Shortly afterwards its obsolete machines were replaced by SPs and SVAs.

139ª Squadriglia was set up by combining two *sezione* of the Regia Marina equipped with Pomilios that themselves had been formed as the Centro Formazione Squadriglie di Ghedi in 1917. It was relocated to Cascina Farello and used for escorting seaplanes over the Gulf of Trieste. For a short while after its formation it was equipped with six Nieuports of French manufacture.

Nieuports in Macedonia

On 15 April 1916 the 7ª Squadriglie Artiglieria was renumbered 47ª Squadriglia; it was equipped with Farmans and based at Oleis. It was transferred to Macedonia on 10 January 1917, and by 27 February occupied Krumian airfield. On 8 June, four Nieuports formed a *sezione caccia* at Dudular under the command of Massola, and carried out reconnaissance duties. Mentions of Nieuports are few. On 16 August 1917, Bassio and Massola carried out a search for a missing Nieuport without success. On 17 August 1917 an attack was carried out by eleven Farmans, eleven French Nieuports and three Italian Nieuports. The unit had returned to Italy by 6 October 1917.

83ª Squadriglia was formed on 5 May 1917 as a special unit, with its *sezione* operating separately. Two *sezione* stayed in Italy, but 1ª Sezione embarked from Taranto for Macedonia on the *Savioa* on 16 May. On 1 June it moved to Dudular with one Nieuport (2273), and it received four others shortly afterwards. On 8 June it transferred to Kremsan, and carried out its first mission on the 22 June. Up to November the unit carried out 189 sorties and was involved in fifteen combats, with one victory in September claimed by Miracca over an Albatros.

On 10 November 1917, 1ª Sezione of 83ª Squadriglia was reformed as 73ª Squadriglia in Salonicco; it remained under the command of Bonavoglia, supporting 35ª Divisione. With two other pilots, it was equipped with Nieuport 11s and 17s and one Spad. It was stationed 20km (12 miles) south of Monastir. On 1 January 1918, Bonavoglia was gravely wounded and was replaced in command by Righi. In the early spring the unit received some Neuport 27s, and experienced varied fortunes: on 4 April one of these was damaged by De Biasi, and one week later another was written off in bad weather when it suffered engine failure and crashed outside the airfield boundary. On 25 May the unit became part of the new XXI Gruppo, and that spring began to operate another Spad. On 26 June, Randi in a Nieuport 27 was forced to land outside the airfield boundary due to engine failure. The unit suffered many problems with the quality of materials and scarcity of parts, particularly with the Nieuport 27. Nevertheless it carried out 384 sorties, and was involved in twenty-seven aerial combats. It returned to Italy in August 1919 to disband.

Nieuports in Albania

A Nieuport *sezione* was formed on 23 September 1916 at Durazzo with XVI Corpo d'Armata and transported to Albania, commanded by G. Sabelli with two other pilots. It was located at Tahyraqua, and was assigned to VIII Gruppo on 9 December 1916. Due to very poor weather conditions it did not commence operations until February 1917. By May 1917 its strength had been increased to six pilots. It was reformed as 85ª Squadriglia on 25 September at Valona under the command of Pellegrino, and received its allocation of Nieuports in October. During the course of 1917 it had carried out ninety-seven sorties and had been involved in three combats during October: Gerard on the 13th, Bacula on the 15th, and Cena on the 26th. In February the unit was transferred from Tahyraqua to Piskupi. On 17 April Cortesi was killed when he was shot down in flames by an enemy aircraft. That month the Nieuport 17s were replaced by six Hanriot HD.1s and by a further twenty-four Hanriots in May.

Seaplane *Squadriglie* of the Regia Marina

In the spring of 1916 the Regia Marina had two Lohner seaplanes at a base at Grado, ten Albatros seaplanes and a few other machines at Venezia, nine machines at Porto Corsini, one at Brindisi, four Curtiss on the *Regia Nave Europa* and eighteen machines at the flying school at Taranto. At the beginning of 1917 the Regia Marina had six Nieuport-Macchi L.2s stationed at Grado, eight L.1s and three L.2s at Venezia, five L.1s at Varano, four L.1s and six L.2s at Brindisi, and six L.1s and a single L.2 with the *Regia Nave Europa*. Throughout 1917, naval aircraft were increasing in quantity and quality, with increased numbers of personnel to match. The number of seaplanes on strength at the beginning of 1917 had increased to 115 by July, and 125 by August. These totals included two Nieuport-Macchi L.1s and thirty-seven L.3s in July, and six L.1s, two L.2s and fifty-five L.3s in August. These were based at Grado, Venezia, Porto Corsini, Varano, Brindisi, Otranto and S. Maria di Leuca, with the six L.1s and one L.2 at the flying school at Taranto. In addition to the FBA and Macchi L.3 flying boats, the units were allocated some Macchi M.5s for escort duties.

Those seaplane *squadriglie* equipped with Nieuport-Macchi seaplanes were concentrated around Venezia in the northern Adriatic, and Brindisi in the south, with some along the coast between these two areas at Porto Corsini near Ravenna, and Ancona. The activities of these units at Venezia were diverse, and included defending the sky above the city from air attack, photo reconnaissance of the upper Adriatic, including the Austrian ports of Pola and Trieste, and the protection of friendly naval forces. Also, operations were carried out against the ships of the Austrian navy, from small torpedo boats to capital ships such as the battleships *Wien* and *Monarch*. From time to time the units were also involved in directing the fire of artillery during the regular outbreaks of fighting along the Front. Sometimes the seaplanes were required to land on the sea to rescue their own compatriots, or even enemy pilots who had been forced down or whose machines had suffered engine failure.

The *squadriglie* at Venezia included 251ª and 252ª at S. Andrea, 253ª at Grado, and 259ª. 251ª was formed in April 1917 from the personnel of 1ª Squadriglia Idrovolante and its aircraft, consisting of FBAs and two serviceable L.3s. By 1 July 1917 the unit also had an M.5 (4867) on strength, and by the end of August the number of L.3s had increased to six. An inventory on 1 January 1918 showed that the unit had nine L.3s in service and three under repair, but three L.3s (including 3437 and 4823) were subsequently lost through accidents during that month. In the spring, the first of the new Macchi M.8s appeared on the scene. On 22 April, L.3 (7354) was forced down by an Austrian seaplane during an operation against the battleship *Tegetthoff*, escorted by destroyers. A similar fate nearly befell L.3 (4842) on 5 November, but it managed to land and moor under the protection of a friendly armed barge. By 1 June 1918 the Squadriglia had eight Macchi L.3s.

252ª was also formed in April 1917 and equipped with FBA seaplanes, but these had been replaced by Macchi L.3s by the second half of October. At this time these machines were attached to III Armata and provided with army observers and radio-telephony to direct the artillery fire of British and Italian monitors operating along the coast. Three L.3s (including 4827 and 4829) were lost during November. By 1 January 1918 the unit had seven Macchi L.3s on charge (including 7303, 7304, 7335, 7336 and 7353), but one was destroyed in a landing accident later that month. By 14 June the unit still had five L.3s available, and these had been joined by two M.8s. One of the M.8s (19018) was lost during an attack on Pola on the night of 21 August. The unit was much involved during the final offensive in October, directing artillery fire and bombing and machine-gunning enemy positions during the Austrian retreat. During these activities three M.8s (19012, 19014 and 19023) were damaged. During 1918, 252ª carried out 758 missions and took 4,000 photographs. It finished the war with five M.8s on strength.

253ª was formed in the spring of 1917 on Isola di Gorgo near Grado, from elements of 1ª Squadriglia Idrovolante, with an FBA and nine Macchi L.3s (3404, 3405 and 3407 to 3413). The unit was situated just 1km from the Front and ten minutes flying away from Trieste, where, using binoculars, Austrian planes could be seen taking off. At the time of the Eleventh Battle of the Isonzo, during which the unit carried out offensive patrols over the Front, the unit had one FBA, ten L.3s and two M.5s (4866 and 4868). 259ª was formed in June 1917 from 3ª Squadriglia Idrovolante at Venezia, with FBAs and L.3s. On 5 November, L.3 (4862) crashed in flames when shot down by an Albatros while attacking the bridge at Latisana. Altogether the unit lost seven L.3s during this period. On 1 January 1918 the unit had five L.3s on strength and by 20 March had at least one M.5 on strength. In September 1918 the unit received some new M.8s, and by 4 November 1918 it had four L.3s and four M.8s.

Between Venezia and Brindisi were stationed 263ª Squadriglia at Porto Corsini, which had been reformed as an American naval squadron, and 264ª at Ancona. The latter unit had been formed on 19 November 1917 from a unit based at the local seaplane station. It was initially equipped with fifteen FBAs, but by 1 June 1918 it had four M.5s in addition to eight remaining FBAs. On 5 September 1918, three of the M.5s combined to shoot down an enemy seaplane. 289ª was formed later at Varano with L.3s and M.8s, but was almost immediately disbanded.

The units at Brindisi, including 254ª, 255ª and 265ª, were mainly involved in protecting the convoys reinforcing the Italian forces in Albania and Macedonia from submarine attack, the interdiction of enemy shipping, and the bombing of Austrian bases along the Dalmation coast. 254ª was formed in the spring of 1917 from the Squadriglia Idrovolanti di Varano, and was based on the coast near Varano north of Gargono. On 1 May 1917 its inventory consisted of four L.1s, four L.3s and two FBAs, and on 1 June 1918, one L.1, eight L.3s, six FBAs and four M.5s. 255ª was formed during April 1917 at Brindisi from the personnel and equipment of the local seaplane station. It was initially equipped with twenty FBAs, but soon included L.3s in its inventory. On 7 June 1917, one of these L.3s (3440) was shot down by an Austrian seaplane. By the beginning of September the unit had received a *sezione* of five L.3s, and three more arrived in October. One of these (3427) was lost in an accident on 13 September, and an M.5 (7075) was lost on 25 November. On 1 January 1918 the unit had fourteen FBAs, one L.3, eight M.5s and a Sopwith. One of the M.5s (7079) was fitted with a 25.4mm cannon. On 25 July, L.3 (7388) was lost during an attack on Durazzo. 265ª was formed at the beginning of 1918 with four L.3s, and received more later. On 30 August 1918, one was shot down by groundfire when eight L.3s took part in a raid on Durazzo. The unit was equipped with L.3s and M.8s at the end of the war.

Two other Squadriglie, 256ª and 257ª, based to the south of Brindisi, were involved in similar duties. 256ª was formed from the Statione Idrovolanti di Otranto on 1 July 1917; unfortunately on the following day it lost one of its L.3s (3447).

On 1 September its inventory consisted of six L.3s – 3414 to 3417, 4847 and 4853 – but 4853 was lost on 16 September. The unit received some M.5s early in 1918. On 20 April 1918 M.5 (7229) was destroyed when it was blown by high winds onto rocks near the slipway. On 1 September the unit had ten FBAs and ten M.5s. On 7 November 1918, an M.5 (13040) collided with another aircraft and was lost. 257[a] was formed in April 1917 at Brindisi with ten FBAs, and transferred to Valona on 14 May opposite the Straits of Otranto to protect naval ships. On 1 June 1918 its aircraft were fifteen FBAs and two M.5s (7082 and 7083). By 25 October 1918 the unit had increased its inventory of M.5s to twelve, which were then transferred immediately to form 288[a] Squadriglia.

In addition to the units based at seaplane stations, 258[a] was formed in the spring of 1917 and embarked on the seaplane carrier *Regia Nave Europa* equipped with FBAs. In November the unit received its first two M.5s (7066 and 7084), and by 1 January 1918 its inventory consisted of two M.5s and eight FBAs. The vessel was involved in escort work, during which an enemy seaplane K.177 was shot down in combat, with two FBAs and an M.5. A second enemy seaplane was shot down on 27 June 1918.

By the end of the war the Marina had 103 aeroplanes and 241 seaplanes along the Adriatic, and a further five aeroplanes and 140 seaplanes involved in protecting transportation. A large proportion of the seaplanes were Nieuport-Macchis.

Scout *Squadriglie* of the Regia Marina

Nieuport scout and Nieuport-Macchi seaplane *squadriglie* of the Regia Marina were renumbered on 19 January 1917. *Squadriglie* used for offensive purposes were allocated numbers 200 to 220, scout *squadriglie* 221 to 250, and seaplane *squadriglie* 251 onwards. *Squadriglie* in the first range were equipped only with bombers, but both of the scout *squadriglie* had Nieuports at some stage in their existence. 241[a] was formed at Venezia Lido in the spring of 1918 with nine Hanriots and three Nieuport 10s and 17s (3699, 7430 and 7432), and began its first sorties in May. However, it was the Hanriots that conducted virtually all of the missions of escorting L.3 and M.8 seaplanes. 242[a] was formed at Sarzana on 4 April 1918 from the Sezione per la Defesa di la Spezia, and was equipped with Nieuport 11s (including 2125). The unit suffered a series of problems with these aircraft and their engines, and was re-equipped with SVAs during September.

At the end of 1917 the Regia Marina had a total of 119 aircraft at its main bases at Venezia, Porto Corsini, Ancona, Varano, Brindisi and Valona, and on the *Regia Nave Europa*, and a further 103 at the fifteen stations of the Ispettorato Difesa del Traffico Nazionale.

The first M.5s were assigned to existing *squadriglie*, but as greater numbers became available, a dedicated Gruppo Idrovolante da Caccia, or seaplane scout group, was based at Venezia, consisting of 260[a] formed on 1 November, and 261[a] formed in December 1917. In addition, 262[a] was formed at the beginning of 1918 at Brindisi. These units carried out patrols, scouting and reconnaissance work, 261[a] accomplishing sixty-eight such sorties in January 1918.

260[a] suffered its first casualty on 3 November 1917. However, on the 17th, the first victory for an M.5 was shared by two pilots of 260[a] over a Brandenburg (K.211). The Austrian pilot was rescued from the sea by an M.5, though he had to lie down on the fuselage decking behind the pilot. Two days later M.5 (7068) was captured intact by the enemy when it ran out of fuel while chasing two Austrian aircraft. It was flown in enemy hands until 23 February 1918, when it crashed in Trieste harbour. On 8 December 1917 an M.5 (7029) of 261[a] was lost to anti-aircraft fire. Inventories show that on 1 January 1918, 260[a] had five M.5s on strength (6059, 7058, 7071, 7062 and 7065), and on 1 April 1918 261[a] had eight M.5s on strength. On 22 April two M.5s of 260[a] shot down an enemy seaplane while escorting a bomber formation.

May 1918 was a very busy month, in which the M.5 earned its reputation as a seaplane scout that could hold its own with its land-based equivalents. On 1 May an M.5 shot down an Austrian seaplane, and three days later, five M.5s from 260[a] shot down two Austrian Phöenix D.Is (A78 and A91) and forced down another flown by the Austrian ace Banfield. On 14 May seven aircraft from 261[a] shared two victories (A70 and A85) but lost an M.5 in the process. On 22 May, the crew of a Macchi L.3 of 260[a] shot down Phöenix D.I (A115).

As explained earlier, in June the Austrians launched their last desperate attempt to win the war, and the Italians threw all their available resources into the battle, including the seaplane *squadriglie*. These units lost one of their number on 15 June when they were called upon to attack ground targets and kite balloons. Away from the Front, on 9 June 1918, a Macchi of 262[a] Squadriglia shot down one of fourteen Austrian seaplanes from Durazzo, attacking the unit's airfield at Brindisi and the naval vessels in the Straits of Otranto.

At the end of the war, 260[a] comprised one M.7 and ten M.5s, having altogether lost seven M.5s and one L.3, and 261[a] had one Hanriot seaplane and ten M.5s on strength, of which nine were serviceable. The bureaucratic process of forming *squadriglie* continued after the Armistice, but these were soon disbanded. The units involved were 288[a], formed at Valona towards the end of 1918, with some SVAs and twelve M.5s taken from 257[a] and 258[a] Squadriglie; 290[a] formed at Varano with M.5s and SVAs; and 292[a], formed at Brindisi with M.5s.

Towards the end of the war, M.7s started to become available, although only three were delivered by the time of the Armistice.

Postwar Service

As the M.5 and its variants had been superseded in production before the end of the war, its postwar service was not extensive. On 30 September 1919 there were still 242 M.5s, and twenty-nine M.5*bis* on the inventory, but only eighty-seven were serviceable.

On 28 March 1923, the army and navy air arms were merged into the new Regia Aeronautica. By then, the majority of the remaining M.5 seaplanes were serving at Brindisi, and the former Austro-Hungarian base at Pola. The 1923–24 seaplane programme had concentrated the remaining M.5*bis* aircraft at Taranto and Venezia, each with an establishment of nine aircraft, and had withdrawn the rest from front-line use. By 15 July 1924, all the M.5s had been withdrawn, leaving just a few M.5*bis* in service.

No M.5 was accepted onto the civil register, and the only competitive event in which any were entered was the Giro Aereo di Sicilia held on 14 September 1919. Only five entrants completed the course around the island, one of which was the M.5 flown by C. Cattaneo, which came second in a time of 5hr 18min 56sec. Another M.5 stalled and crashed into a house, and a third crashed near the finishing line, both pilots being injured.

CHAPTER EIGHT

Nieuports with the American Expeditionary Force and Other Air Forces

(*Above*) **Nieuport aircraft of the USAS Third Instruction Centre lined up at Issoudun aerodrome on 21 May 1918.** via Paul Leaman

Nieuport 80 of the USAS. Philip Jarrett

In 1917 Col Raynal C. Bolling, head of the Bolling Mission, was charged by the US government to procure suitable aircraft for the fledgling air force; in late August he therefore ordered 5,000 combat planes from France. A detailed selection had not been made, but it was intended that some of these were to be Nieuports. However, the strategic materials for their construction, which the United States had agreed to furnish, was very late in arriving, and so the planes were never delivered; as a result the contract was renegotiated in the spring of 1918. Furthermore, because of delays in the production of aircraft sourced in the United States, the American Expeditionary Force (AEF) had to take whatever the French were able to provide, when bearing in mind their own priorities. It also became evident by late 1917 that training in the United States would be limited, and that much would have to take place in Europe. As cadets became available and the AEF took over the airfields allocated to them, it managed to obtain a conglomerate of French trainer types and obsolescent combat machines, some of which were new and some old, and these were used to train pilots and observers.

In late 1917 Nieuport had not been successful in developing a scout that could have been considered competitive with other types on offer; some of the company's production capacity was therefore available to fulfil American orders, and so it was obviously in a better position to supply aircraft. As a result, the AEF were able to obtain many Nieuport trainers and also Nieuport 28 scouts, a type for which neither the French nor the British had a requirement.

As a result, the AEF in Europe acquired seventy-five Nieuport 17s, 197 Nieuport 21s and fifty Nieuport 23s (or the equivalent Nieuport 80 series) for training purposes, deliveries starting in September 1917 and January 1918 respectively. All but three of the Nieuport 23s had the 80hp Le Rhône 9C in place of the standard 110hp Le Rhône 9Jb. One Nieuport 17*bis* was acquired from French sources in October

147

Nieuport 17 '31' of the USAS, used for training purposes. Jean Devaux, via Stuart Leslie

1918, and although this was too late for the type to be considered for production, it was nevertheless sent to the United States for study. A British-built Nieuport 17*bis* was also sent, but its fate is unknown.

The AEF also acquired 121 Nieuport 24s, 140 Nieuport 24*bis* and 287 Nieuport 27s. Twelve Nieuport 24s, forty Nieuport 24s and seventy-five Nieuport 27s had 80hp Le Rhônes, and the rest had 120hp Le Rhônes. All but a few were used for training duties in France. It was not uncommon for some of these aircraft to be hybrids of the various types, due to cannibalization for spares. At least one Nieuport 27 was later sent to the USA for evaluation. One was given the US serial 94098 and was tested at McCook Field, where it was given the station identification number P-153.

The French came to consider the Nieuport 28 to be inferior to the Spad XIII, and it never saw service with the Aviation Militaire. Although the American Expeditionary Force (AEF) also hoped to receive the Spad XIII, because it was in such desperate need of aircraft it was obliged to receive Nieuport 28s instead, and took a total of 297.

The allocation of the Nieuport 28 by the French to the Air Service caused considerable controversy within the AEF. Benjamin Foulois, the Chief of the Air Service, considered it to be a second-rate machine, and advised Gen J.J. Pershing that he strongly disapproved of equipping any of his units with the aircraft. However, since the United States had failed in its commitments to supply the French with the necessary raw materials to manufacture aircraft, it was in no position to force the issue. And as it was evident that the Germans were preparing for a new offensive, it became a matter of necessity to take whatever could be quickly made available. In any case, while the American airmen were aware of the Nieuport's performance shortcomings, the more serious structural problems had not yet come to light.

The First Pursuit Group of the Air Service was the first to be established, and to begin with comprised the 94th and 95th Aero Squadrons. The units were based at Villeneuve les Vertus, near Toul. The Toul sector, which was relatively quiet compared with the British and French fronts, was chosen by Gen Pershing to allow his men to undergo training without coming up against experienced German units. Part of the training was to assign squadron members to courses at the various French airframe and motor manufacturers, including Nieuport and Gnome.

The first impressions of the Nieuport 28 during the initial work-up period were positive. Col W. Mitchell, who was overseeing the Air Service's operations at the front, reported to Foulois that:

> The Nieuport 28 with the Gnome motor has proved to be very satisfactory as a pursuit airplane. I believe that this airplane will not be obsolescent as a single-seater next year. I will therefore recommend that its construction and that of the Gnome Monosoupape be continued with all speed for the use of the American Air Service in France.

The first American squadron to receive Nieuport 28s was the 95th Aero Squadron at the end of February 1918, followed shortly by the 94th Aero Squadron. The latter received twenty-two Nieuports between 15 and 22 March, flown in by pilots of the 95th. The early deliveries of Nieuports to both squadrons were not equipped with guns, but unarmed patrols were nevertheless flown over the lines from their aerodrome at Villeneuve to keep up morale, the 94th making a flight on 6 March, and the 95th following suit on 15 March. Soon after that the pilots of the 95th were withdrawn to receive gunnery training, and did not return to the Front until 2 May. It therefore befell the 94th to fly the first armed patrol on 28 March, having in the meantime received enough guns to provide one per aircraft.

Unfortunately the 94th lost two of their Nieuports in a hangar fire, and several others were badly damaged. This delayed its move to Epiez, where it spent a week before being placed under the direction of the French VIIIth Army and moving to Gengoult aerodrome some 4km (2 miles) from Toul on 9 April. Five days later, Capt David McKelvie Peterson led 1st Lts Edward Rickenbacker and Reed Chambers over the lines. Peterson himself aborted his effort because of thick mist, but Rickenbacker and Chambers continued the patrol between Pont-à-Mousson and St Mihiel, attracting a lot of flak in the process. After the two Americans returned to their airfield, two German aeroplanes of Jagdstaffel 64, apparently lost due to the poor visibility, appeared over the airfield. These were intercepted by two Nieuports, N6164 and N6184, flown by 1st Lt D. Campbell and 2nd Lt A. Winslow, respectively. Within five minutes Campbell had claimed a Pfalz D.IIIa, flown by Vizefeldwebel Antoni Wroniecki, who survived badly burnt, and Winslow had brought down an Albatros D.Va flown by Unteroffizier Simon. On 29 April Rickenbacker in N6159 scored his first victory when he shared the destruction of a Pfalz with J.N. Hall.

On 3 May the 94th lost 2nd Lt C.W. Chapman. While his patrol was engaging four Albatros scouts, a German two-seater attacked him from behind and he burst into flames, crashing near Amerncourt. On 7 May, Rickenbacker brought down a Pfalz D.IIIa, and on 15 May, Capt Peterson scored two victories; after this, Peterson was transferred to take command of the 95th. He soon scored another victory when on 17 May he brought down an LVG C.VI of Fl. Abt (A)

(*Above*) **Nieuport 27 (possibly US serial number 94098), acquired by the USAS in November 1917. Probably photographed at McCook Field.** USAF, via Paul Leaman

46b over the German lines. 1st Lt P.B. Kurtz was also killed when on 22 May he was shot down just north of Gengoult whilst in combat with three Albatros scouts. Campbell, with 1st Lt James Meissner, destroyed a two-seater of Fl. Abt (A) 242 on 31 May. The squadron suffered its last fatality whilst flying Nieuports when 2nd Lt P.W. Davis was shot down in flames on 2 June; this was credited to Ltn Hengst of Jasta 64(w).

On 19 May, Maj Lufbery, the leading American ace at the time, with sixteen victories all obtained when he was with the Escadrille Lafayette, was killed in combat in a Nieuport 28. A German two-seater from the Reihenbildtruppe of Armee Abteilung C, crewed by Gefr Kirschbaum and Ltn Scheibe, crossed the Allied lines and was attacked first by 1st Lt Oscar Gude in N6185, who used up all his ammunition, and then by Maj Lufbery in N6185, borrowed from 2nd Lt Philip Davis. Lufbery's Nieuport was hit in the fuel tank, and Lufberry himself either jumped or fell from his burning machine to his death. The Germans were forced to land by Sgt Dupré of Escadrille Spa 68, though only after they had first managed to kill Adjudant Pierre

Two views of Nieuport 28s (N6298) under test at McCook Field, USA. JMB/GLS collection, and Greg Van Wyngarden

149

Two views of Nieuport 28s in service with 95th AS at Toul on 22 June 1918. Greg Van Wyngarden

Baudry, from the same escadrille. Then on 22 May, 1st Lt P.B. Kurtz (N6185) was killed when his aircraft caught fire in the air as he returned from a patrol; this was possibly due to weakness in the fuel feed pipe, a problem later to become much more apparent (and this would possibly constitute the first loss due to this cause).

By the end of July, First Pursuit Group had been credited with 114 victories, although the actual score was not so generous, consisting of seven by the 95th, twenty-one by the 94th, sixteen by the 27th, and nine by the 147th. Altogether the 94th lost four killed, three shot down and taken prisoner, and three others wounded. The squadron received a total of thirty-six Nieuport 28s before it traded in its Nieuports for Spads towards the end of July 1918.

It was during May and early June that a structural weakness in the Nieuport 28 became apparent. On 2 May, Lt J. Meissner lost the fabric from his upper wing whilst coming out of a high-speed dive, though he was able to control his aircraft (N6144) sufficiently to land safely, thanks to the ailerons being on the lower wing. On 7 May, Capt J.N. Hall in N6153 also suffered failure of the fabric of his upper wing: he was in a steep dive and about to shoot at an enemy aircraft when he heard the sounds of wood cracking and fabric tearing. After pulling out of the dive he saw that his upper starboard wing was broken and the fabric was tearing further in the slipstream. Unfortunately as he was nursing his aircraft back to base his engine was hit by AA fire, and he crash-landed behind enemy lines. Then on 17 May, Rickenbacker similarly lost the fabric from the upper starboard wing of N6169 while making a rolling pull-out from a dive, following his second victory. He reported that the entire spread of canvas of the top wing was torn off and disappeared behind him. And on 30 May, Meissner in N6144 lost the fabric from a wing after achieving his second victory, as did Lt W.V. Casgrain in N6152 – but he was less fortunate, going down between the lines where he was made prisoner. On 2 June, Lt Cunningham of the 94th in N6163 lost the front of his wing whilst diving on an enemy machine, but managed to land safely. Yet another incident involved Lt W. Heinrich of the 95th in N6160. Thus there were at least seven incidents of wing stripping – and there may have been others where the pilot did not survive to tell the tale.

June was generally quiet, but nevertheless the First Pursuit Group managed to obtain six confirmed victories during the month. By this time the group included the newly arrived 27th and 147th Aero Squadrons in addition to the 94th and 95th. On 28 June, it moved from the Toul sector to Touquin aerodrome some 30km (20 miles) south of Château Thierry; this was in expectation of a German offensive in the Marne region. So far the Americans had given a good account of themselves, but now they were up against sterner opposition: the Jastas of JG I.

And the Americans were soon in action. On 2 July, 27th Aero Sqn, led by 1st Lt Donald Hudson, took off at 6.15am and an hour later was in hot contest with nine Fokker D.VIIs of Jastas 4 and 10. The squadron claimed four enemy aircraft shot down, although the Germans reported no losses. One of the Jasta 10 pilots killed 1st Lt Edward Elliott, while Ltn Ernst Udet brought down N6347 (No. 3), piloted by 2nd Lt Walter Wanamaker, who was injured and taken prisoner. Two Nieuports piloted by Lt W. Hoover and 2nd Lt J. MacArthur were claimed by the Germans, but in fact made it back to their home aerodrome. Meanwhile 147th Aero Sqn claimed six Pfalz scouts without loss, although no record has been found of any German loss.

The Germans launched their expected offensive on 15 July 1918, and by the end of that month the Americans had lost eight pilots taken prisoner and nine killed in action, one of the latter being 1st Lt Quentin Roosevelt of 95th Aero Sqn, the son of a former president, shot down on the 14th. The 94th and 95th Aero Sqns began to replace their Nieuports by Spad 13s in mid-July, but 27th Aero Sqn soldiered on with its Nieuports. On 1 August, eighteen of the latter squadron's Nieuports were escorting two Salmson 2A.2s reconnoitring the Fère-en-Tardenois area, when they were jumped on by pilots of JG I. None of 27th Aero Sqn's claims were confirmed by German records, but the squadron lost 1st Lts Charles Sands and Jason Hunt killed, 1st Lt R.C. Martin taken prisoner, and 1st Lt Oliver Beauchamp fatally injured in a crash on landing. In a separate incident, 1st Lt Charles McElvain wounded Ltn dR Günther Schuster, but was himself brought down near Arcy by Ltn dR Alfred Fleischer.

The incidents of wing failures were now a subject of controversy in the higher levels of Command. Coincidentally, Brig Gen B. Foulois replaced Billy Mitchell as Chief of the Air Service First Army on 29 May 1918. Mitchell strongly resented being replaced and was uncooperative in handing over his responsibilities, to the extent that Foulois requested his immediate recall to the United States. Brig Gen B. Foulois had always opposed the use of the Nieuport, and since he now had in his possession the reports on these incidents from Capt Du Doré, Maj A.M. Atkinson and Maj J. Huffer, he also now had all the evidence he required to insist on the replacement of the Nieuport 28 in the inventory of the First Pursuit Group. He forwarded his recommendation to replace the Nieuport on 12 June, stating that the aircraft's weaknesses were of such a serious nature that it posed a considerable risk of unnecessary loss of life. He requested that the aircraft be replaced at the front by Spads or an equivalent British type, and that they be relegated to training duties where they could be used safely.

In the First Pursuit Group, the members of the 94th and 95th ASs were very pleased with receiving Spads. However, Maj H. Hartney and Maj G. Bonnell, who commanded the 27th and 147th AS respectively, were less pleased, as they had been aware of the problem before they left England and appreciated that if properly handled, the Nieuport with its good manoeuvrability could outperform other machines of the same vintage. This was likely true when the Nieuport 28 was

(*Above*) **1st Lt Eddie Rickenbacker with the stripped wing panel from Nieuport 28 (N6169) that survived the incident on 17 May 1918.** Greg Van Wyngarden

(*Right*) **Lt James Meissner posing in front of his Nieuport 28 after losing the fabric from his upper wing.** Greg Van Wyngarden

A restored Nieuport 28 once owned by Paul Mantz. via Paul Leaman

compared with the Pfalz D.IIIa and Albatros D.V, which were both designs from early 1917; but the Fokker D.VII was, of course, in a different class altogether.

Col Dunwoody, the Air Service's Chief of Supply in Paris, interceded on their behalf, proposing that an outstanding order for 600 Nieuport 28s should not be cancelled, particularly as his technicians had now put together some twenty-three changes to overcome the aircraft's deficiencies. Foulois agreed that, in recognition of the current military emergencies, the order should not be cancelled, but insisted that a rigorous inspection regime be implemented at the receiving depot at Orly, and that the service of the aircraft should be restricted to the less arduous duties at the Front. With these aircraft the Vickers gun was replaced by the Marlin.

Soon after the events of 1 August, the change of the First Pursuit Group's Nieuports for Spad 13s was complete. The pilots of the 94th and 95th Aero Sqns welcomed their new mounts. Although the pilots of the 27th and 145th AS were at first pleased to receive Nieuports transferred from the 94th and 95th, these were also soon replaced by Spads. Maj Geoffrey Bonnell, commander of the 147th, protested so much over the change that he was replaced by 1st Lt James Meissner, who, having twice lost wing fabric when flying Nieuports, was naturally much in favour of the replacements.

After the war, thirty-one Nieuport 28s were returned to the United States for use by the armed forces. These (numbers 6125–6356) were derived from the only batch made by Loire et Olivier and were designated 28As, having an improved throttle, strengthened leading edges and undercarriage shock cord and cables, gun mounts for the Marlin machine-gun, and an auxiliary fuel tank at the bottom of the fuselage. The army used eighteen as trainers for a short time, and one was allocated to the Marines. Twelve (serials A5794–5805) were transferred to the navy, where they were equipped with inflatable underwing flotation bags and hydrovanes in front of the undercarriage to prevent nosing-over on ditching. The navy Nieuports were flown from platforms fitted to the forward gun turrets of battleships.

Four genuine Nieuport 28s found their way onto the civilian market. These were navy surplus sold in 1920–21. Three of these were operated by Emery Rogers & Co, Earl Daugherty and Eddie Martin. The latter's was much modified, including having clipped wings, by Joe York in 1924–25. The Rogers Airport Co. aircraft went to Garland Lincoln in 1928, and on to Paul Mantz around 1937. Lincoln also owned a second Nieuport at one stage, this one sporting I-struts. It has been reported that up to six appeared in movies, including the flying sequences for the 1930 movie *The Dawn Patrol*, and four were used in ground scenes in the 1938 remake. However, it is likely that only four were originals, and that the others were dummies.

Seaplane Bases

The Americans received two of the early production Macchi M.5s for evaluation. The first (4870) was shipped from Genoa on 1 August 1917 on the steamer *Duca degli Abruzzi*, and arrived in America in mid-August. This machine, together with several other Italian types, was sent to Langley Field, and it had been assembled ready for testing by mid-September. It was sent, together with another M.5 (possibly 4871), to NAS Hampton Roads, Virginia. However, nothing further happened, as official policy changed direction.

On 19 December 1917, Lt Cdr J.L. Callan arrived in Rome to discuss with the head of the Ispettorato Sommergibili ed Aviazione (Inspectorate of Submarines and Aviation) the problems of training American naval students in Italy, and the taking over by American naval aviation forces of certain stations in Italy, with the object of operating them in the same manner as those in France. The initial offer comprised the seaplane stations at Porto Corsini near Ravenna and Pescara for operations, and at Bolsena for training. Bolsena was commissioned as a US NAS on 21 February 1918. It was equipped with FBA flying boats for initial training, Macchi L.3s for continuation training, and M.5s for more advanced work. The operational stations were to be equipped with nine FBA flying boats for patrol work, six SVA seaplanes for defence, and twelve M.5s. The Italian authorities also wanted the Americans to take over an airfield at San Severo, equipped with eighty Caproni bombers, but this did not materialize. Furthermore the construction of the station at Pescara was not fully completed by the Armistice, and was never handed over to the Americans.

Thus the only American seaplane station established was the one at Porto Corsini, then occupied by 263ª Squadriglia. This unit was formed on 10 November 1917 from 2ª Squadriglia Idrovolanti di Grado, for protection against the incursion of enemy seaplanes and for attacks on Pola. It then consisted of FBAs and a couple of M.5s, which by 1 June 1918 had increased to thirteen FBAs and two M.5s (4875 and 7070).

On 24 July 1918, Lt Cdr W.B. Haviland arrived at Porto Corsini from Pauillac with thirty-five officers, 300 men and 250 tons of equipment. These numbers were later augmented by graduates from the flying school at Bolsena. The following night the Austrians had intended to greet the Americans by bombing the station, but luckily mistook the target. The station was commissioned a week later, but the Americans were soon complaining about the lack of equipment and facilities. Of the thirty seaplanes handed over, only eight were serviceable. Of these, fifteen were M.5s and five were M.8s. Only three M.5s were serviceable, and of the remainder, seven were found to require factory overhaul. Only a limited amount of work could be carried out locally due to lack of spares: for instance, while there were plenty of propellers, the spare wings were of the old type, and not interchangeable. Nevertheless by 28 August there were thirteen serviceable seaplanes, including four M.5s and four M.8s. On 6 September, six new M.5s were delivered, but they had been poorly crated and roughly handled on the railway, so each had to be thoroughly inspected and overhauled on the base before use. The same applied to the engines, which had been assembled by the Franco Tosi factory.

The Americans were soon to be given a taste of warfare when on 11 August 1918, QM J.L. Goggins was killed when he crashed his M.5 near Porto Corsini. On 18 August the unit, together with two Macchi L.3s from 265ª Squadriglia, took part in the search for the airship A.1 that had got lost on its way to Cattaro. Three days later it took part in a serious dogfight: four M.5s were escorting an M.8 that had been dropping leaflets over Pola, when they engaged five enemy scouts. Ens Voorhees had to drop out with a jammed gun, but Ens G. Ludlow, A. Parker and C.H. Hammann managed to break up the enemy formation; however, Ludlow was forced to make an emergency landing on the sea with a damaged engine and radiator some 8km (5 miles) from the coast. After opening the photographic port, slashing the wings and kicking holes in the side of the hull, he was rescued by Hammann who had landed alongside. But Hammann must have damaged his hull in the choppy sea, because after touching down normally at Porto Corsini, his machine suddenly nosed over, slightly injuring both pilots. On 15 September two more aircrew were killed when Ens L.J. Bergen and Gnr T.L. Murphy crashed in an M.8 while testing wireless apparatus. During the following operations the unit, with a typical strength of sixteen to eighteen aircraft, settled down to routine patrols with occasional raids on Pola, clocking up an average of forty to fifty sorties per week. On 1 January 1919 the base and its complement of aircraft were returned to the Italians.

On 2 December 1918, the secretary of the navy accepted as a gift the two M.5s that had found their way to the United States over a year, and on 22 January these were given the serials A-5574 and A-5575. Sadly the latter was destroyed and its pilot Ens Hammann killed on 14 June 1919 when it spun in from a low height while practising for an air show.

Nieuports with the Aviation Militaire Belge

When the war began, the Belgian Compagnie des Aviateurs had thirty-seven qualified pilots and eight civilian pilots in two escadrilles, with two more being formed. The two operational units had their landing grounds at Ans and Belgrade, close to the forts at Liège and Namur respectively. Each escadrille was equipped with four 80hp Henri Farmans. Eight more Farmans were subsequently delivered to units to replace unserviceable machines. As the Belgian army fell back before the German onslaught, its air force was relocated, with Escadrille I at Coxyde, Escadrilles II and III at Houthem near Dunkerque, and Escadrille IV at Ostende. In April 1915 the force was renamed the Aviation Militaire Belge. Belgium received its first Nieuport 10s on 17 June 1915. One each was allocated to Escadrilles I and IV, and two to Escadrille II. Several were operated later by the Franco-Belgian Escadrille at Hondsschoote. The first mission in a Nieuport was flown by 2nd Lt H. Crombez of Escadrille IV on 26 August, and the first combat success was scored by 2nd Lt J. Olieslagers of Escadrille II on 12 September.

It was decided on 18 January 1916 to form dedicated scout units: thus Escadrille I became the 1ière Escadrille de Chasse on 22 February, and in June the unit moved from Coxyde to Les Moëres. There, the Nieuport 10s were replaced by Nieuport 11s in August. Also in August a second scout unit was formed, Escadrille V becoming the 5ième Escadrille de Chasse. This unit became

2nd Lt Edmund Thieffry with his Nieuport 23 of 5ième (Comete) Escadrille. via Paul Leaman

Nieuport 23 of 5ième (Comete) Escadrille.

operational the following month, and stayed at Coxyde until the summer of 1917 when it, too, moved to Les Moëres. By then, both Escadrilles were operating Nieuport 17s from a batch of twelve ordered by the Belgian authorities, and 1ière Escadrille had at least one Nieuport 23 on strength, and 5ième had others. A few Nieuport 16s were also allocated: for instance, one was given to Willy Coppens when he joined 1ière Escadrille at Les Moëres, and despite his misgivings concerning its nose-heaviness, he was still using the type as late as August 1917. However, by August and September, the 1ière began to replace its Nieuports with Hanriot H.D.1s and some Sopwith Camels, and the 5ième with Spad 7s. Belgium also bought a single Nieuport 81 for evaluation.

Coppens did not achieve any victories with his Nieuport, but four others did: Lt A.E.A. de Meulemeester scored seven out of his total of eleven on Nieuports; Lt J. Olieslagers scored one confirmed victory in a Nieuport 10, and another in a Nieuport 11 out of a total of six; 2nd Lt E. Thieffry scored six out of a total of ten; and 2nd Lt Kervyn de Lettenhove two out of four. Single victories were also scored by 2nd Lt C.E.L. Ciselet, 2nd Lt Baron P.L.M.G. de Chaestret de Haneffe, and 2nd Lt M.P.A.J-B. Medaets.

Other Operators of Nieuport Aircraft

Argentina

Argentina purchased a Nieuport IIG and a Nieuport IVG (dubbed 'La Argentina') in 1912. Both aircraft served with the Escuela de Aviacion Militar.

Two Nieuport 28s were obtained in 1919. One crashed while trying to cross the Andes, and the other was reported unable to fly because of a warped fuselage. Several more were obtained later the same year and remained in service until 1922.

In March 1919, a Macchi M.5 was demonstrated at Varese to an Argentinian delegation, but no orders were forthcoming. One was sent to Argentina in 1919 with the Italian Aeronautical Mission. After being turned down by Paraquay, it was presented to the Argentinian Navy, but was never used.

Brazil

The Brazilian Escola de Aviacao Militar received twenty Nieuport 21s in 1920, which were used as advanced trainers. Sixteen serial numbers are known: 2101–4, 2107, 2108, 7090, 7096, 7109, 7112, 7114, 7117, 7118, 7123, 7128 and 7129. Two Nieuport 21s were assigned to the 1st Companhia de Parque de Aviacao, and were used operationally during the San Paulo revolution of June 1924 before returning to Campo dos Afonsos the following month. They were subsequently incorporated into the Destacamento de Aviacao, and sent back to San Paulo in August and September 1924. The Nieuport 21s were retired at the end of that year.

Six Nieuport 24s were purchased in 1919, and were assigned to the Escola de Aviacao Militar at Campo dos Afonsos. They were given serials 3042, 3064, 3318, 3889, 4648 and 5149. They were withdrawn from service in 1924.

A French mission to Brazil in November 1918 brought ten single-seat Nieuport 80E1s, which were given serials 8001 to 8010. They were used at the Escola de Aviacao Militar at Campos dos Afonsos until they were struck off charge in 1924. Brazil received nine Nieuport 81E2s in 1919, that were given serials 7513 and 8101–8108, and assigned to the Escola de Aviacao Militar in Campos dos Afonsos. Some were later converted to taxi trainers (penguins). They remained in service until 1924. The Escola de Aviacao Militar in Campos dos Afonsos also received fourteen Nieuport 83E2s in 1919; they were given the serial numbers 8877, 8889, 8890, 8894, 8901, 8902, 8908, 8909, 8910, 8915, 8917, 8919, 8921 and 8922, and remained in service until 1924.

Chile

The Chilean Air Service purchased a single Nieuport 12 in 1918, and one Nieuport 17 in 1919.

Columbia

Columbia acquired four Nieuport 17s in 1921, which served with the Escuela Militar de Aviacion until 1925.

Finland

A single Russian-built Nieuport 10 was captured by Finland in 1918, and two more were added when their pilots defected. Two of these were given serials D.63/18 and D.64/18, and remained in Finnish service until 1919. They saw action in the Viipuri area with Lento-osasto 2. One Nieuport 17 was flown to Finland in 1918. Nieuport 17s also went to Finland after the war ended. Two Russian pilots with Duksbuilt Nieuport 23s defected to Finland in 1918. These aircraft were given serials D.61/18 and D.62/18, and remained in service until 1920.

Greece

A Nieuport IVG, owned by E. Argyropoulos and christened 'Alkyon', was the first aeroplane flown in Greece. Its maiden flight was on 2 August 1912, and it was subsequently assigned to First Flying Squadron at Larissa during the First Balkan War. It is believed to have been destroyed in 1912.

Greece purchased about twenty Nieuport 24bis fighters; along with some Spad 7s, these equipped 531 Mira squadron based at Gorgupi in March 1918. There

(*Above*) **Nieuport 17 (D86/18), one of three acquired by Finland in 1918.**

(*Above right*) **Nieuport 11 (N214), one of twelve built in Holland with 80hp Thulin engines.** F. Gerdessen, via Stuart Leslie

A Nieuport 17 (N220), one of five acquired by Holland in 1918. P.L. Gray, via Stuart Leslie

were still about twelve on strength by the end of 1918, and they were finally withdrawn from service in 1924. They were joined by some Nieuport 28s in 1919, which served until 1922.

Guatemala

A French mission took at least one Nieuport 28 to Guatemala in 1920. It was assigned to the Cuerpo de Aviacion Militar and used as a trainer at the Campo de la Aurora.

Holland

A damaged Nieuport 11 (3981) of A Sqn 1 Wing of the RNAS force-landed at Cadzand on 26 September 1917. It was bought for £1,700 on the 23rd, and became LA40, then N213 and N230. It was sent on 17 March 1918 to the Nederlandsche Automobil en Vlieguigfabriek Trompenburg (NV Dutch Motor Car and Aeroplane Factory) at Trompenburg in Amsterdam, and used as a pattern for licence building. Five aircraft (N215 to N219) were delivered in 1918 and served until 1925. A further twenty were ordered and allocated serials N230 to N249, but only twelve were delivered in 1918. They were so poorly constructed that they were never used in service.

Holland's Luchtvaart Afdeling introduced five Nieuport 17s as advanced trainers in 1918; these were given serials N220 to N224. One (N220) was re-engined with an 80hp Thulin engine. These were struck off charge in 1925.

Some Nieuport 28s served with the Royal Hellenic Air Force in the 1920s.

Hungary

A single Nieuport 17 was captured on 15 May 1919 when a Rumanian machine landed behind Hungarian lines. It was used by the 8th Voros Repuloszazad.

Japan

Japan was a major user of Nieuports, probably the second largest after France. The first to be acquired was a single Nieuport (probably a Type VIM), purchased in 1913 by a Japanese officer who had been trained in France; it was a two-seater with a 100hp Gnome engine. In 1914 it was sent, together with four MF.7s, to Tsingtao as part of the Provisional Air Corps Unit, and flew reconnaissance missions. Some Nieuport 17s went to Japan after the war ended.

Japan obtained several Nieuport 24s from France in 1917. The army had a distinct preference for manoeuvrability as compared with outright performance, and were quite satisfied with the aircraft; they therefore arranged for production under licence by the Tokorozawa branch of the Army Supply Depot beginning in March 1919, and later by Nakajima. The Le Rhône engines were built under licence by Tokyo Gasuden. A total of 102 were built from 1921 to 1923 by Nakajima. The aircraft were initially known as the Type Ni-24, but in November 1921 they were redesignated Army Type Ko. 3 to conform to a new army designation system. Those with 120hp Le Rhône engines entered operational service with fighter squadrons in June 1922, replacing the *Hei 1* (the Spad 13), and these remained until December 1926 when they were replaced by Nieuport 29s. Some were built with 80hp Le Rhône engines and were used as fighter trainers. As the *Ko. 3* was phased out of service, some went into the civil market and were used as single-seat sports aircraft until around 1933. The Japanese acquired at least one Nieuport 27 after the war; the Itoh Tsurubane No. 2 aerobatic aircraft, produced by Tomotari Innagaki, was a modified version.

A single Nieuport 80 was bought after the war. Forty Nieuport 81E.2s and several Nieuport Type 83s were imported in 1919 by a French aviation mission. Because the aircraft were required in greater numbers than could be imported, the army signed a licence agreement, and production was started at Tokorozawa; however, this was soon transferred to civil constructors. The army supplied the drawings, and the aircraft were essentially identical to French-manufactured machines. Mitsubishi built Nieuport 81E.2s under the designation *Ko.1*, the first being completed by May 1922. The Type 83E.2 was built by Nakajima as the *Ko.2*, the first being completed in March 1922. Some *Ko.1*s were used by the air regiments. Both types were used by the army flying schools at Tokorozawa and Kagamigahara until around 1926, and after that, several were released to civil flying schools.

At least sixty-two Nieuport 24/27s, thirty-two Nieuport 81s, twenty Nieuport 83s and a single Nieuport 82 found themselves on the Japanese civil register.

Portugal

The Escuela Militar de Aviaco received seven Nieuport 83E.2s purchased in 1916. The Escola de Aeronautica Militar received three Nieuport 80E.2s in 1919.

Siam

Siam purchased four Nieuport IVGs in 1914; these were based at Don Muang airfield and served as trainers. It also acquired at least two Nieuport 11s (serials 4 and 23) postwar; these were used as trainers until 1933, as was a Nieuport 12 (serial 1) obtained from France after the war. At least one Nieuport 17 was used by the Royal Siamese Aeronautical Service.

(*Above*) **French-built Nieuport 24 in Japanese service, probably at Tokorogawa. The first Nieuport 24 to go to Japan arrived there in 1917.** JMB/GLS collection

Nieuport 24 (Japanese designation *Ko. 3*) built in Japan at the army factory, photographed at Tokorogawa in 1925. The aircraft entered service with fighter squadrons in May 1922. JMB/GLS collection

(*Above*) **A Nieuport 24 (*Ko. 3*) on the Japanese civil register. This is believed to have been registered to Sigimoto, and was powered by an 80hp Le Rhône engine.** JMB/GLS collection

Cropped Nieuport 12 used for taxiing practice at the 'Nungesser' school, in Japan during the 1920s. Philip Jarrett

156

Spain

Spain had one Nieuport IIN (christened *pinguino*, or penguin) and two Nieuport IIGs in service with the flying school at Cuatro Vientos in 1912, where they remained operational until 1914. They were very popular as compared with the Farman biplanes already at the school. Shortly after delivery, Capt Herrare flew one of these from Guadalajara to Cuatro Vientos in a record thirty-five minutes. In April 1913, a single Nieuport IVG (serial 6) and four Nieuport IVMs (serials 4, 5, 7 and 8) were purchased; at first they were assigned to the Escuela Nieuport de Peu, and were used for training. The first operational *escuela*, formed at Tetuán on 22 October 1913, included three Type IVGs. It moved to Zezulan in May 1914, and the Nieuports remained operational until 1917. On 2 November 1913, 1st Lt S. Alonso, accompanied by Sagasta, became the first to overfly the city of Tetuán. On 13 February Capt Herrera, accompanied by O. Echagüe as observer, carried out a flight between Tetuán and Seville, overflying Gibraltar, which drew a formal protest from the British government. The *escuela* moved to Zeluán in May 1914, and the Nieuport IVMs remained in service until 1917.

Towards the end of 1919 the Hispano Británica SA flying school was formed in Madrid using a DH.6 and two Nieuport 10s obtained in France at a give-away price. On 26 February 1920, the two Nieuports were given the first civil registrations M-AAAA and M-AAAB. Not much is known about their use, although one was re-registered M-ABAA in the name of a company director, D. Antonio Sanz: it was the star of an air show at Valdespartera, where it was flown in an aerobatic display by two pilots, T. Collier and Lt F. Bernáldez. P. Carballo, who had flown with the Aviation Militaire during the war and had formed an agricultural development company with his father in the Ebro delta, acquired two Nieuport 10s from France and flew them from his country estate. Both these aircraft were sold to J. Canudas, who cannibalized one machine to produce a single airworthy aircraft. This was registered M-AOOA, and gave valuable service from its base in Barcelona until 1935.

Sweden

Sweden purchased two Nieuport IVGs, one in 1912 and the second in 1913. They were the first aircraft supplied to the Flygkompanier, and were given serials M1 and M2. Nieuport M1 was struck off charge in April 1918, and M2 crashed on 29 May 1916. One Nieuport floatplane (possibly a VIH) was purchased by the Marine Flyvasende in 1913. Assigned serial N.1, it was struck off charge in 1916.

Switzerland

Five Nieuport 23s were obtained by the Fliegertruppe in 1917 and were given serials 601 to 605. They became the Fliegertruppe's front-line fighters, and remained in service until 1921. In that year 601 was tested to destruction, and it was discovered that the Nieuports could no longer meet the structural requirements of the force. All of this type were therefore withdrawn from service.

Switzerland acquired one Nieuport 28 on 28 June 1918 when 2nd Lt James Ashenden of 147th Aero Sqn strayed over the border and force-landed between Derendingen and Seitingen. Ashenden was interned, and the damaged Nieuport was repaired and given the serial number 607. This machine was retired from the Fleigertruppe in 1925 due to fatigue. In this aeroplane, Oblt Robert Ackermann beat twenty-two other competitors from five countries to win the aerobatic competition at the First International Aeronautical meeting at Dübendorf in 1922. This performance led the Swiss to purchase an additional fourteen Nieuport 28s for use as fighter trainers and aerobatic machines. They were given serials 685 to 698. These were finally scrapped in 1930 except two that survived in museums.

Nieuport 17 in Swiss service. Philip Jarrett

One of a number of Nieuport 28s operated by the Swiss air force. via Paul Leaman

(*Above*) **Line-up of Nieuport 28s in Swiss service.** Philip Jarrett

Nieuport 27 in postwar Turkish service. Philip Jarrett

Turkey

Prior to World War I, the Ottoman Empire attempted to reinforce their motley collection of Blériots, Deperdussins and Ponniers by ordering three Blériot XIs with clipped wings (called 'Pingouins') to be used for training, twenty Morane Saulnier Type L Parasols for the army, and fifteen Nieuport VI floatplanes for the navy. Of these, only the Blériots and two of the Nieuports were delivered. An inventory in 1914 confirmed that the two Nieuport VI floatplanes were still on strength at that time: one operated from a base at Canakkale, where it carried out a trial flight on 17 August 1914, and it then flew reconnaissance sorties to observe the British fleet on 5 and 20 September, and 2, 14 and 19 October. The second Nieuport arrived at Canakkale and carried out a last reconnaissance mission on 5 November 1914, the day before the declaration of war between the Ottoman Empire and the Allies. For reasons that are unclear, the Nieuports were replaced by a Blériot shortly afterwards. The Turks also operated another monoplane named after the Turkish minister of war, *Maahmud Sevkat Pasa*: this was painted on one side of the fuselage in the Western alphabet, and on the other side in Arabic.

The only other Nieuports operated by the Turks were two Nieuport 17s, which were amongst twelve Russian and British aircraft captured during the war. These were apparently found on a Russian vessel in the Black Sea on 7 May 1918. They were repainted in Turkish insignia, given the serial numbers K.1 and K.2, and allocated to the Ninth Squadron. One of these was used at Yesilköy, and joined three other aircraft in the defence of Istanbul against British raids between 18 and 25 October just before the war ended.

Turkey bought some Nieuports after the war was over, one at least being a 24/27 hybrid.

Uruguay

In 1921, six Nieuport 83s were obtained and based at Paso de Mendoza; and during the late 1920s, twenty-four Nieuport 27s were obtained, and also based at Paso de Mendoza.

Other Operators

The Bulgarians operated some Nieuports, and the Germans and Austrians flew captured examples.

CHAPTER NINE

Postwar Developments of Wartime Designs

After the war, Nieuport built two series of aircraft, one of monoplanes and the other of biplanes, the design of which began while the course of the war was still uncertain. Full-scale production of Nieuport biplane scouts during the war ended with the Nieuport 28. However, several prototypes were built during the later part of 1917 and the early part of 1918, which allowed experimentation on different concepts; this in turn led to the design of the Nieuport 29 biplane, built after the war in many military and civil versions. It became the principal single-seater put into production in the immediate postwar period, it equipped French escadrilles for more than ten years, and was extensively exported and constructed under licence overseas. Two prototypes based on the Nieuport 29 and equipped with floats appeared towards the end of 1918: one formed the basis of the racing seaplanes, and the second became the forerunner of the Ni D-32Rh used by the Marine. A few were converted into Ni D-29B-1 light bombers, and a lightened version became the Ni D-29ET-1, built in numbers as trainers. Later, Gustav Delage and his staff developed the Ni D-62 fighter that equipped the Aviation Militaire during the 1930s; but this story is not within the scope of this book.

No other Nieuport 29 derivatives reached series production status for the military. However, various prototypes, including the Ni D-40C-1 and Ni D-29*bis*, optimized as high- and low-altitude interceptors, appeared from 1921 onwards.

With orders for military aircraft becoming hard to come by after the war, Nieuport, in common with other manufacturers, turned its attention to modifying its designs for racing and record-breaking purposes; in this it achieved a considerable reputation, which undoubtedly improved prospects for sales overseas. The first such machines were the Ni D-29 seaplane racers entered for the 1919 Schneider Trophy Race. Other such machines included the Ni D-29V ('Vitesse'), the Ni D-40R high-altitude record breaker and the racing sesquiplanes, the 'Madon', Ni D-31Rh and the Coupe Deutsch entrants. The sesquiplane concept was taken further through the Ni D-37C-1, Ni D-41 and Ni D-42S, but these designs differed to such an extent in shape and configuration that they could no longer be considered developments of the wartime designs, and so are not described in this book.

Precursors of the Nieuport-Delage 29

Towards the end of 1917, the Nieuport company had two prototypes with lightweight nine-cylinder rotary engines under test, one of these a 165hp Gnome 9N monosoupape engine. This was of a similar layout to the Nieuport 28, but had a fuselage of monocoque construction, a much simplified cabane strut arrangement consisting of just two struts in tandem, and a new shape of fin and rudder and tailplane similar to that which was to become the hallmark of the Nieuport 29 series. It achieved a speed of 198km/h (123mph) at 2,000m (6,560ft), in which its performance was comparable to the Nieuport 28. A second machine was fitted with a 170hp Le Rhône 9R: this performed slightly better than the Nieuport 28, but not sufficiently to justify series production. In any case, the two engines were not yet in production at that time.

In parallel with the tests of these machines, another prototype began trials in November 1917. This machine looked like a slightly larger version of the Nieuport 28, with a wing area of 21sq m (226sq ft) and fitted with a rotary engine with eleven cylinders, the 200hp Clerget 11F. The wings were different from the Nieuport 28 in that the lower wing had slightly more dihedral than the upper. With an empty weight of 530kg (1,170lb) and a loaded weight of 850kg (1,875lb), including two Vickers machine-guns, the maximum speed was found to be 200km/h (125mph) at 4,000m (13,120ft), a height that was reached in twelve minutes.

Up to this time, Gustav Delage's designs had been powered by rotary air-cooled engines. However, by the middle of 1917 it was becoming apparent that the rotary engine was reaching the limit of its development potential. It was only natural, therefore, that Delage would look to a water-cooled engine as a means of providing a reliable source of greater power. It was estimated that with a Lorraine-Dietrich water-cooled engine of 220hp, an aircraft with a span of 9.25m (30ft), a wing area of 21sq m (226sq ft) and a loaded weight of 850kg (1,875lb) could attain a speed of 220km/h (137mph) at 4,000m (13,120ft).

The first machine to appear with a water-cooled engine was powered by a 240hp Lorraine-Dietrich 8Bd V-8 engine. It had more than a superficial resemblance to the Nieuport 28, with a similar undercarriage, a fuselage of rounded cross-section, and a similarly shaped tailplane and fin and rudder. The wings were constant chord with rounded wingtips, but differed from the Nieuport 28 in that they were relatively widely spaced on long interplane and centre-section struts, which raised the upper wing well above the fuselage. The engine drove a four-bladed propeller, and its radiator was placed between the closely cowled banks of cylinders, which must have severely restricted the forward view. The aircraft was somewhat ungainly in appearance, suggesting that it was put together in a hurry to test the concept. Tests began in October 1917, and proved that the ideas were on the right lines. The tests were then terminated to await the arrival of a refined version, expected to appear in January 1918.

Tests on this second machine actually began in February 1918, and carried on until April. It was fitted with an uprated Lorraine-Dietrich 8Bd. of 275hp. It again seemed to be based on the Nieuport 28, but both wings were slightly swept back, perhaps indicating that there may have been a problem with the centre of gravity of the first prototype. The upper wing had been lowered to a more normal position, and both upper and lower wings were fitted with balanced ailerons. The radiator was repositioned on the upper wing out of sight of the pilot.

In early 1918 a similar machine to the one described above appeared, fitted with a 300hp Hispano-Suiza 8Fb V-8 watercooled engine; testing commenced in March, along with the Lorraine-Dietrich powered aircraft, and continued until May. The machine had the same wing area of 21sq m (226sq ft), but was much heavier than the

Prototype with a 240hp Lorraine-Dietrich, Nieuport 28-style fin and rudder, and a centrally mounted radiator. *Jean Noël, via Stuart Leslie and Philip Jarrett*

Data on Nieuport 29 Predecessors and Prototypes		Gnome 9N	Clerget 11F	Lorraine 8Bb	Nieuport 29/01	Nieuport 29/02
Engine:		165hp Gnome 9N	200hp Clerget 11F	275hp Lorraine-Dietrich 8Bb	300hp Hispano-Suiza 8Fb	300hp Hispano-Suiza 8Fb
Dimensions:	Wing span, m (ft)			9.25 (30)		
	Length, m (ft)			7 (23)		
	Wing area, sq m (sq ft)		21 (226)	21 (226)	24.7 (266)	26.84 (288.8)
Weights:	Weight empty, kg (lb)		530 (1,170)	535 (1,180)	867 (1,911)	
	Weight loaded, kg (lb)	640 (1,410)	850 (1,875)	850 (1,875)		1,106 (2,439)
Performance:	Maximum speed, km/h (mph):					
	at sea level					226 (140)
	at 1,000m (3,280ft)			201 (125)	224 (139)	
	at 2,000m (6,560ft)	198 (123)		199 (123.6)	218 (135)	222 (138)
	at 3,000m (9,850ft)			196 (121.7)	215 (133.6)	218 (135)
	at 4,000m (13,120ft)		200 (124)	192 (119)	211 (131)	213 (132)
	at 5,000m (16,400ft)			185 (115)	204 (126.7)	205 (127)
	at 6,000m (19,690ft)			170 (105.6)	195 (121)	
	Minimum speed, km/h (mph):					
	at sea level			168 (104)	144 (89)	
	Time to height:					
	1,000m (3,280ft)			2min	2min 30sec	2min 21sec
	2,000m (6,560ft)			6min 38sec	5min 21sec	4min 37sec
	3,000m (9,850ft)	7min 33sec		11min 24sec	8min 49sec	7min 35sec
	4,000m (13,120ft)		12min	18min 9sec	13min 5sec	10min 59sec
	5,000m (16,400ft)			26min 44sec	18min 40sec	15min 2sec
	6,000m (19,690ft)			45min	21min 10sec	
	Service ceiling, m (ft)			6,500 (21,330)	7,400 (24,280)	7,700 (25,265)
	Endurance	2hr 25min	2hr 50min			

160

others, having an empty weight of 600kg (1,320lb) and a loaded weight of 950kg (2,100lb). Again it was fitted with twin Vickers guns, but this machine had a pair of radiators fitted under the lower wings.

Two of the new features that were to be incorporated into the Nieuport 29 series were shown by two of these aircraft: in one it was the 300hp Hispano-Suiza water-cooled engine, and in the Le Rhône-powered prototype it was the monocoque construction of the fuselage.

The Nieuport-Delage 29 and its Use by the French Military

The programme of work to develop the new fighter that was to become the Ni.D-29C-1 or Nieuport 29 was effectively in response to a Programme des Avions Nouveaux issued by the Service Technique de l'Aéronautique (STAé) in May 1918. The outline specification was as follows:

armament:	two machine-guns firing through the airscrew arc, or one cannon
endurance:	two hours
useful load:	165kg (364lb) for pilot, equipment and armament
maximum speed:	240km/h (149mph) at 3,000m (9,850ft)
service ceiling:	7,500m (24,600ft) reducing to 7,000m (23,000ft) with a cannon fitted
strength coefficient:	5.5

To meet these parameters the design office, directed by G. Delage and A. Mary, started the development of a new machine, and built several prototypes to test the novel features that would be incorporated. The basis of the new design was the monocoque fuselage, a mode of construction that permitted a stronger and more streamlined fuselage, to obtain a structure more resistant to bullets, and sufficiently robust to accept an engine of 300hp. As described above, the engine, the second feature necessary to meet the requirements of the future scout, was being tested during May 1918 in a prototype with a fuselage of traditional construction.

Second prototype with a 275hp Lorraine-Dietrich engine with the radiator set in the upper wing. Jean Noël, via Stuart Leslie

Almost contemporary with the Lorraine-powered second prototype, this machine was fitted with a 300hp Hispano-Suiza. Jean Noël, via Stuart Leslie

When the prototype appeared it had only a superficial resemblance to the Nieuport 28. It was a single-bay biplane with wings squared off at the tips, and a wing area of 24.6sq m (265sq ft). The prototype was flown by pilots of the STAé in July 1918, with a view to comparing several different airframes fitted with the same

POSTWAR DEVELOPMENTS OF WARTIME DESIGNS

	Martinsyde C-I	Sopwith Dolphin C-1	Nieuport 29C-1 (2nd specn)	Nieuport 29C-1	SPAD 21C-1	SPAD-Herbemont 20C-1
Engine (300hp):	Hispano 8 Fb No.200.010	Hispano 8 Fb No.200.044	Hispano 8 Fb	Hispano 8 Fb	Hispano 8 Fb No.200.008	Hispano 8 Fb 200020
Propeller:	Lang DRGL 5270A	Lumiere 144 No.3	Lumiere 144C No.3	Lumiere 144C No.3	Chauviere 67.469	Chauviere No.74677
diameter, m (ft)	2.69 (8.8)	2.49 (8.17)	2.49 (8.17)		2.58 (8.46)	
pitch, m (ft)	2.01 (6.6)	2.12 (6.96)	2.12 (6.96)		2.215 (7.27)	
blade width, m (ft)	0.1905 (0.625)	0.1745 (0.573)	0.1745 (0.573)		0.1705 (0.559)	
Performance:						
Maximum speed, km/h @ rev/min:						
at sea level	214 @ 1825	217 @ 1800	216 @ 1910	236 @ 1960	216.8 @ 1770	228.6 @ 1870
at 1,000m (3,280ft)					220.5 @ 1800	
at 2,000m (6,560ft)			218 @ 1925		220 @ 1800	228 @ 1870
at 3,000m (8,850ft)	220 @ 1830	223 @ 1835	215 @ 195		218 @ 1780	223 @ 1840
at 4,000m (13,120ft)	216 @ 1810	219 @ 1815	211 @ 1880		214 @ 1750	217 @ 1800
at 5,000m (16,400ft)	209 @ 1780	213 @ 1780	204 @ 1845		205 @ 1700	209 @ 1760
at 6,000m (19,690ft)	197 @ 1735		193 @ 1805		190 @ 1640	200 @ 1710
Time to height, min/sec @ rev/min:						
1,000m (3,280ft)	2/22 @ 1600	2/38 @ 1620	2/30 @1775	1/56 @ 1775	2/48 @ 1565	2/25 @ 1690
2,000m (6,560ft)	4/56 @ 1590	5/27 @ 1630	5/21 @ 1775	4/19 @ 1765	5/40 @ 1565	5/29 @ 1690
3,000m (8,850ft)	8/08 @ 1580	8/35 @ 1635	8/49 @ 1765	6/37 @ 1755	8/51 @ 1570	8/24 @ 1680
4,000m (13,120ft)	11/39 @ 1575	12/29 @ 1610	13/05 @ 1745	9/53 @ 1750	13/03 @ 1580	12/21 @ 1665
5,000m (16,400ft)	16/38 @ 1570	17/33 @ 1610	18/40 @ 1735	13/26 @ 1740	18/18 @ 1600	17/45 @ 1650
6,000m (19,690ft)	23/54 @ 1560		23/08 @ 1725	18/46 @ 1740		26/49 @ 1625
Service ceiling, m	8,000–8,200 (26,000–26,900)	7,500–7,900 (24,600–26,000)	7,000–7,400 (23,000–24,300)	7,800–8,000 (25,600–26,000)	6,800–7,000 (22,300–23,000)	7,000–7,200 (23,000–23,600)
Test conditions:						
loaded wt, kg (lb)	1,118 (2,465)	1,037 (2,287)	1,143 (2,520)	1,106 (2,439)	1,047 (2,309)	1,206 (2,659)
fuel, kg (lb)	339 (747) +20	339 (747) +20	339 (747) +20	339 (747) + 20	290 (639)	339 (747) + 20
wing area, m²	30.8 (331)	25 (269)	24.7 (266)	26 (280)	23.5 (253)	29.07 (313)
wing loading, kg/m²	36.3	41.5	46.5	42	44.5	41.5
date of test	21/22.7.18	27.6.18	24.7.18	01.10.18	28 & 30.7.18	31.8.18
serial number	4256	3615		12002		
STAé Bulletin	No.7 July '18	No.7 July '18	No.7 July '18	No.9 Sept '18	No.7 July '18	No.9 Sept '18

Hispano engine: these were the Spad 21, a re-engined Sopwith Dolphin, and a Martinsyde Buzzard. The Nieuport was fastest, with a speed of 218km/h (135mph) at 2,000m (6,560ft). However, its climbing performance was less spectacular because it weighed some 100kg (220lb) more than the Spad, reaching 5,000m (16,400ft) in 18min 40sec, compared with 18min 18sec, and was outclassed by the Martinsyde that reached the same altitude in 16min 38sec.

In order to improve the climb performance, 42kg (93lb) was removed from the gross weight by reducing the useful load to 339kg (747lb) and by removing 20kg (44lb) of armour from the tankage. Another aspect that helped the designers to meet the climb performance was a reclassification of the fighter categories by Général Duval of the STAé into two categories:

C.1 High Altitude for interception at 7,000m (23,000ft) (ceiling 9,000m (29,500ft)); and

C.1 Medium Altitude for interception at 4,000m (13,000ft) (ceiling 6,500m (21,327ft)).

The improved performance at high altitude became possible with the appearance of the Rateau turbocharger that had been under development since 1917. The wing loading was also decreased, by increasing the wing area from 24.70sq m (266sq ft) to 26.84sq m (289sq ft). The increase in wingspan meant that an extra pair of interplane struts was needed on each side to form a two-bay structure.

In September the prototype obtained much improved results in the STAé tests. It climbed to 5,000m (16,400ft) in 13min 26sec, improving significantly on the time achieved by the first prototype and beating the previous best, the Martinsyde, by 3min. The maximum speed (236km/h – 147mph) was superior to all other contestants. Due to an incident during testing the remaining tests were not carried out at this time, but were delayed until after further modifications were carried out to the aircraft.

162

The fuselage was reinforced by a transverse cross-member immediately behind the engine, and the sockets for the interplane struts were strengthened. The ailerons, which had been fitted to the ends of both upper and lower wings, were replaced by balanced ailerons on the lower wing only. It was also fitted with a slightly taller rudder of increased area. The war ended before this work was completed, and it was not until May 1919 that test-flying resumed with one of the prototypes (No. 22002). The results of these tests showed that whereas the landing speed was lower, the times to altitude had increased slightly, and were now inferior to the Martinsyde: in fact the maximum speed was comparable to the Spad. When flown by Lt Casale on 14 June 1919, the machine attained an altitude of 9,123m (29,932ft), significantly better than the C.1 specification. The flying qualities were judged to be excellent, with balanced controls, praiseworthy handling and excellent visibility during take-off and landing.

The Nieuport 29 was a single-seat, two-bay biplane with wings of equal span. The fuselage shell was made by hot-glued strips

(*Above*) Two views of the first Nieuport-Delage 29 prototype, with the original revised shape of empennage, single-bay wings and radiators, with rectangular intakes beneath the wings. Jean Noël, via Stuart Leslie

(*Left*) The second prototype (N12002) of those with two-bay wings, ailerons on the upper and lower surfaces, and under-wing Lamblin cylindrical radiators: these differed from the first such prototype in having a more pointed rudder. Jean Noël, via Stuart Leslie

of tulipwood 50mm wide and 0.8mm thick, wrapped in a spiral around a mould, which included the fin and fixed parts of the tailplane. For the fuselage, a total of six layers were stuck alternately at 90 degrees to give a thickness of 5.4mm, tapering to three layers for a thickness of 2.7mm at the rear. The fin and tailplane, moulded with the fuselage, were also made of three layers. The fuselage was strengthened by an internal structure comprising sixteen spruce longerons and four bulkheads of 10mm plywood. The bulkheads reinforced the areas where attachment points were positioned for the lower wings, undercarriage and cabane struts. The engine mountings consisted of two vertical and two horizontal struts, the latter extending rearwards to support the pilot's seat. The whole fuselage was covered in linen and given a coat of cellulose lacquer.

The two wings were of equal span and chord, and were rectangular with rounded corners. The structure of each consisted of two spruce spars 65cm (25½in) apart, with plywood ribs, twenty-six on each side for the upper wing and twenty-seven for each lower wing, cross-braced with piano wire. The leading edge of spruce was covered by plywood back to the front spar. The wings were covered in linen, with the stitching along the ribs covered by strips of fabric, and given three coats of varnish. The interplane struts were profiled from spruce. The struts carried inscriptions 'Type 29 D' or 'Type 29G' for left- or right-hand struts respectively, and also the manufacturer's logo. The upper wings were joined by sockets and pins on the spars articulated on their axes to assist location on the inverted-V cabane struts. The lower wings were attached to the fuselage by sockets fixed to the ends of the spars. Balanced ailerons were fitted only to the lower wing and were made of spruce covered in linen. They were actuated via levers and connecting rods by means of a torsion tube inside the fuselage. The balanced elevators were hinged to the rear of the integral tailplane and were trimmed by an aluminium tab that was adjusted on the ground. The rudder was mounted and trimmed similarly, and was constructed of a framework of spruce, covered in board and linen.

The undercarriage was formed of two V-struts consisting of six laminations of wood, hot-glued together and fixed to the fuselage shell by brackets attached to the internal plywood formers. They were connected by forked joints to a transverse split axle that was articulated in the middle and which was sprung by bungee cord. The axle carried two wheels fitted with 700 × 100mm pneumatic tyres.

The Hispano-Suiza engine was a derivative of the 200hp 8Fd. It was a water-cooled V-8 engine with the cylinders mounted in two pairs set at 90 degrees. The steel cylinders were mounted in an aluminium block and had a bore of 140mm and a stroke of 150mm. It gave a power output of 320hp for a weight of 275kg (606lb). The power-to-weight ratio of more than unity was very advanced for its time. Cooling was effected by twin Lamblin radiators, each bolted between a V of the undercarriage struts. A small square of gauze in the nose covered an aluminium duct that led cooling air to ventilate the engine compartment. Their streamlined form was stated by the manufacturer to give ' … an advantage of some 25km/h [15mph] over conventional radiators, whilst at the same time their position afforded protection against combat damage'. A fuel tank of 147ltr (32gal) capacity was installed between the engine and cockpit. Fuel was pumped by means of

The third prototype with two-bay wings, with longer span and narrower chord ailerons. Jean Noël, via Stuart Leslie

Experimental Nieuport 29 (N12025) with one Lamblin and one frontal radiator. Philip Jarrett

a Weymann pump to two gravity tanks of 30ltr (6.6gal) capacity set in the upper wings. The oil tank of 22ltr (4.8gal) capacity was placed directly under the engine between the two vertical struts, and was corrugated to give an increased surface area to assist cooling.

The armament consisted of two 7.7mm Vickers machine-guns firing through the propeller arc and fixed to an aluminium mounting on top of the fuselage. The fore and aft fixings were designed for rapid removal of the gun.

Due to the retrenchment that occurred following the end of the war, it was not until 1920 that the Nieuport 29 was ordered into quantity production. This aircraft was destined to be produced not only by the Nieuport factory at Issy-les-Moulineaux, but also by many other French manufacturers, including Potez, Levasseur, Blériot, Letord, Farman, Schreck and Buscaylet, and other overseas constructors under licence.

The first production version was distinguished by three factors: the cowling was more pointed at the front, there was revised pipework for the oil system, and a Lumière 144C propeller of 2.5m (8ft) diameter. The first machines began to appear off the production line in 1922, and equipped the Spa 37, 81 and 93 Escadrilles based in Germany. Later it was the turn of the Escadrilles of the 1^{ière}, 2ième and 3ième Régiments d'Aviation based at Thionville, Strasbourg and Châteauroux respectively. By 1925, re-equipment of the Armée de l'Air with the Nieuport 29 was complete, with the delivery of a total of 250 machines to twenty-five escadrilles, although some of these were also equipped with Spad 81s.

The aircraft had a good reputation with the military pilots, who appreciated its excellent flying qualities, its robustness, and the reliability of its engine. However, the aircraft was not without fault. In particular, a report issued on 26 November 1923 by the Inspector General de l'Aéronautique criticized the design in two major respects: firstly, visibility from the cockpit was poor, which meant that other aircraft could pass unnoticed – obviously this did not auger well for success in aerial combat should the occasion arise; and secondly, the part of the fuselage to which the guns were fixed could distort when the guns were fired, leading to a deviation of the shot. Furthermore the Hispano-Suiza engine did not have sufficent power for the Nieuport 29 to intercept such machines as the Breguet XIX fitted with the 450hp Renault. Early modifications did not improve the problem with the armament, although later the gun supports were anchored to a metal structure in a streamlined, humped fairing. Another modification consisted of raising the cockpit coaming to allow a parachute pack to be fitted, accommodated in the pilot's seat. The windscreen was also modified to give increased protection to the pilot from the slipstream.

Nieuport 29 in French service (N12104).
Paul Leaman and Philip Jarrett

Although at the outset there was some concern over the integrity of the monocoque fuselage construction, in general it gave few problems in service. There were some instances of failed engine mountings, delamination of the tail structure, and warping of the plywood, but in the main these faults were attributed to sub-contractors rather than the parent factory. For instance, in machines constructed by licensees there were other faults that could be attributed to the fact that inexperienced, non-specialist workers were employed. In particular there were some problems with the position of the centre of gravity; however, these were overcome by adjusting the balance of the machine by reducing the number of laminations, and thus the thickness and weight of certain parts of the fuselage shell.

The Nieuport 29 was destined to remain in service longer than the general staff intended. This was because they failed to find a suitable replacement in the fighter competition of 1924, and because of the delay in implementing the results of the 1925 competition. Although an order was placed in 1923 for eighty Spad 81s and eighty Dewoitine D-1s with the intention of replacing the Spad 13 and 20, due to problems in service with the fragile undercarriage of the former, production of the Nieuport 29 was extended. It was not until 1928 that the last machines were delivered, by which time the type was being taken out of service and the production of the Nieuport Ni D-42/62 started. Altogether, more than 700 Nieuport 29s were built for the Aéronautique Militaire Française, with the delivery of the last twenty in 1926. Total production figures as high as 1,250 have been quoted, when including licence production, though these have not been substantiated.

Service of the Nieuport-Delage 29 in Other Countries

Argentina

A small number of Nieuport 29s were received by Argentina from France and assigned to the Gruppo de Aviaciòn 1 of the Aviaciòn Militar; these were used mainly for reconnaissance purposes. The period of use was brief due to problems in service.

Belgium

In Belgium, the Aviation Militaire Belge acquired a batch of twenty Nieuport 29s from France, and then supplemented these by another eighty-seven built under licence by SABCA; these were delivered from January 1924 and October 1926, and were used mainly by the 9th and 10th Escadrilles. The Belgians also used some ET.1 trainer versions fitted with 180hp Hispano-Suiza engines.

Italy

Italy acquired the manufacturing licence for the Nieuport 29 in 1923, and after receiving six machines directly from France, Macchi and Caproni built a further 175; these equipped a number of fighter units between 1924 and 1927. The initial imported batch was allocated the experimental serial numbers MM34, MM35, MM36, MM37, MM58 and MM59. Fifty built by Macchi between July 1923 and March 1924, and fifty from Caproni delivered between August 1923 and June 1924, were given serials 1000 to 1049 and 1050 to 1099 respectively. Then Macchi and Caproni each built a further thirty in 1924, with serials in the range 1100 to 1199. A final batch of fifteen was built by Macchi in 1929 and given serials 1700 to 1714. The aircraft were initially allocated in 1924/5 to 76ª, 84ª and 91ª Squadriglia of 7 Gruppo, and 70ª, 74ª and 75ª of 23 Gruppo. The squadron allocations changed slightly in 1926, and the Nieuport 29 was withdrawn from frontline duties and consigned to training units the following year.

Japan

The Japanese army imported some Nieuport 29s in 1923 to replace the *Hei. 1* and *Ko. 3* as the standard fighter. Nakajima then obtained a licence to build them as the *Ko. 4*. The first was built from imported components in 1923 and, with a few modifications, production continued until January 1932, 608 being delivered to the army. The first entered service in 1925 and remained as standard equipment until about 1933, when it was replaced by the Nakajima Type 91. Although its performance was generally satisfactory, pilots preferred the earlier designs due to the N. 29's tendency to side-slip and its relatively high landing speed, coupled with an unreliable engine. Type *Ko. 4* machines were assigned to the following Japanese army units: two squadrons of the 1st Air Regiment, three squadrons of the 3rd Air Regiment, two squadrons of the 4th Air Regiment, and one squadron each of the 7th and 8th Air Regiments. They took part in the Manchurian and Shanghai incidents during the Sino-Japanese conflict, but encountered no aerial opposition. After release from military service, some went to civil operators and remained in flying schools until as late as 1937.

Data on the Nieuport-Delage 29		
Engine:		320hp Hispano-Suiza 8Fd
Propeller:		2.5m Lummière 144C
Dimensions:	Span, upper, m (ft)	9.65 (31.7)
	Chord, m (ft)	1.50 (5.7)
	Length, m (ft)	6.50 (21.3)
	Tailplane span, m	3.2 (10.5)
	Aileron area, sq m (sq ft)	2.4 (25.8)
	Wing area, sq m (sq ft)	26.84 (288.8)
Weights:	Empty, kg (lb)	740 (1,654)
	Loaded, kg (lb)	1,100 (2,426)
Performance:	Max speed, km/h (mph):	
	at sea level	230 (143)
	at 1,000m (3,280ft)	224 (139)
	Climb to 6,000m (19,800ft)	18min 38sec
	Service ceiling, m (ft)	7,500 (24,600)
	Fuel tank capacity, ltr (gal)	147 (32)
	Oil tank capacity, ltr (gal)	22 (4.8)
	Endurance, hr	2

Spain

The Nieuport 29 gave an impressive performance at the Spanish competition in 1923, and as a result around forty were ordered for the Servicio de Aeronáutica. The first arrived at Getafe at the end of that year where a fighter squadron was formed under Capt J.G. Gallarza. During the following summer, eight of these machines were sent to Melilla to replace Martinsyde Buzzards in the squadron there under Capt F.V. Camino. These aircraft were returned to the Spanish mainland in November 1925, where they gradually reduced in numbers due to accidents and wear and tear, to be replaced by Nieuport 52s during 1931.

Sweden

Sweden acquired ten Nieuport 29s for the Flygvapnet in 1926: these were given the designation J2, and all were assigned to F3, based at Malslatt. Due to the recognized problems, these were never used in front-line service, and were sent to the F5 training squadron at Ljungbyhed during 1928/9.

Thailand

The Royal Air Force in Siam obtained a number of Nieuport 29s in 1920, and equipped the 1st Pursuit Group along with some Spad XIIIs. Some Nieuports were used as late as 1940 against Vichy forces.

The Nieuport-Delage 32Rh

Two prototypes equipped with floats and based on the Ni D-29C-1 appeared towards the end of 1918. One, initially known as the Ni D-29M (M = Marine), became the prototype for the Ni D-32Rh (Rh = Le Rhône). This aircraft was put forward against a requirement issued by the Ministère de la Marine in September 1919 for a '*monoplace d'escadre*'. The Marine were looking for a single-seat fighter that would be capable of taking off from the deck of a carrier or from a platform built over the turret of a cruiser. The first priority was therefore not speed, but the ability to take off without difficulty. Other contenders for the order were the Hanriot 12 and Spad 15, though the former was quickly discarded as it was powered by only an 80hp Le Rhône, whereas the Spad and the Nieuport were both powered by the 180hp Le Rhône. The choice of the Le Rhône, which weighed 166kg (366lb) as compared with 271kg (598lb) for the Hispano, enabled the wing loading to be considerably reduced. Without armament the Ni D-32 weighed 857kg (1,890lb), as compared with 1,100kg (2,246lb) for the Ni D-29.

The Nieuport was selected over the Spad, and by October 1921 two 'Nieuport 180 cv Rhône' were in service with the Aviation d'Escadre at Saint Raphaël (later to become Escadrille C-10) under L.V. Teste, and orders had been placed for another eight. The first was the prototype brought up to production standard. Fleet numbers for eight of these were in the range AE 13 to AE 20. These stayed in service until towards the end of 1924. Two or three were allocated to the CEPA, and one or more of these were still around in July 1923.

The wings of the prototype were like the Ni D-29, with overhanging ailerons, but this feature was removed from production machines, whilst at the same time the wing area was increased from 27sq m (290sq ft) to 30sq m (323sq ft) by widening the chord. However, the maximum speed was only 194km/h (120mph), which might have been sufficient to engage airships, but not other aircraft. Tankage was fitted to allow an endurance of more than four hours, but in practice this could be as low as fifteen minutes if the fuel load had to be reduced to guarantee take-off.

Tests were carried out in cooperation with the CEPA; however, the early ones from a platform fitted to *La Bretagne* were not encouraging. In one test on the 27 March 1920, the engine was difficult to start and did not give the power expected,

Nieuport-Delage 32 prototype, with the extended ailerons. Philip Jarrett

producing only about 150hp, and to achieve take-off the parent vessel had to manœuvre into the wind to give at least 10 knots headwind. The platform was very small, being about 13 × 5m (43 × 16ft), and in practice did not prove strong enough. These difficulties were experienced despite the aircraft having no armament, and moreover being a single-seater that would be unable to effectively carry out reconnaissance duties. A further series of seven tests were carried out in September 1922, using an available length of 18m (59ft); some were carried out by L.V. Teste, who had only flown the Ni D-32 once before, and it was found that the aircraft was very sensitive to turbulence.

These tests were supplemented by others carried out ashore, either at Saint Raphaël or at Palyvestre. In particular, safety features were examined, and flotation tests were carried out, the latter aimed at keeping the aircraft afloat with the engine out of the water should it come down in the sea. The tests were similar to some carried out by the RNAS, and used two large, inflatable fabric bags fitted under the lower wings. It was necessary to jettison the wheels before hitting the water, and a hydrofoil was positioned in front of the landing gear to prevent the aircraft from capsizing as it hit the water. The incidence of the hydrofoil was adjusted by the lever that also released the wheels. This system was abandoned in favour of a simple metal blade fitted under the tail that was set at an angle to the water sufficient to keep the tail down.

Nieuport-Delage 40C-1 and Ni DC-1

As part of the 1921 programme, Nieuport, along with other manufacturers, submitted a design for a high altitude interceptor with the intention of fitting the engine with the Rateau turbocharger to boost power at altitude. In the event, Rateau had problems tuning the turbocharger, and as a result this device was not fitted to this aircraft. Designated the Ni D-40, the design differed from the Ni D-29C-1 in having a redesigned engine cowling that sloped down slightly towards the front, and as a result improved the pilot's view. The fuselage length was increased from 6.44 to 6.7m (21 to 22ft), and the rudder was given a more pointed shape. This prototype did not receive an order, but it led to the Ni D-40R, an aircraft of increased span and length designed for an attempt on the world altitude record.

Data on the Nieuport-Delage Ni D-32Rh		
Engine:		180hp Le Rhône
Dimensions:	Span, upper, m (ft)	9.7 (31.8)
	Length, m (ft)	6.7 (22)
	Wing area, sq m (sq ft)	30 (323)
Weights:	Empty, kg (lb)	603 (1,330)
	Loaded, kg (lb)	857 (1,890)
Performance:	Endurance, hr	4.5

At the Paris Salon of December 1922, Nieuport-Astra presented two specialized versions of the Ni D-29 designed for operation at high and low altitudes respectively. The single-seat, high altitude fighter version was designated the Ni DC-1 'Cellule 1923', and was introduced as a development of the Ni D-40C-1. It was distinguished from the Ni D-29 by a small increase in span of 10cm (4in), and in chord from 1.50 to 1.60m (4.9 to 5.2ft), resulting in an increase in the wing area from 26.8 to 29.8sq m (288 to 320sq ft), and a reduction in wing loading to 40kg/sq m (8.2lb/sq ft). The aircraft was further modified by increasing the height of the rudder and reducing its width – thus leaving the overall area the same. This shape was revived some months later on the racing sesquiplane that carried the Nieuport colours in the Coupe Deutsche. This prototype, like the Ni D-40, was not equipped with a Rateau turbocharger. It was exhibited in Madrid during March 1923 in a competition organized by the Spanish military, but no order was forthcoming, the Spanish preferring the standard Ni D-29.

The Nieuport-Delage 29bis

The low altitude version introduced at the 1922 Paris Salon was distinguished by a single-bay wing structure with a reduced wing area. Compared with the Ni D-29, the span was significantly reduced, from 9.7 to 8.0m (31ft 10in to 26ft 3in), and its wing area from 26.8 to 21sq m (288 to 226sq ft), to give a wing loading of 44kg (9.02lb/sq ft) as compared with 52.5kg (10.77lb/sq ft). This machine, known as the Ni D-29bis, was presented at the Concours International at Madrid, but despite an outstanding presentation, was not ordered.

Another experimental prototype appeared in 1924 with a wing structure and reduced span similar to the 29bis. But there were other significant differences: for instance, it had a 390hp Hispano-Suiza engine fitted with a redesigned streamlined metal engine cowling and spinner. The frontal intake for the carburettor was replaced by four small intakes spaced round the top of the front of the cowling. A new radiator installation was incorporated, with two rectangular Lamblin radiators placed along the fronts of the undercarriage legs, similar to those of the Nie D-42 during its course of development. The wings did not possess dihedral, nor a cut-out section in the lower wing. The inverted-V cabane struts were replaced by splayed-out N-struts and a wide central strut. The fin resembled that of the 29bis, except that the ventral fin had been omitted, and the horizontal tailplane did not have the overhanging aerodynamic balance.

The aircraft was entered in the Beaumont Cup of June 1924 under the name 'Nieuport-Delage 380hp Biplane', but did not take part. It was also withdrawn, for reasons unknown, during the previous month from attempts to break the world speed record. Although it was unsuccessful, it acted as a prototype for the Ni D-42C-1, and provided valuable information on the new systems that had been incorporated, such as the separate carburettor intakes, streamlined cowling and the new Lamblin radiators. All these changes were found on the Ni D-42S monoplane that was being developed in parallel.

The Nieuport-Delage 29B-1

A limited number of Ni D-29s were modified to take eight to ten 10kg (20lb) bombs under the designation Ni D-29B-1; these were used in Morocco for a limited period during 1925 as army cooperation and

Experimental version of the Nieuport-Delage 29 with a 390hp Hispano-Suiza engine.

counter-insurgency aircraft. A section of three was formed at Casablanca on 1 November 1925, and together with a bomber force consisting of Breguets and Hanriots, placed under the direction of Sadi Lecointe, who had been seconded from Nieuport-Astra where he was a test pilot. They were used in an attempt to dissuade Abd el-Krim, chief of the Rif guerrilla forces for independence, from recruiting pilots and setting up his own air arm, also to collect information about the movement of his forces, and to operate against ground targets. The section was very active during November, and accomplished around seventy missions, including bombing from altitude; these attacks were made with adequate precision, despite lacking a suitable bombsight, and ground attacks were also made with bombs and machine-guns to assist army operations. In spite of good results obtained in Morocco, and the very successful use of aircraft in similar circumstances by the RAF, the Armée de l'Air did not use aircraft in a similar way until World War Two.

The Nieuport-Delage 29 ET.1

The Ni D-29 ET.1 was a lightened and lower-powered version of the Ni D-29C-1. The intention was to use it as an advanced single-seat fighter trainer, and it was presented in a competition organized by the director of army aviation. This model differed from the Ni D-29 by being fitted with a 180hp Hispano-Suiza engine, though this resulted in only a modest performance. However, the lower cowling and the removal of the machine-guns did at least improve the pilot's view.

There were entries from four other designers – the Spad 72, Caudron 77, Hanriot 27 and Gourdou monoplane – but the Ni D-29 ET.1 won the competition, and as a consequence of this, 100 examples were built under licence by SABCA in Belgium. The Ni D-29ET.1 was used side-by-side with the 300hp Ni D-29 for training in flying schools in France and Belgium during the 1930s. With a total weight of 970kg (2,139lb) as compared with 1,100kg (2,426lb) for the N29C-1, and a wing loading of 36kg/sq m (7.3lb/sq ft) as compared with 41kg/sq m (8.4lb/sq ft), the 29 ET.1 had a presentable maximum speed of 196km/h (122mph), a speed of 186km/h (116mph) at 4,000m (13,120ft), and a service ceiling of 6,000m (19,690ft).

The Nieuport-Delage 29 Seaplane Racers

Two examples of the Ni D-29 were equipped with floats and prepared for the Schneider Trophy Race due to be held at Bournemouth on 10 September 1919. The two machines differed in their wing structure and float configuration: one, given the racing number '4', was prepared by Gustav Delage's assistant, Chasserias. He used the two-bay wing structure with overhanging ailerons of the standard Ni D-29C-1, which was then fitted with two short, broad floats with twin steps and a tail-float. The other machine had the racing number '2' and was fitted with clipped wings, with the wing area reduced from 26 to 22sq m (280 to 237sq ft), and two single-stepped floats of sufficient length to avoid the need for a tail-float.

The two floatplanes undertook their debut in September, with tests on the Seine at Argenteuil. The conditions proved difficult because the bridges on the river were found to be too closely spaced for testing such high performance machines. Thus during one of the tests, J. Casale badly damaged the floats of '2' during a hard landing, and H. Mallard all but wrote off '4' when he hit one of the piers of a bridge when landing in semi-darkness. However, the tests conducted up to this time were promising, so by working

Nieuport-Delage 29C-1 floatplane number '2' at Cowes, ready for the 1919 Schneider Trophy Race held at Bournemouth. Note the single-bay clipped wings and long twin floats. Philip Jarrett

day and night, the two machines were repaired and made ready for the race.

On 7 September, three days before the race was due to begin, Casale took off from Argenteuil in the new machine; despite thick fog he crossed the Channel, and then attempted to land at Cowes where the contestants were based. Having selected a sheltered area to land on the Medina river away from rough sea in the Cowes Roads, he hit a buoy and partially submerged. He was rescued and towed ashore, where the aircraft was repaired by Sam Saunders and his men using a new engine and floats despatched from France. However, he once again damaged a float and developed a leak, and this caused him to be the last competitor to reach Bournemouth. Meanwhile on 7 September, Mallard, who had made a stop at Le Havre, had engine failure 80km (50 miles) from the coast, and force-landed in the sea. He spent one night in the water clinging to the wreckage of his machine before he was rescued by a British naval vessel.

The start of the race was delayed until Casale arrived. When his turn came to compete, the leakage in the float proved too great and he was forced to beach his listing aircraft before it sank. As it happened, thick mist and incompetent management caused the race to be declared void.

The next year, Nieuport entered an Ni D-29C-1 with the racing number '25' and of three-float configuration in the 1920 Trophy Race at Monaco. It did not compete, however, as Nieuport wanted to concentrate on the Gordon Bennett Race that followed shortly after.

A Nieuport with short main floats and a short tail-float was entered for the 1921 Schneider Trophy held in Venice. But it never got there, because during Sadi Lecointe's first landing following a navigability trial, a spreader bar between the floats broke, the floats folded upwards and the wings collapsed. This effectively ended the floatplane's career. But although the Ni D-29 seaplanes were unsuccessful, valuable experience was gained, which was applied to other record-breaking aircraft.

Nieuport-Delage 29V and 29V*bis*

With orders for military aircraft collapsing at the end of the war, manufacturers turned to modifying their designs into racing machines or record-breaking aircraft as a means of attracting the attention of potential customers at home and abroad, and the Nieuport company was no exception.

Nieuport-Delage 29C-1 number '25' being made ready for the 1920 Monaco Trophy Race – in which it did not, however, compete. Note the two-bay wings and tail-float.
Philip Jarrett

For the first Coupe Deutsche de la Meurthe after the war in 1919, Nieuport-Astra entered two prototypes, one a monoplane powered by a 180hp Le Rhône, piloted by Jensen, and the other a modified Ni D-29 piloted by de Romanet. Against them were ranged a Spad-Herbemont piloted by Sadi Lecointe, and a Gourdou 180. The aircraft piloted by de Romanet was called the Ni D-29V (for *vitesse*) and was specially modified for the competition. Any excess weight was removed, including armament, and the tanks were filled with just enough petrol to complete the course. The wingspan was reduced to 6m (20ft) and the resultant wing area from 26.75 to 13sq m (287.8 to 140sq ft). The Hispano-Suiza engine was fine-tuned to give 320hp at 1,980rev/min. The right-hand Lamblin radiator was replaced by a rectangular radiator placed on top of the cowling between the two banks of cylinders. The machine was painted black, polished to a high gloss, and given the racing number '6'. On 23 October, during the first lap of the race, de Romanet succeeded in attaining an unofficial record speed of 268km/h (166.5mph) – though immediately after this the race was postponed for three months due to extremely poor weather conditions. By then, Sadi Lecointe had rejoined Nieuport-Astra from Blériot, and it was he who at the end of 1919 was charged with defending the colours of the company in the Ni D-29V. Kirsch piloted a second example.

The year 1920 started with a series of duels between Sadi Lecointe and Casale in a Spad. On 1 February, the former managed to achieve a homologated world record of 275.862km/h (171.421mph) – but this was beaten three weeks later by Casale with a speed of 283km/h (175.9mph).

After their unsuccessful entry in the 1920 Monaco Trophy Race, Sadi Lecointe flew a Nieuport 29 with the civil registration F-ABAV at the 1920 Olympiad held in Antwerp in early September, and won the speed test.

Nieuport entered two Ni D-29Vs for the Gordon Bennett Cup beginning on 25 September. These were almost identical to the 1919 machines, but differed in having a more angular-shaped tail fin and rudder, a more streamlined engine cowling, and a return to the twin Lamblin radiators. The Hispano engines had a compression ratio of 4.7, which gave little more than 260hp, pistons to give a compression ratio of 5.3 being required to deliver normal rated performance. The two machines were

Nieuport-Delage 29V number '10', winner of the 1920 Gordon Bennett Race and holder of two world speed records, October 1920. Philip Jarrett

distinguished by different wing configurations: Kirsch's aircraft retained the same arrangement as the 1919 machine, whereas that of Sadi Lecointe had the wing area reduced to 12.3sq m (132.3sq ft). During tests prior to the race, the wing area of this machine had been reduced to 11sq m (118sq ft) by clipping the wings to a span of 5.46m (17.9ft). The tests showed that the machine was in fact some 30km/h (18.6mph) slower, probably due to increased induced drag, and Sadi Lecointe opted for a compromise of retaining the 5.46m (17.9ft) span for the upper wing, but reverting to the 6m (19.6ft) span for the lower wing. This machine had a landing speed of 120km/h (74.6mph) and required over 400m (1,300ft) to come to a stop. Sadi Lecointe's machine had double lift wires compared with the single ones fitted to Kirsch's machine. Both machines were painted white, the only difference being that one machine had a blue tail, and the other had a red one. They carried the racing numbers '10' for Sadi Lecointe and '11' for Kirsch.

Eleven competitors were entered: these were three Americans (Curtiss, Verville and Dayton-Wright); three British (Martinsyde Semiquaver, British Nieuport and Sopwith); and five French (two Nieuports, two Spad 20*bis*, piloted by Casale and de Romanet, and a Borel piloted by Barrault). Eliminating trials to reduce the French entrants to three began on 25 September. On the first attempt, Sadi Lecointe was worried about his engine coolant temperatures and landed in a field, puncturing a tyre. He was rescued by Courcelles, a famous racing driver, who drove Lecointe's mechanic Jean Bernard to find him. In his second attempt, Sadi Lecointe achieved a closed circuit record of 279km/h (173 miles) over 100km (62 miles), and Kirsch was only 1sec slower. On 28 September, the day of the race, the weather began poorly, but gradually improved. Kirsch took off first, but his attempt failed due to oiled sparking plugs. However, Sadi Lecointe won with a speed of 271.5km/h (168.7mph), with de Romanet second.

The rivalry between de Romanet and Sadi Lecointe continued. On 10 October, de Romanet attained a speed of 292km/h (181mph), but the next day Sadi Lecointe reached 296.6km/h (184.3mph). This speed was achieved over a 1km course at a height of only 10m (32ft). Six days later, Sadi Lecointe at Villacoublay attained a speed of 302.529km/h (187.99mph), the first time that 300km/h had been exceeded.

The duel between Sadi Lecointe and de Romanet had not ended, because the latter pilot modified his machine by sloping the windscreen and lowering its headrest, changes that allowed him to reach 309km/h (192mph), thus beating the official record by 17km/h (10.5mph). Sadi Lecointe responded by carrying out such modifications a stage further, eliminating the cockpit opening completely by covering it with a sliding hatch, lowering the seat to the bottom of the fuselage, and fitting windows on the sides of the fuselage to give a restricted sideways view. One of the two Lamblin radiators was also removed, and the aircraft was repolished. On 12 December Sadi Lecointe had the last word when in poor conditions and at a height of just 4m (13ft), despite the restricted visibility, he achieved a speed of 313.043km/h (194.525mph), thereby breaking the previous record by 11km/h (6.8mph).

The Ni D-29V*bis*, as it was now called, was entered in the Aerial Derby due to take place in July 1921. However, during the preceding April a wheel broke during a landing, and the aircraft was damaged beyond repair, Sadi Lecointe being lucky to escape with just a broken arm. It was replaced by the second Ni D-29V, the old '10' from the Gordon Bennett Cup, in which Sadi Lecointe carried off the Gran Premio d'Italia d'Aviazione at Brescia on 4 September at an average speed of 280km/h (174mph), beating Brack-Papa into second place. A single Ni D-29V, carrying the racing number '5', and two of the new Nieuport sesquiplanes participated in the Coupe Deutsche of 1921. On 1 October 1921, the first to take off was Sadi Lecointe in one of the sesquiplanes, and he achieved a speed of 314km/h (195mph) over the first 50km (30 miles) before his propeller shattered, eliminating him from the race. Staying the course, Kirsch in his sesquiplane won with a speed of 278.3km/h (172.9mph), with Fernand

POSTWAR DEVELOPMENTS OF WARTIME DESIGNS

Lasne, a newcomer to Nieuport, coming second in the Ni D-29V at a speed of 257.2km/h (159.8mph).

1922 was the last year in which the Ni D-29V*bis* participated, because despite all the improvements that had been incorporated, it had reached the limit of its potential. Three Nieuports were present at the Coupe Deutsche that year: the Ni D-29V, piloted by Berthelin and carrying the number '4', the sesquiplane, and the new Ni D-41 cantilever monoplane. Because of technical difficulties with the latter, Sadi Lecointe switched to the sesquiplane, and Lasne replaced Berthelin in the Ni D-29V. After attaining a speed of 325km/h (202mph), the sesquiplane was eliminated due to trouble with a sparking plug. All the other entrants were eliminated except for Lasne who, with his old Ni D-28V, was declared the winner at a speed of 289km/h (180mph). The Coupe Deutsch was awarded outright to Nieuport-Astra.

Nieuport-Delage 29V number '4', being started with an 'Odier' starter. Philip Jarrett

Nieuport-Delage 40R

One of the early Ni D-29C-1s (12010) was equipped in January 1919 with a Rateau turbocharger with the aim of improving its high altitude performance, and if possible to attack the world altitude record. This machine was modified with a large mounting for the turbocharger, strengthened cabane struts, and the fitting of enlarged Lamblin radiators that required the front undercarriage legs to be curved forwards. Many tests were carried out on this installation by Casale during the spring of 1919. From one such test on 28 May, the aircraft reached an altitude of 9,150m (30,050ft), and this was followed by another test on 7 June when an altitude of 9,250m (30,350ft) was attained. Lastly on 14 June, Casale reached an altitude of 9,520m (31,235ft) thereby establishing a new world altitude record. However, this was beaten the following year on 27 February 1920 for America by Schroeder in a Packhard-Lepère, who reached 10,093m (33,115ft). It was not until 1923 that France was able to regain this record.

The tests continued through 1920. During one of the flights on 19 March, Lt Weiss of the Armée de l'Air made a gradual climb that was interrupted at 7,000m (23,000ft) by a broken impeller. The machine went into a dive for thirty-eight seconds, during which time it lost a great deal of height, the pilot finally regaining control at 3,400m (11,000ft) despite losing part of his machine's elevator. More than a year later, on 24 June 1921, the company test pilot Kirsch succeeded in reaching an altitude of 9,800m (32,150ft). Unlike earlier tests, for this attempt the machine was fitted with an impeller designed for medium altitudes. He attained 9,000m (30,000ft) in only forty-five minutes, but progress was then very slow and the last 800m (2,600ft) took a further thirty-five minutes. Another attempt was made on 15 July when Kirsch took off from Le Bourget and reached a height of 10,600m (34,800ft), easily beating Schroeder's record, but unfortunately the result was not recognized by the FAI as Kirsche, having landed at Montmirail, had not landed at the place where he took off.

On 18 September, the altitude record was again raised by another American, Lt McReady, who reached a height of 10,518m (34,510ft) in a Packhard-Lepère. To restore France's prestige, it was decided by the Under-Secretary for State for Aviation, Laurent-Eynac, to grant three prizes of 50,000Fr to any constructor who achieved a notable performance. Although it did not have the blessing of the General

Nieuport-Delage 40R high-altitude machine at Villacoublay in 1923.

172

Staff, Nieuport-Delage decided to construct a machine, designated the Ni D-40R, derived from the Ni D-40C-1 military high-altitude fighter. The idea was to significantly increase the wing area and reduce the weight to improve the wing loading while increasing the power of the engine at altitude by supercharging rather than turbocharging.

The Ni D-40R utilized the fuselage of the Ni D-40C-1, which was essentially that of the Ni D-29 with a more streamlined cowling. However, this was about the only feature that the two types had in common. The main difference was that the later design had an entirely new wing, with much larger dimensions. The span of the two-bay structure was increased from 9.70m to 14m (31.8ft to 50ft), and the chord from 1.25m to 1.40m (4.1ft to 4.6ft), giving a wing area of 34sq m (366sq ft) compared with 26.84sq m (288.8sq ft). Only the lower wing was given dihedral, and the two wings were slightly closer together, 1.30m (4.2ft) as compared with 1.40m (4.6ft). The interplane struts were of aluminium, and the cabane struts were of N configuration. The area of the fin and rudder were slightly increased, resulting in an increase of fuselage length from 6.60m to 6.80m (21ft 8in to 22ft 4in). The undercarriage legs were lengthened to allow for a larger propeller, and the shock absorbers were deleted to save weight, thereby requiring the aircraft to be positioned for take-off by trailer. Along with other measures, the empty weight was reduced to 746kg (1,645lb) and the fuel restricted to 80kg (176lb), giving a total weight of 980kg (2,160lb) and a wing loading of 27.9kg/m² (5.72lb/sq ft). The engine was a Hispano 8Fb, supercharged to give a power of 400hp at 2,000rev/min, which turned a two-bladed Régy propeller.

Like the Ni D-29V, the fuel was doped with benzene to improve the octane rating and allow a higher compression ratio. The fuel reverted to normal gasoline above 5,000m (16,400ft), where the more rarefied air reduced the effective cylinder pressure on compression.

The Ni D-40R made its first flight towards the end of July 1923 in the hands of Sadi Lecointe, after which the fuselage was painted white with the inscription 'Nieuport-Delage' in large black letters along the fuselage and under the lower wing. The company pilot had been acclimatizing himself in a glass low-pressure chamber, dressed in a fur coat and breathing oxygen at a pressure equivalent to 12,000m (40,000ft) altitude. He then began a series of flights in which he gradually attained greater altitudes. Then on 1 August 1923, he took off from Villecoublay for a climb that registered 10,800m (35,435ft), higher than the current world record; but after verification of the barograph, this height was reduced to 10,127m (33,227ft). A new attempt was therefore necessary, and this was carried out on 5 September, when a height of 10,741m (35,241ft) was achieved. Judging that the aircraft could do better, Sadi Lecointe made two more attempts, achieving 10,772m (35,343ft) on 8 September, and 11,145m (36,567ft) on 30 October above Issy-les-Moulineaux. This latter height was a record that was valid for both aircraft and free-flight balloons, and it was not bettered for four years. However, the Ni D-40R was not at the end of its career. Some months after the record, the machine was fitted with a pair of floats at the factory, and on 11 March 1924, flown by Sadi Lecointe, it took off from the Seine and two hours later beat the world seaplane altitude record with a height of 8,980m (29,463ft).

The Nieuport-Delage Racing Sesquiplanes

Parallel with the development of the Ni D-29V, Delage and Mary, the directors of the design office were developing their sesquiplane concept for racing purposes by improving power and performance, without worrying too much about providing good visibility for the pilot which until then had been an important consideration in designing against a military requirement.

The wings were thickened to allow the accommodation of more robust spars in order to reduce the need for struts and bracing wires. These could not be eliminated entirely, as the STAé had stipulated sufficient strength in the structure to resist forces of 12g. It was therefore necessary to retain two struts under the wing, which were supported by a small auxiliary wing between the undercarriage wheels.

The machine had an untapered wing with rounded tips set in the upper part of the fuselage. It had two spars made of spruce and wrapped in linen, and wing ribs built up from 1.5mm mahogany plywood webs, with steel tube and steel strap cross-members. It was covered in plywood, and then linen to give a smooth profile. A span of 8m (26ft) gave the wing a surface area of 12.7sq m (137sq ft), and a wing loading of 77kg/m² (15.8lb/sq ft). The fuselage was of monocoque construction, as before. The auxiliary wing between the wheels had a thick profile, and an area about a tenth of that of the wing, and it supported single struts from each wing set at about mid-span. The engine was a Hispano 8Fb, similar to that in the Ni D-29V but supercharged to give 320–340hp at 1,800rev/min. It was fed by a 180ltr (40gal) tank placed close to the centre of gravity in front of the pilot. Two Lamblin radiators

Data on Speed and Altitude Record-Breaking Machines		Ni D-29V (1920)	Ni D-29V (1922)	Ni D-40C-1	Ni D-40R
Engine:		320hp Hispano	320hp Hispano	300hp Hispano	400hp Hispano
Dimensions:	Wingspan, upper, m (ft)	6.05 (19.8)	5.46 (17.9) (lower 6.05 (19.8))	9.7 (31.8)	14.0 (50)
	Wing chord, m (ft)	1.02 (3.3)	1.02 (3.3) (lower 1.26 (4.1))	1.25 (4.1)	1.4 (4.6)
	Length, m (ft)	6.2 (20.3)	6.2 (20.3)	6.6 (21.6)	6.8 (22.3)
	Wing area, sq m (sq ft)	13.2 (142)	12.3 (132)	26.84 (288.8)	34 (366)
Weights:	Empty, kg (lb)	620 (1,367)	690 (1,520)	851 (1,876)	746 (1,645)
	Fuel load, kg (lb)	72 (159)	160 (353)	145 (320)	82 (180)
	Loaded, kg (lb)	834 (1,839)	936 (2,063)	1,190 (2,624)	948 (2,090)
	Wing loading, kg/m²	63.18	76.10	44	27.9
	Power loading, hp/m²	3.21	2.92	3.9	2.38

were installed under the fuselage between the undercarriage legs. The propeller was a 2.3m (7.5ft) diameter Lumière.

Two prototypes were constructed for the 1921 Coupe Deutsch: they were finished in highly polished white paint, number '6' with a red fin and rudder, and number '7' with a blue fin and rudder; they were piloted by Sadi Lecointe and Kirsch respectively. The Ni D-29V also took part, piloted by Lasne. The Nieuport machines were ranged against the Monge, piloted by de Romanet, a Hanriot piloted by Rost, a Fiat piloted by Brack-Papa, and a Sopwith Camel piloted by James. The Monge crashed before the race, killing de Romanet, the Hanriot and Fiat were eliminated for technical reasons, and the Camel pilot withdrew during the race. This left just the three Nieuports in the contest.

During the preliminary tests on 26 September, Sadi Lecointe managed to attain a speed of 330.275km/h (205.233mph), beating the record previously held by the Ni D-29V in 1920. The race itself began on 1 October at Etampes, when Sadi Lecointe covered the first 50km (30 miles) at 313km/h (194mph), but crash-landed at Germonville with a shattered propeller, probably due to a bird strike. The machine careered along the ground for 50m (150ft) and was almost destroyed. Sadi Lecointe suffered an injured right eye and a broken wrist, but soon recovered without permanent injury. Kirsch and Lasne continued the race, which was won by Kirsch at an average speed of 278km/h (173mph) over 300km (186 miles), compared with 257.4km/h (159.9mph) for Lasne. During the course of the race Kirsch had set a new 200km (124mph) closed circuit record.

Kirsch had left his attempt late in the day, and being relatively inexperienced with the aircraft, took the turns cautiously and conserved the engine to be sure to finish. Even so, at the end of the race, on landing at around 145km/h (90mph), he bounced, stalled the engine and porpoised along the downward slope, eventually slewing round and coming to a halt. In fact it was not surprising that Kirsch lost concentration at the end, because heat from the engine had raised the temperature of the cockpit to around 90°F, making the metallic parts scalding hot and giving the pilot blistered feet!

The regulations for the Coupe Deutsch the following year were the same as before, except the qualifying speed was to be 280km/h (174mph) over the 300km (186 miles). To improve the performance of his sesquiplane, Mary made further efforts to reduce drag and improve the power output from the Hispano engine. This was raised to 370hp at 1,900rev/min by raising the compression ratio to 6, achieved by using benzene as fuel which has excellent anti-knock characteristics. The engine was fitted with a Zenith carburettor and a Régy propeller. The wing-tips were squared off while retaining the same span and wing area, but the aerofoil, previously with an almost flat under-surface, was changed to a Göttingen 416 bi-concave aerofoil. The machine was christened 'Eugène Gilbert' after a prewar racing hero who had been killed in the war. On 10 September, Sadi Lecointe flew 100km (62miles) at an average speed of 325.491km/h (202.260mph), and nine days before the race on 21 September, he achieved 341.239km/h (212.046mph) to take the world speed record. In the race the machine was due to be flown by Lasne as Sadi Lecointe was scheduled to fly the Ni D-41, a new prototype. However, the latter machine was not ready in time, so Sadi Lecointe switched to the sesquiplane, now numbered '5', and Lasne took the Ni D-29V that had been allocated the number '4'.

Many incidents occurred during the race, causing many to abandon the contest. These included Sadi Lecointe, who experienced engine failure when a sparking plug blew out of its socket and pierced the cowling. He crash-landed on the grass of the aerodrome, hit a rut while still travelling fast and turned over, luckily without injuring himself. Lasne went round at a more lesurely pace and was the only competitor to finish, at an average speed of 289km/h (180mph).

By then the Hispano engine had reached the limit of its potential, and the Coupe Deutsch had come to an end. Nieuport had won the race two years' running, and had gained a great deal of international prestige and financial benefit as a result.

On 18 October, a new era began when the world speed record went to America: a Curtiss R-6, with a 450hp Curtiss D-12 engine and piloted by General Billy Mitchell, attained a speed of 358.8km/h (222.9mph). The directors of the Nieuport company decided to attempt to regain the record by heavily modifying the

Nieuport-Delage sesquiplane 'Eugène Gilbert' number '5', flown by Sadi Lecointe in the 1922 Coupe Deutsche; it did not finish. Philip Jarrett

sesquiplane. Because the sesquiplane had a very high landing speed of around 180km/h (112mph), it was necessary to fly the machine to Istres where the facilities were more appropriate. Fitted with a new Régy propeller, Sadi Lecointe carried out many test flights during December, but could not exceed 348km/h (216mph), a speed attained on 31 December. The machine was returned to its hangar to receive a new kind of radiator, designed to improve cooling and reduce drag. Gustave Delage estimated that the Lamblin radiators contributed something like 30 per cent of the drag, and arranged for the Moreux company to fit a new type of radiator based on a concept developed by Curtiss. The radiators consisted of two thin sheets of brass, corrugated and turned in such a way as to link together in a smooth exterior surface that extended along the bottom of the wing. The sharp leading edge was the return header, and the feed header was a flattened span-wise tube just ahead of the aileron. However, the cooling surface proved to be sufficient only for short sprints, and did not give adequate cooling for sustained flight. The other important modification was the use of an American engine, the Wright H-3, which was more compact and lighter than the Hispano. This delivered 410hp and had been destined for the Ni D-41, the development of which had been abandoned a few months earlier. The tail surfaces were enlarged to give better control at the higher levels of torque, which led to a small increase in fuselage length. In an effort to reduce the landing run, the conventional tail-skid was replaced by a steel design that was designed to dig into the ground.

Piloted by Sadi Lecointe, the modified 'Eugène Gilbert' renewed its tests at Istres during January 1923, and on 15 February beat Mitchell's world record with a speed of 375km/h (233mph) over 1km. This record did not last long, however, as on 29 March the record was again raised, this time to 380km/h (236mph) by Maugham in a Curtiss R-6 fitted with a 500hp engine and a fixed pitch metal propeller. Later, with its Curtiss D-12A engine modified to give 600hp, the Curtiss R-2C-1, piloted first by Lt Brow and then by Lt Williams, achieved 417.590km/h (259.490mph) and 429.025km/h (266.596mph) respectively. It was not possible to match such speeds with the sesquiplane, and Delage ordered Sadi Lecointe to stop further test flights, preferring instead to make fresh attempts with a new prototype, the Ni D-42S.

The Nieuport-Delage sesquiplane 'Eugène Gilbert' of 1923, prepared for the 1923 Coupe Deutsche. Musée de l'Air

The modified Nieuport-Delage sesquiplane of 1923, with the Lamblin radiators replaced by flush radiators in the wing. Philip Jarrett

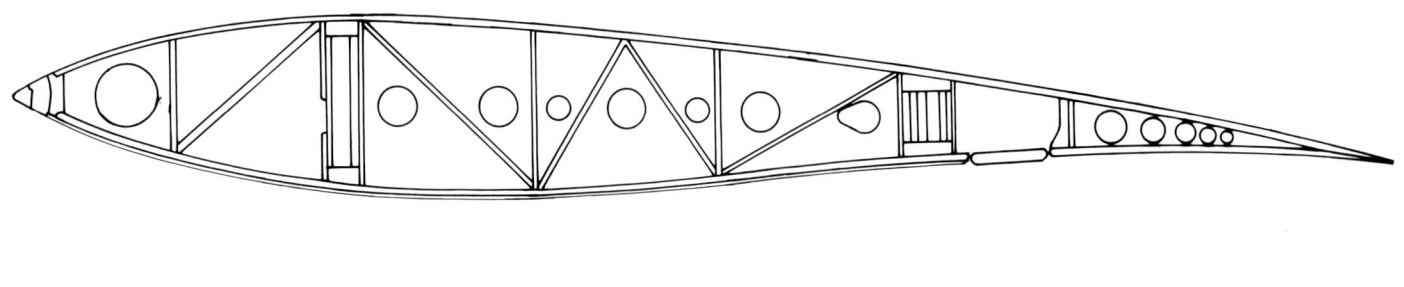

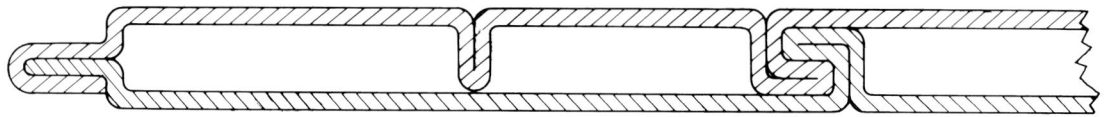

(*Above*) Wing radiator of late-1922 sesquiplane racer showing position of radiator on lower wing skin and section across the Moreau radiator. Mick Davis

(*Below*) 1924 version of the Nieuport-Delage 42S, winner of the 1924 and 1925 Coupe Beaumont races. Philip Jarrett

The Nieuport-Delage 42S

By 1923 it was apparent that the Hispano-Suiza V-8 engine had reached the end of its development potential. French engine manufacturers, including Lorraine, Renault and Gnome-Rhône, were making engines that could produce more than 450hp, but all of these were bulkier and heavier than would be acceptable for a racing machine. Marc Birkigt, the Hispano-Suiza chief engineer, in trying to develop the basic design further, added a further bank of four cylinders to the V-8 to produce a twelve-cylinder engine of W-configuration, designated the 12Ga in military parlance. This engine, destined to power the Bernard V-2 racer, was relatively light and was also of a similar length to the V-8, which made installation into existing airframes a practical proposition; however, its frontal area was considerably greater.

Birkigt also designed a V-12 engine, using cylinders of the same bore and stroke as those of the V-8, and this was the engine that Delage adopted for his next racer, the Nieuport-Delage 42S. This engine was longer, but of smaller frontal area than the W-12 engine. Its inlet ports were on the inside of the V and were fed by three carburettors on each side placed outside the V, with their throttles inline and connected to a common linkage. Air was taken in through the oil cooler bolted to the bottom of the crankcase and distributed to the carburettors, each of which fed just two cylinders by means of pipes passing through the cylinder block. Individual exhaust ports

176

were mounted on the outside of the cylinder blocks. This arrangement must have ensured excellent fuel/air mixture preparation and distribution – although volumetric efficiency must have suffered because of the heated mixture. The engine was produced in two versions, the 12Gb and 12Hb, with compression ratios of 5.3 and 6.2 respectively. During its fifty-hour type test the 12Gb produced 505hp at 1,800rev/min, and 545hp at 2,000rev/min, and could deliver as much as 575 to 600hp.

The Nieuport-Delage 42S was built solely in an attempt to regain the world speed record. Although it was classed as a sesquiplane, it could have been considered as a monoplane, as its auxiliary wing was little more than an axle fairing and support for the undercarriage legs and wing struts. The machine was larger than its predecessors. The monocoque fuselage was built as before from laminated 0.9mm strips of tulipwood in two halves, divided horizontally, and stiffened by longitudinal stringers and plywood bulkheads. A duralumin keel was fitted with metal bulkheads that supported the pilot's seat, the wing structure and undercarriage and the duralumin engine bearers. The engine, tuned to give 600hp at 2,000rev/min, was closely cowled, and flush radiators were fitted above and below the wings, covering nearly the whole surface. The wing was built in one piece, and was built up from twin box-spars of spruce, plywood ribs and spruce stringers, and covered in ply and linen. The inner part of the wing was braced by duralumin tubes, and the outer parts by piano wire. The ailerons were hinged to a spruce false spar and were operated by a torque tube. The tail surfaces were now elliptical in shape and their controls were operated by cables. The undercarriage legs were made of beech and tulipwood.

Sadi Lecointe began his attempts on the world speed record on 12 June 1924, and these continued unsuccessfully until 7 July. However, he did achieve success in the 1924 Coupe Beaumont held on 23 June at Istres. The Coupe Beaumont was first announced in 1923, but was cancelled through lack of foreign entries. The response was better in 1924, but all the entrants except the Nieuport withdrew before the race, leaving Sadi Lecointe to fly over the course unopposed to win the 75,000Fr first prize. After completing the 300km (186 mile) course at an average speed of 311.239km/h (193.404mph), he continued a further 200km (124 miles) to beat the existing 500km (310 miles) closed circuit world record at 306.696km/h (190.580mph). However, it proved impossible to coax much extra speed out of the design, and further record-breaking attempts were abandoned.

Two other sesquiplanes were designed for military and record-breaking purposes, the Ni D-37C-1 and Ni D-41 respectively, but neither can be considered as developments of wartime designs. Likewise military designs, designated the Ni D-42C-1 and Ni D-42C-2, were later developed that were much larger and of a different configuration to the 42S. None of these developments are described in this book.

Nieuport 29 Derivative Race Winners and Record Breakers

Circuit of Paris 1919	1st Count de Romanet at 268.631km/h (166.927mph)	Nieuport-Delage 29V
Circuit of Paris 1920	1st Sadi Lecointe at 266.314km/h (165.487mph)	Nieuport-Delage 29V
Coupe Deutsch 1921	1st Kirsch at 289km/h (180mph)	Sesquiplane No.7
	2nd Lasne at 257.4km/h (159.9mph)	Nieuport-Delage 29V
Coupe Deutsch 1922	1st Lasne at 289km/h (180mph)	Nieuport-Delage 29V
Coupe Beaumont 1924	1st Sadi-Leconte at 311.239km/h (193.404mph)	Nieuport-Delage 42S

Date	Record	km/h (mph)	Pilot	Aircraft
07.02.20	World speed record km/h (mph)	275.862 (171.420)	Sadi Lecointe	Nieuport NiD-29V
10.10.20	World speed record km/h (mph)	296.694 (184.366)	Sadi Lecointe	Nieuport NiD-29V
20.10.20	World speed record km/h (mph)	302.529 (187.992)	Sadi Lecointe	Nieuport NiD-29V
12.12.20	World speed record km/h (mph)	313.043 (194.524)	Sadi Lecointe	Nieuport NiD-29Vbis
26.09.21	World speed record km/h (mph)	330.275 (205.233)	Sadi Lecointe	Sesquiplane No.5
21.09.22	World speed record km/h (mph)	341.239 (212.046)	Sadi Lecointe	Sesquiplane No.5
15.02.23	World speed record km/h (mph)	3375.000 (233.025)	Sadi Lecointe	Sesquiplane 'E. Gilbert'
05.09.23	World altitude record	10,743m (35,248ft)	Sadi Lecointe	Ni D-40R
30.10.23	World altitude record	11,145m (36,567ft)	Sadi Lecointe	Ni D-40R
15.06.24	World altitude record for seaplanes	8,980m (29,463ft)	Sadi Lecointe	Ni D-40R seaplane

Data of Nieuport-Delage Sesquiplanes

		Coupe Deutsch 1921	Coupe Deutsch 1923	Ni D-42S
Engine:		320hp Hispano	410hp Wright H-3	600hp Hispano 12Gb
Propeller:		Régy	Régy	
Dimensions:	Wingspan, m (ft)	8.00 (26)	8.00 (26)	9.50 (31)
	Lower wingspan, m (ft)	1.70 (5.5)		
	Length, m (ft)	6.10 (20)	6.20 (20.3)	7.30 (24)
	Height, m (ft)	2.0 (6.5)	2.0 (6.5)	2.2 (7.2)
	Wing area, sq m (sq ft)	11 (118)	11 (118)	14 + 1.5 (46 + 5)
Weights:	Weight empty, kg (lb)	1,170 (2,580)		
	Fuel load, kg (lb)	159 (350)	170 (375)	
	Weight loaded, kg (lb)	980 (2,160)	1,014 (2,236)	1,440 (3,175)
	Wing loading, kg/m²	89	92.3	93
	Power loading, hp/m²	3.06	2.48	2.4
Performance:	Maximum speed, km/h (mph)	313 (194)	375 (233)	312 (193.8)

The Nieuport-Tellier Flying Boats

As related in the first chapter, Nieuport took a controlling interest in the Tellier company late in 1918 and the current and subsequent Tellier designs were re-designated. Thus the Nieuport BM (Bimoteur) was similar to the Tellier T.5, the Nieuport S was similar to the Tellier 350hp Sunbeam or T.4, the Tellier T.7 became known as the Nieuport TM (Trimoteur), and the Tellier *Vonna* project became the Nieuport 4R 450 in the company catalogue.

The Tellier T.4 and T.5 were larger versions of the earlier T.3, of which more than 260 were built and saw service with the Aviation Maritime from February 1917 and also with navies in Japan, Portugal, Russia and the United States. The T.4 was fitted with a single 350hp Sunbeam V-12 Maori, and the T.5, which was slightly longer, was fitted with two 250hp Hispano-Suiza 8b engines in tandem.

The Nieuport BM

The T.5 or Nieuport BM was designed to carry a 47mm Hotchkiss cannon and 300kg (660lb) of bombs. It was intended as an anti-submarine aircraft, having the capacity to disable a submarine with the cannon and finish it off with the bombs. The overall layout consisted of a hull, with the gunner's position in the nose, and a cockpit with two side-by-side seats just in front of the wings. The wings were of unequal span, with the lower wing set on the upper longerons of the hull. The tailplane was positioned halfway up the fin.

The hull consisted of three watertight compartments and was furnished with two steps. It was made of three layers of mahogany from the nose to the first step, two layers of mahogany between the steps, and of plywood of progressively decreasing thickness to the tail. The three-bay wings were of constant chord, the upper wing being fitted with ailerons that projected beyond the wing trailing edge, and the lower wing had dihedral. The wing spars were constructed from metal tubing, and supported ribs made of ash strengthened with plywood. The wings were covered in linen and coated with Emaillite. A Y-shaped strut stretched from a single point on the top of the fin to two anchor points on the trailing edge of the upper wing, and was supported where it divided by a vertical strut from the hull. A pair of floats was supported below the middle pair of wing struts at about mid-span. The tandem 250hp Hispano-Suiza engines were uncowled and mounted above the hull between the wings. Two Chausson radiators were fitted between the forward engine and the upper wing. The fuel tanks, holding 620ltr (136gal), were located behind the pilot's cockpit.

The prototype T.5 first flew in January 1918. Various payloads were tested, including 800kg (1,764lb), 1,000kg (2,205lb) and 1,215kg (2,679lb). It was found to fly well on one engine whilst carrying a load of 711kg (1,568lb). In early 1918 it was dismantled and sent to Saint Raphaël for further testing by the Aviation Maritime. A considerable number were ordered, but production was slow, and only about ten were placed in service.

To gain experience for a projected transatlantic flight, on 19 July 1919 Capt Marchal of the Aéronautique Militaire and his mechanic carried out the first non-stop crossing of the Mediterranean by flying boat from Saint Raphaël to Bizerte, some 730km (450 miles), in 10hr 30min. In April 1920, three Tellier flying boats took part in the Monaco meeting: these were two T.4s powered by 350hp Sunbeams – '45' piloted by E.V. Sala and '46' piloted by E.V. Renault – and a T.5 powered by two Hispano-Suizas – '47' piloted by L.V. Hurel. Unfortunately none was successful, as '45' came down in the sea 65km (40 miles) from Cagliari, '46' crashed into the sea 35km (22 miles) from Bizerte, and '47' suffered with a leaking hull and remained parked on the quayside.

The Nieuport TM

In January 1918, the Aéronautique Maritime issued a specification for an ocean-going reconnaissance flying boat. It called for a crew of four, with provision for a transmitter/receiver, a 75mm cannon with thirty-five rounds, and two machine-guns. The Tellier submission, the T.7, or Nieuport TM as it became, was of a similar

Nieuport-Tellier BM '47' on the quayside at Monaco after failing to participate in the 1920 Monaco meeting due to a leaking hull. Philip Jarrett

configuration to the earlier machines but was much larger, with a biplane tailplane, and was powered by three 250hp Hispano-Suizas in place of the intended 350hp Lorraine-Dietrich 12D V-12 engines, which were unavailable at the time the prototype was completed. The three engines were mounted between the wings, the centre tractor engine being flanked by two pushers. Construction began in April or May 1918, and was completed before the Armistice. The first flight took place from the Seine at Meulan towards the end of December 1918. Although it was underpowered, the aircraft took off and flew satisfactorily, the fact that it did not have to carry the weight of the cannon compensating for the lower-rated engines.

Several days later, in January 1919, whilst trying to negotiate a difficult manœuvre when under tow, the aircraft sank and lay immersed for several days before it could be raised. It was repaired at the factory, then dismantled and sent to Saint Raphaël, where official trials began during May. At first the flying boat refused to take off, due to the weight of water absorbed by the airframe during its immersion, as well as the weight of the structural reinforcements carried out while the aircraft was under repair following the accident. The fuselage was dried out, and three Lorraine Dietrich engines with four-bladed wooden propellers were fitted, after which trials proceeded satisfactorily. The cannon was fitted during the first months of 1920, and many firing tests were carried out in the air with complete success. Following these tests the cannon was removed, and the aircraft remained at Saint Raphaël for two more years.

The Nieuport 4R 450

Capt Anselme Marshal wrote on 23 July 1918 to M. Dumesnil, the Under Secretary of State of the Aéronautique Militaire et Maritime, proposing that a transatlantic flight be attempted with a military machine totally of French construction. To meet this requirement Tellier proposed the Vonna, a large triplane flying boat of some 13 to 15 tonnes, powered by four Panhard et Levasseur V-12 engines of 325–350hp, mounted in tandem pairs on the middle wing either side of the fuselage. A crew of three was to be accommodated in a cockpit placed in front of the wings.

A novel form of navigation was to be used, which would pinpoint the position of the aircraft to within 15km (9 miles). The crew would transmit their position on an hourly basis. There would be two bases en route, one on St Paul Island, connected by cable to the Cape Verde Islands and from there to Dakar, and the other on Fernando de Norhona Island, connected by cable to Saint Louis in Senegal. It was intended to build two machines with two spare engines. It was planned that one machine would fly to Dakar as a starting point, and the other would be shipped there. With the understanding of the Under Secretary of State of the Marine and its chief engineer Fortant, a detailed study was made, and agreement to manufacture was made. The Nieuport company formed a design bureau, and assigned fifteen engineers and designers under the direction of Alphonse Tellier and Robert Duhamel.

The hulls and centre sections and parts of the wings had been manufactured, and the engines had been delivered by the summer of 1919; but at this time Tellier became ill, and retired as technical director. The construction of the two machines was suspended, and the project was abandoned. In an attempt to resurrect it, Marchal went to the United States to raise funds, but he died there following an illness on 27 June 1921. The Vonna remained in the Nieuport catalogue under the name Nieuport 4R 450, but no further interest was shown.

The Nieuport S

This machine was based on the Tellier 350hp Sunbeam, a T.4 with a revised wing and engine. It is unlikely that any were produced by Nieuport, the only known orders having been passed to E. Dubonnet and Gonnet & Wilock.

One of these flying boats appeared in the Gran Prix de Monaco of 1920. It carried the racing number '5' and had 'Nieuport' inscribed on its tail. The 350hp engine of the Tellier had been replaced by a 450hp Darracq-Coatalen water-cooled V-12 engine driving a wooden four-bladed propeller. The frontal radiator had been replaced by streamlined cowling, and cooling was accomplished by means of three Lamblin radiators placed in the propeller slipstream. The wing area was increased by 10sq m (107sq ft), and the ailerons were fitted to the lower wing and operated by a torsion bar. The forward crew position was deleted, the bow made pointed, and all three crew-members were accommodated in a cockpit in front of the wings.

The machine, piloted by Sadi Lecointe the Nieuport test pilot, flew in to Monaco from St Raphaël on the evening of 19 April. The following day the machine easily met the qualifying height of 2,000m (6,650ft) in 45min, attaining a height of 5,300m (17,400ft) in 43min with a full load of fuel and 400kg (880lb) of ballast, and two days later it achieved 2,200m (7,200ft) in 30min. On 23 April it attained 6,350m (20,800ft) in 63min, but did not beat the current record of 6,500m (21,300ft) held by Jean Casale in a Spad-Herbemont. The following day it took off with Capt Coli as navigator and a mechanic. After a call at Ajaccio in Corsica, it arrived at Bizerte in 14hr 48min after crossing the Mediterranean in 7hr 57min at an average speed of 122km/h (76mph). The flying boat left for

A 350hp Sunbeam Tellier T.4 at Monaco. The Nieuport S of Sadi Lecointe was similar, but powered by a 450hp Darracq-Coatalen engine. Philip Jarrett

		Nieuport BM	Nieuport TM	Nieuport 4R 450	Nieuport S
Engine:		2 250hp Hispano-Suiza	3 350hp Lorraine	4 325hp Panhard et Levassor	450hp Darracq-Coatalen
Dimensions:	Span, upper, m (ft)	23 (75)	30 (98)	40 (131)	23 (75)
	Length, m (ft)	15.8 (51.8)	21.45 (70)	21.5 (70.5)	14.64 (48)
	Height, m (ft)	4 (13)	5.89 (19)	9.5 (31)	4 (13)
	Wing area, sq m (sq ft)	86.5 (930)	156 (1,678)	342 (3,680)	84.5 (909)
Weights:	Empty, kg (lb)	2,350 (5,180)	4,650 (10,250)	9,400 (20,730)	2,250 (4,960)
	Loaded, kg (lb)	3,550 (7,830)	7,100 (15,650)	16,000 (35,280)	3,400 (7,500)
	Wing loading, kg/m^2	41	45.5	46.78	40.2
	Power loading, kg/hp	7.1	7.8	11.85	9.7
Performance:	Max speed, km/h (mph):				
	at sea level	130 (80)	125–130 (77–80)		130–135 (80–84)
	Endurance, hr	4	6		

Sousse in Tunisia on 25 April with the intention of returning directly, but a propeller change was necessary in Sousse, and on 30 April the engine broke down, causing the machine to be withdrawn from the competition. After the engine had been changed the aircraft left Sousse for Bizerte on 6 June, taking around five hours. Starting on 10 June, it returned to France via Alicante and Barcelona. The eventual fate of the aircraft is not known.

An amphibian version of the Nieuport S was illustrated in commercial literature of the time, but it is unlikely that it was built. It was to be powered by a 430hp Darracq-Coatalen 12A.

British Nieuport Designs

Most of the early production undertaken by the Nieuport and General Company during the war was of the Sopwith Camel, of which some 300 were built: 200 mainly fitted with the 140hp Clerget 9Bf engine and given serials C.1–200 under contract nos A.S.14412 and A.S.17565 of 21 June 1917; fifty allocated serials F.3196–3245 under contract no. 35a/590/C.881 of 7 May 1918; and fifty allocated serials F.3918–3967 under contract no. 35a/1154/C.1107 of 17 May 1918, the last two batches mainly fitted with the 130hp Clerget 9B.

British-Nieuport began three designs during the war, which are best covered together in this chapter because most of their testing took place after the conflict had ended.

After the war the company also produced 100 Sopwith Snipes with serials E6937 to E7036, under contract no. 35a/435/C305 dated 20 March 1918; these were delivered between January and March 1919.

(*Above*) **Nieuport BN-1 (C2484).**
Philip Jarrett

Nieuport BN-1 cockpit.
Philip Jarrett

The Nieuport B.N.1

The first indigenous design, begun in March 1918, was the B.N.1 single-seater fighter powered by a Bentley B.R.2 rotary engine. The aircraft had unstaggered, cross-braced, two-bay wings of unequal chord with two pairs of single interplane I-struts. When it first appeared it was fitted with a large conical spinner, but this was later removed. The fuselage was a simple box girder with rounded top decking and side fairings behind the engine cowling. It incorporated some S.E.5a components, including the under-fin and tail-skid. The armament was similar to other aircraft of the period, including the Sopwith Snipe, and consisted of twin fuselage-mounted Vickers guns and a single Lewis gun mounted at a slight upward angle above the centre section. The latter could be pulled downwards for reloading and for firing upwards.

The first prototype, fitted with the sixth B.R.2 built, was sent to Martlesham on 1 March 1918, but the engine ran inconsistently. It then went to Sutton's Farm on 9 March for comparative tests with the similarly powered Sopwith Snipe, Boulton Paul Bobolink and Austin Osprey. The Osprey proved the most manoeuvrable, but the Nieuport was easily the fastest. With the Sopwith company's reputation already well established with the Camel, it was likely that it would still win future contracts despite the better performance of the Nieuport. In any case, the matter was decided when the sole Nieuport caught fire whilst flying from Sutton's Farm and was completely destroyed. Two further machines were built, but too late to influence the production decision. The aircraft was not developed following the official adoption of the Sopwith Snipe, and the company's efforts were concentrated on the Nighthawk.

The unconventional interplane I-struts used on the B.N.1 had previously been used by Folland in the S.E.4, which he had designed whilst at Farnborough. His colleagues there had cast doubts regarding the structural stiffness of such a layout, and it had been replaced by conventional interplane struts in the S.E.4a derivative. It was natural, therefore, that in incorporating the I-strut concept into a commercial design, care should be taken to ensure that the structural strength was adequate. The structural strength was therefore static-tested at Farnborough to determine the ultimate strength whilst subject to the loads experienced in a vertical dive.

Folland's interplane struts comprised streamlined upright spruce shafts to which horizontal walnut ends were fitted with a scarf joint, and held by narrow aluminium plates secured by hollow rivets. These ends rested across the surface of the wing spars and were secured by vertical bolts. The torsional couples imposed by diving were represented by artificial down-loads on the front spar and up-loads on the rear spar of increasing magnitude. Compression creases formed in the leading edge of the struts at the top, and the trailing edge failed in tension at a total load on the rear spars of 3,323kg (7,325lb). Although this represented a suitable safety margin compared with the designed all-up weight of 885kg (1,950lb), the strength was not as great as a conventionally strutted two-bay wing. The I-strut layout was therefore abandoned for the Nighthawk design.

The Nieuport Nighthawk

The second fighter designed by H.P. Folland was the Nighthawk powered by the 320hp A.B.C. Dragonfly engine. The Nighthawk also had two-bay wings but, as described above, had a more conventional structure compared with the B.N.1.

The fuselage was again of girder construction, with four main longerons of ash, lightened in some places by spindling; the spacers were of square-section spruce, rounded at the ends to fit into circular sockets. It was cross-braced with tie-rods. The front fuselage was streamlined by using light longitudinal stringers on three-ply formers. The front of the fuselage terminated in a near-circular engine plate of plywood, reinforced on its front face by a steel plate through which passed the steel bolts securing the engine. The engine plate was secured to the upper main longerons with steel strips. The fuel tanks were placed in streamlined fairings to the side of the fuselage, and could be easily removed by taking off the side panels and undoing the retaining straps. A gravity tank was placed in the centre section of the upper wing. The pilot was protected from the slipstream by a V-shaped windscreen. The control column and rudder bar were adjustable in relation to the pilot's seat. The undercarriage was of a conventional V-strut type, with the rubber-sprung axle housed in a three-ply fairing. The stearable tail-skid and many fuselage fittings were taken from the S.E.5a. The aircraft was armed with two synchronized fuselage-mounted Vickers guns belt-fed via chutes from the lower fuselage.

The wings were staggered and connected by four pairs of interplane struts with wire cross-bracing. The two main spars were of spruce spindled out to an I-section. Most ribs were of lightweight spruce webs and flanges, but the compression ribs inline with the interplane struts were I-section spruce. Ailerons were fitted to both upper and lower wings, hinged to false spars. The

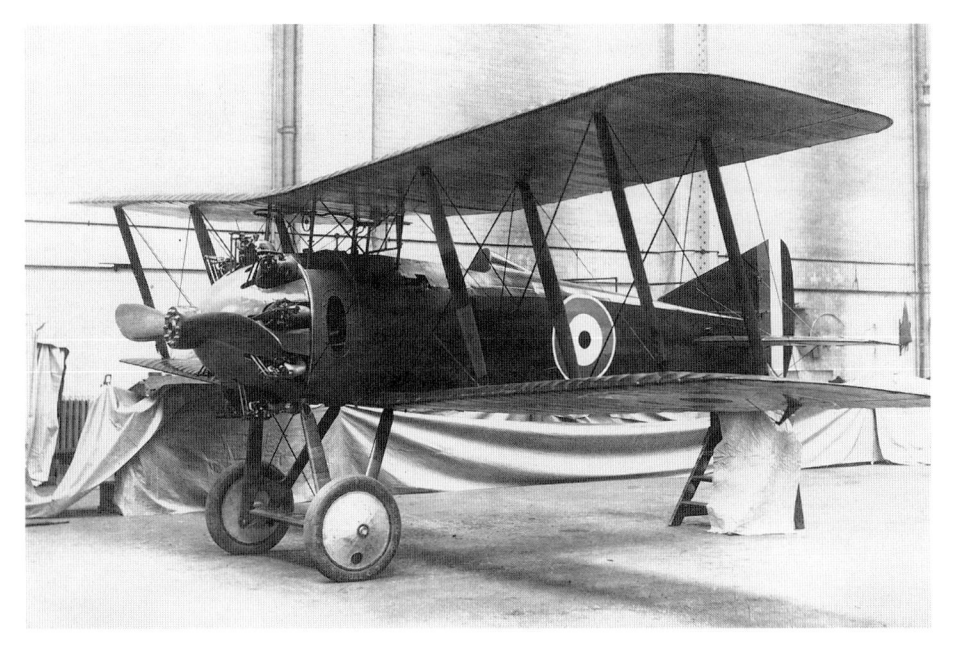

Nieuport Nighthawk prototype. Philip Jarrett

centre section was supported by four struts of spruce. The tailplane was hinged round its rear spar, and could be trimmed by a screw jack in the cockpit. One feature of the design was the first use of tubular rivets, which were much lighter and projected less than the nuts and bolts that they replaced.

The Nieuport was very agile and fast with a good rate of climb, and it would have been an excellent fighting machine but for its unreliable engine. The Nighthawk was the first design to be ordered with the Dragonfly

Nieuport Nighthawk production machine.
Philip Jarrett

engine, and it went into large-scale production towards the end of 1918, some subcontracted with the Grahame-White Company. However, the Dragonfly engine suffered from dynamic unbalance and severe vibration, which generally led to mechanical failure after just a few hours flying. These problems, which were not confined just to the Nighthawk, led to the cancellation of most of the Nighthawk production.

Some Nighthawks were used for experimental purposes; for instance, F2911 went to Martlesham Heath for performance tests between June 1919 and February 1920, H8553 went to Grain on 13 March 1920 for flotation gear tests, and another was used for testing crash-proof fuel tanks. The type was obsolete by the spring of 1923 and was withdrawn.

Some of the undelivered airframes were rebuilt by the R.A.E. These were initially fitted with the Dragonfly engine, and several were used for testing undercarriage modifications (J2405), engine exhaust and silencer system tests (J2415) and in general (J2413), endurance tests (J2414) and parachute tests (J2416). Two of these (J2405 and J2416) were later re-engined with the Jaguar. Three others (J6925 to J6927, now fitted with the 325hp Jaguar II or 385hp Jaguar III) joined Sopwith Snipes in service with No.8 Sqn RAF and No.1 Sqn at Hinaidi in Iraq during 1923.

The Nieuport London

Like the contemporary Avro 533 Manchester, Boulton & Paul Bourges, the D.H. 11 Oxford and the Sopwith Cobham, the Nieuport London was designed to be powered by two A.B.C. Dragonfly engines. However, whereas the others were intended as high-speed day bombers, the London was designed as a night bomber. Design was started by H.P. Folland in 1918, but the prototype (H.1740) did not fly until 1920.

The London was a triplane, and was designed to be cheap and simple to construct. It was built entirely of wood, and the number of metal fittings was kept to a minimum. The structural members were a mixture of deal, pine and cypress. Wooden pegs and dowels were used, and joints were fastened with nails and brass wire. Most metal fittings were of pressed steel, and welding was kept to an absolute minimum. The rectangular-section fuselage was formed of four longerons and spacers, the joints between them consisting of triangular pieces of three-ply slotted in, glued and fixed with wooden pegs. Load-bearing areas were strengthened with diagonal wooden strips. This structure was covered with 6mm (¼in) tongue-and-groove boarding that was nailed in place and then covered in fabric and varnished.

Each wing spar consisted of two planks of spruce about 1.25cm (½in) apart, with the outer surfaces spindled out and joined together by wooden blocks at load-bearing areas such as the interplane strut attachments. The ribs were of a lattice construction. Both the wings and tail unit were fabric covered. The twin-bay wings were equally spaced, with the middle wing just above the fuselage, and were rigged without stagger with a very simple arrangement of vertical struts. All the control surfaces were horn balanced. To begin with, all the mainplanes were fitted with ailerons, but as the aircraft proved to be responsive to the controls, only those on the lower plane were retained and the other wings rebuilt and the control system much simplified. The tail unit sported a curved fin, an angular rudder and an under-fin similar to the earlier British Nieuport designs. All the control surfaces were the same shape and interchangeable. The wide-track undercarriage consisted of two single wheel units positioned under the engine nacelles, with each axle supported at the ends by two V-struts, one attached to the wing spars and the other to the lower longerons of the fuselage. The tail-skid consisted of an inverted A made of tubular steel, pivoted about the cross-member and sprung with rubber between the ends of the two struts and the lower fuselage longerons.

The two Dragonfly engines were fitted into streamlined nacelles and mounted midway between the middle and lower wings. Each engine plate was of a similar design to the Nighthawk, but was positioned by means of two pairs of V-struts with the apices joined to the front and rear spars of the middle and lower wings. The oil tanks were placed in the nacelles behind the engines, but the two cylindrical fuel tanks, each consisting of a main and a header tank, were placed in the fuselage. It was intended to build a second prototype, designated the London Mk. II, to be fitted with Armstrong Siddeley Puma engines in case the problems with the Dragonfly engines proved insurmountable; however, it is unlikely that the second prototype was ever built.

Three seats were provided for the crew of two, two of which were side by side just in front of the mainplanes. If attacked, one crew-member was expected to leave his seat and make his way to the gunner's position in the nose where the armament consisted of a pair of Lewis guns mounted on a Scarff ring. The machine was designed to carry a load of nine 113kg (250lb) bombs arranged in sets of three.

By the time the first airframe was completed with the Dragonfly engines, the war was over and no military orders were forthcoming. Instead it was proposed to convert the London into a transport aircraft with accommodation for thirteen passengers, or more than a ton of mails or freight. But development of the London ceased when

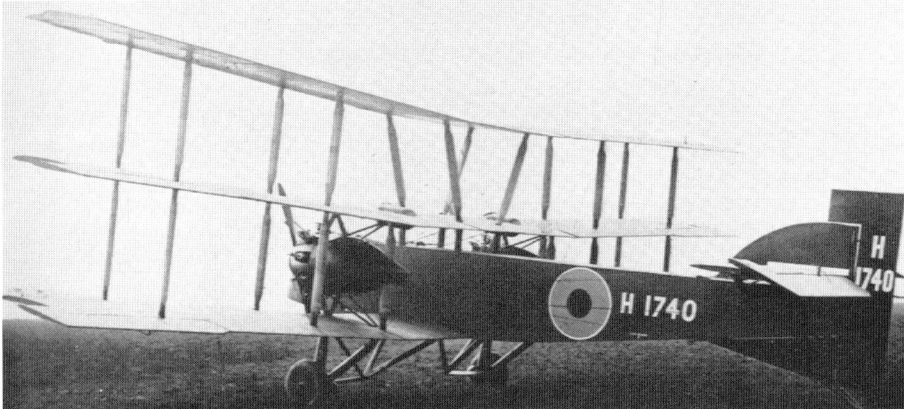

Nieuport London. Philip Jarrett

Nieuport L.C.1 Nieuhawk (K.151) with a 320hp A.B.C. Dragonfly engine entered for the 1919 Aerial Derby; it failed to finish. Philip Jarrett

the Nieuport and General Aircraft Company closed down in 1920.

The Nieuport Nieuhawk

The two-seat Nieuport Nieuhawk was built from single-seat fighter components; it was tested by Capt L.R. Tait-Cox in the summer of 1919. It was entered in the 1919 Aerial Derby with Lt L.R. Tait-Cox as pilot, but its Dragonfly engine failed half-way round the second lap. It was later flown at the meeting by Jimmy James in an impressive show of aerobatics. It was then prepared for a demonstration in India, and was freighted over at the end of the year. It was painted in a blue and yellow check pattern and given the serial K.151.

Gloster Sparrowhawk II (Mars III) JN.401, for the Japanese navy. Philip Jarrett

Gloster Developments of the Nighthawk

The Gloucestershire Aircraft Company took over the Nieuport Nighthawk design in 1920 and converted a considerable number of airframes to various configurations; these were christened 'Mars', and given a series of mark numbers.

Following the visit of the British Air Mission to Japan in January 1921, the Japanese navy ordered fifty modified Nighthawk airframes powered by 230hp Bentley BR.2 rotary engines. Thirty of these were Sparrowhawk I (Mars II) single-seat land-based fighters, ten were two-seat Sparrowhawk II (Mars III) trainers, and ten were Sparrowhawk III (Mars IV) single-seat shipborne fighters. Spares and components equivalent to forty more airframes were also sent. All three marques saw extensive service, and were not retired until 1928. The naval fighters operated from platforms built over the turrets of capital ships.

Some Nighthawk airframes were re-engined with Jaguar and Jupiter engines as the Mars VI series, including two (H8532 and H8534) with the 325hp Jaguar III engine, and one (H8544) with the 380hp Jaguar IV. From May 1921, H8534 was used at Martlesham for extensive tests with its original engine, clocking about fifty hours, before a Jaguar IV engine was fitted and a further thirty-two hours were accumulated. H8544 was tested at Farnborough from 14 July 1922, where it was joined by several others. One Jupiter-powered Mars VI was sent to Iraq for high-temperature trials, and three or four more were sent to the Middle East for the same reason. One aircraft went to 1 Sqn, another went to 8 Sqn and a third, probably powered by a Jupiter engine, was flown to the Hinaidi depot. At least sixteen were re-engined in total.

Although the Mars VI Nighthawk did not enter squadron service in the RAF, twenty with Jaguar engines were ordered by the Greek government in 1922; these reached Salonika early in 1923. Ten of these entered service with E Fighter Squadron, but this unit was disbanded when the Greco-Turkish Peace Treaty was signed on 24 July 1923. The Nighthawks were subsequently transferred to A Aircraft Squadron, which was gradually expanded into a regiment. The Nighthawks remained in first-line service until 1938, when they were relegated to training duties.

The company also developed the design into the Nightjar (Mars X) shipborne fighter, for use on aircraft carriers. It used basic Nighthawk components, and was identical in construction except for modifications to take the Bentley BR.2 rotary engine, and to the undercarriage to make it suitable for carrier operation. The undercarriage had a wider track and a longer stroke, and the axle casing was fitted with claws to engage the fore and aft arrester wires then used on aircraft carriers. Armament consisted of twin Vickers guns. Although intended for naval use, twenty-two airframes were requisitioned for RAF service, and sufficient spares were retained to keep twelve in service for two years (including H8535 to H8543, H8545 and J6930 to J6941). Some of these aircraft briefly saw service with 203 Sqn at Leuchars. Six Nightjars were operated from HMS *Argus* during a crisis in the Middle East in September 1922.

Several racing and record-breaking aircraft were converted from the basic Nighthawk airframe. The Nieuport Goshawk established a new British record of 267.7km/h (166.4mph), despite retaining the unreliable Dragonfly engine. The Mars I, fitted with a neatly cowled 450hp Napier Lion engine, won the 1921 Aerial Derby bearing the civil registration G-EAXZ. Going through a series of modifications the aircraft repeated the success in 1922 and 1923. Mounted on floats, it acted as a trainer for the pilots of the High Speed Flight to gain experience for the 1925 and 1927 Schneider Trophy races. It was scrapped in 1927.

Serials of Postwar British Nieuport Aircraft

C3484–C3486: Three British Nieuport B.N.1 (320hp A.B.C. Dragonfly 1) built by Nieuport & General, Cricklewood to Type A.1 (a) Specification under contract no. AS.41282.

F2909–F2911: Three Nieuport Nighthawk (320hp A.B.C. Dragonfly I) built by Nieuport and General to Specification A.1 (c) under contract no. 35a/912/C728, dated 25 April 1918.

H1740–H1745: Six British Nieuport London Mk. I (two 320hp A.B.C. Dragonfly I) built by Nieuport & General, Cricklewood to Type VII Specification under contract no. 35a/2030/C2278. Four of these (H1742–H1745) were cancelled.

Nieuport Nightjar. Philip Jarrett

POSTWAR DEVELOPMENTS OF WARTIME DESIGNS

		B.N.1	Nighthawk	London
Engine:		230hp Bentley B.R.2	320hp A.B.C. Dragonfly I	Two 320hp A.B.C. Dragonfly I
Dimensions:	Wingspan, m (ft)	8.5 (28.0)	8.5 (28.0)	18 (59.5)
	Chord, upper, m (ft)	1.8 (6.0)	1.6 (5.25)	
	Chord, lower, m (ft)	1.45 (4.17)	1.6 (5.25)	
	Wing gap, m (ft)		1.4 (4.5)	
	Tailspan, m (ft)		2.7 (9.0)	
	Length, m (ft)	5.6 (18.5)	5.6 (18.5)	11.4 (37.5)
	Height, m (ft)	2.7 (9.0)	2.9 (9.5)	5.3 (17.5)
	Propeller diam, m (ft)	2.8 (9.25)	2.7 (9.0)	
	Wing area, sq m (sq ft)	24 (260)	25.6 (276)	102 (1,100)
	Tailplane area, sq m (sq ft)	2.6 (28.0)	2.6 (28.0)	9.7 (104)
	Fin & rudder area, sq m (sq ft)	0.94 (10.2)	0.97 (10.5)	4.6 (50)
Weights:	Empty, kg (lb)		771 (1,700)	
	Loaded, kg (lb)	920 (2,030)	1,006 (2,218)	
	Petrol, ltr (gal)	164 (36)	182 (40)	796 (175)
	Oil		18 (4)	
Performance	Max speed, km/h (mph):			
	at sea level		243 (151)	160 (100)
	at 2,000m (6,500ft)		225 (140)	
	at 3,000m (10,000ft)		223 (138.5)	
	at 4,500m (15,000ft)	204 (127)	216 (134)	
	at 6,000m (20,000ft)		209 (130)	
	Climb to:			
	1,500m (5,000ft)		3min	
	2,000m (6,500ft)		4min 10sec	
	3,000m (10,000ft)		7min 10sec	30min
	4,500m (15,000ft)	16m	12min 40sec	
	6,000m (20,000ft)		20min	
	Ceiling, m (ft)	8,000 (26,000)	7,500 (24,500)	
	Endurance, hr	3	3	4

H8513–H8662: 150 Nieuport Nighthawk (320hp A.B.C. Dragonfly I) ordered from Nieuport and General under contract no. 35a/2739/C3053 dated 28 August 1918. H8533 and H8553 were used, H8513–H8531 and H8546–H8552 were put in store, H8532 and H8534–H8545 were rebuilt, H8555–H8662 were cancelled.

H8532, H8534 and H8544: Three Gloster Nighthawk (Mars VI) (325hp Jaguar III or 385hp Jaguar IV) under contract no. 346773/22 to D of R Type I Specification.
HH8535–HH8543 and H8545: Ten Gloster Nightjar (Mars X) (230hp Bentley B.R.2) under contract no. 373763/22, dated 8 January 1923 to RAF Type XX Specification.
J2392–J2541: 150 Nieuport Nighthawk ordered on contract no. 35a/3461/C.4064 dated 1 November 1918. J2392–J2416 completed, J2417–J2461 cancelled but completed as spares, J2462–J2541 cancelled 15 April 1919.
J6801–J6848: Forty-eight Nieuport Nighthawk ordered on contract nos 378663/20 and APT52332, reserved for rebuilds by

Nieuport Goshawk (G-EAEQ) with a 320hp A.B.C. Dragonfly engine that took the British Speed Record at 267.7km/h (166.4mph) at Martlesham Heath on 17 June 1920. Philip Jarrett

		Macchi M.9bis
Engine:		250hp Isotta-Fraschini V.6
Dimensions:	Span, upper, m (ft)	15.45 (50.69)
	Length, m (ft)	9.5 (31.2)
	Wing area, sq m (sq ft)	44.57 (479.57)
Weights:	Empty, kg (lb)	1,100 (2,426)
	Loaded, kg (lb)	1,620 (3,572)
Performance:	Cruising speed, km/h (mph)	160 (100)
	Maximum speed, km/h (mph):	
	at sea level	180 (112)
	Service ceiling, m (ft)	5500 (18,000)
	Range, km (miles)	170 (106)
	Endurance, hr	3

R.A.E but not used.

J6925–J6927: Three Gloster Nighthawk (Mars VI) ordered on contract no. 340272/22, dated 13 October 1922.

J6928–J6929: Two Nieuport Nighthawks, R.A.E rebuilds not taken up.

J6930–J6941: Twelve Gloster Nightjars (Mars X) ordered on contract no. 373763/22 dated 8 January 1923.

Postwar Nieuport-Macchi Designs

Nieuport-Macchi M.9 and M.12

The M.9 was a scaled-up version of the M.8, with a six-cylinder 250hp Isotta-Fraschini inline water-cooled engine and improved armament; it was used for anti-submarine patrols. After the war the M.9 was exported to Spain and Brazil.

The first civil Nieuport-Macchi machine to appear was the M.9bis, a passenger version of the military aircraft with a four-seat cabin that was completely enclosed and fitted with large windows, situated forward of the wings. Most of these aircraft were fitted with the standard engine, but at least two were fitted with a 300hp Hispano-Suiza engine built by Fiat under licence and designated the M.9ter.

The final seaplane produced by Macchi during the war was the M.12, designed by Buzio. It was intended as a fast, long-range seaplane for unescorted bombing missions and anti-submarine duties. It featured a twin-boom rear fuselage. A passageway allowed a gunner to move from the front turret to a rear turret, which gave an unrestricted view to the rear allowing coverage from a stern attack. In 1919 the M.12bis was produced, a civil version of the M.12 with the fuselage converted to give accommodation in an enclosed cabin for three passengers.

Postwar Service of Civil Nieuport-Macchi Aircraft

Two civil conversions of the Nieuport-Macchi M.3 were operated on the Swiss lakes by Ad Astra Aero. CH 12 was burnt at Lugano in 1922, and CH 15 was withdrawn from use the same year. Three M.9s were also operated in Switzerland: CH 19 and CH 20 by Ad Astra Aero, and CH 96 by Aero Lausanne. The latter two were in fact M.9ters powered by 300hp Fiat engines. One M.9bis was owned privately in Italy and given the registration I-BAEG.

The Società Italiana di Transporti Aerei (or Sociedade Italo-Brasileira de Transportes Aéreos) briefly operated two Macchi flying boats in Brazil. The Italians arrived in Rio de Janeiro in November 1919 with an M.7 and an M.9 together with a Caproni bomber. The M.9 was destroyed when John Pinder, formerly of Handley Page, made a forced landing on a lagoon in South Catarina whilst attempting to fly from Rio to Buenos Aires. The M.7 was donated to the Brazilian military on 2 November 1920.

(*Above left*) **Nieuport L.S.3 Goshawk (G-EASK) entered for the 1921 Aerial Derby.** Philip Jarrett

(*Left*) **Macchi M.12.** Giorgio Apostolo

Bibliography

Alegi, G. *Macchi M.5* (Windsock Datafile No.86, Albatros Publications, 2001).

Alexandrov, A. (ed. H. Woodman) *Russian Naval Nieuports 1917–20* (Windsock International 15.6. pp.12–15, 16.1. pp.16–20, 16.2. pp.27–32, Albatros Publications).

Andersson, L. *Soviet Aircraft & Aviation, 1917–1941* (Putnam 1994, pp.11–15, 183–5, 326–7).

Andrews, C.F. *The Nieuport 17* (Profile Publications No. 49, 1965).

Apostolo, G. *Aermacchi, from Nieuports to AMX* (1991, pp. 6–51).

Avram, V. *L'Aviation Roumaine 1916–1918* (Avions 7, Sep. 1993 pp.29–33; 8, Oct. 1993 pp.24–31).

Blume, G. and Casirati, A. *L'Aviation Italienne dans la Campagne de Macédonie et d'Albanie, 1915–1918* (Avions 30, Sep. 1995, pp.33–5; 31, Oct. 1995, pp.31–3; 32, Nov. 1995, 17–8, 33, Dec. 1995, pp.20–1).

Bodemer, A. and Laugier, R. *Les Moteurs á Pistons Aéronautiques Français (1900/1960) Volume 1* (Docavia Volume 24, p.88).

Bowers, P.M. *The Nieuport N.28C-1* (Profile Publications No. 79, 1966).

Bruce, J.M. *British Aeroplanes 1914–18* (Putnam, 1957, pp.317–22).

Bruce, J.M. *The Aeroplanes of the Royal Flying Corps (Military Wing)* (Putnam, 1982, pp.315–38).

Bruce, J.M. *Nieuport Aircraft of World War One* (Arms & Armour Press, 1988).

Bruce, J.M. *Nieuport 10–12* (Windsock Datafile 68, Albatros Publications, 1998).

Bruce, J.M. *Nieuport 17* (Windsock Datafile 20, Albatros Publications, 1990).

Bruce, J.M. *Nieuport Fighters* (Windsock Datafile Special Vols 1 & 2, Albatros Publications, 1993/4).

Bruce, J.M. *Nieuport Triplanes* (W.W.I Aero No. 115, Jul. 1987, pp.40–5).

Cavanagh, R.L. *The 94th and its Nieuports* (US Cross & Cockade, pp.193–222).

Cejka, Z. (ed. B. Klaeylé) *Les Chasseurs Nieuport Tchécoslovaques* (Avions 94, Jan. 2001, pp.38–47; Avions 95, Feb. 2001, pp.42–7).

Corret, C.-A.J. *L'Aéronautique Navale à Fréjus-Saint-Rapaël, 1912–1995* (Ardhan, 1995, pp.12–44).

Cronin, R. *Royal Navy Shipboard Aircraft Developments 1912–1931* (Air-Britain, 1990).

Foxworth, T.G. *The Speed Seekers* (Macdonald & Janes, 1975, pp.107–128).

Frandsen, A. *Nieuport 28, Broken Wings in the Pursuit Group* (W.W.I Aero 165, Aug. 1999, pp.33–51).

Frey, R.D. *The Nieuport 28 Described* (US Cross & Cockade 12, 2, summer 1971, pp.116–128).

Gentilli, R. and Varriale, P. *I Reparti dell'aviazione italiana nella Grande Guerra* (Aeronautica Militare, 1999).

Geust, C.-F. and Petrov, G. *Camouflage & Markings of Russian and Soviet Aircraft until 1941* (Apali, 1999).

George, M. and Sheppard, V. *Russia's Air Forces in War and Revolution 1914–1920 Parts I & II*, (Cross & Cockade 17, 4, 1986, pp.145–153 and 18, 2, 1987, pp.49–54).

Guttman, J. *Nieuport 28* (Windsock Datafile 36, Albatros Publications, 1992).

James, D.N. *Gloster Aircraft since 1917* (Putnam, 1971, pp.68–88).

Jones, I. *An Air Fighter's Scrapbook* (1938, Greenhill reprint 1990).

Keimel, R. *Flugzeuge der Österreichischen Firma Lohner 1909–1923* (TMW, 1990, pp.265–81).

King, B. *Royal Naval Air Service 1912–1918* (Hikoki, 1997, p.58).

Klaeylé, B. and Osché, P. *Guynemer, Les Avions d'un As* (Avion, 1999).

Klaeylé, B. *Nieuport Aircraft 1915–18*, (Pegase 94, Jul. 1999, pp.16–30 & 95, October 1999, pp.4–14).

Kopanski, T. *Les Nieuport Polonais de la Guerre Russo-Polonaise* (Avions, No. 2, Apr., 1993, pp.13–20).

Layman, R.D. *Naval Aviation in the First World War, Its Impact and Influence* (Chatham, 1996, pp.128–32).

Le Roy, T. *L'Escadrille de Port-Said* (Avions, 34, Jan. 1996, pp.29–31; 35, Feb. 1996, pp.18–21; 36, Mar. 1996, pp.31–6).

Macmillan, Wg Cdr N. *Into the Blue* (Jarrolds, 1969).

Mason, H.M. *The Lafayette Escadrille* (Smithmark, 1964).

Morareau, L., Feuilloy, R., Courtinat, J.-l., Le Roy, T., and Rossignol, J.-P. *L'Aviation Maritime Française Pendant la Grande Guerre* (Ardhan, 1999).

Nelson, S.F. *Nieuport 'Vee'-Strutters* (US Cross & Cockade, pp.237–80).

Nicolle, D. *L'Aviation 'Francaise' du Sultan; Les Unités Aériennes Ottomanes 1912–1915* (Avions 27, Jun. 1995, pp.16–19; 28, Jul. 1995, pp.30–33; 29, Aug. 1995, pp.15–20).

O'Connor, M. *P.F. Fullard, Nieuport Exponent* (Cross & Cockade Journal, 13, 2, 1982, pp.63–9).

Rosenthal, L., Marchand, A., Borget, M. and Bénichon, M. *Nieuport 1909–1950* (Docavia Volume 38, 1999).

Scott, A.J.L. *Sixty Squadron RAF, 1916–1919* (1910, Greenhill reprint 1990).

Shavrov, V.B. *Istoriya konstruktsii samoletov v SSSR do 1938* (Moscow, 1978).

Shaw, M. *No.1 Squadron* (Ian Allan, 1971, pp.19–32).

Shirley, N.C. *United States Naval Aviation 1910–1918* (Schiffer, 2000, pp.132–140).

Silió, J.V. *Aviones Españolas desde 1910* (Aena, 1995, pp.32–3, 52–3, 82–3, 112–3, 460).

Stroud, J. *European Transport Aircraft since 1910* (Putnam, 1966, pp.422–6).

Sturtivant, R. and Page, G. *Royal Navy Aircraft Serials and Units, 1911–1919* (Air-Britain, 1992).

Thompson, D. and Sturtivant, R. *Royal Air Force Aircraft J1–J9999 and WWI Survivors* (Air-Britain, 1987, pp.30–1, 182).

Villard, H.S. *Blue Ribbon of the Air, The Gordon Bennett Races* (Smithsonian, 1987, pp.109–27).

Woodman, H. *The Russian 1912 Military Aircraft Competition* (Windsock International 16, 4, Jul./Aug. 2000, pp.14–19).

Woodman, H. *Avions-Torpilleurs, Le Prieur's rockets* (Windsock 10, 3, May/Jun. 1994, Albatros Publications, pp.8–14).

Woodman, H. *Early Aircraft Armament, The Aeroplane and the Gun up to 1918* (Arms & Armour Press, 1989).

Woodman, H. *Imperial Russia*, manuscript undated.

Wright, P. *Herbert Rutter Simms* (Cross & Cockade Journal 13, 3, 1982, pp.112–123).

Periodicals

The Aero: Vol III, No.61, 20.7.10, p.57; III, 63, 3.8.10, 88; III, 75, 26.10.10, 328; III, 76, 2.11.10, 350; III, 80, 30.11.10, 425; V, Apr. 1911, 15–16; V, 99, Jun. 1911, 68–70; V, 100, Jul. 1911, supplement between 106–7; V, 101, Aug. 1911, 136–7; V, 103, Oct. 1911, 188, 190; V, 104, Nov. 1911, 211–17; V, 105, Dec. 1911, 240–1; VI, 106, Jan. 1912, 15; VI, 107, Feb. 1912, 46; VI, 108, Mar. 1912, 73, 85; VI, 112, Jul. 1912, 187–91, 201; VI, 114, Sep. 1912, 266–8; VI, 116, Nov. 1912, 328; VII, 119, Feb. 1913, 59; VII, 120, Mar. 1913, 78–9, 88; VII, 123, Apr. 1913, 123; VII, 122, May 1913, 131.

Aerofan: No.61, Apr.–Jun. 1997, pp.103–7; 63, Oct.–Dec. 1997, 244–7; 67, Oct.–Dec. 1998, 194–203.

Avions: No.12 Feb. 94, pp.18–22; 13, Mar. 94, 17–21; 14, Apr. 94, 35–8; 17, Jul. 94, 30–3; 18, Aug. 94, 6–9; 19, Sep. 94, 14–16; 20, Oct. 94, 43–6; 29, Aug. 95, 15–20; 37, Apr. 96, 19–22; 38, May 96, 31–5; 44, Nov. 96, 12–14; 50, May 97, 36–41; 54, Aug. 97, 33–5; 72, Mar. 99, 51–9; 74, May 99, 50–6; 75, Jun. 99, 53–8; 79, Oct. 99, 43–7; 83, Feb. 00, 18–23; 85, Apr. 00, 17–21.

Cross & Cockade Journal: Vol. 5, No. 4, 1974, p.176; 8, 4, 1977, 150–1; 12, 3, 1981, 137–8; 16, 1, 1985, 20; 18, 3, 1987, 120–2; 19, 2, 1988, 97–8; 23, 4, 1992, 172; 24, 3, 1993, 113–36, 137–57; 26, 1, 1995, 1–928; 3, 1997, 144–58.

Flight: Vol. II, No.81, 16.7.1910, pp.548–51; II, 103, 17.12.10, 1028; III, 107, 14.1.11, 36; III, 126, 27.5.11, 455–60; III, 127, 3.6.11, 479–80; III, 130, 24.6.11, 555–6; III, 131, 1.7.11, 574; III, 132, 8.7.11, 583; III, 132, 8.7.11, 595; III, 134, 22.7.11, 627–36; III, 135, 29.7.11, 652–61; III, 144, 30.9.11, xii; III, 145, 7.10.11, 862–3, 876; III, 146, 14.10.11, 896; III 152, 25.11.11, 1017; III, 153, 1033; III, 153, 2.12.11, 1051; III, 154, 9.12.11, ix; III, 156, 23.12.11, 1110–4; IV, 158, 6.1.12, vi, 8–9; IV, 178, 25.5.12, 473; IV, 192, 31.8.12, 799; IV, 202, 9.11.12, 1023–8; V, 210, 4.1.12, 18, V, 212, 18.1.12, 76; V, 215, 8.2.12, 148; V, 216, 15.2.12, 185–6; V, 221, 22.3.12, 339; V, 225, 19.4.12, 430–1, 432–9; V, 228, 10.5.13, 523; V, 237, 12.7.13, 768–9; V, 243, 23.8.13, 942–3; V, 244, 30.8.13, 961; V, 245, 6.9.13, 992; V, 256, 22.11.13; V, 258, 6.12.13, 1331; V, 259, 13.12.13, 1349, 1355; VI, 262, 3.1.14, 6–7; VI, 265, 24.1.14, viii; VI, 266, 30.1.14; 113; VI, 272, 14.3.14; 261–2, 267; VI, 273, 21.3.14, 305; VI, 274, 28.3.14, viii, 332–4; XI, 570, 4.12.19, 1191; XI, 27.11.19, 1524–32; XII, 577,15.1.20, 65–7; XII, 592, 29.4.20, 467–70; XII, 593, 6.5.20, 491–6; XII, 605, 19.7.20; XII, 615, 7.10.20, 1055–9; XII, 623, 2.12.201231–9; XIII, 543, 21.4.21, 276; XIII, 656, 21.7.21,483, 490–2; XIII, 667,6.10.21, 663; XIII, 672, 10.11.21, 731.

Windsock International: Vol. 5, No. 4, Winter 1989, pp.24–6; 7, 1 Jan./Feb. 1991, 24–7; 8, 1, Jan./Feb. 1992, 12–15; 8, 3, May/Jun. 1992, 24–8; 9, 4, Jul./Aug. 1993, 14–15; 9, 5, Sep./Oct. 1993, 36–7; 9, 6, Nov./Dec. 1993, 24–6; 10, 3, May/Jun. 1994; 12, 6, Nov./Dec. 1996, 7–8; 13, 1, Jan./Feb. 1997, 4; 15, 2, Mar./Apr. 1995, 14–19; 16, 3, May/Jun. 2000, 6–12.

World War One Aero: No. 111, Sept 1986, p.31–40; 119, Apr. 1988, 14–16.

Index

Abakanowicz, Lt P. 128
A.B.C. Dragonfly engine 15, 181–3, 186
Abd-el-Krim 12, 169
Abeele 99
Ackermann, Oblt R. 157
Ad Astra Aero 187
Adams, Flt Cdr S. 103
Adige 85
Aegean 99–100
Aenne Rickmers (*see* HMS Anne)
Aerial Derby:
 1919 184
 1921 171
Aero Club of America 8
Aero Lausanne 187
Aéro-Club de France 8
Aéro-Club of France Grand Prix 22
Aeromarittima 75
Aéronautique Militaire 11, 178
Aeroplane Experimental Station, Martlesham Heath 53
Aiello 139, 142
Air Battalion Royal Engineers 93
Airco:
 DH2 103
 DH4 105, 122
 DH.9/9A 123
 DH.11 Oxford 182
Aircraft Disposal Company 15
Airship A.1 153
Aisovizza 132
Ajaccio 77, 179
Albania 136, 140
Albatros 100, 139, 142, 145
 D.III 89
 D.Va 148, 152
 seaplane 144
Aliperta 142
Alkan, SgtMec 38
Alkan gun mounting 38
Alkan synchronization gear 103–4
Alkyon 154
Allasia 139
Allied Military Commission 125
al-Masri, Aziz 131
Alonso, 1st Lt S. 157
Altschuller 7
Ambrogi 83
American Expeditionary Force (AEF) 48, 64, 71, 147–53
Amiots-SECM 12
Amman, Enrico 13
Anatra 11, 16, 114
Ancillotto 141
Ancona 145–6
Andriani 132
Angista 100
Anilite bomb 43
Ans 153
Antivari, Montenegro 78
Antoinette 7
Anzani flying school 12
Aquilino 143
Arbuzov, 2nd Lt 124
Arcade 143
Archangel 111, 121, 129
Arensburg 117–18
Argeev, Staff Capt Pavel 113–15
Argenteuill 11, 169–70
Argentina 154, 166
 1 Gruppo de Aviaciòn 166
Argyropoulos, E. 24, 154
Armée de l'Air 172
Armistice 126, 146
Armstrong Siddeley:
 Jaguar 182, 184
 Puma 183
Arrigoni 138
Arsiè 142

Ashenden, 2nd Lt J. 157
Asiago 134
Astra 11, 28
Astrakhan 122
Ateliers d'Aviation R. Savary et H. de la Fresnaye 11, 47–8, 107
Atkinson, Maj A.M. 65, 151
Attili 138
Aubry, Capt 77
Austin Osprey 181
Austria-Hungary 14, 78, 119, 131, 141
 FLG1 139
 Flik 2 133–4
 Flik 11 142
 Flik 12 134, 137, 139, 142
 Flik 15 137
 Flik 16 136
 Flik 19 133, 135
 Flik 23 137
 Flik 28 136
 Flik 32 139, 142
 Flik 35 137, 139
 Flik 55 141
 Flik 56J 142
 Monarch 145
 Wien 145
Aviaciòn Militar 166
Aviano 143
Aviatik 87–8
Aviation Competition 1911 9
Aviation Maritime 26, 34, 48, 52, 77–80, 85–6
 Esc. 313 47
 Esc. de Chasse Terrestre du Centre d'Aviation Maritime 85
 Esc. de Port-Said 78–9
 Port Said Detachment 10
Aviation Militaire 11, 34, 37, 43, 48, 50–1, 64, 77, 80–7, 102, 121
 Esc. C-10 167
 Esc. Cigognes 48
 Esc. d'Athene 49
 Esc. de l'intérieur 85
 Esc. de Mestre 82
 Esc. MS.12 38
 Esc. MS.26 31
 Esc. MS.38 11
 Esc. N.3 80–3, 90, 116
 Esc. N.5 82
 Esc. N.12 10, 23, 77, 80–1, 83, 90
 Esc. N.15 80–3, 88, 90
 Esc. N.23 80–3, 90
 Esc. N.26 81–3, 90
 Esc. N.31 82–3, 90
 Esc. N.37 80–4, 90
 Esc. N.38 82, 90
 Esc. N.48 82–3, 90
 Esc. N.49 82–4, 90
 Esc. N.57 81–3, 90
 Esc. N.62 82–3, 90
 Esc. N.65 81, 84–, 88, 90
 Esc. N.67 80–3, 91
 Esc. N.68 83, 91
 Esc. N.69 81–3, 91
 Esc. N.73 82–3, 91
 Esc. N.75 83–4, 91
 Esc. N.76 91
 Esc. N.77 91
 Esc. N.78 83–4, 91
 Esc. N.79 83, 91
 Esc. N.80 83–4, 91
 Esc. N.81 83–4, 91
 Esc. N.82 84–5, 91
 Esc. N.83 84, 91
 Esc. N.84 84, 88, 91
 Esc. N.85 84, 91
 Esc. N.86 84, 91
 Esc. N.87 91
 Esc. N.88 89, 91
 Esc. N.89–N.91 91
 Esc. N.92 82, 85, 91
 Esc. N.93 11, 84, 91
 Esc. N.94 83, 91

Esc. N.95 91
Esc. N.96–N.102 92
Esc. N.103 43, 82–3, 92
Esc. N.112 83–4, 92
Esc. N.124 81–4, 87–90, 92
Esc. N.150–N.162 92
Esc. N.311 85, 92
Esc. N.312–N.314 92
Esc. N.387 92, 121
Esc. N.391 92, 121
Esc. N.392 85, 92
Esc. N.523 92
Esc. N.531 92
Esc. N.561 92
Esc. N.562 92
Esc. N.581 92, 115
Esc. Sherifian 12
Esc. Spa 37 165
Esc. Spa 68 149
Esc. Spa 81 165
Esc. Spa 93 165
Esc. Spa 581 115
GB.1 83
GB.2 80
GB.4 88
GC.11 82–3
GC.12 82–3, 88
GC.13 83, 89
GC.22 85
GC Cachy 80–2
GC Chaux 84
GC de la Somme 82–3
GC Malzéville 80
l'Escadrille Americaine 87–90
l'Escadrille Lafayette 82, 87, 90, 149
Régiments d'Aviation 165
Aviation Militaire Belge 37, 153–4
 1 Esc. de Chasse 153
 5 Esc. de Chasse 153
 10 Esc. 166
Compagnie des Aviateurs 153
Esc. I 153
Esc. II 153
Esc. III 153
Esc. IV 153
Franco-Belgian Esc. 153
Avro 533 Manchester 182

Bacalan flying school 11
Bacula 144
Baftalovsky 116
Bainsizza 137, 143
Baklanov, Lt P. 128
Baldock 94
Ball, Albert 48
Balloon Factory, Farnborough 28
Baltic Fleet 117
Bands, FSL G.K. 100
Baracca 133, 136–7, 139
Baracchini 139
Barattini 134
Barbosi 120
Bar-le-Duc 81, 87
Barrault 171
Barrington-Kennet, Lt 93–4
Barthélemy de Saizieu, LV L. 95, 97
Bassio 144
Battle of Caporetto 139–40, 142–3
Battle of Champagne 84
Battle of Chemin des Dames 84
Battle of Guise 77
Battle of Ortigara 136
Battle of Piave 140–2
Battle of the Somme 80, 83, 100, 103
Battle of Ypres 90
Baudry, Flt Lt R.G.A. 102
Bazaine, Léon P.M. 11, 13
Beardmore 34, 101

Beare, Flt Lt S.G 100
Beauchamp, 1st Lt O. 151
Beersheba 96
Behonne 87
Belgian Seaplane Trial, Tamise sur Escaut 1913 24
Belgium 48, 166
Belgrade 153
Bell-Davis, Flt Cdr R. 99
Bellina 141
Belluno 137
Belofastov, Capt 116
Belorussia 121–2
Bembridge 95
Bentley B.R.2 engine 15, 181, 184
Berchem Ste Agathe 98
Bergen, Ens L.J. 153
Bernáldez, Lt F. 157
Bernard, General 23
Bernard, Jean 171
Berthelot, Gen H. 119
Bessarabia 120
Besson, FSL F. 99
Biansizza 143
Biego di Costa Bissara, Constantino 13
Bir El Abd 97
Birkigt, Marc 176
Bizerte 78, 178–9
Black Sea 122, 158
Black Sea Air Division 119
Black Sea Fleet 117
Blanchis 143
Blankenberge 102
Blériot aircraft 11, 21, 28, 109, 119, 131, 133, 158, 165
Blériot-Spad 12
Bléry, Capt P. 120
Blida, Algeria 7
Bolling, Col R.C. 147
Bolognesi 138
Bolsena flying school 153
Bolshevik Revolution 121, 126
Bolzano 138
Bonavoglia 144
Bône 78
Bone, FSL J.T. 98
Bone, Flt Cdr R.J. 99
Bonifacio 78
Borel, Duperon, Niepce et Fetterer 11, 171
Borgnano 138–9
Bortashevich, V.V. 16
Borzesti 120
Boston Meeting 1911 22
Boulton & Paul:
 Bobolink 181
 Bourges 182
Bournemouth 170
Bowden cable 81
Boyau 83
Brack-Papa 171, 174
Brandenburg C.I 114, 120, 133–9, 142, 146
Brasov 119
Bray Dunes 98
Brazil 52, 154
 1 Companhia de Parque de Aviacao 154
 Destacamento de Aviacao 154
 Escola de Aviacao Miltar 154
Breguet aircraft 77, 93
 XIX 165
Breguet-Michelin 119–20
Brenta 85
Bretagne 86
Brimont 77
Brindisi 142
Bristol Jupiter engine 15
British Air Mission to Japan 184
British Aviation Commission 106
British Nieuport (*see* Nieuport & General Aircraft Co)

Brocourt 81
Broili 138
Brusilov, Gen 116
Buc 8, 105
Bucharest 103, 119
Bucovini 120
Bugulma 124
Bulgaria 95, 158
Buk 100
Bureau of Commissars for Aviation and Aeronautics 121
Buriago 141
Burke, Maj C.J. 94
Buscaylet 11, 165
Busche 138
Buzcacz 115
Buzio, Felice 13, 14, 139

Cabruna 142
Cachy 43, 81, 88
Cadzand 103, 155
Caffyn, Lt C.H.F.M. 48
Calais 102
Callan, Lt Cdr J.L. 152
Calori 139
Calshot 7
Calzavara 14
Campanaro 141
Campbell, Sgt A.C. 89
Campbell, Lt D. 65, 148–9
Campo de la Aurora 155
Campo dos Afonsos 154
Campoformido 131–4
Canakkale 158
Canziano 137
Cape Verde Is 179
Caproni aircraft 131, 133–4, 135–6, 140, 153, 166
Carabelli 142
carboliseur 59
Carr, Capt 122
Carso 132
Casablanca 169
Casale, Lt J. 163, 169, 172, 179
Cascina Bianca 134
Cascina Farello 134–6, 138–9
Caselli 136
Casgrain, Lt W.V. 150
Caspian Sea 122
Castenedolo 141
Castle Bromwich 101
Cattaro 153
Caudron 77–8, 119–20, 169
 G.3 10, 82, 133, 136
 G.4 80, 99, 139
Cavazzo Carnico 137
Cazeaux School of Aerial Gunnery 118
Cellé-sur-Ouese 21
Cena 137
Central Powers 95, 112
Centre d'aviation maritime, Saint Raphaël 77
CEPA 167
Cephalonia 78, 97
Cerutti 141–2
Cevignano 137, 139
CFS Upavon 93, 101
Châlons-sur-Vesles 77
Chambe, Capt R. 120
Chambers, Lt Reed 65, 148
Champaigne 80
Chantiers Aéro-Maritimes de la Seine (CAMS) 12
Chapman, 2nd Lt C.W. 148
Chapman, Sgt V.E. 87
Chasserias 169
Chassério 24
Châteauroux 165
Chaudun 89
Chauvière propeller 56
Chaux 84
Chelna station 124
Chemin-les-Dames 90
Cherdakhy station 124

Chiaperotti 133–5
Chile 154
Chiri 142–3
Chita 130
Cintré, LV A. 78, 95
Ciotti 139
Cipriani 132
Ciprianisca 138
Circuit d'Anjou 1912 19
Circuit de l'Est 8
Circuit of Britain 1911 21
Circuit of Europe 1911 21
Ciselet, 2nd Lt C.E.L. 154
Citroën 7
Cizeck 7
Clauriano 132
Clerget engines:
 110hp 95
 7Z 80hp 71, 82, 96
 9B 120/130hp 34, 49–50, 54, 56, 59, 106, 118
 9Z/110hp 45, 50, 83, 106
 11E 200hp 64, 159–60
Cochran-Patrick, Capt C.J.K. 104
Collier, T. 157
Columbia 154
Columbian Escuela Militar de Aviacion 154
Comazzi 132
Comina 135–6, 139, 143
Commissar for National Defence 121
Compagnie Générale Transaérienne 11
Concours International, Madrid 168
cône de pénétration 34, 58
Conner, Capt D.G. 94
Consonni 135
Constantini 143
Construzione Aeromarine SA 14
Construzioni Aeromarittime 76
Coppens, Willy 41, 54
Corbett, Sub-Lt The Hon A.C. 102
Corfu 86
Cormon 143
Corsi, Roberto 13
Cortesi 144
Coupe Beaumont:
 1924 177
 1925 12
Coupe Deutsch:
 1919 68, 170
 1921 11, 168, 174
 1922 172, 174
Coupe Gordon Bennett:
 1910 8
 1911 19, 21
 1913 20
 1914 30
 1920 170
 1921 171
Courcelles 171
Courtney, Sqn Ldr C.L. 50, 54
Cowdin, Sgt Elliott 101
Cowes Roads 170
Cox, Flt Lt G.A. 103
Coxyde 153–4
Craiu, Lt V. 120
Craonne 77
Crombez, Lt H. 153
Cuatro Vientos 157
Cucchetti 138
Cunningham, Lt 150
Curtiss 171, 175
 D-1A 600hp engine 174
 D-12 450hp engine 174
 flying boat 144
 R-6 174
Czechoslovakia 123
 1 Aviation Detachment 123
 2 Aviation Company 125
 3 Czech Division of Fusiliers 125

189

INDEX

Dakar 179
Dallas, FSL R.S. 102
Dalmatian coast 145
Daly, FSL I. de B. 99
Dardenelles 78
Darracq engines 8, 17
Darracq-Coatalen 12A 450hp 179–80
Daugherty, E. 152
Davis, 2nd Lt P.W. 149
Dayton-Wright 171
De Bernardi 135
de Carolis 135
de Caumont La Force, Lt 7–8
de Chaestret de Haneffe, 2nd Lt Baron P.L.M.G. 154
de Courcelles, Adj Henri 53, 57
de Jong 7
De Laage de Meux, Lt Alfred 87–9
de Laborde, LV 78
de l'Escaille, LV 26, 77–8
de Lettenhove, 2nd Lt Kervyn 154
de Marmier, Lt F 57
De Martini, Giovanni 13
de Meulemeester, Lt A.E.A. 154
de Romanet 170–1, 174
De Rossi di Santa Rosa 132
de Turenne 83
de Vergnette de la Motte, Lt Col 119
Dedulin, Ens Alexander 123–5
Delage, LV A. 95–6
Delage, Gustave 9–13, 30, 55, 161, 175
Delesalle, Sous-Lt 85
Dell'Oro 139
Denikin 119, 123, 129
Depasse, Henri 7, 19
Deperdussin 20, 93, 158
  Type XI 9
Desbordes 7
designation systems 6
Destrem, EV 26, 77, 78
Deullin 11, 83
Deutsch de la Meurthe, Henri 9, 11, 28
Dewoitine D-1 166
di Imolesi 137
Di Moriago 142
Diderot 86
Dixmude 102
Dobrova 136
Dollfus, Lt 98
Domesnes 117
Don Muang 156
Donadio 142
Dormé 11, 83
Dornberg 134
Dover 98
Dover Patrol 99
Doyen, Professor 9
Dragnaeuusti 103
Dragusanu, Sub-Lt M. 120
Droglandt 101
Du Doré, Capt 64, 151
Dubonnet, E. 179
Duca degli Abruzzi 152
Dudular 144
Duhamel, Robert 11
Dukinfield-Jones, A. 99
Duks factory 11, 16, 23, 33, 37, 111–12, 117–18, 129
Dumoulin, Françoise 7
Dunkerque 47, 54, 98–100
Dunn, Capt F.G. 57
Dunne D.8 28
Dunne, Lt J.W. 28
Dunwoody, Col. 152
Dupré, Sgt 149
Durazzo 144–6
Duval, Gen 86, 162
Dvina river 118, 122–3

Eastchurch 21, 28, 99
Eastchurch Naval Flying School 93
Echagüe, O. 157
École Polytechnique 7
École Supérieure d'Electricité 7

Egyptian Survey Department 96
Ekaterinbourg Offensive 124
Elettro-Ferroviera 11, 37
Eleventh Battle of the Isonzo 138
Elliott, 1st Lt E. 150
Emaillite dope 178
Emery Rogers & Co 152
Enisei river 122
Epiez 148
Eppeville 89
Erna river 121
Eschwege, von 103
Escuela de Aviacioíon Militar 24
Escuela de Peu 24
Espanet 9, 22–6
Esposti 139
Estienne, Col 9
Estonia 126
Estonian Aviation Company 126
Etampes 9
Étévé gun mounting 34, 41
Euler 37
Evampliev, N.N. 118, 122

Faber, Ltz K. 100
Fairey IIIC 123
Falkenhain 81
Fancello 142
Fargo Bottom 94
Farman 10, 11, 77, 88, 123, 131, 136, 141, 144, 165
  VII 110
  XVI 111
  XXII 111
  30 123–5
Farman, Henri 7
Farman, Maurice 7
Farnborough 94, 108, 181
FBA 80, 145–6, 152–3
Feber, Ferdinand 7
Fedoseev, Lt 119
Felice, Carlo 13
Félix, Cdr 28
Feltre 142
Féquant, Philippe 88
Fère-en-Tarnenois 151
Fernando de Norhona Is 179
Fiat 174
  25.4mm cannon 75, 145
  A.10 engine 146
Fifth Battle of the Isonzo 134
Filippov, V.N. 118
Finland 48, 154
  Lento-osasto 2 154
First Aeronautical meeting 1922, Dübendorf 157
First Balkan War 154
First Battle of the Isonzo 132
First Pursuit Group AS 148–51
Fiume 134
Fleischer, Ltn R.A. 151
Fokker 100
  D.VII 71, 150, 152
  Dr.I 52
  E.III 37, 81, 87–8, 102, 120
Folland, H.P. 15, 181–2
Fonzaso 141
Fornagiari 138, 143
Fort Douaumont 40
Fortant 179
Fossalunga 138
Foster gun mounting 47, 104
Fougier 142
Foulois, Brig Gen B. 65, 148, 151
Fournié, LV 77
Fox, Lt 94
France (*see also* Aviation Maritime, Aviation Militaire) 95
  Aeronautical Corps 28
  Military Aeroplane Trials 1911, Reims 21
  Military Manœuvres:
    1911 9
    1912 77
    1913 77
  Navy Competition 1913, St Malo 24
Campinas 78, 97

Foudre 77–8, 95–6
Jean Bart 86
La Bretagne 167
Liamone 78
Montcalm 97
Franco Tosi factory 153
Freidrichshafen FF33 99–100, 118
Fry, Lt W.M. 48
Fulton, Capt J.D.B. 93
Furniss, FSL H.A. 100

Gadda 142
Galassi 142
Galbraith, FSL D.M.B. 102–3
Galician Front 103
Gallipoli 95, 97, 100
Galyshev, Capt 118
Ganfardine 141
Garos, Roland 9
Gasson, FSL C.B. 95
GAZ No.1 factory 16
Genêt, Sgt E.C.C. 89
Gengoult 148–9
Genoa 152
Gentili 137
Gerard 144
Germany 78
  Breslau 78
  Fl. Abt(A) 46b 148
  Fl. Abt(A) 242 148
  Goeben 78
  Jasta 4 150
  Jasta 10 150
  Jasta 25 99
  Jasta 64 148
  JGI 150–1
  Spring Offensive 1918 108
Germonville 174
Gerrard, Capt E.L. 93
Gerrard, Ft Lt T.F.N. 102
Ghelfi 135
Ghidotti 137
Ghizzoni 136
Giacomelli 143
Giammarco 132
Giannotti 142
Gibraltar 78, 157
Gigli 143
Gilewicz, Lt J. 126–7
Gilsher 2nd Lt J.V. 116
Giori 135, 137
Giovine 132
Giro Aerea di Sicilia 146
Gloucestershire Aircraft Company 15
Gnome engines:
  50hp 93
  70hp 16, 94
  160hp 24
  180hp 64
  9N 160hp 159–60
  Monosoupape 160hp 33, 67, 148
Gobé, Armand 7, 9, 22, 24
Goggins, QM J.L. 153
Gomel 122
Gonde, Capt M. 120
Gonnet & Wilock 179
Gordesco 139
Gorgupi 154
Gorizia 134, 143
Gotha 85
Gourdou:
  180 170
  8b 178–9
  monoplane 169
Gradis 11
Gradisca 131, 137
Grado 144–5
Graham, FSL C.W. 98
Grahame-White, Claude 22, 94–5
Grahame-White Co 182
Grall, QM H. 95–6
Gran Premio d'Italia d'Aviazione, Brescia 1921 171
Grand Prix de Monaco 1920 179
Grand Prix d'Hydroaeroplanes de Monaco 1913 25
Grande Semaine d'Aviation de Reims 8
Grappa 141

Great Britain (*see also* RFC, RNAS, RN) 10
Greece 154, 184
  1 Flying Sqn 154
  531 Mira Sqn 154
  A Aircraft Sqn 184
  E Fighter Sqn 184
Grigorovitch
  M.9 118
  M.15 118
Grisolera 142
Grudziadz Advanced Pilot's School 129
Gruppo Idrovolante da Caccia 146
Guadaljara 157
Guatemalan Cuerpo de Aviacion Militar 155
Gude, 1st Lt O. 149
Guglielmi 139
Guierre, LV Georges 85
Guillaux, E. 101
Guillot 9
Gulf of Aqaba 96
Gulf of Finland 122
Gunnery School, Eastchurch 107
Gusev, Lt 124
Gusiatina 115
Gustin 7
Guynemer 11, 48, 83

Haapsala 126
Habillon, QM 85
Habsheim 88
Hall, Adj W.B. 87
Hall, J.N. 148, 150
Hammann, Ens C.H. 153
Hampson, AMI A. 99
Handley Page 106
Handley-Page, Sir F. 15
Hánek, Sgt F. 125
Hanriot 12, 27, 174
  12 167
  HD.1 14, 139–44, 154
  HD.2 86
  seaplane 146
Happe, Capt 87
Hapsal 118
Hartney, Maj H. 151
Hatfield 94
Haviland, Lt Cdr W.B. 88–9, 153
Hazet radiator 41
Heinrich, Lt W. 150
Heiro 150hp 72
Helen, Emmanuel 19, 22
Hendon 106
Hengst, Ltn 149
Henri Farman aircraft 9, 119, 153
Herbert, Capt T.R. 96
Herrare, Capt 157
Heurtaux 11
Hinkle, Sgt E.F. 89
Hiouthulst Forest 85
Hirschauer, Gen 10
Hispano-Suiza 54
  150hp 41, 44–5
  180hp 166
  200hp 42
  220hp 43
  250hp 44
  300hp 160–1
  8Aa 175hp 42
  12Ga/b/12Hb 176–7
  V-12 176
Holland 48, 103, 155
  Luchtvaart Afdeling 155
Hondsschoote 153
Hoover, Lt W. 150
Hoper, FSL K.V. 99
Hoskier, Sgt R.W. 89
Houthem 153
Hudson, 1st Lt D. 150
Huffer, Major J. 65, 151
Hungary 155
  8 Voros Repuloszazad 155
Hunt, J. 151
Hyde, 2nd Lt E.P. 100

Il'ya Muromets 129
Imbros 95, 98–9, 100, 103
Imolesi 141

Imperial Army Air Service 110
Imperial Russia 109
Ince, FSL A.S. 98
Industrie Meridionali 14, 76
Innes-Kerr, Capt Lord Robert 102
International Michelin Cup 1913 23
Iordan, V.V. 112
Irben 117
Isle de la Jatte 11
Isles de Lérins 77
Isola di Arturo 143
Isola di Gorgo 145
Isola Morosini 132
Isonzo river 131
Isotta-Franchini engines:
  150hp 14
  V4B 160hp 72
  V6 250hp 75–6
Issy-les-Moulineaux 10, 11, 165
Istrana 137–8, 140, 143
Italy 10, 14, 60, 74, 131, 166
  Ispettorato Difesa del Traffico Nazionale 146
  Ispettorato Sommergibili ed Aviazione 75, 152
  Regia Aeronautica 14, 146
  Regia Marina 140, 144
  Sezione per la Defensa di la Spezia 146
  1ª Flottiglia Aeroplani 23, 131
  1ª Gruppo Sqd di Artilleria 133
  1ª Sqd Caccia 133–4
  1ª Sqd Idrovolante 145
  1ª Sqd Nieuport 131
  2ª Gruppo Sqd di Artilleria 133
  2ª Sqd Blériot 131
  2ª Sqd Caccia 133–4
  2ª Sqd Idrovolanti di Grado 153
  3ª Gruppo Sqd di Artilleria 133
  3ª Sqd Idrovolante 145
  5ª Sezione da Difesa 143
  5ª Sqd Nieuport 131, 133
  6ª Sqd Nieuport 131–2
  7ª Sqd Artilieria 144
  7ª Sqd Nieuport 131
  8ª Sqd Nieuport 131–3
  25ª Sqd 142
  32ª Sqd 133, 136, 144
  35ª Sqd 133, 136
  37ª Sqd 141
  47ª Sqd 144
  50ª Sqd 141
  61ª Sqd 141
  70ª Sqd 133, 135–7, 139–40, 143, 166
  71ª Sqd 134–7, 141
  72ª Sqd 140–1
  73ª Sqd 136, 140–1, 144
  74ª Sqd 140–2, 166
  75ª Sqd 135–7, 140–1, 144, 166
  76ª Sqd 135, 139–40, 143, 166
  77ª Sqd 135–9, 142
  78ª Sqd 135–9, 141, 143
  79ª Sqd 137–41
  80ª Sqd 137, 139–40
  81ª Sqd 139–41, 143
  82ª Sqd 136–7, 139–40, 142
  83ª Sqd 136–7, 139–42, 144
  84ª Sqd 137, 139, 142, 166
  85ª Sqd 136, 140–1, 144
  86ª Sqd 140
  90ª Sqd 139
  91ª Sqd 137, 139–40, 166
  108ª Sqd 144
  110ª Sqd 144
  122ª Sqd SAML 144
  139ª Sqd 144
  241ª Sqd 146
  242ª Sqd 146
  251ª Sqd–259ª Sqd 145
  260ª Sqd 75, 146
  261ª Sqd 146
  262ª Sqd 146

  263ª Sqd 145, 153
  265ª 145, 153
  288ª Sqd 145
  290ª Sqd 146
  292ª Sqd 146
  Centro Formazione Sqd di Arcardia 138–9, 142
  Gruppo Difesa Aerea Veneto-Emilia 143
  Masse de Caccia 140–2
  RN *Europa* 144–6
  Sezione Defesa Bologna 143
  Sezione Defesa Brindisi 143–4
  Sottogruppo Aeroplani di Borgnani 143
  Sqd Idrovolanti di Varano 145
Itoh Tsurubane No.2 156

Jacob, Flt Lt A.F.F. 103
Jacques Schneider Cup 1913 26
Jaeger-France 13
Japan 10, 155–6, 166
  Air Regiments 146
  Army Flying Schools:
    Kagamigahara 156
    Tokorozawa 156
  Army Supply Depot, Tokorozawa 155
Jdersko 156
Jensen, Keith 68
Johnson, Adj C.C. 89
Jurkiewicz, Lt A. 126

Kacha Field 109, 114
Kacha fighter school 16
Kama river 122
Kantara 97
Kapférer, Henry 11
Kataloi-Tulca 119
Kavalkin 60hp engine 23
Kazakov 122–3
Kazan 124
Keeble, FSL 99
Keller 139
Kent, L.M. 95
Kerensky 113
Kiliya 119
Kim, Jnr Lt 119
Kindyakouka station 124
Kirsch, Georges 7, 11, 171–2, 174
Kirschbaum, Gef 149
Knopp, Viktor 123
Kokorin, Ens 115
Kolchak, Vice Adm A.V. 117, 124
Komorowski, Lt W. 126
Kosice 125
Kozakov, Staff Capt Alexander 33, 113–14
Koziatyn 129
Krakow Pilot's School 128
Krasnoe-Selo 111, 117–18
Kronstadt 121–2
Krumian 144
Kruten, Capt Evgraf 113, 115
Kuivast 118
Kurtz, 1st Lt P.B. 149–50

La Ferté-St-Aubin 11
La Société Générale d'Aerolocomotion 7
La Spezia 78
Ladoga lake 122
Lagarina valley 134
Lago di Caldonazzo 141
Lago di Doberdò
Lago di Pietra Rossa 132
Lagoda, Sgt C. 129
Lake Barawil 97
Lake Drisviaty 114
Lake Scutari 78
Lamblin radiator 164, 168, 170–1, 175, 179
Langley Field 152
Larissa 154
Larkhill 93
Lasne, Fernand 11, 171–2, 174
Latham, Hubert 7
Latvia 125–6

INDEX

Laurent-Eynac, Victor 12, 172
Le Bourget 172
Le Gall 97
Le Garrec, QM 85
Le Panne 98
Le Prieur, Lt Y.P.G. 39
Le Prieur rockets 39–40, 48, 88, 136, 141–2, 144
Le Rhône engines 107, 155
  9C/80hp 31, 37–8, 41, 49, 51–3, 71, 83, 133, 147–8, 167
  9Da/90hp 51
  9J/110hp 33, 38, 41, 45, 47–8, 50–1, 53, 61, 117
  9Jb/120/130hp 33, 49, 55, 118, 123, 127, 147–8
  9N/170/hp180hp 67, 159, 167–8
Lebed 12 118
Lebedev, V.A. 16
Leblanc 21
Lecointe, Sadi 170–7, 179
Ledger 97
Legagneux, Maurice 9
Legion d'Honneur 9
Legros, F. 57
Leman 114
Lemnos 95
Leningrad 129–30
Leonardi 142
Les Moëres 154
Letord 11, 165
Levasseur 165
Levasseur 549 propeller 56
Levasseur, QM J. 78, 95
Levavasseur, André 7, 11
Lewis gun 34, 36, 39, 41, 43, 47–8, 50–1, 81, 104, 118, 127
Liepaja 125
Lincoln, G. 152
Lithuanian-Belorussian front 128
Lloyd 125
Lloyd C.III 134
Locker-Lampson, Oliver 103
Loda 126
Lohner Type L 14, 72, 74, 136, 139, 144
Loiko, Ivan 116
Loire et Olivier 152
Longmore, Wg Cdr A.M. 98
Loque 143
Loraine, Capt Eustace 94
Loraine, Robert 94
Lorraine-Dietrich 12
  180hp 41, 43
  240hp 159–60
  275hp 160–1
Lovell, Adj W. 89
Lubny aviation park 123
Lucentini 142
Ludlow, Ens G. 153
Lufbery, Maj G.R. 88–9, 149
Lumière 144C propeller 165
Lutsk 114
Luxeuil-les-Bains 82, 87
Luzk 115
LVG 102, 127
  C.VI 148
Lvov 127
Lyncker, Oblt von 99

Maahmud Sevkat Pasa 158
MacArthur, 2nd Lt J. 150
Macchi 137, 166
Macchi, Giulio 13
Macedonia 136, 139–40, 144
MacMillan, Wg Cdr N. 102
Madon 48, 83
Madrid 8
Madrid Rally 1902 7
Magalea, Sub-Lt 120
Maggiora, Clemente 14, 29
Magistrini 138
Makeenok, 2nd Lt D.A. 116
Malancourt 87
Mallard, H. 26, 169–70
Malpensa airfield 14
Manchuria 166
Mancini 141
Mannock, Edward 48
Marasesti-Oituz Front 120
Marazzani 138

Marchal, Capt A. 36, 178–9
Marcon 142
Mariakerke 102
Marr, Sgt K. 89
Martin, E. 152
Martin, 1st Lt R.C. 151
Martinsyde:
  C.1 Buzzard 162, 167
  Semiquaver 171
Martlesham Heath 181–2, 186
Marvin, FSL J.D. 99
Mary, A. 161, 174
Masala 142, 144
Masson, FSL D.H. 87–8, 103
Matecki, Lt J. 127
Maugham 176
Maurice Farman 11 14, 82
  40 119
  MF.7 155
Maxim machine-gun 112, 114
Maxwell, Lt Gen Sir John G. 95
Mazio, Capt 131
McConnell, Sgt J.R. 88–9
McCook Field 148
McElvain, 1st Lt C. 151
McReady, Lt 172
Medaets, 2nd Lt M.P.A.J-B. 154
Medana 141
Medeuzza 133
Meinikov, N.S. 122
Meissner, 1st Lt J. 149, 150, 151, 152
Melc, 2nd Lt 124
Mele 141
Melilla 167
Meller, Y.A. 16
Mellone 143
Meulan 77
Middle East 106, 108
Mihail, Lt G. 120
Mikhailovich, The Grand Duke Alexander 109
Mikhailovskaya station 124
Military Aviation Laboratory, Vincennes 9
Minsk 126–7
Mitchell, Col W. 148, 151, 174
Mitsubishi Ko.1 156
Mogilev 111
Molina, Paulo 13
Monaco Rally 1914 26
Monaco Trophy Race 1920 170, 178–9
Monastir 144
Monfalcone 131
Monge 174
Monte Grappa 140
Monte Stol 139
Monte Verena 139, 142
Monti & Martini 75
Montirail 172
Montmain 28
Moon Island 118
Morane Saulnier:
  Parasol 10, 77, 80, 89, 111, 116, 123, 158
  monoplane 9, 10, 86, 89, 114–15
  BB 102
  N 81
Moreau gun mounting 38
Moretto 134
Moreux radiator 175–6
Morgan, Flt Lt H.E. 100
Morozov, Jnr Lt 119
Mortimer Singer Prize 93
Mosca factory 11, 16
Moscow 111
Moscow Air School 116
Mourmelon 7
Mt Kuk 136
Mt San Michele 134
Mt Vodice 136
Mudros 95, 97, 99
Mulhouse 87
Mullens, Sub-Lt C.J.A. 100
Mulock, FSL R.H. 98, 102
Muntenescu, Sub-Lt 120
Murmansk 111, 122, 129
Murphy, Ens T.L.153

Nadezhdin, Capt V.M. 118

Nakajima 155
  Hei .1 155, 166
  Ko.1 156
  Ko.3 58, 155, 166
  Ko.4 166
  Type 91 166
Nancy 80
Nannini 135
Napier Lion 184
Nardini 138, 143
NAS Hampton Roads 152
Nasta, Sub-Lt E. 120
Natale 143
Navarre 11
Nederlandsche Automobil en Vleieguigfabriek Trompenburg 155
Nelidov, 2nd Lt A.A. 118
Nelli 143
Nesbizh 115
Nice 78
Nicelli 141–2
Nicholas II, Tsar 113
Nieuport, Charles 7, 9
Nieuport, Edouard 7, 21
Nieuport advertisement 8
Nieuport & General Aircraft Co. 15, 106, 171
  B.N.1 15, 180–1, 186
  Goshawk 186
  London 15, 182–4, 186
  Nieuhawk 184
  Nighthawk 15, 181–2, 184, 186
  Nightjar 15, 184–6
  Sparrowhawk 184
Nieuport aircraft:
  10 10, 11, 14, 30–33, 36, 52, 80–1, 98, 102, 112, 114, 116–17, 121–2, 124, 129–30, 133–4, 146, 153–4
  11 11, 14, 16, 37–39, 41, 80–2, 87, 98, 102–3, 108, 112–13, 115–16, 119–21, 126, 130, 135–9, 142–3, 146, 153, 155
  11C 53
  12/12bis 11, 33–36, 41, 83, 85–6, 88, 99–103, 108, 119, 121, 126, 130, 154–5
  13 37, 69, 113
  14 41–4
  15 43–4
  16 37–41, 48, 82, 85–6, 103–4, 108, 114, 154
  17/17bis 11, 14, 38, 45–53, 83–6, 88, 99, 104–8, 113, 115, 117–24, 126–30, 135–43, 146–8, 154–5, 158
  18 44–5
  19 45
  20 36, 99, 101–2, 108
  21(17B) 51–2, 102–3, 113–17, 119, 122, 124–6, 129–30, 147, 154
  22 45, 61
  23/23bis/École 49, 52, 83–5, 105–6, 108, 114, 120, 122–3, 125–30, 147, 154, 157
  24/24bis 11, 54–8, 61, 85–7, 105, 107–8, 114, 118, 120, 122–3, 126–9, 140, 148, 154–5
  25 59, 122, 130
  27 11, 59–61, 88, 105–8, 130, 139–43, 148, 155, 158
  28 11, 61–6, 69, 86, 120, 148–52, 154–5, 157
  29 11, 155
  32 52
  52 167
  80 23, 37, 69–71, 82, 143, 147, 154–6
  81 37, 69–71, 82, 154–6
  82 45, 69–71
  83 69–71, 82, 154–6, 158
  84 69, 71
  100hp Gnome 21
  165hp Gnome Monosoupape 65
  180hp Lorraine Dietrich 41, 43
  200hp Hispano-Suiza 42
  1910 monoplane 17, 23
  II/IID/IIN/IIG 17–19, 23, 94, 108, 130, 154, 157
  III 20
  IV/IVG/IVM 16, 19–24, 77, 93–5, 109–11, 116, 154, 156–7
  VI 24–6, 77–9, 108, 155, 158
  X 26, 77–80
  XI 27
  XIII 27–8
  'de Vitesse' 19
  Destroyer 24
  floatplanes 9, 10, 24–6, 29, 95–8
  monoplanes 9, 22, 93, 131–3
  'Obus' 20, 23
  Pusher Seaplane 28–9
  S 179–80
  single-seat scout prototype 58
  Triplanes 52–4, 108
Nieuport engines 19, 94
Nieuport-Astra 10, 11
Nieuport-Delage:
  165hp Gnome 9N prototype 159–60
  170hp Le Rhône prototype 159
  200hp Clerget 11F prototype 159–60
  240hp Lorraine-Dietrich prototype 159–60
  275hp Lorraine-Dietrich prototype 160–1
  300hp Hispano-Suiza prototype 160–1
  380hp Biplane 168
  29 159–67
  29 seaplane racers 169–70
  29B-1 159, 168–9
  29bis 159, 168
  29C 159
  29ET.1 159, 166, 169
  29V/Vbis 159, 170–3
  30T2 11
  31 68–9, 159
  32M/Rh 159, 167–8
  37 159, 177
  40/40R/DC-1 159, 168, 172–3
  41 159, 175, 177
  42 166, 168, 177
  42S 159
  62 11, 159, 166
  Eugene Gilbert 12,159
  J2 167
  Madon 67–9, 159
Nieuport-Dunne 28
Nieuport-Duplex 7
Nieuport-Macchi 11, 13–14, 27, 33, 37, 72–3, 48
  10 134
  10.000 14
  11 135
  L.1 14, 72, 145
  L.2 14, 72, 145
  L.3 (M.3) 14, 73–4, 136, 145–6, 152–3, 187
  M.4 14, 73
  M.5/M.5bis/5M 14, 74–6, 140, 145–6, 152–4
  M.6 14, 73–4
  M.7/7bis/ter/AR 14, 74–6, 146, 187
  M.8 14, 145–6, 153
  M.9/9bis/9ter 14, 187
  M.12/bis 14, 187
  M.14 14
  M.15 14
  M.24 14
  Parasol 10, 28–9, 133
Nieuport-Tellier
  BM (T.5) 178, 180
  TM (T.7) 11, 178–80
Nistra river 120
Nivelle Offensive 89
Nizhny Novgorod 122
Nokolsky, S.D. 122
Noblette Farm 90
North Russian Expeditionary Force 122

Northern Aircraft Flying School, Windermere 95
Norton, FSL E.W. 99
Novelli 139
Novocherkassk 116–18, 129
Novorossitsk 123
Nowo-Swieciany 127
Novyi Peterhof 122
Nungesser, Sous-Lt C. 40, 48, 50, 59, 83, 87

Oberndorf 88
Odessa 103, 119, 123, 129
Odessa Aviation School 116
Oeffag C.II 116
Oezel Island 118
Okhremenko, SLT V.M. 118
Okna 116
Oleis 142
Olieslagers, 2nd Lt J. 153–4
Olivera 153
Olivieri 142
Olomouc Aircraft Works 125
Olympia Show:
  1911 19
  1914 26
Olympiad 1920 170
Omizzolo 142
Omsk 125
Onega lake 122
Opcina 134
Orlov, 2nd Lt Ivan 116
Orly 65
Ostende 103, 153
Otranto 145
Ots, Ens J. 126

Packhard-Lepère 172
Padova 138, 141
Palestine 95
Palpacelli 141
Palyvestre 168
Paraquay 154
Paris 8
Paris Salon:
  1911 22
  1913 23–4, 28
  1922 168
Paris to Madrid Race 21
Paris Vélodrome d'Hiver 11
Paris-Deauville race 1913 26
Paris-Rome–Turin race 1911 21
Parker, Ens A. 153
Parsons, Sub-Lt E.C. 88
Partridge, Lt 97
Paso de Mendoza 158
Pasubio 136
Patriarca, Count 14
Pau flying school 71
Pauckett, Sub-Lt 120
Paul 97
Pavelka, Sgt P. 88
Peberdy, Flt Lt W.H. 103
Pellanda 143
Pellegrino 144
Pelletier d'Orsy 11
Penny, Lt A.R. 48
Penza 123
Pershing, Gen J.J. 148
Pervomaisk 130
Pescara 152
Peterhofte airstrip 126
Peterson, Capt D. Mc. 148
Petain, Gen 86
Petre, Flt Cdr J.J. 106
Petrograd 111, 117, 121
Petrov, Lt V.V. 118
Pfalz D.III 148, 150, 152
Philbert, Sub-Lt 86
Philippeville 78
Phoënix:
  C.I 142
  D.I 146
Piaggio 138–9
Piatra Neamt 119
Piave 85, 131, 140–2
Picardie 80
Piccio 135, 141
Pinder, J. 187
Pinsard 11, 83
Pishvanov, W/O 116
Piskapi 141
Plesetskaya 122
Podmelec 143
Poianella 142

Pola 145, 153
Poland 126–9
  1 Aviation Sqn 126–8
  2 Air Regiment 128
  4 Aviation Sqn 126–7
  5 Aviation Sqn 127–9
  6 Aviation Sqn 127
  14 Aviation Sqn 128–9
  Szyrinkin Sqn 128
Polock 128
Ponnier 20, 158
Pont-à-Mousson 148
Popescu, Sub-Lt M. 120
Popov, 2nd Lt 127
Porcelengo 142
Port Said 97
Portal, Sub-Lt R.H. 100
Port-au-Prince 8
Porto Corsini 72, 144–6, 152–3
Portugal 156
  Escola de Aeronautica Militar 156
  Escuela Militar de Aviaco 156
Potamos 86
Potez 11, 165
Powles, FSL G.P. 103
Prévost, Maurice 27
Prieditis, Sgt J. 126
Prince, Adj FH 88
Prince, Sub-Lt N. 87–8
Programme des Avions Nouveaux 161
Prokofiev, Lt A.N. (see Seversky)
Proscini 134
Prosecco 136
Protopopescu, Capt S. 120
Pryjamino 128
Przemysl 127–9
Punta Sdobba 139

Rabenfels (see HMS Raven II)
Royal Aircraft Factory:
  BE3 94
  SE4/4a 181
  SE5/5a 105, 107–8, 181
Randi 144
Rankine Dart 35
Rateau turbocharger 168, 172
Ravenel 89
Ravenna 145, 152
Régy propeller 56, 173–5
Reims 77
Reinggart, Oblt 100
Renault engines:
  80hp 14
  150hp 43
  12F 220hp 43–4
  450hp 165
REP 28
  Type III 8
Rettori 143
Reutter, Fl P. 100
Reynaud, LV 77
Royal Flying Corps 3, 93, 103
  1 AD St Omer 101, 103–5
  1 ASD 108
  1 Sqn 46, 60, 101–3, 105, 107–8
  2 AD, Candas 48, 53, 55, 57, 59, 101, 104–5, 107
  2 Slavo-British Sqn 122
  3 Sqn 94, 103
  11 Sqn 36, 48, 53, 57, 98–9, 103–4
  14 Sqn 106
  28RS 101
  29 Sqn 55, 60, 99, 104–8
  39 Sqn 102
  40 Sqn 55, 105, 107
  45 Sqn 102
  46 Sqn 101–2
  60 Sqn 48, 104–6
  66 Sqn 142
  111 Sqn 108
  113 Sqn 106
  Military Wing 94
  X AD, Abukir 108
Riali 142
Richenbacker, 1st Lt E. 65, 148, 150
Ridd, Cpl 93–4

191

INDEX

Ridge-Whitworth bicycle 7
Riga 125
Righi 144
Rigone, G. 141
Rispal 7
Riva Grassa 142
Rizzotto 138, 142
Roberti, Lt G. 14
Roberts, Sub-Lt A.E.H. 100
Rocchi 132
Rockwell, Sub-Lt K.Y. 87–8
Rocques, Gen 9
Roland C.II 88
Rome 8
Roose, Lt A. 126
Roosevelt, 1st Lt Q. 151
Ross, S/Cdr R.P. 95
Rossi 136, 142
Rost 174
Rostov 129
Rovno 83
Royal Navy:
 HMS Anne 96–7
 HMS Argus 184
 HMS Ark Royal 78
 HMS Ben-My-Chree 97
 HMS Diana 96
 HMS Doris 96
 HMS Empress 97
 HMS Euryalus 97
 HMS Minerva 96
 HMS Nairana 122–3
 HMS Raven II 78, 96–7
 HMS Reliance 97
 RIMS Hardinge 97
Royal Naval Air Service 11, 34, 36–7, 45, 53–4, 98–9, 102, 106–7, 118
 1(N) Sqn 31
 1 Wing 39, 98, 100
 2 Wing 99, 102–3
 3 Wing 88, 95, 99
 4 Wing 98
 6(N) Sqn 51, 102–3, 106–7
 9(N) Sqn 102
 11(N) Sqn 54, 102, 107
 A Sqn 2 Wing 103
 A Sqn 4 Wing 99
 B Sqn 1 Wing 102
 CSD White City 95
 CSD Wormwood Scrubs 95
 D Sqn 2 Wing 100
 Dover Patrol Flight 31
 Dunkerque 33–4
 RNAS Windermere 95
 S Sqn 103
Royal Naval Review, Portland 93
Royal Siamese Aeronautical Service 156
Rudini 138
Rudorfer 125
Ruffo 135–7
Rumania 100, 103, 115–16, 119–21
 F.1–F.3 Sqns 119
 N.1 Sqn 120
 N.3 Sqn 120
 N.10 Sqn 120
 N.11 Sqn 120
Rumsey, Sgt Lawrence 87
Russia 10, 33, 48, 52, 95, 109–130
 1 Air Division 114
 1 Aviation Company 110
 1 Baltic Air Brigade 118
 1 Fighter Air Section 116
 1 Turkistan Air Section 111–13
 2 Air Division 115–16
 2 Air Section 114
 2 Baltic Fighter Air Section 118
 2 Fighter Air Section 112, 115
 3 Air Section 115
 3 Corps 115
 3 Fighter Air Section 112
 4 Air Section 114–15
 4 Fighter Air Section 113
 5 Fighter Air Section 112
 6 Aviation Division 113
 6 Corps Aviation Division 119
 7 Aeronautics Company, Kiev 109
 7 Air Section 115
 7 Fighter Air Section 116
 8 Air Section 115
 9 Fighter Air Section 116
 10 Fighter Air Section 113, 116
 12 Fighter Air Section 112
 13 Air Section 119
 19 Air Section 114
 25 Air Section 115
 Army Air Sections 111–12
 Army Aviation Corps 112, 114–17
 Artillery Air Sections 112
 Balloonists School, Volkov Field 109
 Baltic Air Division 117–18
 Black Sea Air Division 117
 Corps Air Sections 112
 Fighter Air Sections 112
 Gatchina military flying school 109
 Petrapavlovsk 122
 Sevastopol 122
 Sevastopol School of Aeronautics 109
 Siberian Aeronautics Battalion 109
 Siberian Air Sections 111–12
 Volunteer Air Fleet (VHF) 109
Russian White Army 119
Russo-Baltic Wagon Works 16, 111
Russo-Polish War 116

S. Andrea 145
S. Luca di Treviso 141
S. Maria di Leuca 145
S. Maria la Longa 131–2, 135, 139, 142
Sabatino 134
SABCA 166, 169
Sabelli, G. 144
Sadi Lecointe 11–12, 170–4
Safonov, Lt M.I. 118–19
Saint Pol-sur-Mer 85
Saint Raphaël 77, 167–8, 178
Salisbury Plain 94
Salmson 110hp engine 28
Salmson 2A.2 151
Salonika 137, 141
SAML 137, 141
Samson, Cdr 78
Samson, Lt C.R. 93
San Luca 141
San Martino del Carso 137
San Michele di Coneglano 142
San Pietro 142
San Pietro di Godego 85
San Severo 153
Sandell, Sub-Lt A. 100
Sands, 1st Lt C. 151
Santa Caterina 134, 136, 139, 142
Santa Maria, Lt 45
Sanz, D. Antonio 157
Saunders, S. 170
Savioa 144
Scarff gun mounting 183
Scarff-Dibovsky 101
Scheibe, Lt 149
Schepotiev, B.A. 118
Schetinin 110
Schetinin factory 16, 23, 117
Schneider, Frank 7
Schneider Trophy:
 1919 169
 1921 170
 1925/1926 184
Schopotiev, 2nd Lt B.A. 122
Schreck 11, 165
Schroeder 172
Sea of Azov 122
Second Aeronautical Exhibition 1912, St Petersburg 109
Second Battle of the Isonzo 132
Seguin 16
Selenga river 122
Senard 90
Serbia 121
Serdobsk 123
Sergievsky, Lt Boris 115–16
Service Fabrication Aéronautique (SFA) 36, 80, 83, 107
Service Technique de l'Aéronautique (STAé) 12, 43, 53, 56, 68, 161
Servicio de Aeronáutica 167
Sevastopol 129
Seversky, A.N. 118–19
Seville 157
Sewell, Major J.P.C. 56
Shamary station 124
Shanghai 166
Shephard, Bdr Gen Gordon 107
Sheremetev 121
Shishkevich, Maj Gen 110
Shishkovsky, F.P. 112
Shrewton 94
Shteven, 2nd Lt D.I. 118
Siam 156
Siberia 122
Siemens-Schuckert 37
Sikorsky S6B 110
Simbirsk 114
Simferopol 114
Simms, FSL H.R. 98, 100, 102
Simon 148
Sinai Peninsular 96
Sino-Japanese War 166
Sir William Beardmore & Co. 99
Sixth Battle of the Isonzo 134
Skompass 138
Smirnov 114
Smylie, FSL G.F. 99
Smyrna 100
Società Anonima Nieuport-Macchi (see Nieuport-Macchi)
Società Italiana di Transporti Aerei, Brazil 187
Société A. Tellier et Cie 11
Société Aéronautique Bordelais 12
Société Anonyme des Establissements Nieuport 9, 107
Société Anonyme Française de Construction Aéronautiques 48
Société Astra (see Astra)
Société Dyle et Bacalan 11
Société Générale Aéronautique (SGA) 12
Société Nationale de Construction Aéronautique du Sud-Ouest (SNCAO) 13
Société Nieuport et Deplante 9
Société pour la Construction et l'Entretien d'Avions 47
Sommer, Roger 7
Sommer monoplane 93
Sopwith 123–4, 171
 1½-Strutter 85, 88, 105, 120–1, 123, 126
 Baby 123
 Camel 123, 154
 Dolphin C-1 162
 Pup 102
 Scout 57
 Snipe 123, 180–1
 Triplane 52, 85
Sopwith-Kauper Syn Mech 106
Sorrentino 139
Soubiran, R. 88
Sousse 179
Soviet Air Force 129–30
 1 Fighter Air Sqn 122
 1 Higher Military Pilot's School 130
 1 Irkovtsk Detachment 124
 1 Light Bomber Sqn 130
 1 Military Pilot's School 130
 1 Northern Fighter Unit 122
 1 Tvessk Aviation Group 124
 2 Fighter Air Sqn 122
 2 Fighter Sqn, Kiev 129–30
 2 Fighter Sqn, Moscow 129–30
 2 Flight 130
 2 Military Pilot's School 130
 2 Naval Flight 130
 2 Northern Fighter Unit 122
 3 Artillery Air Sqn 126
 3 Bolshevik Sqn 127
 4 Fighter Sqn, Minsk 129–30
 4 Flight 130
 5 Flight 130
 7 Soviet Fighter Air Flight 124
 8 Flight 130
 12 Aviation Reconnaissance Section 130
 14 Flight 130
 17 Aviation Reconnaissance Section 130
 19 Flight 130
 Byelomorsky Flying Boat Detachment 122
 Caspian Hydroaviation Unit 122
 Dnepr Hydroaviation Unit 122
 Kamsky Flying Boat Detachment 122
 Northern Hydroaviation Battalion 122
 Serpukhov School 130
 Volga-Caspian Aviation Group 122
SP2 141, 143
SP3 143–4
Spad aircraft 136–8, 141, 143–4
 7 54, 87, 89, 115–16, 121, 129, 154
 12 87
 13 58, 64, 86–7, 139, 148, 150, 152, 155, 166–7
 15 167
 20/20bis 162, 166, 171
 21 162
 72 169
 81 166
 A.2 82, 115
Spad-Herbemont 170, 179
Spain 157, 167
 Aviation Militaire 157
 Escuela Nieuport de Peu 157
SS Balmoral Castle 98
St Andrew, hospital ship 95
St Cyr 8
St Just-en-Chaussée 89
St Mihiel 148
St Paul Island 179
St Pol-sur-Mer 90, 98
St Raphaël 179
Stanislav 115
Staragora 139
Starskii 115
Statione Idrovolanti di Otranto 145
Stavros 100
Stenay 77
Stephens, FSL T.G.M. 95
Stirling, Capt 96
Stoppani 138
Straits of Otranto 78, 146
Strasbourg 165
Strizhevsky, W/O Vladimir 116
Suez Canal 78, 95–7
Sugana valley 134
Suk, W/O Grigory 116
Sulina 119
Sunbeam 350hp Maori V-12 178
Suresnes 9
Sutton's Farm 181

SVA 139–41, 146
 seaplane 153
Sweden 10, 157, 167
 F5 Sqn 167
 Marine Flyvasende 157
Switzerland 157
 Fliegertruppe 62, 157
Szczepanski, Obs K. 129

Tacchini 133–4
Taganrog Naval Aviation School 117
Tahyraqua 137, 144
Tait-Cox, Capt L.R. 184
Talbot, Flt Lt G.R.H. 99
Taliedo 133
Tallinin 126
Talmaci 119
Taranto 145
Tarnopol 116
TBD Demir Hissar 97
Tcheliabinsk 125
Tegetthoff 145
Tellier:
 4R 450 11
 T.3/T.4/T.5/T.7 178–9
Tellier, Alphonse 11
Tenedos 78, 95, 99
Tenth Battle of the Isonzo 136
Tesei 136
Tesio 141
Teste, LV 168
Tetuán 157
Thai 1 pursuit Group 167
Thailand 167
Thasos 103
Thaw, Lt W. 87, 89–90
The Dawn Patrol 152
Thénault, Capt Georges 87
Thermi 100
Thetford 93
Thieffry, Adj E. 49, 154
Thionville 157
Third Battle of the Isonzo 132
Thomas 11
Thorold, FSL H.K. 100
Thulin 80hp engine 37, 155
Tivoli 138
Tokyo Gasuden 155
Tombette 135
Tomson, Ens P.M. 116
Tonini, Alessandro 14, 76
Toul 148
Touquin 150
Trans-Siberian Railway 123
Travers, FSL H.G. 99
Treaty of Brest-Litovsk 121
Trenchard, Maj Gen 105
Trentino 134, 140
Trieste 134, 145–6
Trincornot de Rose, Maj 81
Triple Alliance 78
Trompenburg factory 37
Trouillet 97
Tserel 117–18
Tsingtao 155
Turk 9 Sqn 158
Turkey 95, 158

Udet, Ltn E. 150
Udine 131, 137
Ufficio Vigilanza Costruzioni Aviatorie 14
Uheerske Hradiste 125
Ukraine 52, 121–3, 129–30
 1 Ukraine Air Sqn 129
Uktus station 124
United Kingdom 10
United States 10, 21, 52
United States Air Service 11, 31, 60, 90
 27th AS 150, 152
 31st AS 52
 94th AS 65, 148–51
 95th AS 148–51
 147th AS 150, 152, 157
 First Pursuit Group 65
Uruguay 11

Vacher, QM 85
Vadelaincourt 83
Vakulovsky, Lt K. 116
Val Seren 142
Valdespartera 157
Vall d'Assa 138, 141–2
Valleika, Lt A. 125
Valona 144, 146
Varano 145–6
Vardar river 120
Varsovie 128–9
Varsovie Mechanics School 128
Venanzi su Salzano 131
Venezia 82, 85, 144–5, 170
Verdun 9, 80–1, 90, 112
Verkhnaya Chasouina 124
Verkhnyaya Toima 122
Verona 137
Veronesi 143
Vertekop 121
Verville 171
Vicenza 134–6
Vichy government 12, 167
Vickers FB.19 116
Vickers gun 33, 47–51, 63, 75, 101, 106, 118, 127, 152, 159, 165
Vidzerne 125
Viipuri 154
Villacoublay 23, 28, 101, 107, 173
Villaverla 137
Villeneuve les Vertus 148
Vilnius 126
Vladimirov, Ens P. 124
Vladimirovich, V. 33
Vladivostok 122–3, 25
Voisin 3, 7, 10, 77, 99, 111, 115, 119, 133, 136, 142 3 82, 112
 LA/LAS 123
Vola 138
Volga river 122
Vologda 121
Voorhees, Esn 153

Wadi Gaza 97
Waldon, Capt L.B. 96
Wanamaker, 2nd Lt W. 150
Ware, Lt 98
Weiss, Lt 172
Westende 102
Westgate 95
Weymann, Charles 7–8, 21, 24–6
Whetland, FSL A.J. 103
White 33 Hussite Aviation Detachment 124–5
White Russia 121, 126, 129
 Independent Aviation Detachment/First Hussites 124
 Samarian First Detachment 123
Williams, Flt Lt E.W. 102
Williams, Lt 175
Willis, Sgt H.B. 89
Willman, Lt W. 126
Wilson, S/Sgt 94
Wingate-Grey, Lt A.G. 107
Winslow, 2nd Lt A. 148
Wolsit company 13
Wolyn 128
Wood, Flt Lt C.E. 100
World Altitude Record 14, 172
Wright aeroplane 111
Wright H-3 410hp engine 175
Wroniecki, A. 148
Wyllie, FSL 99

Yakovitsky, Lt N.A. 118, 122
Yakovlev, Jnr Lt V.L. 118
Yanchenko, E. Vasili 116
Yesilköy 158
York, J. 152

Zanibelli 14
Zari 75
Zeebrugge 99–100, 103
Zeluán 157
Zemette 7
Zenith carburettor 174
Zherebtsov, Jnr Lt 118
Zodzin 128
Zoppi 132

192